The Gospel of John in Greek and Latin

in Greek and Latin

A Comparative Intermediate Reader

Greek and Latin Text with Running Vocabulary
and Commentary

Virginia Grinch
Evan Hayes
Stephen Nimis

The Gospel of John in Greek and Latin: A Comparative Intermediate Reader
Greek and Latin Text with Running Vocabulary and Commentary

First Edition

© 2018 by Virginia Grinch, Evan Hayes, and Stephen Nimis

ISBN-10: 1940997925

ISBN-13: 9781940997926

Published by Faenum Publishing, Ltd.

Cover Design: Evan Hayes

Fonts: GFS Porson
         Garamond

editor@faenumpublishing.com

TABLE OF CONTENTS

Acknowledgments

The idea for this project grew out of work that we, the authors, did with support from Miami University's Undergraduate Summer Scholars Program, for which we thank Martha Weber and the Office of Advanced Research and Scholarship. Work on the series, of which this volume is a part, was generously funded by the Joanna Jackson Goldman Memorial Prize through the Honors Program at Miami University. We owe a great deal to Carolyn Haynes and the 2010 Honors & Scholars Program Advisory Committee for their interest and confidence in the project.

The technical aspects of the project were made possible through the invaluable advice and support of Bill Hayes, Christopher Kuo, and Daniel Meyers. The equipment and staff of Miami University's Interactive Language Resource Center were a great help along the way. We are also indebted to the Perseus Project, especially Gregory Crane and Bridget Almas, for their technical help and resources. We also profited greatly from advice and help on the POD process from Geoffrey Steadman. All responsibility for errors, however, rests with the authors themselves.

INTRODUCTION

The aim of this book is to make the Gospel of John accessible simultaneously to intermediate students of Ancient Greek and Latin. There are lots of resources available for the study of John's gospel, particularly in Greek, but this edition juxtaposes the Greek text to one of its most famous translations: the rendering into Latin by St. Jerome known as the *Vulgate*. The running vocabulary and grammatical commentary are meant to provide everything necessary to read each page, so that readers can progress through the text, improving their knowledge of Greek and/or Latin while reading one of the key texts of early Christianity. For those who know both Greek and Latin, it will be possible to use one language as a resource to read the other. Meanwhile, the *Vulgate* is a key index of how the Greek text was understood by early Christians in the Latin west.

The Gospel of John is a great text for intermediate readers of both Greek and Latin. It is one of our best examples of *koine* Greek, the *lingua franca* of the eastern Mediterranean for centuries after the time of Alexander the Great. The sentence structure is very simple and there is a great deal of repetition in vocabulary and syntax. The Latin translation follows the Greek closely, translating word for word as much as possible, so that it is a fascinating exercise in translation. St. Jerome did not produce a fresh translation of the New Testament, but was asked by the Pope to regularize the many translations current at the time. As he explains in his own preface, Jerome was constrained by tradition and could not deviate significantly from these older versions, known collectively as the *vetus Latina*.

The Gospel of John narrates the life of Jesus in a way distinct in many features from the other three "synoptic" gospels, so-called because of their strong similarities in content and form. The majority of John's gospel is unique, while episodes such as the last supper and Jesus' encounter with John the Baptist are treated very differently. Most striking are the opening lines identifying Jesus with the divine *Logos*. The divinity of Jesus is emphasized throughout, describing him with such key phrases as "the bread of life," "the light of the world," "the good shepherd," "the resurrection and the life," "the way, the truth and the life." John gives special emphasis to Mary Magdalene's experience of the resurrection, does not record any of the many parables found in the other gospels, nor the

Lord's Prayer, nor important discourses found in the other gospels, such as the Sermon on the Mount.

The gospel is based on the personal testimony of "the disciple whom Jesus loved" as he is called in book 21. For a long time tradition held that the apostle John was the author of this gospel, but biblical scholars now generally agree that it was composed by some kind of community inspired by John the apostle near the end of the first century CE.

How to use this book

The page by page vocabularies gloss all but the most common words. We have endeavored to make these glossaries as useful as possible without becoming fulsome. Words occurring frequently in the text that are not glossed, or not glossed in every instance, can be found in an appendix in the back, but it is our hope that most readers will not need to use this appendix often. In addition, proper names are presented in an appendix and only given in the page by page glossaries when they occur for the first time.

The commentary is almost exclusively grammatical, explaining subordinate clauses, unusual verb forms, and idioms. An introduction on the language and style of the Greek text and its Latin translation highlights the most important differences from the norms of classical Greek and Latin. Starting on page xvi there is a side by side comparison of Greek and Latin characteristics of New Testament grammar with examples. These are elaborations of grammatical points made in the page-by-page commentaries. The commentaries are meant to be a safety net to supply what is necessary for reading each page, and for this reason there is a good deal of repetition. They are not meant to be read continuously, but to be consulted when necessary.

A good strategy is to read a passage in Greek or Latin, check the glossary for unusual words and consult the commentary as a last resort. For those knowing both Latin and Greek, it is possible to observe the parallels between the two languages up close.

An Important Disclaimer:

This volume is a self-published "Print on Demand" (POD) book, and it has not been vetted or edited in the usual way by publishing professionals. There are sure to be some factual and typographical errors in the text, for which we apologize in advance. The volume is also available only through online distributors, since each book is printed when ordered online. However, this publishing

channel and format also account for the low price of the book; and it is a simple matter to make changes when they come to our attention. For this reason, any corrections or suggestions for improvement are welcome and will be addressed as quickly as possible in future versions of the text.

Please e-mail corrections or suggestions to editor@faenumpublishing.com.

About the Authors:

Virginia Grinch is a graduate in Classics and History at Miami University. She received an MA in History at the University of New Hampshire.

Evan Hayes is a graduate in Classics and Philosophy at Miami University and the 2011 Joanna Jackson Goldman Scholar.

Stephen Nimis is an Emeritus Professor of Classics at Miami University and Professor and Chair of English and Comparative Literature at the American University in Cairo.

The Language of the Gospel of John: Greek

The Gospel of John is one of our best examples of *koine* Greek, the *lingua franca* of the eastern Mediterranean during the Hellenistic and Roman periods of the Greek language. Used for a variety of administrative purposes, *koine* is the ancestor of Byzantine medieval Greek and modern Greek. This *koine* was also used in various literary works, where more of the features of classical Greek dialects were preserved, particularly in verse. A revival of interest in the classical Attic dialect in the second century CE led to a strong classicizing movement, called the "second sophistic." But the Greek of the New Testament writers, especially John, was not affected by this movement and departs from the classical canons of usage in many ways. For example, the emergence of *koine* coincides with the diminishing use of the optative mood, and indeed there are no examples of the optative in John at all. Other important differences include the use of simple sentences instead of subordination, a greater amount of directly reported dialogue, the decreased use of particles, an increase in the use of pronouns and demonstratives, a decline in the use of the dative case, often replaced by prepositional phrases, and the increased use of periphrastic expressions.

The Language of the Gospel of John: Latin

St. Jerome (347 – 420 CE), a deeply learned man who had had a classical education, was asked to revise and correct the then current Latin translations of the *Bible* in order to produce a definitive version, which is now known as the *Vulgate*. In doing so, he was constrained by the already existing translations (the *vetus Latina*), which had sought in general to produce as literal a translation as possible. This meant departing from the canons of use typical of classical Latin syntax in many respects, just as the *koine* Greek of John departed from classical usage. The result is a kind of "humble style" (*sermo humilis*) which was felt to be appropriate for the new intellectual and spiritual world of Christianity, a world where "the first shall be last," where the wisdom of men is folly, and where God became man and suffered for his own creatures. The "haughtiness" of pagan antiquity was legible in the canons of classical rhetoric and philosophy; and as Jerome's contemporary Augustine wrote, it was pride that made him despise the *Bible* before his conversion. Christians throughout the middle ages often studied and imitated pagan Latin works, but the plain Latin of the New Testament became an alternate model of writing about the most serious matters.

Grammatical and stylistic features of John's Gospel: Greek and Latin

1. Use of direct speech

Major narrative forms in antiquity did not include the amount of direct dialogue that John uses. Speeches, often elaborate and carefully crafted, are quite common in epic and history, but not the short exchanges that abound in the New Testament, which smack of the theater. Note the following common expressions used in these exchanges:

ἀπεκρίθη: ao. pass. of ἀποκρίνομαι	*respondit*	"s/he answered"
ἀπεκρίθησαν: ao. pass. of ἀποκρίνομαι	*responderunt*	"they answered"
εἶπον: ao. of λέγω	*dixi, dixerunt*	"I said," "they said"
εἶπε: ao. of λέγω	*dixit*	"s/he said"
εἶπαν: ao. 3 pl. of λέγω	*dixerunt*	"they said"
λέγων/λέγουσα: pr. part. of λέγω	*dicens*	"saying"
εἴπων/εἴπουσα	*cum dixisset*	"having said," "when s/he had said"
various forms of λαλέω	*loquor*	"he says," etc.

2. Sentence structure

The syntax of the book of John is disarmingly simple, closer, it is generally believed, to spoken Greek than most surviving literature. The word order seems aimed at clarity rather than elegance, as is the use of extra pronouns, demonstratives and prepositions. Most of these characteristics make the Greek seem more similar to English. The Latin translation follows the Greek word order as much as possible and regularly translates pronouns and prepositions, resulting in an equally mannered Latin prose compared to the terseness generally sought for by classical authors.

3. Below are some unusual examples of the use of prepositions
with their Latin equivalents:

a.   Koine made greater use of prepositions to express relationships that were
     more typically (but not exclusively) expressed with cases alone in Attic
     Greek.

17:20	διὰ τοῦ λόγου: "by means of the message" (for dative of means)	*per verbum*: (for ablative of means)
21:10	Ἐνέγκατε ἀπὸ τῶν ὀψαρίων: "bring (some) of the fish" (for partitive genitive)	*Afferte de piscibus*: (for partitive genitive)
6:50	καταβαίνων ἵνα τις ἐξ αὐτοῦ φάγῃ: "descending so that if anyone eats of it" (for partitive genitive)	*descendens, ut, si quis ex ipso manducaverit*: (for partitive genitive)
6:71	εἷς ἐκ τῶν δώδεκα: "one of the twelve" (for partitive genitive)	*unus ex Duodecim*: (for partitive genitive)
21:8	μακρὰν ἀπὸ τῆς γῆς: "far *from the sea*" (for genitive of separation)	*longe a terra*: (for ablative of separation)

b.   There is an increased use of "improper" prepositions, usually derived from
     adverbs.

| 3:22 | ἐγγὺς τοῦ πλοίου: "next to the ship" | *proximum navi* |
| 3:31 | ἐπάνω πάντων: "above all" | *supra omnes* |

c.   There is a reduction in the use of the dative case.

| 8:25-6 | λαλῶ ὑμῖν ... λαλῶ εἰς τὸν κόσμον. I speak *to you* ... I speak *to the world*. | *loquor vobis ... loquor ad mundum* |
| 2:11 | ἐπίστευσαν εἰς αὐτὸν οἱ μαθηταὶ: the disciples believed *in him* | *crediderunt in eum discipuli eius* |

d.   Different cases no longer change the meaning of prepositions.

13:25	ἐπὶ τὸ στῆθος: "on his breast"	*supra pectus*
6:19	περιπατοῦντα ἐπὶ τῆς θαλάσσης: "walking *on the sea*"	*ambulantem super mare*
8:6	κατέγραφεν εἰς τὴν γῆν: "he wrote *on the ground*"	*scribebat in terra*
1:18	ὁ ὢν εἰς τὸν κόλπον: "being in the lap"	*qui est in sinum*
3:15-16	ὁ πιστεύων ἐν αὐτῷ ... ὁ πιστεύων εἰς αὐτὸν: "the one believing in him"	*qui credit in ipso... qui credit in eum*

4. Indirect Statement

Of the three main forms of indirect statement in Greek, John uses ὅτι plus the indicative the most, no matter what verb is introducing the statement. Jerome regularly translates ὅτι with the conjunction *quia*, which was rarely used for indirect statement in classical Latin. The accusative infinitive form of indirect statement, the most common in Latin, is rarely used in the book of John. In some cases, the conjunction *quia* retains its normal causal force (*because*), a force that the conjunction ὅτι can also have in Greek. For details and examples of indirect statement see below.

5. Indirect Question

The verbs in indirect questions in Greek are normally in the indicative, but can be changed to the corresponding tense of the optative in secondary sequence (i.e. after a main verb that is a past tense). Since there are no optatives in John, all indirect questions are in the indicative. In Latin, indirect questions are normally in the subjunctive, following the sequences of tenses.

ἠρώτων <u>πῶς ἀνέβλεψεν</u>	interrogabant <u>quomodo vidisset</u>	"They were asking *how he had seen*"

But John also uses ἵνα plus the subjunctive for indirect questions, for which Jerome uses *ut* plus the subjunctive:

ἠρώτησεν ... ἵνα ἄρη τὸ σῶμα τοῦ Ἰησοῦ·	rogavit... ut tolleret corpus Iesu	"He asked to take the body of Jesus"

6. Conditions

Contrafactual conditions in John follow the rules of classical usage; and Jerome follows the comparable rules of classical Latin. However, future and general conditions are more complicated. In classical Greek there are two future conditions (less and more vivid), one using the optative, one using the subjunctive. Since John does not use the optative, there are only "future more vivid" conditions in this gospel, which must cover a greater range of probability.

In addition, John uses the form of the so-called "present general condition" in some contexts that clearly refer to the future. Both kinds of condition (future more vivid and present general) have the same form of the protasis (ἐὰν plus the subjunctive), differing only in the tense of the apodosis. Jerome regularly translates these protases with the future perfect indicative, which is the normal form of the future more vivid condition in Latin. Jerome thus rarely uses the ususal Latin forms of present general conditions. See below for more details and examples.

7. Expansion of the use of ἵνα plus the subjunctive and *ut* plus the subjunctive

In Attic Greek, ἵνα and the subjunctive is used regularly in purpose clauses in primary sequence (i.e., after main verbs in the present and future tenses). In John, this combination is used after any tense, can express purpose, result, or a combination of the two. Such clauses can also be used as complements in a variety of ways, as appositional or explanatory phrases, in indirect statement and command, where classical usage would deploy a participle or infinitive. Jerome translates all these expressions with *ut* plus the subjunctive, expanding the use of that combination as well. The distinction in Latin between negative result clauses (*ut non* + subjunctive) and negative purpose clauses (*ne* + subjunctive) is not observed. Jerome does, however, observe the sequence of tenses in Latin. See below for examples.

8. Participles

Whereas Greek has a full complement of participle forms, Latin lacks an active participle in the past and a passive participle in the present, so that often it was not possible to translate participles directly. In addition, Greek participles generally indicate verbal aspect (complete, incomplete, simple) rather than time, whereas Latin participles regularly indicate time. For attributive participles, Jerome often uses a relative clause with a finite verb.

ἀλλ᾽ ὁ πέμψας με ... μοι εἶπεν:	sed, *qui misit me* ... ille mihi dixit	"but *the one who sent* me said to me."

For circumstantial participles, he often uses a *cum* circumstantial clause:

καὶ ποιήσας φραγέλλιον ἐκ σχοινίων πάντας ἐξέβαλεν:	et *cum fecisset* flagellum de funiculis, omnes eiecit:	"and *when he had made* a whip from rope, he cast out all."

For examples and more details, see below.

9. Tense, aspect, mood

i.   The Latin perfect indicative must do double duty for the Greek aorist tense and the present perfect tense: hence *dixit* can mean "he spoke (just once)" or "he has spoken." Greek has two different forms for these two aspects, which Jerome must thus always translate with the perfect tense.

καὶ ἐμαρτύρησεν Ἰωάνης λέγων ὅτι τεθέαμαι τὸ πνεῦμα καταβαῖνον ὡς περιστερὰν ἐξ οὐρανοῦ, καὶ ἔμεινεν ἐπ᾽ αὐτόν·	et testimonium *perhibuit* Iohannes dicens quia *vidi* Spiritum descendentem quasi columbam de caelo et *mansit* super eum.	"and John *witnessed* saying that "*I have seen* the spirit descending like a dove from heaven, and it *remained* over him."

ii.   The pluperfect tense is used by Jerome to translate aorist tenses in relative clauses (as we often do in English).

| πάντα ἑωρακότες ὅσα ἐποίησεν | cum omnia vidissent _quae_ _fecerat_ | "when they had seen what he had done" |

iii.   Greek uses the optative in subordinate clauses after past tenses, the subjunctive after present and future tenses; Greek thus has a _sequence of moods_.

Latin uses the subjunctive in subordinate clauses, with the perfect and present after future and present tenses, the imperfect and pluperfect after past tenses: Latin thus has a _sequence of tenses_.

Jerome follows the rules for the sequence of tenses in Latin (but not always), whereas the Greek has the subjunctive after all tenses, there being no optative at all in John.

iv.   The subjunctive in Greek is timeless and indicates only different verbal aspects (complete, incomplete, simple action); the subjunctive in Latin indicates time relative to the main verb. Greek temporal or conditional clauses with the subjunctive are regularly translated by the future perfect indicative, irrespective of the tense of the Greek subjunctive.

v.   The Latin perfect subjunctive is very similar in form to the future perfect indicative, as can be see in the following chart:

future perfect active		perfect subjunctive	
dixero	dixerimus	dixerim	dixerĭmus
dixeris	dixeritis	dixerīs	dixerītis
dixerit	dixerint	dixerit	dixerint

In non-rhythmical prose, where the quantity of the syllables cannot be determined, only the first person singular form is different, and it would be easy to see how they might be confused. However, the perfect subjunctive seems to be restricted to relative clauses in John and in the _Vulgate_ in general. But note the following famous passage from I Corinthians 13 and the shift between future perfect indicative and perfect subjunctive:

Et si habuero prophetiam, et noverim mysteria omnia ... nihil sum.

Introduction

10. Periphrastic expressions

Periphrastic expressions (combinations of a participle and a form of the verb "to be") are not common in classical Greek, but are more common both in *koine* and in Latin. John uses more such expressions than are usual, and these are easily translated into Latin.

Perfect Passive:

γεγραμμένον ἐστίν	ἐστιν εἰργασμένα	ἀπεσταλμένος εἰμὶ
scriptum est	*sunt facta*	*missus sum*
"it has been written"	"they have been done"	"I have been sent"

Pluperfect Passive:

ἀπεσταλμένοι ἦσαν	ἦν βεβλημένος
missi fuerant	*missus fuerat*
"they have been sent"	"he had been sent"

Imperfect:

ὅπου ἦν ὁ Ἰωάνης βαπτίζων	Εἰ μὴ ἦν οὗτος κακὸν ποιῶν
ubi erat Ioannes baptizans	*Si non esset hic malefactor*
"where John was baptizing"	"unless he were doing evil"

The Greek verb μέλλω, "to be about to" has no equivalent in Latin, so the future participle is used with various forms of the verb *esse* to translate it.

γνοὺς ὅτι μέλλουσιν ἔρχεσθαι:	*cum cognovisset quia venturi essent:*	"When they had learned that they were about to come."

10. Proper Names

The proper names occurring in the book of John, as with the rest of the New Testament, are derived from three languages: Hebrew (and its later Aramaic form), Greek, and Latin. These can cause some confusion, especially when names are declined at one point in the text and treated as indeclinable at another. Generally, transliterations and derivations of Hebrew names are indeclinable, and can end in any letter:

Ἀβραάμ, Ἰακώβ, Ἰσραήλ, Συχάρ

However, some Hebrew and Aramaic names are Hellenized and inflected. For example:

Nominative	Ἰησοῦς	Iēsus	Μωϋσῆς	Moyses
Genitive	Ἰησοῦ	Iēsū	Μωϋσέως	Moysis
Dative	Ἰησοῦ	Iēsū	Μωϋσεῖ	Moysi
Accusative	Ἰησοῦν	Iēsum	Μωϋσῆν	Moysen
Ablative		Iēsū		Moyse
Vocative	Ἰησοῦ	Iēsū	Μωϋσῆ	Moyse

	-ας Hebrew Names		-ᾶς Aramaic Names	
Nominative	Ἠλίας	Ēliās	Βαραββᾶς	Barabbas
Genitive	Ἠλίου	Ēliae	Βαραββᾶ	Barabbae
Dative	Ἠλίᾳ	Ēliae	Βαραββᾷ	Barabbae
Accusative	Ἠλίαν	Ēliān	Βαραββᾶν	Barabban
Ablative		Ēliā		Barabba
Vocative	Ἠλία	Ēliā	Βαραββᾶς	Barabba

Occasionally a name will appear in multiple forms. For example, the name Jerusalem occurs in John's Greek as a regularly declined neuter plural noun: τά Ἱεροσόλυμα, -ύμων (though elsewhere in the New Testament is indeclinable feminine ἡ Ἱερουσολήμ occurs frequently). Jerome's Latin alternates between the singular and plural forms depending on the case (*in Hierosolymis*, abl. pl; *iuxta Hierosolymam*, acc. s.)

Greek and Latin names are regularly declined:

	Latin		Greek	
Nominative	Πιλᾶτος	Pīlātus	Πέτρος	Petrus
Genitive	Πιλᾶτου	Pīlātī	Πέτρου	Petrī
Dative	Πιλᾶτῳ	Pīlātō	Πέτρῳ	Petrō
Accusative	Πιλᾶτον	Pīlātum	Πέτρον	Petrum
Ablative		Pīlātō		Petrō
Vocative	Πιλᾶτε	Pīlāte	Πέτρε	Petre

For a complete list of proper names, see the list at the end of the volume.

Introduction

Of the many resources available for the study of John's Gospel, the following were most useful for this project:

Auerbach, Eric. *Literary Latin and its Public in Late Latin Antiquity and in the Middle Ages*. Princeton University Press: Princeton, NJ, 1993

Boyer, James. "Second Class Conditions in New Testament Greek." *Grace Theological Journal* 3.1 (1982) 81-88.

Houghton, H. A. G. *The Latin New Testament: A Guide to its Early History, Texts, Manuscripts*. Oxford University Press: Oxford, 2016.

Wallace, Daniel B. *Greek Grammar: Beyond the Basics: An Exegeetical Syntax of the New Testament*. Zondervan: Nashville, TN, 1996

More detailed discussions with examples

1. Indirect statement: Greek

Greek had three forms of indirect statement, depending on the main verb.

i. Verbs of saying can take ὅτι (or ὡς) + the indicative

ii. Verbs of believing and thinking (and also saying) take the accusative + infinitive construction

iii. Verbs of knowing and perceiving take the accusative + participle construction

In John, the most common form of indirect statement is ὅτι plus the indicative, which had become more common in *koine* after all kinds of verbs.

4:51	ὑπήντησαν αὐτῷ λέγοντες ὅτι ὁ παῖς αὐτοῦ ζῇ	"they rushed to him saying *that his child was living*"
3:2	οἴδαμεν ὅτι ἀπὸ θεοῦ ἐλήλυθας	"we know *that you have come* from God"
1:34	καὶ μεμαρτύρηκα ὅτι οὗτός ἐστιν ὁ υἱὸς τοῦ θεοῦ	"and I testified *that this one is* the son of God"
4:1	ἔγνω ὁ κύριος ὅτι ἤκουσαν οἱ Φαρισαῖοι ὅτι Ἰησοῦς πλείονας μαθητὰς ποιεῖ.	"Jesus knew *that the Pharisees heard that Jesus made* many disciples"
4:19	θεωρῶ ὅτι προφήτης εἶ σύ.	"I see *that you are* a prophet"

The accusative infinitive construction occurs less frequently:

12:18	ἤκουσαν τοῦτο αὐτὸν πεποιηκέναι τὸ σημεῖον	"They heard *that he had made this sign*."
12:29	ἔλεγεν βροντὴν γεγονέναι	"The crowd said *that there was thunder*."
21:25	οὐδ' αὐτὸν οἶμαι τὸν κόσμον χωρήσειν	"I do not think *that the world itself would hold (them)*."

The accusative + participle also occurs after verbs of perceiving and knowing:

19:24	εἶδον ἤδη αὐτὸν τεθνηκότα	They saw *that he was already dead*

This should be distinguished from those cases (more numerous in John) where the accusative-participle construction emphasizes the actual act of preceiving rather than intellectual perception. This is more like the circumstantial use of the participle:

1. Indirect Statement: Latin

In classical Latin, the accusative + infinitive was by far the most common form of indirect statement. The use of causal conjunctions *quia, quod* and *quoniam* to introduce indirect statement, common in Late Latin, is rare in classical Latin.

Jerome follows the syntax of the Greek original closely in translating indirect statement, regularly translating ὅτι as *quia*, despite the fact that this is uncommon in classical Latin.

4:51	ὑπήντησαν αὐτῷ λέγοντες ὅτι ὁ παῖς αὐτοῦ ζῇ	*occurrerunt ei dicentes quia puer eius vivit*
3:2	οἴδαμεν ὅτι ἀπὸ θεοῦ ἐλήλυθας	*scimus quia a Deo venisti*
1:34	καὶ μεμαρτύρηκα ὅτι οὗτός ἐστιν ὁ υἱὸς τοῦ θεοῦ	*et testimonium perhibui quia hic est Filius Dei*
4:1	ἔγνω ὁ κύριος ὅτι ἤκουσαν οἱ Φαρισαῖοι ὅτι Ἰησοῦς πλείονας μαθητὰς ποιεῖ.	*cognovit Iesus quia audierunt pharisaei quia Iesus plures discipulos facit*
4:19	θεωρῶ ὅτι προφήτης εἶ σύ.	*video quia propheta es tu*

Jerome translates an accusative infinitive with the same form in Latin.

12:18	ἤκουσαν τοῦτο αὐτὸν πεποιηκέναι τὸ σημεῖον	*audierunt eum fecisse hoc signum*
12:29	ἔλεγεν βροντὴν γεγονέναι	*dicebat tonitruum factum esse*
21:25	οὐδ᾿ αὐτὸν οἶμαι τὸν κόσμον χωρήσειν	*nec ipsum arbitror mundum capere eos*

The one instance of the participle in indirect statement is translated with a periphrastic infinitive, which hues close to the Greek.

19:24	εἶδον ἤδη αὐτὸν τεθνηκότα	*viderunt eum iam mortuum* (sc. *esse*)

Those cases where the accusative-participle construction emphasizes the actual act of perceiving rather than intellectual perception, and is thus not strictly speaking in indirect discourse, is parallel to Greek usage.

1:33 ἐφ᾽ ὃν ἂν ἴδῃς τὸ πνεῦμα καταβαῖνον καὶ μένον: "upon whomever you see the spirit *descending and abiding*"

Only the context can distinguish this circumstantial use from indirect statement, but the difference in English is clear:

"I see that he is descending" (*indirect statement*)

vs.

"I see him descending" (*circumstantial*)

Contrast both of these cases with the attributive participle as a direct object:

13:11 ᾔδει γὰρ τὸν παραδιδόντα: "for he knew *the one betraying*," i.e. he knew who the traitor was.

2. Conditions in Greek

i. ***Contrary to fact conditions*** in John follow the rules of classical usage.

8:42 Εἰ ὁ θεὸς πατὴρ ὑμῶν ἦν ἠγαπᾶτε ἂν ἐμέ   "If God were your father, you would love me."

11:32 εἰ ἦς ὧδε οὐκ ἂν μου ἀπέθανεν ὁ ἀδελφός   "If you had been here, my brother would not have died."

ii. ***Future conditions***: In classical Greek, there were two main future conditions, which grammarians call the "more vivid" and the "less vivid." The less-vivid used the potential optative in the apodosis and expressed a *possible premise*; the more-vivid type used the future indicative in the apodosis and expressed a *probable premise*. With the loss of the optative in *koine*, the future more vivid form began to represent a broader range of probablilty, from likely to unlikely. The protasis of such conditions typically used ἐάν with the subjunctive. This combination is marked in our commentary as "future more vivid," following the conventions of standard grammars, but can sometimes imply conditions that are highly improbable.

Future more vivid conditions

protasis	apodosis
5:43 ἐὰν ἄλλος ἔλθῃ ἐν τῷ ὀνόματι τῷ ἰδίῳ...	ἐκεῖνον λήμψεσθε
"If someone comes in his own name...	you will accept that one."
6:51 ἐάν τις φάγῃ ἐκ τούτου τοῦ ἄρτου...	ζήσει εἰς τὸν αἰῶνα
"If someone eats from this bread...	he will live forever."

1:33 ἐφ’ ὅν ἀν ἴδῃς τὸ πνεῦμα καταβαἴνον καὶ μένον: *Super quem videris Spiritum descendentem et manentem*

Note how Jerome translates an attributive participle when it is the direct object of a verb of knowing:

13:11 ἤδει γὰρ τὸν παραδιδόντα: *Sciebat enim quisnam esset, qui traderet*

2. Conditions in Latin

i. In the case of **contrary to fact conditions**, Jerome follows the rules of classical Latin.

8:42   *Si Deus pater vester esset, diligeretis me*   "If God were your father, you would love me."

11:32   *si fuisses hic, non esset mortuus frater meus*   "If you had been here, my brother would not be dead."

ii. **Future conditions:** In classical Latin, there were two main future conditions, which grammarians call the "more vivid" and the "less vivid." The less-vivid used the subjunctive in the protasis and apodosis, and expressed a *possible premise*; the more-vivid type used the future indicative in the protasis and apodosis, and expressed a *probable premise*. Since there are no "less-vivid" conditions in the Greek, there are none in the *Vulgate* as well, but the "more vivid" type now has a broader range of meaning. We have marked these conditions in our commentary as "future more vivid," following the conventions of standard grammars, but they can sometimes imply conditions that are highly improbable.

Future more vivid conditions

protasis	apodosis
5:43 *Si alius venerit in nomine suo...*	*illum accipietis*
"If someone comes in his own name..."	you will accept that one."
6:51 *Si quis manducaverit ex hoc pane...*	*vivet in aeternum*
"If someone eats from this bread..."	he will live forever."

iii. Present general conditions: In classical Greek, the same kind of protasis (ἐὰν with the subjunctive) can be used with a present tense in the apodosis to form a "present general" or "indefinite" condition, and this combination is so-marked in our commentary. However, many examples in John clearly refer to the future and some New Testament scholars (Boyer, Wallace) argue that all protases with ἐὰν + the subjunctive refer to the future and should be classed together. Indeed, even in classical Greek the present indicative could be used in the protasis of future more vivid conditions.

Present General or Indefinite

	protasis	apodosis
3:3	ἐὰν μή τις γεννηθῇ ἄνωθεν...	οὐ δύναται ἰδεῖν τὴν βασιλείαν τοῦ θεοῦ
	Nisi quis natus fuerit desuper...	*non potest videre regnum Dei*
	"Unless someone is born from above...	he is not able to enter into the kingdom of God."
6:53	ἐὰν μὴ φάγητε τὴν σάρκα...	οὐκ ἔχετε ζωὴν ἐν ἑαυτοῖς
	Nisi manducaveritis carnem...	*non habetis vitam in vobismetipsis*
	"Unless you eat the flesh...	you do not have life in you."

iii. Present general conditions: In classical Latin there were several ways to express a present general condition:

protasis	apodosis
Perfect Indicative: *si quid dixit...* "If ever he says anything...	
	Present Indicative:
Present Subjunctive 2nd singular: *si hoc dicas...* "If ever one says anything...	...*creditur.* ...he is believed."
Present Indicative: *si hoc dicit...* "Every time he says this...	

In a few instances, Jerome translates a condition that is in the present general form in Greek with the present indicative in the protasis. In the vast majority of cases, however, he translates the protasis with the future perfect indicative. Thus ἐὰν + the subjunctive is regularly translated with the future perfect indicative, irrespective of the form of the apodosis.

Present General or Indefinite

	protasis	apodosis
3:3	*Nisi quis natus fuerit desuper* "Unless someone is born from above...	*non potest videre regnum Dei* he is not able to enter into the kingdom of God.
6:53	*Nisi manducaveritis carnem* "Unless you eat the flesh...	*non habetis vitam in vobismetipsis* you do not have life in you

3. General or indefinite clauses in Greek

Indefinite relative and temporal clauses are usually expressed with a relative pronoun or temporal conjunction with ἄν and the subjunctive. The main verb can be either future or present, much like conditional clauses with ἐάν and the subjunctive in the protasis. In either case these clauses will be identified in the commentary as general relative or general temporal clauses, because of the indefinite or generalizing force of the expression: "whenever something happens," or "when something happens, whenever that is."

Temporal Clause	Main Clause
ὅταν ἔλθῃ ἐκεῖνος	ἀναγγελεῖ ἡμῖν ἅπαντα
"When he has come (whenever that is)...	he will send to us all things."

ὃς δ᾽ ἂν πίῃ ἐκ τοῦ ὕδατος οὗ ἐγὼ δώσω αὐτῷ	οὐ μὴ διψήσει εἰς τὸν αἰῶνα
"Whoever drinks from the water I will give...	will certainly never thirst ever."

4. ἵνα and the subjunctive

In Attic Greek, ἵνα and the subjunctive is used regularly in purpose clauses in primary sequence (i.e., after main verbs in the present and future tenses). In John, this combination is used after any tense, can express purpose, result, or a combination of the two. Such clauses can also be used as complements in a variety of ways, as appositional or explanatory phrases, in indirect statement and command, where classical usage would deploy a participle or infinitive. These differences are typical of developments in *koine* Greek (Horrock 1997; Wallace 1996). Here are some examples:

i. Subjunctive in secondary sequence (instead of optative)

1:7	οὗτος ἦλθεν ... ἵνα μαρτυρήσῃ περὶ τοῦ φωτός.	"This one came ... in order to witness about the light."

3. General or indefinite clauses in Latin

Indefinite relative and temporal clauses that have *ἄν* and the subjunctive in Greek are regularly translated with *cum* or a relative pronoun with the future perfect, parallel to present general and future more vivid protases:

Temporal Clause	Main Clause
ὅταν ἔλθῃ ἐκεῖνος	ἀναγγελεῖ ἡμῖν ἅπαντα
cum venerit ille	*nobis annuntiabit omnia*
"*When he has come* (whenever that is)...	he will send to us all things."

ὃς δ' ἂν πίῃ ἐκ τοῦ ὕδατος οὗ ἐγὼ δώσω αὐτῷ	οὐ μὴ διψήσει εἰς τὸν αἰῶνα
qui autem biberit ex aqua, quam ego dabo ei	*non sitiet in aeternum*
"*Whoever drinks* from the water I will give...	will certainly never thirst ever."

Related to these clauses are "relative clauses of characteristic," which describe a class or type rather than an individual, and which do employ the subjunctive. Indeed, the last example, *qui biberit*, could be thought of as such a clause meaning, "a man *who has drunk* from the water I will give." Such clauses often indicate purpose or result:

5:45   *est qui accuset vos: Moses*
ἔστιν ὁ κατηγορῶν ὑμῶν: Μωυσῆς
this is the one would accuse you: Moses

4. *ut* and the subjunctive

In Classical Latin, *ut* and the subjunctive is used regularly in purpose and result clauses, being distinguished only in the negative (*ne* vs. *ut non*). The tense of the subjunctive follows the sequence of tenses in Latin. Jerome uses this combination to translate any Greek clause using ἵνα plus the subjunctive, which can be used to express purpose, result, or a combination of the two in the gospel of John. Such clauses can also be used as complements in a variety of ways, as appositional or explanatory phrases, in indirect statement and command. In following the Greek closely, the *Vulgate* often deviates from standard usage. Although Jerome does not always observe the difference between *ut non* and *ne*, he regularly observes the sequence of tenses. Here are some examples.

i. Jerome follows the sequence of tenses in Latin.

1:7   *hic venit ... ut testimonium perhiberet de lumine.*   "This one came ... in order to witness about the light."

ii. Epexegetic clause (instead of an epexegetic infinitive)

1:27   οὐκ εἰμὶ ἐγὼ ἄξιος ἵνα λύσω αὐτοῦ   "I am not worthy to loose the
τὸν ἱμάντα τοῦ ὑποδήματος.   strap of his sandal."

2:25   οὐ χρείαν εἶχεν ἵνα τις μαρτυρήσῃ.   "He did not have need to
witness."

iii. Noun clause used as a predicate or subject

4:34   Ἐμὸν βρῶμά ἐστιν ἵνα ποιήσω τὸ   "My bread is *that I do* the will
θέλημα τοῦ πέμψαντός με.   of the one who sent me."

11:50   συμφέρει ὑμῖν ἵνα εἷς ἄνθρωπος   "*For one man to die* is
ἀποθάνῃ.   expedient for you."

iv. Noun clause in apposition to a noun or pronoun

6:29   Τοῦτό ἐστιν τὸ ἔργον τοῦ θεοῦ ἵνα   "The work of god is this, *that
πιστεύητε εἰς ὃν ἀπέστειλεν ἐκεῖνος.   you believe* in the one whom
that one sent."

13:34   ἐντολὴν καινὴν δίδωμι ὑμῖν ἵνα   "I give you a new command,
ἀγαπᾶτε ἀλλήλους.   *that you love one another.*"

v. Indirect command

4:47   ἠρώτα ἵνα καταβῇ καὶ ἰάσηται   "He asked *that he come down
αὐτοῦ τὸν υἱόν.   and heal* his son."

vi. Supplementing or complementing a verb (instead of a participle or infinitive)

8:56   Ἀβραὰμ ὁ πατὴρ ὑμῶν   "Abraham your father rejoiced
ἠγαλλιάσατο ἵνα ἴδῃ τὴν ἡμέραν   *to see* this day."
τὴν ἐμήν·

9:22   ἤδη γὰρ συνετέθειντο οἱ Ἰουδαῖοι   "The Jews had already decided
ἵνα ... ἀποσυνάγωγος γένηται.   *that he would become driven
from the synagogue.*"

11:53   ἐβουλεύσαντο ἵνα ἀποκτείνωσιν   "They plotted *to kill* him."
αὐτόν.

vii. Result clause

9:2   τίς ἥμαρτεν ... ἵνα τυφλὸς   "Who sinned ... so that he was
γεννηθῇ;   born blind?"

ii. Epexegetic clause (instead of an epexegetic infinitive)

1:27	*ego non sum dignus, ut solvam eius corrigiam calceamenti*	"I am not worthy *to loose* the strap of his sandal."
2:25	*opus ei non erat, ut quis testimonium perhiberet*	"He did not have need *to witness*."

iii. Noun clause used as a predicate or subject

4:34	*Meus cibus est, ut faciam voluntatem eius, qui misit me*	"My bread is *that I do* the will of the one who sent me."
11:50	*expedit vobis, ut unus moriatur homo*	"*For one man to die* is expedient for you."

iv. Noun clause in apposition to a noun or pronoun

6:29	*Hoc est opus Dei, ut credatis in eum, quem misit ille*	"The work of god is this, *that you believe* in the one whom that one sent."
13:34	*Mandatum novum do vobis, ut diligatis invicem*	"I give you a new command, *that you love one another*."

v. Indirect command

4:47	*rogabat, ut descenderet et sanaret filium eius*	"He asked *that he come down and heal* his son."

vi. Supplementing or complementing a verb (instead of a participle or infinitive)

8:56	*Abraham pater vester exsultavit, ut videret diem meum*	"Abraham your father rejoiced *to see* this day."
9:22	*iam enim conspiraverant Iudaei, ut... extra synagogam fieret*	"The Jews had already decided *that he would become driven from the synagogue*."
11:53	*cogitaverunt, ut interficerent eum*	"They plotted *to kill* him."

vii. Result clause

9:2	*quis peccavit ... ut caecus nasceretur*	"Who sinned ... so that he was born blind?"

viii. Mixture of result and purpose

3:16	τὸν υἱὸν τὸν μονογενῆ ἔδωκεν, ἵνα πᾶς ὁ πιστεύων εἰς αὐτὸν μὴ ἀπόληται ἀλλὰ ἔχῃ ζωὴν αἰώνιον.	"He gave his only-begotten son *so that all who believe in him would not perish, but would have eternal life.*"

5. Greek Participles

Greek participles fall into three broad classes of use, with many other distinctions:

i. Attributive participles modify a noun or pronoun like other adjectives. They usually occur with an article in the attributive position and are often used substantively:

1:12	ἔδωκεν αὐτοῖς ἐξουσίαν τέκνα θεοῦ γενέσθαι, τοῖς πιστεύουσιν εἰς τὸ ὄνομα αὐτοῦ:	"he gave to them the power to become sons of God, *those believing* in his name."
1:33	ἀλλ' ὁ πέμψας με ... μοι εἶπεν	"but the one *who sent me* said to me"

ii. Circumstantial participles are added to a noun or pronoun to set forth some circumstance under which an action takes place. Although agreeing with a noun or pronoun, these participles actually qualify the verb in a sentence, indicating time, manner, means, cause, purpose, concession, condition or attendant circumstance.

1:38	στραφεὶς δὲ ὁ Ἰησοῦς καὶ θεασάμενος αὐτοὺς ἀκολουθοῦντας λέγει αὐτοῖς	"and Jesus, *having turned* and *having seen* them following says to them"

Circumstantial participles can occur in the genitive absolute construction.

2:3	καὶ ὑστερήσαντος οἴνου λέγει ἡ μήτηρ τοῦ Ἰησοῦ πρὸς αὐτόν	"and the wine having run out, the mother of Jesus says to him"

iii. Supplementary participles complete the idea of certain verbs. Often it is the participle itself that expresses the main action:

8:7	ὡς δὲ ἐπέμενον ἐρωτῶντες αὐτόν	"when they persisted *asking* him"

Note also the use of circumstantial participles after verbs of perceiving in the discussion of indirect statement.

viii.   Mixture of result and purpose

| 3:16 | *Filium suum unigenitum daret, ut omnis, qui credit in eum, non pereat, sed habeat vitam aeternam* | "He gave his only-begotten son *so that all who believe in him would not perish, but would have eternal life.*" |

5. Latin Participles

i.   Latin participles can be used as an adjective or a substantive, like the Greek attributive participle, but since Latin lacks a definite article, only the context can distinguish it from circumstantial participles. Jerome generally uses relative clauses to translate Greek attributive participles:

| 1:12 | *dedit eis potestatem filios Dei fieri, his, qui credunt in nomine eius* | "he gave to them the power to become sons of God, *those believing* in his name." |

| 1:33 | *sed, qui misit me ... ille mihi dixit* | "but the one *who sent me* said to me" |

ii.   Latin participles can be used like their Greek counterparts to set forth some circumstance under which an action takes place. Although agreeing with a noun or pronoun, these participles actually qualify the verb in a sentence, indicating time, manner, means, cause, purpose, concession, condition or attendant circumstance.

| 1:38 | *Conversus autem Iesus et videns eos sequentes se dicit eis* | "and Jesus, *having turned* and *having seen* them following says to them" |

Note the differences in tense between the Greek and Latin versions of this verse, because Latin has no active aorist or perfect participle. For the same reason, many circumstantial participles are often rendered by *cum* circumstantial clauses with finite verbs. See p. ix above.

Circumstantial participles can occur in the ablative absolute construction.

| 2:3 | *Et deficiente vino, dicit mater Iesu ad eum* | "and the wine having run out, the mother of Jesus says to him" |

iii.   Supplementary participles are rare in Latin, where the infinitive is more common:

| 8:7 | *Cum autem perseverarent interrogantes eum* | "when they persisted *asking* him" |

Note also the use of circumstantial participles after verbs of perceiving in the discussion of indirect statement.

6. Distinguishing Subject from Predicate: In Greek

In general a nominative subject will be distinguished from a nominative predicate by the fact that the subject is more known than the predicate. This can be signalled in Greek in the following ways.

1. The subject will be a pronoun, stated or implied (except for interrogative pronouns).

1:8	οὐκ ἦν ἐκεῖνος τὸ φῶς	"that one was not the light"
1:20	ἐγὼ οὐκ εἰμὶ ὁ χριστός	"I am not the annointed one"

2. The subject will have a definite article.

1:1	καὶ θεὸς ἦν ὁ λόγος	"and the Word was God"
1:14	καὶ ὁ λόγος σὰρξ ἐγένετο	"and the Word became flesh"

3. The subject will be a proper name.

4. Where the last two factors are equal, the subject will be first in order.

1:4	ἡ ζωὴ ἦν τὸ φῶς τῶν ἀνθρώπων	"the life was the light of men"
20:31	Ἰησοῦς ἐστιν ὁ χριστὸς	"Jesus is the annointed one"

6. Distinguishing Subject from Predicate:
In Latin

In Latin there is no definite article to distinguish a nominative subject from a nominative predicate. This can lead to some confusion, especially since Jerome rarely changes the word order of the Greek.

ἐν ἀρχῇ   ἦν ὁ λόγος,   καὶ ὁ λόγος ἦν πρὸς τὸν θεόν,   καὶ θεὸς ἦν ὁ λόγος.

In principio   *erat Verbum,*   *et Verbum erat apud Deum,*   *et Deus erat Verbum.*

In the beginning   was the word   and the word was with God   and God was the word.

In Latin the only thing indicating that *Verbum* is the subject of the last phrase is the parallelism with the phrases before it. Note the following examples where the meaning in Latin is less clear.

ἡ ζωὴ ἦν τὸ φῶς τῶν ἀνθρώπων
vita erat lux hominum
"the life was the light of men"

Ἰησοῦς ἐστὶν ὁ χριστὸς
Iesus est Christus
"Jesus is the annointed one"

Glossing Conventions: Latin

Adjectives of two and three terminations will be formatted thus:

> **bonus**, **-a**, **-um**: good
>
> **facilis**, **-e**: easy
>
> **prior**, **prius**: earlier

Single termination adjectives will have the genitive indicated thus:

> **plus**, **pluris** (*gen.*): more

Participles will generally be glossed as a verb, but some participles (particularly where their verbal force has been weakened) are glossed as adjectives or nouns: e.g.

> **decens**, **decentis** (*gen.*): appropriate
>
> **valens**, **valentis** (*gen.*): strong
>
> **paratus**, **-a**, **-um**: prepared
>
> **parens**, **parentis** m/f: a parent
>
> **serpenes**, **-entis** m: a snake

Verbs with regular infinitives are indicated by conjugation number: e.g.,

> **laudo** (1): to praise
>
> **moneo** (2): to warn
>
> **facio** (3): to do
>
> **venio** (4): to come

Where principal parts are predictable, as in the case of most first conjugation verbs, only the conjugation number will be given in the glossary. This format is used even in the case of unpredictable perfect forms, if the word occurring in the text at that point is based on the present stem (present, future, imperfect tenses). Elsewhere the principal parts will be provided as necessary. The following irregular verbs are listed with their infinitive instead of a number: *ferre, nolle, volle, posse.*

Simple syntactical information such as "+ *gen.*" or "+ *inf.*" will often be cited in the glossary with verbs and adjectives. However, the lexical information given for most words is minimal and sometimes specific to the context. To get a broader sense of the peculiarities of language of the gospel, it will be necessary to consult the commentaries or critical literature cited above.

Glossing Conventions: Greek

The glossing conventions for nouns and adjectives is the standard one found in dictionaries, except the genitive is not always given for regular words:

γυνή, γυναικός, ἡ: a woman

but:

μαρτυρία, ἡ: a witness

λόγος, ὁ: a word

Since verbs tend to be the biggest challenge in Greek from a morphological standpoint, they have been treated more fully in the commentary than the corresponding forms in Latin. The page by page vocabularies only list the dictionary forms (present indicative). Those tenses that are predictable from the present stem (imperfect, weak aorist, future, etc.) are not generally noted in the commentary. However, unpredictable forms are given fuller treatment in the commentary, which results in much repetition. But the commentary is meant to be consulted as needed rather than read continuously.

There is a small number of important "defective" verbs that lack forms in the present, and these will be found in the glossary with an indication of the tense in parentheses in the following manner:

ἦλθον: to go (*aor.*), used as the aorist of ἔρχομαι

εἶμι: to go (*fut.*), used as the future of ἔρχομαι

οἶδα: to know (*perf.*), used as the perfect of ὁράω (i.e. "I have seen")

εἶδον: to see (*aor.*), used as the aorist of ὁράω

ὄψομαι: to see (*fut.*), used as the future of ὁράω

ἤνεγχον: to bear (*aor.*), used as the aorist of φέρω

οἴσω: to bear (*fut.*), used as the future of φέρω

ἐρέω: to speak (*fut.*), used as the future of λέγω

εἶπον: to speak (*aor.*), used as the aorist of λέγω

εἴρηκα: to speak (*perf.*), used as the perfect of λέγω

ἔφαγον: to eat (*aor.*), used as the aorist of ἐσθίω

ἔδραμον: to run (*aor.*), used as the aorist of τρέχω

ABBREVIATIONS

abl.	ablative	lit.	literally
abs.	absolute	m.	masculine
acc.	accusative	mid.	middle
act.	active	n.	neuter
adj.	adjective	neg.	negative
adv.	adverb	nom.	nominative
aor.	aorist	obj.	object
attrib.	attributive	part.	participles
cf.	*confer* ("compare")	pass.	passive
circum.	circumstantial	perf.	perfect
cl.	clause	periph.	periphrastic
com.	command	pl.	plural
comp.	comparative	plupf.	pluperfect
cond.	condition	poss.	possession
dat.	dative	pred.	predicate
delib.	deliberative	prep.	preposition
dep.	deponent	pres.	present
epex.	epexegetic	prohib.	prohibition
etc.	*et cetera* ("and the rest")	pron.	pronoun
f.	feminine	purp.	purpose
fut.	future	quest.	question
gen.	genitive	rel.	relative
i.e.	*id est* ("that is")	resp.	respect
imper.	imperative	s.	singular
impers.	impersonal	sc.	*scilicet* ("supply")
impf.	imperfect	st.	statement
ind.	indirect	subj.	subjunctive
indecl.	indeclinable	subst.	substantive
indef.	indefinite	suppl.	supplementary
indic.	indicative	sync.	syncopated
inf.	infinitive	temp.	temporal
interog.	interrogative	voc.	vocative

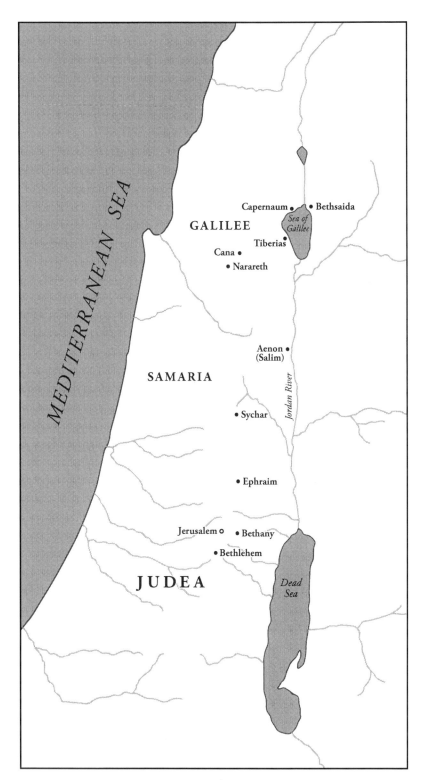

ΚΑΤΑ ΙΩΑΝΝΗΝ ΕΥΑΓΓΕΛΙΟΝ

EVANGELIUM SECUNDUM IOANNEM

Chapter 1

The Word Becomes Flesh

¹ ἐν ἀρχῇ ἦν ὁ λόγος, καὶ ὁ λόγος ἦν πρὸς τὸν θεόν, καὶ θεὸς ἦν ὁ λόγος. ² οὗτος ἦν ἐν ἀρχῇ πρὸς τὸν θεόν. ³ πάντα δι᾽ αὐτοῦ ἐγένετο, καὶ χωρὶς αὐτοῦ ἐγένετο οὐδὲ ἕν. ⁴ ὃ γέγονεν ἐν αὐτῷ ζωὴ ἦν, καὶ ἡ ζωὴ ἦν τὸ φῶς τῶν ἀνθρώπων· ⁵ καὶ τὸ φῶς ἐν τῇ σκοτίᾳ φαίνει, καὶ ἡ σκοτία αὐτὸ οὐ κατέλαβεν.

⁶ ἐγένετο ἄνθρωπος ἀπεσταλμένος παρὰ θεοῦ, ὄνομα αὐτῷ Ἰωάνης· ⁷ οὗτος ἦλθεν εἰς μαρτυρίαν, ἵνα μαρτυρήσῃ περὶ τοῦ φωτός, ἵνα πάντες πιστεύσωσιν δι᾽ αὐτοῦ. ⁸ οὐκ ἦν ἐκεῖνος τὸ φῶς, ἀλλ᾽ ἵνα μαρτυρήσῃ περὶ τοῦ φωτός.

ἄνθρωπος, ὁ: a man, human	λόγος, ὁ: the word
ἀποστέλλω: to send off or away from	μαρτυρέω: to bear witness
ἀρχή, ἡ: first cause, beginning	μαρτυρία, ἡ: witness, testimony, evidence
γίνομαι: to become	ὄνομα, -ατος, τό: name
εἷς, μία, ἕν: one	πιστεύω: to believe in
ζωή, ἡ: life	σκοτία, ἡ: darkness, gloom
ἦλθον: to come (aor.)	φαίνω: to bring to light, shine
θεὸς, ὁ: God	φῶς, φωτός, τό: light
Ἰωάνης, ὁ: John (the Baptist)	χωρίς: without (+ gen.)
καταλαμβάνω: to seize upon, comprehend	

1:1   **θεὸς ἦν ὁ λόγος**: the article indicates the subject, "the Word was God"

1:3   **ἐγένετο**: aor. of γίνομαι, "all things *became*"

1:4   **γέγονεν**: perf. of γίνομαι, "what *has become*"
      ἡ ζωὴ ἦν τὸ φῶς: "the life was the light." When both subject and predicate have a definite article, the subject will usually be the first.

1:5   **αὐτὸ**: acc. n. s., "did not comprehend *it*," i.e. the light
      κατέλαβεν: aor. of κατα-λαμβάνω, "*did* not *comprehend* it"

1:6   **ἀπεσταλμένος**: perf. part. of ἀπο-στέλλω, "having been sent"
      αὐτῷ: dat. of poss., "*his* name"

1:7   **ἵνα μαρτυρήσῃ**: aor. subj. in purpose clause, "in order to witness." John regularly uses the subj. in secondary sequence instead of the optative.
      ἵνα πιστεύσωσιν: aor. subj. mixing purpose and result, "so that all believe"

1:8   **οὐκ ἦν ἐκεῖνος τὸ φῶς**: a pronoun will generally be the subject, "*that one* was not the light"

Chapter 1

The Word Becomes Flesh

¹ In principio erat Verbum, et Verbum erat apud Deum, et Deus erat Verbum. ² Hoc erat in principio apud Deum. ³ Omnia per ipsum facta sunt, et sine ipso factum est nihil, quod factum est; ⁴ in ipso vita erat, et vita erat lux hominum, ⁵ et lux in tenebris lucet, et tenebrae eam non comprehenderunt.

⁶ Fuit homo missus a Deo, cui nomen erat Ioannes; ⁷ hic venit in testimonium, ut testimonium perhiberet de lumine, ut omnes crederent per illum. ⁸ Non erat ille lux, sed ut testimonium perhiberet de lumine.

---

apud: near, among (+ *acc.*)
comprehendo, (3), **-prendi**: to catch, seize, overcome
Deus, **-i** *m*: god
facio, (3), **feci**, **factum**: to make, do
homo, **hominis** *m*: man
Ioannes, **Ioannis** *m*: John (i.e. the Baptist)
luceo, (2): to shine, emit light
lumen, **luminis** *n*: light
lux, **lucis** *f*: light

mitto, (3), **misi**, **missus**: to send
nihil: nothing
nomen, **nominis** *n*: name
omnis, **-e**: each, every
principium, **-i** *n*: beginning
tenebrae, **-arum** *f*: darkness (*pl.*)
testimonium, **-i** *n*: testimony
perhibeo, (2): to present, give
verbum, **-i** *n*: word
vita, **-ae** *f*: life

1:1   **Deus**: nom. predicate, "The Word was *God.*" See the note on predication above on pages xxviii-xxix.

1:3   **nihil, quod factum est**: "nothing which was made" Jerome understood the phrase ὃ γέγονεν as the end of this verse, instead of the beginning of the next one.

1:5   **eam**: "did not comprehend *her*" i.e. the light

1:6   **cui**: relative pron. dat. of possession, "*whose* name"

1:7   **ut perhiberet**: impf. subj. in purp. clause, "in order to witness"
     lumine: "about *the light*," note the variation of *lux* and *lumen*
     ut crederent: impf. subj. mixing purpose and result, "so that all believe"

1:8   **lux**: nom. predicate, "he was not *the light*" a pronoun will usually be the subject, not the predicate

⁹ ἦν τὸ φῶς τὸ ἀληθινόν, ὃ φωτίζει πάντα ἄνθρωπον, ἐρχόμενον εἰς τὸν κόσμον. ¹⁰ ἐν τῷ κόσμῳ ἦν, καὶ ὁ κόσμος δι᾽ αὐτοῦ ἐγένετο, καὶ ὁ κόσμος αὐτὸν οὐκ ἔγνω. ¹¹ Εἰς τὰ ἴδια ἦλθεν, καὶ οἱ ἴδιοι αὐτὸν οὐ παρέλαβον. ¹² ὅσοι δὲ ἔλαβον αὐτόν, ἔδωκεν αὐτοῖς ἐξουσίαν τέκνα θεοῦ γενέσθαι, τοῖς πιστεύουσιν εἰς τὸ ὄνομα αὐτοῦ, ¹³ οἳ οὐκ ἐξ αἱμάτων οὐδὲ ἐκ θελήματος σαρκὸς οὐδὲ ἐκ θελήματος ἀνδρὸς ἀλλ᾽ ἐκ θεοῦ ἐγεννήθησαν.

¹⁴ καὶ ὁ λόγος σὰρξ ἐγένετο καὶ ἐσκήνωσεν ἐν ἡμῖν, καὶ ἐθεασάμεθα τὴν δόξαν αὐτοῦ, δόξαν ὡς μονογενοῦς παρὰ πατρός, πλήρης χάριτος καὶ ἀληθείας·

αἷμα, -ατος, τό: blood	λαμβάνω: to take
ἀληθινός, -ή, -όν: true	μονογενής, -ές: only-begotten, single
γεννάω: to beget, engender	ὅσος, -η, -ον: how many
γινώσκω: to learn to know	παραλαμβάνω: to receive from
δίδωμι: to give	πατήρ, πατρός, ὁ: a father
δόξα, ἡ: glory, opinion	πιστεύω: to believe in (+ *dat.*)
ἐξουσία, ἡ: power or authority	σάρξ, -κος, ἡ: flesh
ἔρχομαι: to come or go	σκηνόω: to encamp, dwell
θεάομαι: to look on, gaze at, view, behold	τέκνον, τό: a child
θέλημα, -ατος, τό: will	πλήρης, -ες: filled with (+ *gen.*)
ἴδιος, -α, -ον: one's own,	φωτίζω: to enlighten, illuminate
κόσμος, ὁ: world	χάρις, ἡ: grace

1:9   **ἐρχόμενον**: pres. part. nom. n. used periphrastically, "the light was *coming*"

1:10   **οὐκ ἔγνω**: aor. of γινώσκω, "did not recognize"

1:11   **εἰς τὰ ἴδια**: n. pl., "into his own (things);" note the use of ἴδιος here instead of the reflexive pronoun, a common change in *koine*.

      οἱ ἴδιοι: "his own people"

      οὐ παρέλαβον: aor. of παρα-λαμβάνω, "did not receive"

1:12   **ἔλαβον**: aor. of λαμβάνω, "those who *received*"

      ἔδωκεν: aor. of δίδωμι, "he gave"

      γενέσθαι: aor. inf. epexegetic after ἐξουσίαν, "the power *to become*"

      τοῖς πιστεύουσιν: pres. part. attributive dat., "gave *to the ones believing*"

1:13   **ἐγεννήθησαν**: aor. pass. of γεννάω, "who *were begotten*"

1:14   **ὡς μονογενοῦς**: gen., "the glory *like that of an only-begotten son* of a father"

      πλήρης: nom. agreeing with λόγος, "full of" + gen.

⁹ Erat lux vera, quae illuminat omnem hominem, veniens in mundum. ¹⁰ In mundo erat, et mundus per ipsum factus est, et mundus eum non cognovit. ¹¹ In propria venit, et sui eum non receperunt. ¹² Quotquot autem acceperunt eum, dedit eis potestatem filios Dei fieri, his, qui credunt in nomine eius, ¹³ qui non ex sanguinibus neque ex voluntate carnis neque ex voluntate viri, sed ex Deo nati sunt.

¹⁴ Et Verbum caro factum est et habitavit in nobis; et vidimus gloriam eius, gloriam quasi Unigeniti a Patre, plenum gratiae et veritatis.

---

accipio, (3), **accepi, acceptus**: to receive, accept
caro, carnis *f.*: flesh
filius, fili *m*: son
fio, (3): to happen, become
gloria, -ae *f.*: glory, fame
gratia, -ae *f.*: grace
habito, (1): to inhabit, live, stay
illumino, (1): to illuminate, light up
mundus, -i *m*: world
nascor, (3), **natus sum**: be produced, born
pater, patris *m*: father

plenus, -a, -um: full of (+ *gen.*)
potestas, potestatis *f.*: power, rule, force
proprius, -a, -um: own, very own
quotquot: however many
recipio, (3), **recepi, receptus**: to receive, accept
sanguis, sanguinis *m*: blood, family
unigenitus, -a, -um: only begotten
veritas, veritatis *f.*: truth, fact
verus, a, um: true
video, (2), **vidi, visus**: to see
voluntas, voluntatis *f.*: will, desire, purpose

1:9   **veniens**: pres. part. used periphrastically, "the light was *coming*"
1:11   **propria**: used like ἴδιος instead of the reflexive pronoun, "into *his own*"
1:12   **fieri**: epexegetic inf. after *potestatem*, "power *to become*"
       in nomine: "believe *in his name*." Both Jerome and John sometimes use the dative after credo/πιστεύω and at other times, as here, use a preposition.
1:14   **in nobis**: "among us"
       quasi Unigeniti: not "as if," but "as being appropriate for an only-begotten"
       plenum: agreeing with verbum, "full of" + gen.

¹⁵ Ἰωάνης μαρτυρεῖ περὶ αὐτοῦ καὶ κέκραγεν λέγων·

«οὗτος ἦν ὃν εἶπον· ὁ ὀπίσω μου ἐρχόμενος ἔμπροσθέν μου

γέγονεν, ὅτι πρῶτός μου ἦν ·» ¹⁶ ὅτι ἐκ τοῦ πληρώματος

αὐτοῦ ἡμεῖς πάντες ἐλάβομεν, καὶ χάριν ἀντὶ χάριτος· ¹⁷ ὅτι

ὁ νόμος διὰ Μωυσέως ἐδόθη, ἡ χάρις καὶ ἡ ἀλήθεια διὰ Ἰησοῦ

Χριστοῦ ἐγένετο. ¹⁸ θεὸν οὐδεὶς ἑώρακεν πώποτε· μονογενὴς

θεὸς ὁ ὢν εἰς τὸν κόλπον τοῦ πατρὸς ἐκεῖνος ἐξηγήσατο.

The Testimony of John the Baptist

¹⁹ καὶ αὕτη ἐστὶν ἡ μαρτυρία τοῦ Ἰωάνου ὅτε ἀπέστειλαν

πρὸς αὐτὸν οἱ Ἰουδαῖοι ἐξ Ἱεροσολύμων ἱερεῖς καὶ Λευείτας

ἵνα ἐρωτήσωσιν αὐτόν «Σὺ τίς εἶ;»

εἶπον: to speak, say (aor.)
ἔμπροσθεν: before, in front
ἐξηγέομαι: to lead out, to declare
ἐρωτάω: to ask, inquire
Ἰησοῦς, -ου, ὁ: Jesus
κόλπος, ὁ: the bosom
κράζω: to cry out
μονογενής, -ές: only-begotten, single
Μωυσῆς, Μωυσέως, ὁ: Moses
νόμος, ὁ: custom, law
ὀπίσω: backwards

ὁράω: to see
πλήρωμα, -ατος, τό: a full measure
πρῶτος, -η, -ον: first
πώποτε: ever yet
χάρις, ἡ: grace
Ἰουδαῖος, ὁ: a Jew
Ἱεροσόλυμα, -ων, τά: Jerusalem
ἱερεύς, ὁ: a priest, sacrificer
Λευείτης, -ου, ὁ: a Levite
χριστός, -ή, -όν: annointed

1:15 κέκραγεν: perf. of κράζω, "John *shouted*"
οὗτος ἦν ὃν εἶπον: "this was (the one) about whom I said"
ὁ ὀπίσω μου ἐρχόμενος: pres. part. attributive, "the one coming behind"
1:16 ἐλάβομεν: aor. of λαμβάνω, "we all received"
ἀντὶ χάριτος: "for the sake of grace," perhaps meaning, "grace in abundance"
1:17 ἐδόθη: aor. pass. of δίδωμι, "it was given"
1:18 ἑώρακεν: perf. of ὁράω, "no one *has seen*"
ὁ ὢν: pres. part. attributive, "the one who is"
ἐξηγήσατο: aor. of ἐξ-ηγέομαι, "that one (the son) *has declared*"
1:19 ἀπέστειλαν: aor. of ἀπο-στέλλω, "when *they sent out* priests and Levites"
ἵνα ἐρωτήσωσιν: weak aor. subj. of ἐρωτάω in purpose clause, "in order to
question"

¹⁵ Ioannes testimonium perhibet de ipso et clamat dicens: "Hic erat, quem dixi: 'Qui post me venturus est, ante me factus est, quia prior me erat'." ¹⁶ Et de plenitudine eius nos omnes accepimus, et gratiam pro gratia; ¹⁷ quia lex per Moysen data est, gratia et veritas per Iesum Christum facta est. ¹⁸ Deum nemo vidit umquam; unigenitus Deus, qui est in sinum Patris, ipse enarravit.

The Testimony of John the Baptist

¹⁹ Et hoc est testimonium Ioannis, quando miserunt ad eum Iudaei ab Hierosolymis sacerdotes et Levitas, ut interrogarent eum: "Tu quis es?"

---

accipio, (3) **accepi, acceptus**: to receive, accept
clamo, (1): to proclaim, declare, shout
enarro, (1): to describe, narrate
Hierosolyma, -orum *n*: Jerusalem
Iesus, Iesu *m*: Jesus
interrogo, (1): to ask, question, interrogate
Iudaeus, -i *m*: Jew, the Jews
Levita, -ae *m*: Levite
lex, legis *f*: law

nemo, neminis *m/f*: no one, nobody
plenitudo, plenitudinis *f*: fullness
prior, prius: ahead, in front; prior
sacerdos, -dotis *m*: a priest
sinus, sinus *m*: bosom, lap
umquam: ever, at any time
unigenitus, -a, -um: only begotten
venio (4): to come
veritas, -tatis *f*: the truth

1:15 **de ipso**: i.e. about the Word
venturus: fut. part. periphrastic, "who is *about to come*"
1:16 **gratiam pro gratia**: "grace for grace," reproducing the ambiguity of the Greek phrase, which perhaps means "grace in abundance"
1:18 **in sinum**: "in the lap" where classical Latin would use "in sinu." Jerome follows the Greek usage.
1:19 **ut interrogarent**: impf. subj. purpose clause, "in order to question him"

²⁰ καὶ ὡμολόγησεν καὶ οὐκ ἠρνήσατο, καὶ ὡμολόγησεν ὅτι «Ἐγὼ οὐκ εἰμὶ ὁ χριστός.»

²¹ καὶ ἠρώτησαν αὐτόν «Τί οὖν; σὺ Ἠλείας εἶ;»

καὶ λέγει «Οὐκ εἰμί.»

«Ὁ προφήτης εἶ σύ;»

καὶ ἀπεκρίθη «Οὔ.»

²² εἶπαν οὖν αὐτῷ «Τίς εἶ; ἵνα ἀπόκρισιν δῶμεν τοῖς πέμψασιν ἡμᾶς· τί λέγεις περὶ σεαυτοῦ;»

²³ ἔφη «Ἐγὼ φωνὴ βοῶντος ἐν τῇ ἐρήμῳ Εὐθύνατε τὴν ὁδὸν Κυρίου, καθὼς εἶπεν Ἡσαίας ὁ προφήτης.»

²⁴ καὶ ἀπεσταλμένοι ἦσαν ἐκ τῶν Φαρισαίων. ²⁵ καὶ ἠρώτησαν αὐτὸν καὶ εἶπαν αὐτῷ «Τί οὖν βαπτίζεις εἰ σὺ οὐκ εἶ ὁ χριστὸς οὐδὲ Ἠλείας οὐδὲ ὁ προφήτης;»

ἀποκρίνομαι: to answer
ἀπόκρισις, ἡ: an answer
ἀποστέλλω: to send away or forth
ἀρνέομαι: to deny, disown
βαπτίζω: to dip in water, baptize
βοάω: to cry aloud, to shout
ἐρῆμος, ὁ: desert
εὐθύνω: to guide straight, direct
Ἠλείας: Elijah the prophet

Ἡσαίας: Isaiah the prophet
καθώς: just as
κυριός, ὁ: lord
ὁδός, ἡ: a way, path
ὁμολογέω: to speak together, agree
πέμπω: to send, despatch
προφήτης, -ου, ὁ: a prophet
Φαρισαῖοι, οἱ: the Pharisees, a Jewish sect
φωνὴ, ἡ:

1:20 ὡμολόγησεν: aor. of ὁμολογέω, "he agreed"
      οὐκ ἠρνήσατο: aor. of ἀρνέομαι, "he did not deny"

1:21 ἠρώτησαν: weak aor. of ἐρωτάω, "they asked"
      ἀπεκρίθη: aor. pass. of ἀπο-κρίνομαι, "he answered"

1:22 εἶπαν: aor. of λέγω with a weak aorist ending, "they said"
      ἵνα δῶμεν: aor. subj. of δίδωμι in result clause, "so that we might give"
      τοῖς πέμψασιν: aor. part. dat. pl. of πέμπω, "to those sending"

1:23 βοῶντος: pres. part. gen. s., "voice *of one crying out*"
      εὐθύνατε: aor. imper. of εὐθύνω, "make straight!"

1:24 ἀπεσταλμένοι ἦσαν: plupf. periphrastic of ἀπο-στέλλω, "they had been sent forth"

1:25 ὁ χριστὸς ...ὁ προφήτης: the definite article in the predicate particularizes, "if you are not *the* annointed one or *the* prophet"

²⁰ Et confessus est et non negavit; et confessus est: "Non sum ego Christus."

²¹ Et interrogaverunt eum: "Quid ergo? Elias es tu?"

Et dicit: "Non sum."

"Propheta es tu?"

Et respondit: "Non."

²² Dixerunt ergo ei: "Quis es? Ut responsum demus his, qui miserunt nos. Quid dicis de teipso?"

²³ Ait: "Ego vox clamantis in deserto: 'Dirigite viam Domini,' sicut dixit Isaias propheta."

²⁴ Et qui missi fuerant, erant ex pharisaeis; ²⁵ et interrogaverunt eum et dixerunt ei: "Quid ergo baptizas, si tu non es Christus neque Elias neque propheta?"

---

baptizo, (1): to baptize	**Elias**: Elijah the prophet
clamo, (1): to cry out	**Isaia, -ae** *m*: Isaiah the prophet
confiteor, (2), **confessus sum**: to agree	**nego**, (1): to deny, say ... not
desertum, -i *n*: desert	**Pharisaeus, -i** *m*: Pharisee
dirigo, (3): to make straight	**propheta, -ae** *m*: prophet
do, (1) **dedi, datus**: to give	**via, -ae** *f*: way, road
dominus, -i *m*: master, lord	**vox, vocis** *f*: voice

1:22   **ut... demus**: pres. subj. purpose clause, "*in order that we may give* a response"

1:23   **vox**: predicate nom., "I am *the voice*"

1:24   **missi fuerant**: plupf. (= *missi erant*), "who *had been sent*"

²⁶ ἀπεκρίθη αὐτοῖς ὁ Ἰωάνης λέγων «Ἐγὼ βαπτίζω ἐν ὕδατι· μέσος ὑμῶν στήκει ὃν ὑμεῖς οὐκ οἴδατε, ²⁷ ὀπίσω μου ἐρχόμενος, οὗ οὐκ εἰμὶ [ἐγὼ] ἄξιος ἵνα λύσω αὐτοῦ τὸν ἱμάντα τοῦ ὑποδήματος.»

²⁸ ταῦτα ἐν Βηθανίᾳ ἐγένετο πέραν τοῦ Ἰορδάνου, ὅπου ἦν ὁ Ἰωάνης βαπτίζων.

The Lamb of God

²⁹ τῇ ἐπαύριον βλέπει τὸν Ἰησοῦν ἐρχόμενον πρὸς αὐτόν, καὶ λέγει «Ἴδε ὁ ἀμνὸς τοῦ θεοῦ ὁ αἴρων τὴν ἁμαρτίαν τοῦ κόσμου. ³⁰ οὗτός ἐστιν ὑπὲρ οὗ ἐγὼ εἶπον Ὀπίσω μου ἔρχεται ἀνὴρ ὃς ἔμπροσθέν μου γέγονεν, ὅτι πρῶτός μου ἦν·

αἴρω: to take up, raise, lift up
ἁμαρτία, ἡ: a failure, fault, sin
ἀμνός, ὁ: a lamb
ἄξιος, -ία, -ον: worthy
Βηθανία, ἡ: Bethany
βλέπω: to see, have the power of sight
εἶδον: to see (*aor.*)
ἐπαύριον: on the morrow
ἱμάς, -αντις, ὁ: a leathern strap or thong
Ἰορδάνος, ὁ: Jordan River

λύω: to loose
μέσος, -η, -ον: middle, in the middle
οἶδα: to know (*perf.*)
ὀπίσω: behind (+ *gen.*)
πέραν: on the other side of (+ *gen.*)
πρῶτός, -ή, -όν: first
στήκω: to stand
ὕδωρ, ὕδατος, τό: water
ὑπόδημα, -ατος, τό: a sandal

1:26 ἀπεκρίθη: aor. pass. of ἀπο-κρίνομαι, "he answered"
 οὐκ οἴδατε (=ἴστε): perf. of εἶδον, "you have not seen," i.e., "you know not"
1:27 οὗ: gen. after ἄξιος, "*of whom* I am not worthy"
 ἵνα λύσω: aor. subj. in noun clause after ἄξιος, in place of an epexegetic inf., "worthy *to loose*"
1:28 ἦν ... βαπτίζων: pres. part. in periphrastic impf., "was baptizing"
1:29 τῇ ἐπαύριον: (sc. ἡμέρᾳ), "on the next day"
 ἐρχόμενον: pres. part. circum. after βλέπει, "sees Jesus *walking*"
 ἴδε: imper. of εἶδον, "behold!"
 ὁ αἴρων: pres. part. attributive, "the one lifting"
1:30 ὑπὲρ οὗ: "this is the one *about whom*"
 πρῶτός μου: "first of me" i.e. before me

²⁶ Respondit eis Ioannes dicens: "Ego baptizo in aqua; medius vestrum stat, quem vos non scitis, ²⁷ qui post me venturus est, cuius ego non sum dignus, ut solvam eius corrigiam calceamenti."

²⁸ Haec in Bethania facta sunt trans Iordanem, ubi erat Ioannes baptizans.

The Lamb of God

²⁹ Altera die videt Iesum venientem ad se et ait: "Ecce agnus Dei, qui tollit peccatum mundi. ³⁰ Hic est, de quo dixi: Post me venit vir, qui ante me factus est, quia prior me erat.

---

agnus, -i *m*: lamb
alter, -a, -um: one (of two), the other
aqua, -ae *f*: water, sea
Bethania, -ae *f*: Bethany
calceamentum, -i *n*: shoe
corrigia, -ae *f*: shoe-lace, tie
dies, -i *m/f*: day
dignus, -a, -um: worthy (+ *gen.*)
ecce: behold! see!

Iordan, Iordanis *f*: Jordan (river)
medius, -a, -um: in the middle of (+ *gen.*)
peccatum, -i *n*: sin
prior, prius: ahead, in front, previous
scio, (4): to know, understand
solvo, (3): to loosen
sto, (1), **steti**, **status**: to stand
tollo, (3): to remove
venio, (4): to come

1:26 **vestrum**: gen. pl., "in the middle *of you*"
1:27 **cuius**: gen. after *dignus*, "*of whom* I am not worthy"
    ut solvam: pres. subj. epexegetic noun clause after *dignus* instead of an infinitive, "worthy *so as to loosen*"
1:28 **baptizans**: pres. part. used periphrastically with *erat*, "John was *baptizing*"
1:30 **venit**: pres. with fut. meaning, "he is coming"

11

³¹ κἀγὼ οὐκ ᾔδειν αὐτόν, ἀλλ' ἵνα φανερωθῇ τῷ Ἰσραὴλ διὰ τοῦτο ἦλθον ἐγὼ ἐν ὕδατι βαπτίζων.»

³² καὶ ἐμαρτύρησεν Ἰωάνης λέγων ὅτι «Τεθέαμαι τὸ πνεῦμα καταβαῖνον ὡς περιστερὰν ἐξ οὐρανοῦ, καὶ ἔμεινεν ἐπ' αὐτόν· ³³ κἀγὼ οὐκ ᾔδειν αὐτόν, ἀλλ' ὁ πέμψας με βαπτίζειν ἐν ὕδατι ἐκεῖνός μοι εἶπεν Ἐφ' ὃν ἂν ἴδῃς τὸ πνεῦμα καταβαῖνον καὶ μένον ἐπ' αὐτόν, οὗτός ἐστιν ὁ βαπτίζων ἐν πνεύματι ἁγίῳ· ³⁴ κἀγὼ ἑώρακα, καὶ μεμαρτύρηκα ὅτι οὗτός ἐστιν ὁ υἱὸς τοῦ θεοῦ.»

ἅγιος, -α, -ον: sacred, holy
θεάομαι: to see
Ἰσραὴλ, ὁ: Israel
καταβαίνω: to step down, go or come down
μαρτυρέω: to be a witness, to bear witness
μένω: to remain

οὐρανός, ὁ: heaven
περιστερά, ἡ: the common pigeon or dove
πνεῦμα, -ατος, τό: spirit
ὕδωρ, ὕδατος, τό: water
υἱός, ὁ: a son
φανερόω: to make manifest

1:31 κἀγὼ: = καὶ ἐγώ
    ᾔδειν: plupf. of οἶδα, "*I did not know* him"
    ἵνα φανερωθῇ: aor. pass. subj. of φανερόω in result/purpose clause, "I came *so he will be revealed*"
1:32 τεθέαμαι: perf. of θεάομαι, "I have seen"
    καταβαῖνον: pres. part. circum., "the spirit *descending*"
    ἔμεινεν: aor. of μένω, "*it rested* on him"
1:33 ὁ πέμψας: aor. part. attributive, "*the one who sent* me"
    βαπτίζειν: pres. inf. indicating purpose, "sent *in order to baptize*"
    ἐφ' ὃν ἂν ἴδῃς: aor. subj. of εἶδον in general relative clause, "on whomever you see"
    καταβαῖνον καὶ μένον; pres. part. circum. after ἴδῃς, "see the spirit *descending and remaining*"
    ὁ βαπτίζων: pres. part. pred., "this is *the one baptizing*"
1:34 ἑώρακα: perf. of ὁράω, "I have seen"
    μεμαρτύρηκα: perf. of μαρτυρέω, "I have witnessed"

³¹ Et ego nesciebam eum, sed ut manifestetur Israel, propterea veni ego in aqua baptizans."

³² Et testimonium perhibuit Ioannes dicens: "Vidi Spiritum descendentem quasi columbam de caelo, et mansit super eum; ³³ et ego nesciebam eum, sed, qui misit me baptizare in aqua, ille mihi dixit: 'Super quem videris Spiritum descendentem et manentem super eum, hic est qui baptizat in Spiritu Sancto.' ³⁴ Et ego vidi et testimonium perhibui quia hic est Filius Dei."

---

aqua, -ae *f.*: water
caelus, -i *m*: heaven, sky
columba, -ae *f.*: dove
descendo, (3): to descend
hic: here, in this place
Israel (*indecl.*): Israel
maneo, (2), mansi, mansus: to remain, stay
manifesto, (1): to reveal, make known

mitto (3) misi, missus: to send
nescio, (4): to not know
perhibeo, (2), perhibui, perhibitus: to give, bestow
propterea: therefore, for this reason
sanctus, -a, -um: consecrated, sacred
spiritus, -us *m*: spirit
video (2) vidi, visus: to see

1:31 **ut manifestetur**: pres. subj. in purpose clause, "I came *in order that* Israel *be revealed*"

1:32 **quasi**: translating ὡς in its adverbial sense, "as if, sort of like"

1:33 **baptizare**: inf. of purpose, "sent me *to baptize*"
quem videris: perf. subj. in relative clause of characteristic, "over (the one) *whom you see*"

1:34 **quia hic est**: vivid form of ind. st., "gave testimony *that he is the son*"

13

The First Disciples

³⁵ τῇ ἐπαύριον πάλιν εἱστήκει Ἰωάνης καὶ ἐκ τῶν μαθητῶν αὐτοῦ δύο, ³⁶ καὶ ἐμβλέψας τῷ Ἰησοῦ περιπατοῦντι λέγει «Ἴδε ὁ ἀμνὸς τοῦ θεοῦ.»

³⁷ καὶ ἤκουσαν οἱ δύο μαθηταὶ αὐτοῦ λαλοῦντος καὶ ἠκολούθησαν τῷ Ἰησοῦ. ³⁸ στραφεὶς δὲ ὁ Ἰησοῦς καὶ θεασάμενος αὐτοὺς ἀκολουθοῦντας λέγει αὐτοῖς «Τί ζητεῖτε;»

οἱ δὲ εἶπαν αὐτῷ «Ῥαββεί, (ὃ λέγεται μεθερμηνευόμενον Διδάσκαλε,) ποῦ μένεις;»

³⁹ λέγει αὐτοῖς «Ἔρχεσθε καὶ ὄψεσθε.» ἦλθαν οὖν καὶ εἶδαν ποῦ μένει, καὶ παρ᾽ αὐτῷ ἔμειναν τὴν ἡμέραν ἐκείνην· ὥρα ἦν ὡς δεκάτη.

ἀκολουθέω: to follow
ἀμνός, ὁ: a lamb
Ἀνδρέας ὁ: Andrew
διδάσκαλος, ὁ: teacher
ἐμβλέπω: to look in the face, look at
ἐπαύριον (adv.): tomorrow
ζητέω: to seek, seek for
λαλέω: to talk

μαθητής, -οῦ, ὁ: a disciple
μεθερμηνεύω: to translate
ὄψομαι: to see (fut.)
πάλιν: again
περιπατέω: to walk about
Ῥαββεί: (Hebr.) teacher
στρέφω: to turn about or aside, turn
ὥρα, ἡ: hour

1:35 εἱστήκει: plupf. of ἵστημι, "John *was standing*"
  δύο: "and so were *two* of his disciples," an example of anacolouthon
1:36 ἐμβλέψας: aor. part. of ἐν-βλέπω, "having looked at" + dat.
1:37 ἤκουσαν: aor. of ἀκούω, "they heard" + gen. of source
  λαλοῦντος: pres. part. circum. gen. after ἤκουσαν, "heard him *speaking*"
  ἠκολούθησαν: aor. pass. of ἀκολούω, "they followed" + dat.
  τῷ Ἰησοῦ: dat. s. as indicated by the article
1:38 στραφεὶς: aor. part. pass. of στρέφω, "having turned"
  ἀκολουθοῦντας: pres. part. circum., "having seen them *following*"
  μεθερμηνευόμενον: pres. part. of μετα-ερμενεύω, "which *being translated*"
1:39 ὄψεσθε: fut., "you will see"
  ἦλθαν ... εἶδαν: aor. with weak aor. ending (=ἦλθον ... εἶδον), "they came ... they saw"
  τὴν ἡμέραν ἐκείνην: acc. of duration, "for that day"
  ὡς: "it was *about* the 10th hour"

14

The First Disciples

³⁵ Altera die iterum stabat Ioannes et ex discipulis eius duo, ³⁶ et respiciens Iesum ambulantem dicit: "Ecce agnus Dei."

³⁷ Et audierunt eum duo discipuli loquentem et secuti sunt Iesum. ³⁸ Conversus autem Iesus et videns eos sequentes se dicit eis: "Quid quaeritis?"

Qui dixerunt ei: "Rabbi — quod dicitur interpretatum Magister — ubi manes?"

³⁹ Dicit eis: "Venite et videbitis." Venerunt ergo et viderunt, ubi maneret, et apud eum manserunt die illo; hora erat quasi decima.

---

agnus, -i *m*: lamb
alter, -a, -um: second, next
ambulo, (1): to walk
apud: near, among (+ *acc.*)
audio, (4): to hear, listen, accept
autem: while, however
converto, (3), **converti, conversus**: to turn
   backwards
decem: tenth
dies, diei *m/f*: day

discipulus, –i *m*: follower, disciple
hora, -ae *f*: hour, time
interpreto (1): translate
iterum: again, for a second time
loquor, (3), **locutus sum**: speak, tell
quaero, (3): to search for, seek
quasi: as if, about
respicio, (3): to look back at, gaze at
sequor, (3), **secutus sum**: follow

1:36   **ambulantem**: pres. part. circumstantial, "looking at him *walking*"

1:37   **loquentem ... sequentes**: note the active participle form of deponent verbs
      loquor and *sequor*, "heard him *speaking* ... seeing them *following*"

1:38   **interpretatum**: perf. part., "which having been translated"

1:39   **ubi maneret**: impf. subj. indirect question, "saw *where he was staying*"
      die illo: abl. instead of acc. for duration, "for that day"

⁴⁰ ἦν Ἀνδρέας ὁ ἀδελφὸς Σίμωνος Πέτρου εἷς ἐκ τῶν δύο τῶν ἀκουσάντων παρὰ Ἰωάνου καὶ ἀκολουθησάντων αὐτῷ· ⁴¹ εὑρίσκει οὗτος πρῶτον τὸν ἀδελφὸν τὸν ἴδιον Σίμωνα καὶ λέγει αὐτῷ «Εὑρήκαμεν τὸν Μεσσίαν» (ὅ ἐστιν μεθερμηνευόμενον Χριστός). ⁴² ἤγαγεν αὐτὸν πρὸς τὸν Ἰησοῦν.

ἐμβλέψας αὐτῷ ὁ Ἰησοῦς εἶπεν «Σὺ εἶ Σίμων ὁ υἱὸς Ἰωάνου, σὺ κληθήσῃ Κηφᾶς» (ὃ ἑρμηνεύεται Πέτρος).

The Calling of Philip and Nathaniel

⁴³ τῇ ἐπαύριον ἠθέλησεν ἐξελθεῖν εἰς τὴν Γαλιλαίαν. καὶ εὑρίσκει Φίλιππον καὶ λέγει αὐτῷ ὁ Ἰησοῦς «Ἀκολούθει μοι.»

ἄγω: to lead or carry, to convey, bring
ἀδελφός, ὁ: brother
Γαλιλαία, ἡ: Galilee
ἐθέλω: to will, wish, purpose
ἐμβλέπω: to look in the face, look at
ἐξῆλθον: to go or come out of (*aor.*)
ἑρμηνεύω: to interpret
εὑρίσκω: to find

καλέω: to call, name
Κηφᾶς, -ᾶ, ὁ (*Hebr.*): a rock
μεθερμηνεύω: to translate
Μεσσία, -ου, ὁ (*Hebr.*): annointed
Πέτρος, ὁ: Peter
Σίμων -ονος, ὁ: Simon
Φίλιππος, ὁ: Philip
Χριστός, ὁ: Christ, the annointed one

1:40 τῶν ἀκουσάντων ... ἀκολουθησάντων: aor. part. attributive gen. pl., "one of the two *who had heard ... who had followed*" + dat.

1:41 εὑρήκαμεν: unaugmented perf. of εὑρίσκω, "we have found"
ἐστιν μεθερμηνευόμενον: pres. part. pass. periphrastic, "which *is translated*"

1:42 ἤγαγεν: aor. of ἄγω, "he led"
ἐμβλέψας: aor. of ἐν-βλέπω, "having seen him"
κληθήσῃ: fut. pass. of καλέω, "you will be called"

1:43 τῇ ἐπαύριον: (sc. ἡμέρᾳ) dat. of time when, "on the next day"
ἠθέλησεν: aor. of ἐθέλω, "he wished" + inf.
ἀκολούθει: pres. imper. of ἀκολουθέω, "follow!"

⁴⁰ Erat Andreas, frater Simonis Petri, unus ex duobus, qui audierant ab Ioanne et secuti fuerant eum. ⁴¹ Invenit hic primum fratrem suum Simonem et dicit ei: "Invenimus Messiam"— quod est interpretatum Christus; ⁴² adduxit eum ad Iesum.

Intuitus eum Iesus dixit: "Tu es Simon filius Ioannis; tu vocaberis Cephas"— quod interpretatur Petrus.

The Calling of Philip and Nathaniel

⁴³ In crastinum voluit exire in Galilaeam et invenit Philippum. Et dicit ei Iesus: "Sequere me."

---

adduco, (3): to lead
Andreas, -ae *m*: Andrew
Christus, -i *m*: Christ
crastinum, -i *n*: tomorrow
exeo, (4): to come, go
frater, fratris *m*: brother
Galilaea, -ae *f*: Galilee
intueor, (2), **intuitus sum**: to look at, consider

invenio, (4), **inveni, inventus**: to find, discover
Petrus, -i *m*: Peter
Philippus, -i *m*: Philip
primum: first
sequor (3) **secutus sum**: follow
Simon, Simonis *m*: Simon
voco, (1): to call
volo, velle, volui: to wish, want

1:40 **secuti fuerant:** plupf. (=*secuti erant*): "who *had followed*"
1: 41 **invenimus Messiam:** perf., "*we have found* the Messiah"
1:42 **vocaberis:** fut. pass., "you will be called"
1: 43 **in crastinum:** "in the morning," where we would expect the ablative

17

⁴⁴ ἦν δὲ ὁ Φίλιππος ἀπὸ Βηθσαιδά, ἐκ τῆς πόλεως Ἀνδρέου καὶ Πέτρου. ⁴⁵ εὑρίσκει Φίλιππος τὸν Ναθαναὴλ καὶ λέγει αὐτῷ «Ὃν ἔγραψεν Μωυσῆς ἐν τῷ νόμῳ καὶ οἱ προφῆται εὑρήκαμεν, Ἰησοῦν υἱὸν τοῦ Ἰωσὴφ τὸν ἀπὸ Ναζαρέτ.»

⁴⁶ καὶ εἶπεν αὐτῷ Ναθαναήλ «Ἐκ Ναζαρὲτ δύναταί τι ἀγαθὸν εἶναι;»

λέγει αὐτῷ ὁ Φίλιππος «Ἔρχου καὶ ἴδε.»

⁴⁷ εἶδεν Ἰησοῦς τὸν Ναθαναὴλ ἐρχόμενον πρὸς αὐτὸν καὶ λέγει περὶ αὐτοῦ «Ἴδε ἀληθῶς Ἰσραηλείτης ἐν ᾧ δόλος οὐκ ἔστιν.»

⁴⁸ λέγει αὐτῷ Ναθαναήλ «Πόθεν με γινώσκεις;»

ἀπεκρίθη Ἰησοῦς καὶ εἶπεν αὐτῷ «Πρὸ τοῦ σε Φίλιππον φωνῆσαι ὄντα ὑπὸ τὴν συκῆν εἶδόν σε.»

⁴⁹ ἀπεκρίθη αὐτῷ Ναθαναήλ «Ῥαββεί, σὺ εἶ ὁ υἱὸς τοῦ θεοῦ, σὺ βασιλεὺς εἶ τοῦ Ἰσραήλ.»

ἀγαθός, -ή, -όν: good
ἀκολουθέω: to follow
βασιλεύς, -έως, ὁ: a king, chief
Βηθσαιδά, ἡ: Bethesda
γράφω: to write
δόλος, ὁ: guile
δύναμαι: to be able, capable, strong enough
Ἰσραηλείτης, ὁ: an Israelite

Ἰωσήφ: Joseph
Ναζαρέτ: Nazareth
Ναθαναήλ, ὁ: Nathanael
πόθεν: whence?
πόλις, πόλεως, ἡ : a city
συκῆ, ἡ: a fig tree
φωνέω: to speak

1:45 ἔγραψεν: aor. of γράφω, "the one whom Moses *wrote about*"
ἐν τῷ νόμῳ καὶ οἱ προφῆται: "in the law and the prophets," i.e. in the Hebrew Bible
1:46 εἶναι: pres. inf. complementing δύναταί, "is anything good able *to be*"
ἔρχου καὶ ἴδε: the imperatives have a conditional force, "if you come, you will see"
1:47 ἐρχόμενον: pres. part. circum., "Jesus saw Nathaniel *coming*"
1:48 πρὸ τοῦ ... φωνῆσαι: aor. inf. articular of φωνέω; the subject is Φίλιππον and the object is σε, "before Philip addressing you"
σε ... ὄντα: pres. part. circum, after εἶδόν, "I saw *you being*"
1:49 ὁ υἱὸς ... σὺ βασιλεὺς: "you are the son ... you are the king." The two statements are parallel, although only the first has a definite article

⁴⁴ Erat autem Philippus a Bethsaida, civitate Andreae et Petri.
⁴⁵ Invenit Philippus Nathanael et dicit ei: "Quem scripsit Moyses
in Lege et Prophetae invenimus, Iesum filium Ioseph a Nazareth."

⁴⁶ Et dixit ei Nathanael: "A Nazareth potest aliquid boni esse?"

Dicit ei Philippus: "Veni et vide."

⁴⁷ Vidit Iesus Nathanael venientem ad se et dicit de eo: "Ecce
vere Israelita, in quo dolus non est."

⁴⁸ Dicit ei Nathanael: "Unde me nosti?"

Respondit Iesus et dixit ei: "Priusquam te Philippus vocaret,
cum esses sub ficu, vidi te."

⁴⁹ Respondit ei Nathanael: "Rabbi, tu es Filius Dei, tu rex es
Israel!"

---

aliquis, aliquid: anyone, anything
Bethsaida: Bethsaida (north of the Sea of Galilee)
bonus, -i *m*: good
civitas, civitatis *f*: city, community
dolus, -i *m*: trick, deceit
ficus, -us *m*: fig tree
Ioseph (*indecl.*): Joseph
Israel (*indecl.*): Israel
Israelita, -ae *m*: Israelite
Nathanael (*indecl.*): Nathanael

Nazareth (*indecl.*): Nazareth, city in Galilee
nosco, (3), novi, notus: to know
possum, posse, potui: be able, can
priusquam: before
rex, regis *m*: king
scribo, (3), scripsi, scriptus: to write
sub: under, beneath (+ *abl.*)
unde: from where
venio, (4): to come
verus, -a, -um: true

1:45   **Ioseph**: gen., "son of *Joseph*"
      in Lege et Prophetae: i.e. in the Hebrew Bible
      quem scripsit... invenimus: "we have found (him) whom Moses wrote"
1:46   **Nathanael**: nom., "*Nathaniel* said to him"
      boni: gen. partitive, "anything *of good*"
1:47   **Nathanael**: acc., "Jesus saw *Nathaniel*"
      vere Israelita: voc., "behold *a true Israelite!*"
1:48   **nosti**: syncopated perf. (= *no(vi)sti*), whence *you knew*"
      vocaret: impf. subj. anticipatory after *priusquam*, "before Philip *was calling* you"
      cum esses: impf. subj. circumstantial clause, "*when you were* under"
1:49   **Israel**: gen., "king *of Israel*"

⁵⁰ ἀπεκρίθη Ἰησοῦς καὶ εἶπεν αὐτῷ «Ὅτι εἶπόν σοι ὅτι εἶδόν σε ὑποκάτω τῆς συκῆς πιστεύεις; μείζω τούτων ὄψῃ.» ⁵¹ καὶ λέγει αὐτῷ «Ἀμὴν ἀμὴν λέγω ὑμῖν, ὄψεσθε τὸν οὐρανὸν ἀνεῳγότα καὶ τοὺς ἀγγέλους τοῦ θεοῦ ἀναβαίνοντας καὶ καταβαίνοντας ἐπὶ τὸν υἱὸν τοῦ ἀνθρώπου.»

Chapter 2

The Wedding at Cana

¹ καὶ τῇ ἡμέρᾳ τῇ τρίτῃ γάμος ἐγένετο ἐν Κανὰ τῆς Γαλιλαίας, καὶ ἦν ἡ μήτηρ τοῦ Ἰησοῦ ἐκεῖ· ² ἐκλήθη δὲ καὶ ὁ Ἰησοῦς καὶ οἱ μαθηταὶ αὐτοῦ εἰς τὸν γάμον. ³ καὶ ὑστερή-σαντος οἴνου λέγει ἡ μήτηρ τοῦ Ἰησοῦ πρὸς αὐτόν «Οἶνον οὐκ ἔχουσιν.»

ἄγγελος, ὁ: a messenger, angel
ἀναβαίνω: to go up
ἀνοίγνυμι: to open
γάμος: a wedding, wedding-feast
ἡμέρα, ἡ: day
καλέω: to summon, invite
Κανά: Cana
καταβαίνω: to go down
μείζων, -ον: greater

μήτηρ, μητρός, ἡ: a mother
οἶνος, ὁ: wine
οὐρανός, ὁ: heaven
ὄψομαι: to see (fut.)
πιστεύω: to trust, believe in
συκῆ, ἡ: a fig tree
τρίτος, -η, -ον: the third
ὑποκάτω: below, under
ὑστερέω: to be behind

1:50　ὅτι εἶπόν: causal after πιστεύεις, "you believe *because I said*"

　　ὅτι εἶδόν σε: ind. st. after εἶπόν, "said *that I saw you*"

　　ὄψῃ: fut. 2 s., "you will see"

　　μείζω: (= μείζο(ν)α) n. pl. acc., "greater things"

　　τούτων: gen. of comparison after μείζω, "greater *than these*"

1:51　ὄψεσθε: fut. 2 pl., "you will see"

　　ἀνεῳγότα: perf. part. circum. after ὄψεσθε, "will see the heaven *having opened*"

　　ἀναβαίνοντας καὶ καταβαίνοντας; pres. part. circum. after ὄψεσθε, "see angels *ascending and descending*"

2:1　τῇ ἡμέρᾳ τῇ τρίτῃ: dat. of time when, "on the third day"

　　ἐγένετο: aor. of γίνομαι, "*there was* a wedding"

2:2　ἐκλήθη: aor. pass. of καλέω, "Jesus *was invited*"

　　καὶ οἱ μαθηταὶ: "and so were his disciples;" note the casual disagreement of subject and verb

2:3　ὑστερήσαντος: aor. part. of ὑστερέω in gen. abs., "the wine *having given out*"

⁵⁰ Respondit Iesus et dixit ei: "Quia dixi tibi: Vidi te sub ficu, credis? Maiora his videbis." ⁵¹ Et dicit ei: "Amen, amen dico vobis: Videbitis caelum apertum et angelos Dei ascendentes et descendentes supra Filium hominis."

Chapter 2

The Wedding at Cana

¹ Et die tertio nuptiae factae sunt in Cana Galilaeae, et erat mater Iesu ibi; ² vocatus est autem et Iesus et discipuli eius ad nuptias. ³ Et deficiente vino, dicit mater Iesu ad eum: "Vinum non habent."

---

angelus, -i *m*: angel, messenger
aperio, (4) aperui, apertus: to open
ascendo, (3): to climb, ascend
caelus, -i *m*: heaven
Cana (*indecl.*): Cana
deficio, (3): to be insufficient, to run out
ibi: there, where

maior, maius: more greatly
mater, matris *f*: mother
nuptia, -ae *f*: marriage
supra: above (+ *acc.*)
tertius -a, -um: third
vinum, -i *n*: wine

1:50   **his**: abl. comparison, "greater than *these*"
1:51   **apertum**: perf. part. circum. after *videbitis*, "see the heaven *to have been opened*"
       ascendendentes ... descendentes: pres. part. circum., "will see angels *ascending and descending*"
2:1   **die tertio**: abl. of time when, "on the third day"
2:2   **vocatus est**: singular although it applies to both *Iesus* and *discipuli eius*.
2:3   **deficiente**: pres. part. in abl. abs., "when the wine *was running out*"

⁴ καὶ λέγει αὐτῇ ὁ Ἰησοῦς «Τί ἐμοὶ καὶ σοί, γύναι; οὔπω ἥκει ἡ ὥρα μου.»

⁵ λέγει ἡ μήτηρ αὐτοῦ τοῖς διακόνοις «Ὅτι ἂν λέγῃ ὑμῖν ποιήσατε.»

⁶ ἦσαν δὲ ἐκεῖ λίθιναι ὑδρίαι ἓξ κατὰ τὸν καθαρισμὸν τῶν Ἰουδαίων κείμεναι, χωροῦσαι ἀνὰ μετρητὰς δύο ἢ τρεῖς.

⁷ λέγει αὐτοῖς ὁ Ἰησοῦς «Γεμίσατε τὰς ὑδρίας ὕδατος·» καὶ ἐγέμισαν αὐτὰς ἕως ἄνω.

⁸ καὶ λέγει αὐτοῖς «Ἀντλήσατε νῦν καὶ φέρετε τῷ ἀρχι- τρικλίνῳ·»

ἀντλέω: to draw out
ἀρχιτρίκλινος, ὁ: steward
γεμίζω: to fill full of
γυνή, -γυναικός, ἡ: a woman
διάκονος, ὁ: a servant, waiting-man
δύο: two
ἓξ: six
ἕως: until, till
ἥκω: to have come, be present, be here
καθαρισμός, ὁ: purification

κεῖμαι: to be placed
λίθινος, -η, -ον: of stone
μετρητής, -οῦ, ὁ: a liquid measure
οὔπω: not yet
τρεῖς: three
ὑδρία, ἡ: a water-pot, pitcher, urn
φέρω: to bear, bring
χωρέω: to make room for
ὥρα, ἡ: hour, time

2:4   τί ἐμοὶ: "what (is this) to me?"
      γύναι: voc. of γυνή
2:5   ὅ τι ἂν λέγῃ: pres. subj. in general relative clause, "whatever he says, do!"
      2:6   ἦσαν ... κείμεναι: pres. part. periphrastic with impf. force, "they
      were placed" i.e. they were lying there
      κατὰ τὸν καθαρισμὸν: "according to the purification rite"
      χωροῦσαι: pres. part. nom. pl. f., "making room for" i.e. holding
2:7   ὕδατος: gen. after γεμισατε, "fill them full of water"
      ἕως ἄνω: "all the way to the top"
      ἀντλήσατε ...φέρετε: imper., "draw out! ...and bring!"
2:8   ἀρχιτρικλίνῳ: dat. ind. obj., "bring to the steward"

⁴ Et dicit ei Iesus: "Quid mihi et tibi, mulier? Nondum venit hora mea."

⁵ Dicit mater eius ministris: "Quodcumque dixerit vobis, facite."

⁶ Erant autem ibi lapideae hydriae sex positae secundum purificationem Iudaeorum, capientes singulae metretas binas vel ternas.

⁷ Dicit eis Iesus: "Implete hydrias aqua." Et impleverunt eas usque ad summum.

⁸ Et dicit eis: "Haurite nunc et ferte architriclino."

---

aqua, -ae *f*: water
architriclinus, -i *m*: one who presides at table; master of a feast
binus, -a, -um: two
capio, (3): to hold, occupy
facio, (3): to make, do
fero, ferre: to bring, carry
haurio, (4): to draw up
hora, -ae *f*: hour, time
hydria, -ae *f*: water-pot
impleo, (2): to fill up
lapideus, -a, -um: of stone; stony

metreta, -ae *f*: Greek liquid measure equal to about 40 liters
minister, -tri *m*: attendant, servant, waiter
mulier, mulieris *f*: woman
nondum: not yet
pono, (3), **posui, positus**: to place, set
purificatio, -ionis *f*: purification
secundum: according to (+ *acc.*)
singulus, -a, -um: every, each one
summum, -i *n*: top
ternus, -a, -um: three
usque: all the way

2:4 **mihi et tibi**: dat. of advantage, "what is this *to me and you*"
   venit: perf., "*has* not yet *come*"
2:5 **quodcumque dixerit**: perf. subj. in general relative clause, "whatever he has tells you"
2:6 **capientes singulae**: "six waterpots *each one holding*"
2:7 **aqua**: abl. of means, "fill them *with water*"
   ferte: pres. imper., "draw and *bring*"

οἱ δὲ ἤνεγκαν. ⁹ ὡς δὲ ἐγεύσατο ὁ ἀρχιτρίκλινος τὸ ὕδωρ οἶνον γεγενημένον, καὶ οὐκ ᾔδει πόθεν ἐστίν, οἱ δὲ διάκονοι ᾔδεισαν οἱ ἠντληκότες τὸ ὕδωρ, φωνεῖ τὸν νυμφίον ὁ ἀρχιτρίκλινος ¹⁰ καὶ λέγει αὐτῷ «Πᾶς ἄνθρωπος πρῶτον τὸν καλὸν οἶνον τίθησιν, καὶ ὅταν μεθυσθῶσιν τὸν ἐλάσσω· σὺ τετήρηκας τὸν καλὸν οἶνον ἕως ἄρτι.»

¹¹ ταύτην ἐποίησεν ἀρχὴν τῶν σημείων ὁ Ἰησοῦς ἐν Κανὰ τῆς Γαλιλαίας καὶ ἐφανέρωσεν τὴν δόξαν αὐτοῦ, καὶ ἐπίστευσαν εἰς αὐτὸν οἱ μαθηταὶ αὐτοῦ.

¹² μετὰ τοῦτο κατέβη εἰς Καφαρναοὺμ αὐτὸς καὶ ἡ μήτηρ αὐτοῦ καὶ οἱ ἀδελφοὶ καὶ οἱ μαθηταὶ αὐτοῦ, καὶ ἐκεῖ ἔμειναν οὐ πολλὰς ἡμέρας.

ἄρτι: just now
ἀρχιτρίκλινος, ὁ: steward
διάκονος, ὁ: a servant, waiting-man
δόξα, ἡ: glory
ἐλάσσων, -ον: lesser, poorer
ἤνεγκα: to bring (aor.)
Καφαρναοὺμ: Capharnaum

μεθύσκω: to make drunk, inebriate
νυμφίος, ὁ: groom
πόθεν: whence?
σημεῖον, τό: a sign, a mark, token
τηρέω: to watch over, protect, keep
τίθημι: to set, put, place
ὡς: when

2:9   γεγενημένον: perf. part. of γίνομαι agreeing with ὕδωρ with pred. οἶνον, "tasted the water *having become* wine"

      πόθεν ἐστίν: ind. quest., "know *whence it is*"

      ᾔδεισαν: plupf. of εἶδον, "they knew"

      οἱ ἠντληκότες: perf. part. attributive., "*the ones having drawn* the water"

2:10 ὅταν μεθυσθῶσιν: aor. subj. in general temporal clause, "whenever they have become drunk"

      τὸν ἐλάσσω ...τὸν καλὸν: "the *lesser* wine ...the *good* wine"

      τετήρηκας: perf. of τηρέω, "you have reserved"

      ἕως ἄρτι: "up until right now"

2:11 ἐπίστευσαν εἰς αὐτὸν: this prep. phrase and the dat. are used interchangeably with πιστεύω

2:12 κατέβη ... ἔμειναν: aor., "he went down ... they remained" note the change in the number of the verbs

      οὐ πολλὰς ἡμέρας: acc. of duration, "for a few days"

Illi autem tulerunt. ⁹ Ut autem gustavit architriclinus aquam

vinum factam et non sciebat unde esset, ministri autem sciebant,

qui haurierant aquam, vocat sponsum architriclinus   ¹⁰ et dicit ei:

"Omnis homo primum bonum vinum ponit et, cum inebriati fuerint,

id quod deterius est; tu servasti bonum vinum usque adhuc."

¹¹ Hoc fecit initium signorum Iesus in Cana Galilaeae et

manifestavit gloriam suam, et crediderunt in eum discipuli eius.

¹² Post hoc descendit Capharnaum ipse et mater eius et fratres

eius et discipuli eius, et ibi manserunt non multis diebus.

---

adhuc: till now
descendo, (3), **descendi, descensus**: to
  descend, go down
fero, ferre, tuli: to carry
gusto, (1), **gustavi, gustatus**: to taste, sip
haurio (4) **hauri, hauritus**: to draw water
inebrio, (1): to intoxicate, make drunk
initium, **-i** *n*: beginning, initial

maneo, (2), **mansi, mansus**: to remain, stay
multus, -a, -um: much, many
primum: at first
servo, (1): to save
signum, -i *n*: sign
sponsus, -i *m*: groom
usque: all the way
vinum, -i *n*: wine

2:9   **vinum**: acc. predicate after *factum*, "water made *wine*"
        unde esset: subj. indirect question after *sciebat*, "whence it was"
2:10   **cum inebriati fuerint**: fut. perf. in general temporal clause, "when they
        become drunk"
        servasti: syncopated perf. (=*servavisti*), "you have served"
        usque adhuc: "all the way up to this point in time"
2:11   **in eum**: note the prep. phrase instead of the dat. case after *crediderunt*
2:12   **descendit**: s. with pl. subject, "*he descended* and so did his mother"
        Capharnaum: acc. place to which
        non multis diebus: abl. of duration where the acc. would be expected, "for not
        many days

25

The Cleansing of the Temple

¹³ καὶ ἐγγὺς ἦν τὸ πάσχα τῶν Ἰουδαίων, καὶ ἀνέβη εἰς Ἱεροσόλυμα ὁ Ἰησοῦς. ¹⁴ καὶ εὗρεν ἐν τῷ ἱερῷ τοὺς πωλοῦντας βόας καὶ πρόβατα καὶ περιστερὰς καὶ τοὺς κερματιστὰς καθημένους, ¹⁵ καὶ ποιήσας φραγέλλιον ἐκ σχοινίων πάντας ἐξέβαλεν ἐκ τοῦ ἱεροῦ τά τε πρόβατα καὶ τοὺς βόας, καὶ τῶν κολλυβιστῶν ἐξέχεεν τὰ κέρματα καὶ τὰς τραπέζας ἀνέτρε-ψεν, ¹⁶ καὶ τοῖς τὰς περιστερὰς πωλοῦσιν εἶπεν «Ἄρατε ταῦτα ἐντεῦθεν, μὴ ποιεῖτε τὸν οἶκον τοῦ πατρός μου οἶκον

αἴρω: to remove
ἀναβαίνω: to go up, mount, to go up to
ἀνατρέπω: to turn up or over, overturn, upset
βοῦς, βοός, ὁ: cow
ἐγγύς: near, at hand
ἐκβάλλω: to throw or cast out of
ἐκχέω: to pour out
ἐντεῦθεν: hence or thence
ἱερόν, τό: temple
Ἱεροσόλυμα, -ων, τά: Jerusalem
κάθημαι: to be seated

κέρμα, -ατος, τό: a slice
κερματιστής, -οῦ, ὁ: a money-changer
κολλυβιστής, -οῦ, ὁ: a small money-changer
οἶκος, ὁ: a house, abode, dwelling
πάσχα, τό (*indecl.*): Passover
περιστερά, ἡ: the common pigeon or dove
πρόβατον, τό: sheep
πωλέω: to exchange or barter
σχοινίον, τό: a cord
τράπεζα, -ης, ἡ: four-legged a table
φραγέλλιον, τό: whip

2:13 ἀνέβη: aor. of ἀνα-βαίνω: "he went up"
2:14 εὗρεν: aor. of εὑρίσκω, "he found"
      τοὺς πωλοῦντας pres. part. attrib. obj. of εὗρεν, "found *those selling*"
      καθημένους: pres. part. circum., "found the money-changers *sitting down*"
2:15 ποιήσας: aor. part. circum. of ποιέω, "he *having made*"
      ἐξέβαλεν: aor. of βάλλω, "he drove out"
      ἐξέχεεν: impf. of ἐκ-χέω, "he was pouring out"
      ἀνέτρεψεν: aor. of ἀνα-τρέφω, "he overturned"
2:16 τοῖς ... πωλοῦσιν: pres. part. dat. pl., "said *to those selling*"
      ἄρατε: aor. imper. of αἴρω, "remove!"
      οἶκον ἐμπορίου: pred. acc. after ποιεῖτε, "don't make it *a house of business*"

The Cleansing of the Temple

¹³ Et prope erat Pascha Iudaeorum, et ascendit Hierosolymam

Iesus. ¹⁴ Et invenit in templo vendentes boves et oves et columbas,

et nummularios sedentes; ¹⁵ et cum fecisset flagellum de funiculis,

omnes eiecit de templo, oves quoque et boves, et nummulariorum

effudit aes et mensas subvertit; ¹⁶ et his, qui columbas vendebant,

dixit: "Auferte ista hinc! Nolite facere domum Patris mei domum

---

aes, aeris *n*: money, pay, fee
ascendo, (3), **ascendi, ascensus**: to ascend
aufero, auferre , apstuli, ablatus: remove, take away
bos, bovis *m/f*: ox, bull, cow
columba, -ae *f*: dove
domus, -us *f*: house
effundo, (3), **effudi, effusus**: to eject, throw out
eicio, (3), **eieci, eiectum**: to cast out, throw out
facio, (3): to make
flagellum, -i *n*: whip, lash
funiculus, -i *m*: thin rope, cord
Hierosolyma, -ae *n*: Jerusalem

hinc: from here
Iudaeus, Iudaei *m*: Jew, the Jews
mensa, -ae *f*: table
nolo, nolle, nolui: be unwilling; refuse to
nummularius, -i *m*: money exchange tables
ovis, ovis *f*: sheep
Pascha, -ae *f*: Passover
prope: near
quoque: likewise
sedeo, (2): to sit, remain
subverto, (3), **subverti, subversus**: to overturn, cause to topple
templum, -i *n*: temple
vendo, (3): to sell

2:13 **Hierosylam:** note the variant spelling of Jesrusalem
2:14 **vendentes ... sedentes**: acc. pres. part., "those selling ... those sitting"
    nummularios: only Hebrew money could be used in the temple as an offering.
2:15 **cum fecisset**: plupf. subj. *cum* circumstantial clause, "when he had made"
2:16 **auferte ... nolite**: imper., "remove! ...don't!" + inf.
    domum negotianis: pred. after *facere*, "make this home a *home of business*!"

ἐμπορίου.» ¹⁷ ἐμνήσθησαν οἱ μαθηταὶ αὐτοῦ ὅτι γεγραμμένον ἐστίν «Ὁ ζῆλος τοῦ οἴκου σου καταφάγεταί με.»

¹⁸ ἀπεκρίθησαν οὖν οἱ Ἰουδαῖοι καὶ εἶπαν αὐτῷ «Τί σημεῖον δεικνύεις ἡμῖν, ὅτι ταῦτα ποιεῖς;»

¹⁹ ἀπεκρίθη Ἰησοῦς καὶ εἶπεν αὐτοῖς «Λύσατε τὸν ναὸν τοῦτον καὶ ἐν τρισὶν ἡμέραις ἐγερῶ αὐτόν.»

²⁰ εἶπαν οὖν οἱ Ἰουδαῖοι «Τεσσεράκοντα καὶ ἓξ ἔτεσιν οἰκοδομήθη ὁ ναὸς οὗτος, καὶ σὺ ἐν τρισὶν ἡμέραις ἐγερεῖς αὐτόν;» ²¹ ἐκεῖνος δὲ ἔλεγεν περὶ τοῦ ναοῦ τοῦ σώματος αὐτοῦ. ²² ὅτε οὖν ἠγέρθη ἐκ νεκρῶν, ἐμνήσθησαν οἱ μαθηταὶ αὐτοῦ ὅτι τοῦτο ἔλεγεν, καὶ ἐπίστευσαν τῇ γραφῇ καὶ τῷ λόγῳ ὃν εἶπεν ὁ Ἰησοῦς.

ἀποκρίνομαι: to answer
γραφή, ἡ: a writing, scripture
δείκνυμι: to bring to light, display, exhibit
ἐγείρω: to raise up
ἐμπόριον, τό: exchange
ἔτος, -εος, τό: a year
ζῆλος, -ου, ὁ: eager rivalry
καταφάγομαι: to eat up, devour (*fut.*)
λύω: to loose

μαθητής, -οῦ, ὁ: disciple
μιμνήσκω: to remind, put
ναός, ναοῦ, ὁ: a temple
νεκρός, ὁ: a dead body, corpse
οἰκοδομέω: to build a house
σῶμα, σώματος, τό: body
τεσσαράκοντα: forty
τρεῖς: three

2:17   **ἐμνήσθησαν**: aor. pass. of **μιμνήσκω**: "they remembered"
     γεγραμμένον ἐστίν: perf. periphrastic of **γράφω**, "that *it was written*" Ps. 6:69
     καταφάγεταί: fut. (=**κατέδεται**), "jealousy *will consume*"
2:18   **ὅτι ταῦτα ποιεῖς**: noun clause explaining **σημεῖον**, "what sign do you show *that you are doing these things?*"
2:19   **λύσατε**: aor. imper. of **λύω**, "loose!"
     ἐν τρισὶν ἡμέραις: "within three days" where the acc. or gen. without a preposition would be expected
     ἐγερῶ: fut. of **ἐγείρω**, "I will raise"
2:20   **ἓξ ἔτεσιν**: dat., "within the course of six years"
     οἰκοδομήθη: aor. pass. unaugmented of **οἰκοδομέω**, "was built"
2:22   **ἠγέρθη**: aor. pass. of **ἐγείρω**, "when he was raised"
     ἐμνήσθησαν: aor. pass. of **μιμνήσκω**, "they remembered"
     τῇ γραφῇ καὶ τῷ λόγῳ: dat. after **ἐπίστευσαν**, "they believed the scripture and his word"

negotiationis." ¹⁷ Recordati sunt discipuli eius quia scriptum est: "Zelus domus tuae comedit me."

¹⁸ Responderunt ergo Iudaei et dixerunt ei: "Quod signum ostendis nobis, quia haec facis?"

¹⁹ Respondit Iesus et dixit eis: "Solvite templum hoc, et in tribus diebus excitabo illud."

²⁰ Dixerunt ergo Iudaei: "Quadraginta et sex annis aedificatum est templum hoc, et tu tribus diebus excitabis illud?" ²¹ Ille autem dicebat de templo corporis sui. ²² Cum ergo resurrexisset a mortuis, recordati sunt discipuli eius quia hoc dicebat, et crediderunt Scripturae et sermoni, quem dixit Iesus.

---

aedifico, (1): to build, erect
annus, **-i** *m*: year
comedo, (3): to eat, consume
corpus, **-oris** *n*: body
credo, (3), **credidi**, **creditus**: to believe, trust
excito, (1): to raise, erect
mortuus, **-i** *m*: corpse, the dead
negotiatio, **-onis** *f*: business
ostendo (3): to show, reveal

quadraginta: forty
recordor, (1): to call to mind, remember
resurgo, (3), **resurrexi**, **resurrectus**: to rise, appear again, resurrect
scriptura, **-ae** *f*: scripture
sermo, **-onis** *m*: diction, speech, the word
sex: six
solvo, (3): to dissolve, break up, destroy
tres, **tria**: three
zelus, **-i** *m*: jealousy; fervor

2:17   **domus tuae**: objective gen., "zeal *for your house*"

2:18   **quia haec facis**: noun clause explaining *signum*, "what sign *that you are doing these things*"

2:20   **annis... diebus**: abl. of time within which, "in the course of forty six years .. in the course of three days"

2:22   **cum... resurrexisset**: plupf. subj. *cum* circumstantial clause, "when he had risen from the dead"

       quia hoc dicebat: indirect statement, "remembered *that he said this*"

       scripturae et sermoni: dat. after *crediderunt*, "believed in *the scripture and this word*"

²³ ὡς δὲ ἦν ἐν τοῖς Ἱεροσολύμοις ἐν τῷ πάσχα ἐν τῇ ἑορτῇ, πολλοὶ ἐπίστευσαν εἰς τὸ ὄνομα αὐτοῦ, θεωροῦντες αὐτοῦ τὰ σημεῖα ἃ ἐποίει· ²⁴ αὐτὸς δὲ Ἰησοῦς οὐκ ἐπίστευεν αὐτὸν αὐτοῖς διὰ τὸ αὐτὸν γινώσκειν πάντας ²⁵ καὶ ὅτι οὐ χρείαν εἶχεν ἵνα τις μαρτυρήσῃ περὶ τοῦ ἀνθρώπου, αὐτὸς γὰρ ἐγίνωσκεν τί ἦν ἐν τῷ ἀνθρώπῳ.

Chapter 3

Jesus and Nicodemus

¹ ἦν δὲ ἄνθρωπος ἐκ τῶν Φαρισαίων, Νικόδημος ὄνομα αὐτῷ, ἄρχων τῶν Ἰουδαίων· ² οὗτος ἦλθεν πρὸς αὐτὸν νυκτὸς καὶ εἶπεν αὐτῷ «Ῥαββεί, οἴδαμεν ὅτι ἀπὸ θεοῦ ἐλήλυθας διδάσκαλος· οὐδεὶς γὰρ δύναται ταῦτα τὰ σημεῖα ποιεῖν ἃ σὺ ποιεῖς, ἐὰν μὴ ᾖ ὁ θεὸς μετ' αὐτοῦ.»

ἄρχων, -οντος, ὁ: a chief
διδάσκαλος, ὁ: a teacher, master
ἑορτή, ἡ: a feast or festival, holiday
ἦλθον: to come (*aor.*)
θεωρέω: to look at, view, behold

μαρτυρέω: to be a witness, to bear witness
Νικόδημος: Nicodemus
νύξ, νυκτός, ἡ: the night
Ῥαββεί: (Hebr.) a teacher
χρεία, ἡ: use, advantage, service

2:23   **ἐν τῷ πάσχα**: "in the (time of the) Passover"
    εἰς τὸ ὄνομα: contrast the use of the prepositional phrase with **ἐπίστευσαν** here with the dative in the previous verse
2:24   **αὐτὸς δὲ Ἰησοῦς**: "Jesus himself"
    αὐτὸν (=έ-αὐτὸν): "did not entrust *himself*"
    αὐτοῖς: dat., "entrust himself *to them*"
    διὰ τὸ αὐτὸν γινώσκειν: pres. inf. articular, "because of him knowing"
    πάντας: acc. pl. m., "knowing *all* (men)"
2:25   **ἵνα τις μαρτυρήσῃ**: aor. subj. in noun clause instead of an infinitive explaining **χρείαν**, "he had no need *to witness*"
    τί ἦν: ind. quest., "knew *what was* in man"
3:2   **νυκτὸς**: gen. of time within which, "in the course of the night"
    οἴδαμεν: = ἴσμεν, "we know"
    ἐλήλυθας: perf., "you have come"
    ἐὰν μὴ ᾖ: pres. subj. of εἰμι in pres. general protasis,"*unless God is* with him"

²³ Cum autem esset Hierosolymis in Pascha, in die festo, multi crediderunt in nomine eius, videntes signa eius, quae faciebat. ²⁴ Ipse autem Iesus non credebat semetipsum eis, eo quod ipse nosset omnes, ²⁵ et quia opus ei non erat, ut quis testimonium perhiberet de homine; ipse enim sciebat quid esset in homine.

Chapter 3

Jesus and Nicodemus

¹ Erat autem homo ex pharisaeis, Nicodemus nomine, princeps Iudaeorum; ² hic venit ad eum nocte et dixit ei: "Rabbi, scimus quia a Deo venisti magister; nemo enim potest haec signa facere, quae tu facis, nisi fuerit Deus cum eo."

---

credo, (3), **credidi, creditus**: to believe, trust
enim: indeed, in fact
festus, -a, -um: festive
magister, magistri *m*: teacher, master
Nicodemus (*indecl.*): Nicodemus
nosco, (3), **novi, notus**: to know

nox, noctis *f*: night
opus, operis *n*: need; work
possum, posse, potui: can, be able
princeps, principis *m*: leader, chief
scio, (4): to know, understand
semetipse, -a, -um: one's own self

2:23 **cum... esset**: impf. subj. *cum* circumstantial clause, "*while he was* in Jerusalem"
    videntes: pres. part. circum., "when they were seeing"
2:24 **se-met-ipsum**: emphatic pron. (= *se*), "he did not entrust *himself* to them"
    quod nosset: syncopated plupf. subj. (= *novisset*) in causal clause explaining *eo*, "on account of this, *that he himself knows* all men"
2:25 **ut... perhiberet**: impf. subj. after *opus*, "not necessary *that anyone give*"
    quid esset: impf. subj. in ind. question, "knew *what was* in the man"
3:2 **quia... venisti**: ind. st., "know *that you have come*"
    nisi...fuerit: fut perf. in pres. general protasis, "unless God is with him"

31

³ ἀπεκρίθη Ἰησοῦς καὶ εἶπεν αὐτῷ «Ἀμὴν ἀμὴν λέγω σοι, ἐὰν μή τις γεννηθῇ ἄνωθεν, οὐ δύναται ἰδεῖν τὴν βασιλείαν τοῦ θεοῦ.»

⁴ λέγει πρὸς αὐτὸν ὁ Νικόδημος «Πῶς δύναται ἄνθρωπος γεννηθῆναι γέρων ὤν; μὴ δύναται εἰς τὴν κοιλίαν τῆς μητρὸς αὐτοῦ δεύτερον εἰσελθεῖν καὶ γεννηθῆναι;»

⁵ ἀπεκρίθη ὁ Ἰησοῦς «Ἀμὴν ἀμὴν λέγω σοι, ἐὰν μή τις γεννηθῇ ἐξ ὕδατος καὶ πνεύματος, οὐ δύναται εἰσελθεῖν εἰς τὴν βασιλείαν τοῦ θεοῦ. ⁶ τὸ γεγεννημένον ἐκ τῆς σαρκὸς σάρξ ἐστιν, καὶ τὸ γεγεννημένον ἐκ τοῦ πνεύματος πνεῦμά ἐστιν. ⁷ μὴ θαυμάσῃς ὅτι εἶπόν σοι Δεῖ ὑμᾶς γεννηθῆναι ἄνωθεν. ⁸ τὸ πνεῦμα ὅπου θέλει πνεῖ, καὶ τὴν φωνὴν αὐτοῦ ἀκούεις, ἀλλ' οὐκ οἶδας πόθεν ἔρχεται καὶ ποῦ ὑπάγει· οὕτως ἐστὶν πᾶς ὁ γεγεννημένος ἐκ τοῦ πνεύματος.»

ἀκούω: to hear (+ *gen.*)
ἄνωθεν: from above, from on high
βασιλεία, ἡ: a kingdom, dominion
γεννάω: to beget, engender
γέρων, -οντος, ὁ: an old man
δεῖ: to be necessary
δεύτερος, -α, -ον: second
εἰσῆλθον: to go in, enter (*aor.*)

θαυμάζω: to wonder, marvel, be astonied
θέλω: to will, wish, purpose
κοιλία, ἡ: the belly
πνέω: to blow
πόθεν: whence?
ὕδωρ, -ατος, τό: water
ὑπάγω: to withdraw
φωνή, ἡ: a sound, tone

3:3　ἐὰν μή τις γεννηθῇ: aor. subj. pass. in pres. general protasis, "unless someone is born anew"

3:4　γεννηθῆναι: aor. pass. inf. after δύναται, "how is a man able *to be born*?"
　　γέρων ὤν: pres. part. circum., "being an old man"
　　μὴ δύναται: expecting a no answer, "surely it is not possible to" + inf.

3:6　τὸ γεγεννημένον: perf. part. of γεννάω, "that which has been born"

3:7　μὴ θαυμάσῃς: aor. subj. of θαυμάζω in prohibition, "don't wonder!"

3:8　ὅπου θέλει: local relative clause, "blows *where it wishes*"
　　πόθεν ἔρχεται: ind. quest., "knows *whence it comes*"
　　ποῦ ὑπάγει: ind. quest., "where it goes" where we would expect ποῖ

³ Respondit Iesus et dixit ei: "Amen, amen dico tibi: Nisi quis natus fuerit desuper, non potest videre regnum Dei."

⁴ Dicit ad eum Nicodemus: "Quomodo potest homo nasci, cum senex sit? Numquid potest in ventrem matris suae iterato introire et nasci?"

⁵ Respondit Iesus: "Amen, amen dico tibi: Nisi quis natus fuerit ex aqua et Spiritu, non potest introire in regnum Dei. ⁶ Quod natum est ex carne, caro est; et, quod natum est ex Spiritu, spiritus est. ⁷ Non mireris quia dixi tibi: Oportet vos nasci denuo. ⁸ Spiritus, ubi vult, spirat, et vocem eius audis, sed non scis unde veniat et quo vadat; sic est omnis, qui natus est ex Spiritu."

---

audio, (4): to hear
caro, **carnis** *f*: flesh
denuo: anew, over again
desuper *(adv.)*: from above
fio, **fieri**, **factus sum**: happen, come about
introeo, (4): to enter, go into
iterato *(adv.)*: again
miro, (1): to be amazed, wonder
nascor, (3), **natus sum**: begotten, born
numquid: is it possible? surely ... not?

oportet, (2): ought, it is necessary (+ *inf.*)
quomodo: how, in what way?
regnum, -i *n*: kingdom
senex, **senis** *m*: an old man
sic: thus, so
spiro, (1), **spiravi**, **spiratus**: to blow
vado, (3), **vasi**: to go
venio, (4): to come
venter, **ventris** *m*: womb

3:3   **nisi quis:** (= *quisque*): "unless someone"
      nisi... fuerit: fut. perf. in general protasis, "*unless he has been* born"
3:4   **cum... sit:** pres. subj. in cum circumstantial clause, "*when he is* old"
      numquid potest: "surely it is not possible to" + inf.
3:5   **nisi...fuerit:** fut. perf. in pres. general protasis, "*unless he is* born"
3:7   **non mireris:** pres. subj. in prohibition, where we would expect *ne*, "do not wonder!"
3:8   **unde veniat et quo vadat:** pres. subj. in indirect question, "know *whence it comes and where it goes*"

⁹ ἀπεκρίθη Νικόδημος καὶ εἶπεν αὐτῷ «Πῶς δύναται ταῦτα γενέσθαι;»

¹⁰ ἀπεκρίθη Ἰησοῦς καὶ εἶπεν αὐτῷ «Σὺ εἶ ὁ διδάσκαλος τοῦ Ἰσραὴλ καὶ ταῦτα οὐ γινώσκεις; ¹¹ ἀμὴν ἀμὴν λέγω σοι ὅτι ὃ οἴδαμεν λαλοῦμεν καὶ ὃ ἑωράκαμεν μαρτυροῦμεν, καὶ τὴν μαρτυρίαν ἡμῶν οὐ λαμβάνετε. ¹² εἰ τὰ ἐπίγεια εἶπον ὑμῖν καὶ οὐ πιστεύετε, πῶς ἐὰν εἴπω ὑμῖν τὰ ἐπουράνια πιστεύσετε; ¹³ καὶ οὐδεὶς ἀναβέβηκεν εἰς τὸν οὐρανὸν εἰ μὴ ὁ ἐκ τοῦ οὐρανοῦ καταβάς, ὁ υἱὸς τοῦ ἀνθρώπου. ¹⁴ καὶ καθὼς Μωυσῆς ὕψωσεν τὸν ὄφιν ἐν τῇ ἐρήμῳ, οὕτως ὑψωθῆναι δεῖ τὸν υἱὸν τοῦ ἀνθρώπου, ¹⁵ ἵνα πᾶς ὁ πιστεύων ἐν αὐτῷ ἔχῃ ζωὴν αἰώνιον.»

αἰώνιος, -ον: lasting for an age
γινώσκω: to know
δεῖ: it is necessary
ἐπίγειος, -ον: earthly
ἐπουράνιος, -ον: in heaven, heavenly
ἐρῆμος, ὁ: desert

ζωή, ἡ: life
καταβαίνω: to go or come down
λαμβάνω: to take
ὄφις, ὁ: a serpent, snake
ὑψόω: to lift high, raise up

3:9 γενέσθαι: aor. inf. of γίνομαι after δύναται, "able *to be*"
3:11 ὃ οἴδαμεν: perf. (=ἴσμεν), "what *we know*"
    ὃ ἑωράκαμεν: perf. of ὁράω, "what *we have seen*"
3:12 τὰ ἐπίγεια: "earthly things"
    ἐὰν εἴπω: aor. subj. in fut. more vivid protasis, "if I tell you"
    πῶς ... πιστεύσετε: fut. serving as a more vivid apodosis, "how will you believe?"
3:13 ἀναβέβηκεν: perf. of ἀνα-βαίνω, "no one *has ascended*"
    ὁ ... καταβάς: aor. part. attrib. of κατα-βαίνω, "except *the one who descended*"
3:14 καθὼς ... οὕτως: "just as ... so also"
    ὕψωσεν: aor. of ὑψόω: "he lifted"
    ὑψωθῆναι: aor. pass. inf. of ὑψόω after δεῖ, "it is necessary for the son *to be lifted up*"
3:15 ἵνα .... ἔχῃ: pres. subj. in clause of purpose and result, "*so that* the believer *has*"

⁹ Respondit Nicodemus et dixit ei: "Quomodo possunt haec fieri?"

¹⁰ Respondit Iesus et dixit ei: "Tu es magister Israel et haec ignoras? ¹¹ Amen, amen dico tibi: Quod scimus, loquimur et, quod vidimus, testamur; et testimonium nostrum non accipitis. ¹² Si terrena dixi vobis, et non creditis, quomodo, si dixero vobis caelestia, credetis? ¹³ Et nemo ascendit in caelum, nisi qui descendit de caelo, Filius hominis. ¹⁴ Et sicut Moyses exaltavit serpentem in deserto, ita exaltari oportet Filium hominis, ¹⁵ ut omnis, qui credit in ipso, habeat vitam aeternam."

---

accipio, (3): to receive, accept
aeternus, -a, -um: eternal, everlasting
caelestis, -e: heavenly, celestial
caelus, -i *m*: heaven
desertum, -i *n*: desert
diligo, (3), **dilexi, dilectus**: to love
exalto, (1): to elevate, raise
filius, fili *m*: son
habeo, (2): to have
ignoro, (1): to not know; be unfamiliar with

Israel (*indecl.*): Israel
magister, -tri *m*: teacher, master
noster, nostra, nostrum: our
oportet, (2), **oportuit**: it is necessary; ought
serpens, serpentis *m/f.*: serpent, snake
terrenus, -a, -um: earthly, worldly
testor, (1): to give as evidence; bear witness
video, (2), **vidi, visus**: to see
vita, -ae *f.*: life

3:10 **Israel**: gen., "teacher *of Israel*"
3:11 **vidimus**: perf., "what *we have seen*"
3:12 **terrena ...caelestia**: acc. pl. n., "earthly things ...heavenly things"
       si dixero: fut. perf. in future more vivid protasis, "if I speak"
3:13 **qui descendit**: perf. in relative clause translating Greek perf. part., "except the one *who has descended*"
3:14 **sicut... ita**: "just as... so also"
       exaltari... Filium: acc. + inf. after *oportet*, "fitting *that the son be exalted*"
3:15 **ut... habeat**: pres. subj. combining purpose and result, "so that anyone have"

35

¹⁶ οὕτως γὰρ ἠγάπησεν ὁ θεὸς τὸν κόσμον ὥστε τὸν υἱὸν τὸν μονογενῆ ἔδωκεν, ἵνα πᾶς ὁ πιστεύων εἰς αὐτὸν μὴ ἀπόληται ἀλλὰ ἔχῃ ζωὴν αἰώνιον. ¹⁷ οὐ γὰρ ἀπέστειλεν ὁ θεὸς τὸν υἱὸν εἰς τὸν κόσμον ἵνα κρίνῃ τὸν κόσμον, ἀλλ᾽ ἵνα σωθῇ ὁ κόσμος δι᾽ αὐτοῦ. ¹⁸ ὁ πιστεύων εἰς αὐτὸν οὐ κρίνεται. ὁ μὴ πιστεύων ἤδη κέκριται, ὅτι μὴ πεπίστευκεν εἰς τὸ ὄνομα τοῦ μονογενοῦς υἱοῦ τοῦ θεοῦ. ¹⁹ αὕτη δέ ἐστιν ἡ κρίσις ὅτι τὸ φῶς ἐλήλυθεν εἰς τὸν κόσμον καὶ ἠγάπησαν οἱ ἄνθρωποι μᾶλλον τὸ σκότος ἢ τὸ φῶς, ἦν γὰρ αὐτῶν πονηρὰ τὰ ἔργα. ²⁰ πᾶς γὰρ ὁ φαῦλα πράσσων μισεῖ τὸ φῶς

ἀγαπάω: to love, be fond of	μισέω: to hate
αἰώνιος, -ον: lasting for an age	μονογενής, -ές: only-begotten, single
ἀπόλλυμι: to destroy utterly, kill, slay	ὄνομα, -ατος, τό: name
ἤδη: now, already	πονηρός, -ά, -όν: toilsome, painful, grievous
ἦλθον: to come or go (aor.)	πράσσω: to do
κόσμος, ὁ: world	σκότος, -εος, τό: darkness, gloom
κρίνω: to judge	σώζω: to save
κρίσις, ἡ: a judgement	φαῦλος, -η, -ον: foul

3:16   ἠγάπησεν: aor. of ἀγαπάω, "he so loved"

 ὥστε ... ἔδωκεν: aor. of δίδωμι in result clause, "so that he gave"

 ἵνα ... μὴ ἀπόληται ... ἔχῃ: subj. showing result and purpose, "so that every believer *not die* ... but *have*"

 ἀπόληται: aor. subj. of ἀπόλλυμι

3:17   ἀπέστειλεν: aor. of ἀπο-στέλλω, "God *sent*"

 ἵνα κρίνῃ: pres. subj. in purpose clause, "in order to judge"

 ἵνα σωθῇ: aor. subj. pass. of σώζω, "*in order for* the world *to be saved*"

 δι᾽ αὐτοῦ: "through him"

3:18   ὁ δὲ μὴ πιστεύων: pres. part., with μὴ indicating condition, "if he does not believe"

 κέκριται: perf. of κρίνομαι: "he is already judged"

 ὅτι μὴ πεπίστευκεν: perf. causal, "because he has not believed"

3:19   ἐλήλυθεν: perf., "the light *has come*"

 μᾶλλον ... ἤ: "more ... than"

3:20   ὁ πράσσων: pres. part. attrib., "every man *doing*"

^{16} Sic enim dilexit Deus mundum, ut Filium suum unigenitum daret, ut omnis, qui credit in eum, non pereat, sed habeat vitam aeternam. ^{17} Non enim misit Deus Filium in mundum, ut iudicet mundum, sed ut salvetur mundus per ipsum. ^{18} Qui credit in eum, non iudicatur; qui autem non credit, iam iudicatus est, quia non credidit in nomen Unigeniti Filii Dei. ^{19} Hoc est autem iudicium: Lux venit in mundum, et dilexerunt homines magis tenebras quam lucem; erant enim eorum mala opera. ^{20} Omnis enim, qui mala agit, odit lucem

---

ago, (3), **egi**, **actus**: to do, act
arguo, (3): to disclose, censure
do, (1): to give
iudicium, -i *n*: judgment
iudico, (1): to judge
lux, **lucis** *f*: light
magis: to greater extent; more

malus, -a, **um**: bad, evil
mitto, (3), **misi**, **missus**: to send
odi, **odisse** (*perf.*): to hate, dislike
pereo, (2): to die
salvo, (1): to save
tenebrae, -arum *f*: darkness
unigenitus, -a, -um: only begotten

3:16 **ut…daret**: impf. subj. result clause, "so that he gave"
    ut…non pereat…habeat: pres. subj. result clause, "*so that he not die* but *have*"
3:17 **ut iudicet**: pres. subj. purpose clause, "in order that he judge"
    ut salvetur: pres. subj. purpose clause, "in order that it be saved"
3:19 **venit**: perf., "he came"
    magis… quam: "more X (*acc.*) than Y (*acc.*)"

καὶ οὐκ ἔρχεται πρὸς τὸ φῶς, ἵνα μὴ ἐλεγχθῇ τὰ ἔργα αὐτοῦ·
²¹ ὁ δὲ ποιῶν τὴν ἀλήθειαν ἔρχεται πρὸς τὸ φῶς, ἵνα φανερωθῇ
αὐτοῦ τὰ ἔργα ὅτι ἐν θεῷ ἐστιν εἰργασμένα.

Jesus and John the Baptist

²² μετὰ ταῦτα ἦλθεν ὁ Ἰησοῦς καὶ οἱ μαθηταὶ αὐτοῦ εἰς
τὴν Ἰουδαίαν γῆν, καὶ ἐκεῖ διέτριβεν μετ' αὐτῶν καὶ ἐβάπτιζεν.
²³ ἦν δὲ καὶ ὁ Ἰωάνης βαπτίζων ἐν Αἰνὼν ἐγγὺς τοῦ Σαλείμ,
ὅτι ὕδατα πολλὰ ἦν ἐκεῖ, καὶ παρεγίνοντο καὶ ἐβαπτίζοντο·
²⁴ οὔπω γὰρ ἦν βεβλημένος εἰς τὴν φυλακὴν Ἰωάνης. ²⁵ ἐγένετο οὖν ζήτησις ἐκ τῶν μαθητῶν Ἰωάνου μετὰ Ἰουδαίου περὶ
καθαρισμοῦ. ²⁶ καὶ ἦλθαν πρὸς τὸν Ἰωάνην καὶ εἶπαν αὐτῷ
«Ῥαββεί, ὃς ἦν μετὰ σοῦ πέραν τοῦ Ἰορδάνου, ᾧ σὺ μεμαρτύρηκας, ἴδε οὗτος βαπτίζει καὶ πάντες ἔρχονται πρὸς αὐτόν.»

Αἰνὼν (*indecl.*): Aenon
βάλλω: to throw
βασπτίζω: to baptize
γῆ, ἡ: earth
διατρίβω: to spend time
ἐλέγχω: to judge, disgrace
ἐργάζομαι: to work, labour
ἔρχομαι: to come or go

ζήτησις, -εως, ἡ: a quarrel, examination
Ἰορδάνος, ὁ: Jordan River
καθαρισμός, ὁ: a purification
οὔπω: not yet
παραγίνομαι: to be near
πέραν: on the other side, across, beyond
Σαλείμ (*indecl.*): Salim
φυλάξ, φυλακός, ὁ: prison

3:20 **ἵνα μὴ ἐλεγχθῇ**: aor. subj. pass. in purpose clause, "lest his deeds be judged"
3:21 **ἵνα φανερωθῇ**: aor. subj. pass. in purpose clause, "so his deeds are made manifest"
   ἐστιν εἰργασμένα: perf. periphrastic of ἐργάζω, "these deeds have been done"
3:22 **διέτριβεν ... ἐβάπτιζεν**: impf., "he was spending time ... he was baptizing"
3:23 **παρεγίνοντο ... ἐβαπτίζοντο**: impf., "they were present ... they were being baptized"
3:24 **ἦν βεβλημένος**: plupf. periphrastic of βάλλω, "he had not yet been cast"
3:25 **μετὰ Ἰουδαίου**: "with a certain Jew" the only time the singular is used in John
3:26 **ἦλθαν ...εἶπαν**: note the weak aorist endings, "they came ...they said"
   ὃς ἦν: "(he) who was" i.e Jesus
   μεμαρτύρηκας: perf. of μαρτυρέω, "the one about whom *you have borne witness*"

et non venit ad lucem, ut non arguantur opera eius; ²¹ qui autem facit veritatem, venit ad lucem, ut manifestentur eius opera, quia in Deo sunt facta.

Jesus and John the Baptist

²² Post haec venit Iesus et discipuli eius in Iudaeam terram, et illic demorabatur cum eis et baptizabat. ²³ Erat autem et Ioannes baptizans in Enon iuxta Salim, quia aquae multae erant illic, et adveniebant et baptizabantur; ²⁴ nondum enim missus fuerat in carcerem Ioannes. ²⁵ Facta est ergo quaestio ex discipulis Ioannis cum Iudaeo de purificatione. ²⁶ Et venerunt ad Ioannem et dixerunt ei: "Rabbi, qui erat tecum trans Iordanem, cui tu testimonium perhibuisti, ecce hic baptizat, et omnes veniunt ad eum!"

---

accipio, (3): to receive, accept, undertake
advenio, (4): to come to, arrive
aqua, -ae *f.*: water
caelus, -i *m*: heaven
carcer, -eris *m*: prison, jail
demoror, (1): to linger, stay
ecce: behold! see!
Enon (*indecl.*): on the left bank of the Jordan
homo, hominis *m*: man
illic: in that place, there
Ioannes, Ioannis *m*: John (i.e. the Baptist)

Iudaeus, -a, -um: Jewish
iuxta: near, near by (+ *acc.*)
manifesto, (1): to reveal, make known
nondum: not yet
purificatio, -onis *f*: purification
quaestio, -onis *f*: question, inquiry
Salim: on the left bank of the Jordan
testimonium, -i *n*: testimony
trans: across, over (+ *acc.*)
veritas, -tatis *f*: truth, honesty

3:20 **ut… arguantur**: pres. subj. mixing result and purpose, "so that they are not disclosed"

3:21 **ut manifestentur**: pres. subj. result clause, "so that they are revealed"

3:22 **venit**: perf. s., although its subject is both *Iesus* and *discipuli*

3:23 **erat … baptizans**: impf. periphrastic, "he was baptizing"

3:24 **missus fuerat**: (= *missus erat*), plupf., "he had not been sent"

3:25 **cum Iudaeo**: "with a certain Jew," perhaps John referring to himself

3:26 **qui … cui … hic …eum**: i.e. Jesus, "*he who* was … *about whom* you presented testimony … *this one* baptizes …and all go to *him*"

²⁷ ἀπεκρίθη Ἰωάνης καὶ εἶπεν «Οὐ δύναται ἄνθρωπος λαμβάνειν οὐδὲν ἐὰν μὴ ᾖ δεδομένον αὐτῷ ἐκ τοῦ οὐρανοῦ. ²⁸ αὐτοὶ
ὑμεῖς μοι μαρτυρεῖτε ὅτι εἶπον Οὐκ εἰμὶ ἐγὼ ὁ χριστός, ἀλλ᾽ ὅτι
Ἀπεσταλμένος εἰμὶ ἔμπροσθεν ἐκείνου. ²⁹ ὁ ἔχων τὴν νύμφην
νυμφίος ἐστίν· ὁ δὲ φίλος τοῦ νυμφίου, ὁ ἑστηκὼς καὶ ἀκούων
αὐτοῦ, χαρᾷ χαίρει διὰ τὴν φωνὴν τοῦ νυμφίου. αὕτη οὖν ἡ χαρὰ
ἡ ἐμὴ πεπλήρωται. ³⁰ ἐκεῖνον δεῖ αὐξάνειν, ἐμὲ δὲ ἐλαττοῦσθαι.»

³¹ ὁ ἄνωθεν ἐρχόμενος ἐπάνω πάντων ἐστίν. ὁ ὢν ἐκ τῆς
γῆς ἐκ τῆς γῆς ἐστιν καὶ ἐκ τῆς γῆς λαλεῖ· ὁ ἐκ τοῦ οὐρανοῦ
ἐρχόμενος ἐπάνω πάντων ἐστίν· ³² ὃ ἑώρακεν καὶ ἤκουσεν
τοῦτο μαρτυρεῖ, καὶ τὴν μαρτυρίαν αὐτοῦ οὐδεὶς λαμβάνει.
³³ ὁ λαβὼν αὐτοῦ τὴν μαρτυρίαν ἐσφράγισεν ὅτι ὁ θεὸς ἀληθής

ἀληθής, -ές: true	νύμφη, ἡ: a young wife, bride
αὐξάνω: to increase, augment	νυμφίος, ὁ: a groom
ἐλαττόω: to lessen, diminish, lower	πληρόω: to make full
ἔμπροσθεν: before, in front (+ gen.)	σφραγίζω: to seal
ἐπάνω: above, atop (+ gen.)	φίλος, ὁ: the beloved, dear
ἵστημι: to make to stand	χαίρω: to rejoice, be glad, be delighted
μαρτυρέω: to bear witness	χαρά, ἡ: joy, delight
μαρτυρία, ἡ: witness, testimony, evidence	χριστός, -ή, -όν: annointed

---

3:27 ἐὰν μὴ ᾖ δεδομένον: perf. subj. periphrastic in present general protasis, "unless
it is given"

3:28 ἀπεσταλμένος εἰμὶ: perf. periphrastic of ἀπο-στέλλω, "I have been sent"
ἔμπροσθεν ἐκείνου: "sent *before this one*"

3:29 ὁ ἑστηκὼς: perf. part. of ἵστημι, "the one standing"
αὐτοῦ: gen. after ἀκούων, "listening *to him*"
χαρᾷ: cognate dative with χαίρει, "he rejoices *with joy*"
πεπλήρωται: perf., "my joy *has been filled up*"

3:30 αὐξάνειν: pres. inf. after δεῖ, "it is necessary for him to increase"
ἐλαττοῦσθαι: pres. inf. pass. also after δεῖ, "but for me to be decreased"

3:31 ἐπάνω: = ἐπι-ἀνω, "above" + gen.

3:33 ὁ λαβὼν: aor. part. attrib. of λαμβάνω, "he who grasped"
ἐσφράγισεν: aor., "*has set his seal*" i.e. has indicated

[27] Respondit Ioannes et dixit: "Non potest homo accipere quidquam, nisi fuerit ei datum de caelo. [28] Ipsi vos mihi testimonium perhibetis, quod dixerim: 'Non sum ego Christus,' sed 'Missus sum ante illum.' [29] Qui habet sponsam, sponsus est; amicus autem sponsi, qui stat et audit eum, gaudio gaudet propter vocem sponsi. Hoc ergo gaudium meum impletum est. [30] Illum oportet crescere, me autem minui."

[31] Qui de sursum venit, supra omnes est; qui est de terra, de terra est et de terra loquitur. Qui de caelo venit, supra omnes est; [32] et quod vidit et audivit, hoc testatur, et testimonium eius nemo accipit. [33] Qui accipit eius testimonium, signavit quia Deus verax

---

accipio, (3) **accepi, acceptus**: to receive, accept
amicus, -i *m*: friend
cresco, (3): to increase, grow
gaudeo, (2): to be glad, rejoice
gaudium, -i *n*: joy, delight
habeo, (2): to have, hold
impleo, (2), **implevi, impletus**: to fill up
minuo, (3), **minui, minutus**: to lessen, diminish
nemo, neminis *m/f*: no one, nobody

oportet, (2): ought to (+ *inf.*)
signo, (1), **signavi, signatus**: to signal
sponsa, -ae *f*: bride
sponsus, -i *m*: groom, bridegroom
sto, (1): to stand, remain
supra (*adv.*): above; over, in authority over
sursum: up, on high
terra, -ae *f*: earth, land
testor, (1): to give as evidence, testify
verax, veracis (*gen.*): truthful
vox, vocis *f*: voice

3:27 **nisi fuerit datum**: fut. perf. in pres. general protasis, "unless it has been given"
3:28 **quod dixerim**: perf. subj. in an alleged ind. st., "give testimony *that I said*"
3:29 **gaudio**: cognate abl. with *gaudet*, "he rejoices *with joy*"
    hoc ...meum: nom., "*this* joy *of mine* is full"
3:30 **minui**: passive infinitive complementing *oportet*, "ought *to be diminished*"
3:31 **de sursum**: note the preposition followed by an adverb, "he who comes *from above*"

41

ἐστιν. ³⁴ ὃν γὰρ ἀπέστειλεν ὁ θεὸς τὰ ῥήματα τοῦ θεοῦ λαλεῖ, οὐ γὰρ ἐκ μέτρου δίδωσιν τὸ πνεῦμα. ³⁵ ὁ πατὴρ ἀγαπᾷ τὸν υἱόν, καὶ πάντα δέδωκεν ἐν τῇ χειρὶ αὐτοῦ. ³⁶ ὁ πιστεύων εἰς τὸν υἱὸν ἔχει ζωὴν αἰώνιον· ὁ δὲ ἀπειθῶν τῷ υἱῷ οὐκ ὄψεται ζωήν, ἀλλ᾽ ἡ ὀργὴ τοῦ θεοῦ μένει ἐπ᾽ αὐτόν.

Chapter 4

Jesus and the Woman of Samaria

¹ ὡς οὖν ἔγνω ὁ κύριος ὅτι ἤκουσαν οἱ Φαρισαῖοι ὅτι Ἰησοῦς πλείονας μαθητὰς ποιεῖ καὶ βαπτίζει [ἢ] Ἰωάνης, ² — καίτοιγε Ἰησοῦς αὐτὸς οὐκ ἐβάπτιζεν ἀλλ᾽ οἱ μαθηταὶ αὐτοῦ, ³ — ἀφῆκεν τὴν Ἰουδαίαν καὶ ἀπῆλθεν πάλιν εἰς τὴν Γαλιλαίαν.

αἰώνιος, -α, -ον: eternal
ἀπειθέω: to be disobedient
ἀπῆλθον: to go away, depart from (aor.)
ἀποστέλλω: to send off or away from
ἀφήκω: to arrive at
ἀφίημι: to send forth, discharge
γινώσκω: to know
δίδωμι: to give
ζωή, ἡ: life
Ἰουδαῖα, ἡ: Judea
κύριος, ὁ: a lord, master

μαθητής, -οῦ, ὁ: a disciple
μένω: to remain, abide
μέτρον, τό: a measure
ὀργή, ἡ: anger
ὄψομαι: to see (fut.)
πιστεύω: to trust, believe in
πνεῦμα, -ατος, τό: spirit
ῥῆμα, -ατος, τό: a word, saying
υἱός, ὁ: a son
χείρ, χειρός, ἡ: the hand

3:34 ἀπέστειλεν: aor. of ἀπο-στέλλω, "whom God *sent*"
οὐ ἐκ μέτρου: "not by measure" i.e. he gives abundantly
3:35 δέδωκεν: perf. of δίδωμι, "he has given"
3:36 τῷ υἱῷ: dat. ind. obj. of ἀπειθῶν, "the one not believing *in the son*"
οὐκ ὄψεται: fut., "will not see"
4:1 ὅτι ...ὅτι: note the embedded ind. st., "he knew *that* they had heard *that*..."
πλείονας ... ἢ: "*more than* John"
4:2 καί-τοι-γε: concessive, "even though"
4:3 ἀφῆκεν: aor. of ἀπο-ἵημι, "he departed" + acc.

est. ³⁴ Quem enim misit Deus, verba Dei loquitur; non enim ad mensuram dat Spiritum.   ³⁵ Pater diligit Filium et omnia dedit in manu eius.   ³⁶ Qui credit in Filium, habet vitam aeternam; qui autem incredulus est Filio, non videbit vitam, sed ira Dei manet super eum.

Chapter 4

Jesus and the Woman of Samaria

¹ Ut ergo cognovit Iesus quia audierunt pharisaei quia Iesus plures discipulos facit et baptizat quam Ioannes   ² — quamquam Iesus ipse non baptizaret sed discipuli eius —   ³ reliquit Iudaeam et abiit iterum in Galilaeam.

---

abeo, (4), **abii**, **abitum**: depart, go forth
Galilaea, **-ae** *f*: Galilee
incredulus, **-a**, **-um**: disbelieving of (+ *dat*.)
ira, **-ae** *f*: anger, wrath
iterum: again, a second time
Iudaea, **-ae** *f*: Judaea
manus, **-us** *f*: hand

mensura, **-ae** *f*: capacity; limit
plus, **pluris** (*gen*.): more
quamquam: although
relinquo, (3), **reliqui**, **relictus**: to leave behind, left
spiritus, **-us** *m*: spirit
verbum, **-i** *n*: word, proverb
vita, **-ae** *f*: life

3:34   **non ... ad mensuram**: "not up to a limit,"i.e. "without limit"
3:35   **in manu eius**: "into his hand," following the Greek case use where an acc. would be expected
4:1   **quia ...quia**: embedded ind. st., "he knew *that* they had heard *that* he had"
       plures... quam: "more...than"
4:2   **baptizaret**: impf. subj. consessive clause with *quamquam*, "*although he was* not *baptizing*"

⁴ ἔδει δὲ αὐτὸν διέρχεσθαι διὰ τῆς Σαμαρίας. ⁵ ἔρχεται οὖν εἰς πόλιν τῆς Σαμαρίας λεγομένην Συχὰρ πλησίον τοῦ χωρίου ὃ ἔδωκεν Ἰακὼβ τῷ Ἰωσὴφ τῷ υἱῷ αὐτοῦ· ⁶ ἦν δὲ ἐκεῖ πηγὴ τοῦ Ἰακώβ. ὁ οὖν Ἰησοῦς κεκοπιακὼς ἐκ τῆς ὁδοιπορίας ἐκαθέζετο οὕτως ἐπὶ τῇ πηγῇ· ὥρα ἦν ὡς ἕκτη.

⁷ ἔρχεται γυνὴ ἐκ τῆς Σαμαρίας ἀντλῆσαι ὕδωρ. ⁸ λέγει αὐτῇ ὁ Ἰησοῦς «Δός μοι πεῖν·» οἱ γὰρ μαθηταὶ αὐτοῦ ἀπε-ληλύθεισαν εἰς τὴν πόλιν, ἵνα τροφὰς ἀγοράσωσιν.

⁹ λέγει οὖν αὐτῷ ἡ γυνὴ ἡ Σαμαρεῖτις «Πῶς σὺ Ἰουδαῖος ὢν παρ' ἐμοῦ πεῖν αἰτεῖς γυναικὸς Σαμαρείτιδος οὔσης;» οὐ γὰρ συνχρῶνται Ἰουδαῖοι Σαμαρείταις.

ἀγοράω: to buy
αἰτέω: to ask, beg
διέρχομαι: to go through, pass through
ἕκτος, -η, -ον: sixth
Ἰακώβ: Jacob
κοπιάω: to be tired, grow weary
ὁδοιπορία, ἡ: a journey, way
πηγή, ἡ: running waters, streams
πίνω: to drink

πλήσιος, -α, -ον: near, close to (+ *gen.*)
πόλις, πόλεως, ἡ: a city
Σαμαρία, ἡ: Samaria
συνχράομαι: to use together, share with (+ *dat.*)
Συχάρ: Suchar
τροφή, ἡ: nourishment, food, victuals
ὕδωρ, ὕδατος, τό: water
χωρίον, τό: a district

4:4 διέρχεσθαι: pres. inf. after ἔδει, "it was necessary for him *to go through*"
4:5 ἔρχεται: note the casual shift to the present tense
4:6 κεκοπιακὼς: perf. part. of κοπιάω, "Jesus, *having become weary*"
     ὡς: "*about* the sixth hour"
4:7 ἀντλῆσαι: aor. inf. of purpose, "comes *in order to draw*"
4:8 δός: aor. imper. of δίδωμι, "give!"
     πεῖν: aor. inf. of purpose after δός, "give me *to drink*"
     ἀπεληλύθεισαν: plupf. of ἀπο-ῆλθον, "they had departed"
     ἵνα ... ἀγοράσωσιν: aor. subj. in purpose clause, "went *to buy*"
4:9 Ἰουδαῖος ὢν: pres. part. concessive, "you *although being a Jew*"
     γυναικὸς οὔσης: part. gen. concessive, "seek from me *although being a woman*"

⁴ Oportebat autem eum transire per Samariam. ⁵ Venit ergo in civitatem Samariae, quae dicitur Sichar, iuxta praedium, quod dedit Iacob Ioseph filio suo; ⁶ erat autem ibi fons Iacob. Iesus ergo fatigatus ex itinere sedebat sic super fontem; hora erat quasi sexta.

⁷ Venit mulier de Samaria haurire aquam. Dicit ei Iesus: "Da mihi bibere;" ⁸ discipuli enim eius abierant in civitatem, ut cibos emerent.

⁹ Dicit ergo ei mulier illa Samaritana: "Quomodo tu, Iudaeus cum sis, bibere a me poscis, quae sum mulier Samaritana?" Non enim coutuntur Iudaei Samaritanis.

---

abeo, (4), abii: depart, go away
bibo, (3): to drink
cibus, -i *m:* food
civitas, civitatis *f:* community
coutor, (3), cousus sum: to associate with, have dealings with (+ *abl.*)
emo, (3): to buy
fatigo, (1): to be weary
fons, fontis *m:* spring, fountain, well
haurio, (4): to draw up
hora, -ae *f:* hour, time
Iacob (*indecl.*): Jacob
Ioseph (*indecl.*): Joseph

iter, itineris *n:* journey
iuxta: near by, close to
mulier, mulieris *f:* woman
oportet, (2): it is necessary (+ *inf.*)
posco, (3), poposci: to ask, demand
praedium, -i *n:* farm, estate
quasi: about
Samaria, -ae *f:* Samaria (middle district of Palestine)
Samaritanus, -a, -um: Samaritan
sextus, -a, -um: sixth
Sichar (*indecl.*): Sychar
transeo, (4): go over, cross

4:5   **Ioseph:** dat., "to his son, Joseph" cf. Genesis 33:18
4:6   **Iacob:** gen., "the fountain *of Jacob*"
      ex itinere: *ex* + gen. expressing cause with superfluous preposition, "having been worried *by the journey*"
4:7   **haurire:** inf. of purpose, "she came *to draw up*"
      bibere: inf. of purpose, "give me *to drink!*"
4:8   **ut... emerent:** impf. subj. purpose clause, "went *in order to buy*"
4:9   **cum sis:** pres. subj. *cum* concessive clause, "*although you are* Jewish"

¹⁰ ἀπεκρίθη Ἰησοῦς καὶ εἶπεν αὐτῇ «Εἰ ᾔδεις τὴν δωρεὰν τοῦ θεοῦ καὶ τίς ἐστιν ὁ λέγων σοι Δός μοι πεῖν, σὺ ἂν ᾔτησας αὐτὸν καὶ ἔδωκεν ἄν σοι ὕδωρ ζῶν.»

¹¹ λέγει αὐτῷ «Κύριε, οὔτε ἄντλημα ἔχεις καὶ τὸ φρέαρ ἐστὶν βαθύ· πόθεν οὖν ἔχεις τὸ ὕδωρ τὸ ζῶν; ¹² μὴ σὺ μείζων εἶ τοῦ πατρὸς ἡμῶν Ἰακώβ, ὃς ἔδωκεν ἡμῖν τὸ φρέαρ καὶ αὐτὸς ἐξ αὐτοῦ ἔπιεν καὶ οἱ υἱοὶ αὐτοῦ καὶ τὰ θρέμματα αὐτοῦ;»

¹³ ἀπεκρίθη Ἰησοῦς καὶ εἶπεν αὐτῇ «Πᾶς ὁ πίνων ἐκ τοῦ ὕδατος τούτου διψήσει πάλιν· ¹⁴ ὃς δ' ἂν πίῃ ἐκ τοῦ ὕδατος οὗ ἐγὼ δώσω αὐτῷ, οὐ μὴ διψήσει εἰς τὸν αἰῶνα, ἀλλὰ τὸ ὕδωρ ὃ δώσω αὐτῷ γενήσεται ἐν αὐτῷ πηγὴ ὕδατος ἁλλομένου εἰς ζωὴν αἰώνιον.»

αἰτέω: to ask, beg
αἰών, -ῶνος, ὁ: age
ἅλλομαι: to spring, leap, bound
ἄντλημα, -ατος, τό: a bucket for drawing water
ἀποκρίνω: to separate, set apart
βαθύς, -εῖα, -ύ: deep or high
διψάω: to thirst
δίψησις, -εως, ἡ: a thirst, longing
δωρεά, ἡ: a gift, present

ζάω: to live
θρέμμα, -ατος, τό: a creature
οἶδα: to know (perf.)
πατήρ, πατρός, ὁ: a father
πηγή, ἡ: running waters, streams
πίνω: to drink
πόθεν: whence?
ὕδωρ, ὕδατος, τό: water
φρέαρ, τό: a well

4:10 εἰ ᾔδεις: plupf. of οἶδα in present contrafactual, "if you (now) knew"
    τίς ἐστιν ὁ λέγων: ind. quest. after ᾔδεις, "if you knew *who is the one speaking*"
    ἂν ᾔτησας ... ἔδωκεν ἄν: aor. in past contrafactual protasis, "you would have asked ...and *he would have given*"
4:11 τὸ ζῶν: pres. part. attributive, "the *living* water"
4:12 μὴ σὺ μείζων εἶ: "are you greater than?" + gen., expecting a negative answer
    αὐτὸς ἐξ αὐτοῦ: "*he himself* drank *from it*"
4:13 ὁ πίνων: pres. part. attributive with indefinite force, "everyone *who drinks*"
4:14 ὃς δ' ἂν πίῃ: aor. subj. of πίνω in a general rel. clause with conditional force, "whoever drinks" i.e. if anyone drinks
    οὐ μὴ + fut. in emphatic denial, "*he certainly will not* thirst"
    εἰς τὸν αἰῶνα: "forever"
    γενήσεται: fut. of γίνομαι, "will become"
    ἁλλομένου: pres. part., "of water *springing up*"

¹⁰ Respondit Iesus et dixit ei: "Si scires donum Dei, et quis est, qui dicit tibi: 'Da mihi bibere,' tu forsitan petisses ab eo, et dedisset tibi aquam vivam."

¹¹ Dicit ei mulier: "Domine, neque in quo haurias habes, et puteus altus est; unde ergo habes aquam vivam? ¹² Numquid tu maior es patre nostro Iacob, qui dedit nobis puteum, et ipse ex eo bibit et filii eius et pecora eius?"

¹³ Respondit Iesus et dixit ei: "Omnis, qui bibit ex aqua hac, sitiet iterum; ¹⁴ qui autem biberit ex aqua, quam ego dabo ei, non sitiet in aeternum; sed aqua, quam dabo ei, fiet in eo fons aquae salientis in vitam aeternam."

---

aeternum, -i n: eternity
aqua, -ae f: water
donum, -i n: gift, present
fons, fontis m: spring, fountain, well
forsitan: perhaps
habeo, (2): to have, hold
haurio, (4), **hausi, haustus**: to draw up
maior, -us: greater

pecus, pecoris n: cattle, herd, flock
peto, (3), **petii**: to beg, entreat, ask
puteus, -i m: well
salio, (3): to leap, gush
sitio, (4), **sitivi**: to be thirsty
unde: from where, whence
vivus, -a, -um: living

4:10 **si scires**: impf. subj. pres. contrary to fact protasis, "If you knew (now)"

  petisses… dedisset: plupf. subj. past contrary to fact apodosis, "then *you would have asked… he would have given*"

4:11 **in quo haurias**: pres. subj. in relative clause of characteristic, "(anything) into which you could draw," with superfluous and confusing preposition

4:14 **qui autem biberit**: perf. subj. in relative clause of characteristic, "anyone who has drunk"

  salientis: pres. part. gen. s., "of water *gushing*"

47

¹⁵ λέγει πρὸς αὐτὸν ἡ γυνή «Κύριε, δός μοι τοῦτο τὸ ὕδωρ, ἵνα μὴ διψῶ μηδὲ διέρχωμαι ἐνθάδε ἀντλεῖν.»

¹⁶ λέγει αὐτῇ «Ὕπαγε φώνησόν σου τὸν ἄνδρα καὶ ἐλθὲ ἐνθάδε.»

¹⁷ ἀπεκρίθη ἡ γυνὴ καὶ εἶπεν αὐτῷ «Οὐκ ἔχω ἄνδρα.»

λέγει αὐτῇ ὁ Ἰησοῦς «Καλῶς εἶπες ὅτι Ἄνδρα οὐκ ἔχω · ¹⁸ πέντε γὰρ ἄνδρας ἔσχες, καὶ νῦν ὃν ἔχεις οὐκ ἔστιν σου ἀνήρ· τοῦτο ἀληθὲς εἴρηκας.»

¹⁹ λέγει αὐτῷ ἡ γυνή «Κύριε, θεωρῶ ὅτι προφήτης εἶ σύ. ²⁰ οἱ πατέρες ἡμῶν ἐν τῷ ὄρει τούτῳ προσεκύνησαν· καὶ ὑμεῖς λέγετε ὅτι ἐν Ἱεροσολύμοις ἐστὶν ὁ τόπος ὅπου προσκυνεῖν δεῖ.»

ἀνήρ, ἀνδρός, ὁ: a man, husband
διέρχομαι: to go through, pass through
εἶπον: to say (aor.)
ἐνθάδε: hither
κάλως: well
ὄρος, -εος, τό: a mountain, hill

πέντε (indecl.): five
προσκυνέω: to worship, worship
προφήτης, -ου, ὁ: a prophet
τόπος, ὁ: a place
ὑπάγω: to withdraw
φωνέω: to summon, call

4:15 ἵνα μὴ διψῶ ... μηδὲ διέρχωμαι: pres. subj. in result clause, "give me *so I won't thirst ... I won't come here*"
ἀντλεῖν: pres. inf. of purpose, "come here *to draw*"
4:16 ὕπαγε: pres. imper., "go!"
φώνησον ... ἐλθέ: aor. imper., "summon! ...come!"
4:17 καλῶς εἶπες: aor., "you spoke well"
4:18 ἔσχες: aor. of ἔχω, "*you had* five husbands"
νῦν ὃν ἔχεις: "(the husband) *whom you now have* is not"
εἴρηκας: perf., "you have spoken"
4:20 προσκυνεῖν: pres. inf. after δεῖ, "where it is necessary *to worship*"
ἐν Ἱεροσυλμοις: prepositional phrase as a pred., "the place is *in Jerusalem*"

48

¹⁵ Dicit ad eum mulier: "Domine, da mihi hanc aquam, ut non sitiam neque veniam huc haurire."

¹⁶ Dicit ei: "Vade, voca virum tuum et veni huc."

¹⁷ Respondit mulier et dixit ei: "Non habeo virum."

Dicit ei Iesus: "Bene dixisti: 'Non habeo virum'; ¹⁸ quinque enim viros habuisti, et nunc, quem habes, non est tuus vir. Hoc vere dixisti."

¹⁹ Dicit ei mulier: "Domine, video quia propheta es tu. ²⁰ Patres nostri in monte hoc adoraverunt, et vos dicitis quia in Hierosolymis est locus, ubi adorare oportet."

---

adoro, (1): to honor, adore, worship
bene: well, rightly
haurio, (4), **hausi**, **haustus**: to draw up
Hierosolyma, **-orum** *n*: Jerusalem
locus, **-i** *m*: place, location
mons, **montis** *m*: mountain
noster, -ra, -**rum**: our
nunc: now
oportet, (2): it is proper; ought

pater, **patris** *m*: father
propheta, **-ae** *m*: prophet
quinque: five
venio, (4): to come
vere: really, truly
video, (2), **vidi**, **visus**: to see
vir, **viri** *m*: husband
voco, (1): to call, summon

4:15   **ut non… sitiam…veniam**: pres. subj. result clause, "so that I not be thirsty …so that I not come," i.e. not need to come

      haurire: inf. purpose, "come *to draw water*"

²¹ λέγει αὐτῇ ὁ Ἰησοῦς «Πίστευέ μοι, γύναι, ὅτι ἔρχεται ὥρα ὅτε οὔτε ἐν τῷ ὄρει τούτῳ οὔτε ἐν Ἱεροσολύμοις προσκυνήσετε τῷ πατρί. ²² ὑμεῖς προσκυνεῖτε ὃ οὐκ οἴδατε, ἡμεῖς προσκυνοῦμεν ὃ οἴδαμεν, ὅτι ἡ σωτηρία ἐκ τῶν Ἰουδαίων ἐστίν· ²³ ἀλλὰ ἔρχεται ὥρα καὶ νῦν ἐστίν, ὅτε οἱ ἀληθινοὶ προσκυνηταὶ προσκυνήσουσιν τῷ πατρὶ ἐν πνεύματι καὶ ἀληθείᾳ, καὶ γὰρ ὁ πατὴρ τοιούτους ζητεῖ τοὺς προσκυνοῦντας αὐτόν· ²⁴ πνεῦμα ὁ θεός, καὶ τοὺς προσκυνοῦντας αὐτὸν ἐν πνεύματι καὶ ἀληθείᾳ δεῖ προσκυνεῖν.»

²⁵ λέγει αὐτῷ ἡ γυνή «Οἶδα ὅτι Μεσσίας ἔρχεται, ὁ λεγόμενος Χριστός· ὅταν ἔλθῃ ἐκεῖνος, ἀναγγελεῖ ἡμῖν ἅπαντα.»

²⁶ λέγει αὐτῇ ὁ Ἰησοῦς «Ἐγώ εἰμι, ὁ λαλῶν σοι.»

ἀλήθεια, ἡ: truth	προσκυνέω: to worship
ἀληθινός, -ή, -όν: true	προσκυνητής, -οῦ, ὁ: a worshipper
ἀναγγέλλω: to carry back tidings of, report	σωτηρία, ἡ: a saving, deliverance
ἅπας, ἅπασα, ἅπαν: quite all, the whole	τοιοῦτος, -αύτη, -οῦτο: such as this
ζητέω: to seek, seek for	τουτῶ: from here, from there
λαλέω: to talk	χριστός, -η, -ον: annointed
Μεσσίας: the annointed one	ὥρα, ἡ: hour, season

4:22 οἴδατε ... οἴδαμεν: perf. with present force, "what *you know* not ... what *we know*"

4:25 ἔλθῃ: aor. subj. in general temporal clause, "when he comes (whenever that will be)"

   ἀναγγελεῖ: fut., "he will send"

4:26 ὁ λαλῶν: pres. part. attributive, "I am he, *the one speaking*"

50

²¹ Dicit ei Iesus: "Crede mihi, mulier, quia venit hora, quando neque in monte hoc neque in Hierosolymis adorabitis Patrem. ²² Vos adoratis, quod nescitis; nos adoramus, quod scimus, quia salus ex Iudaeis est. ²³ Sed venit hora, et nunc est, quando veri adoratores adorabunt Patrem in Spiritu et veritate; nam et Pater tales quaerit, qui adorent eum. ²⁴ Spiritus est Deus, et eos, qui adorant eum, in Spiritu et veritate oportet adorare."

²⁵ Dicit ei mulier: "Scio quia Messias venit, qui dicitur Christus; cum venerit ille, nobis annuntiabit omnia."

²⁶ Dicit ei Iesus: "Ego sum, qui loquor tecum."

---

adoro, (1): to adore, worship
annuntio, (1): to announce, preach
Christus, -i *m*: Christ, the annointed one
credo, (3), **credidi, creditus**: to trust, believe
Messias, -ae *m*: Messiah, the annointed one
nescio, (4): to not know, be ignorant
oportet, (2), **oportuit**: ought

pater, patris *m*: father
quaero, (3): to search for, seek; demand
quando: when
salus, salutis *f*: prosperity, salvation
talis, -e: of such kind
veritas, -tatis *f*: truth
verus, -a, -um: true

4:23   **venit hora:** pres. for future, "*the hour is coming* when they will adore"
     qui adorent eum: pres. subj. in relative clause of characteristic, "such *who worship him*"
4:24   **Deus:** nom. subject, "*God* is the spirit"
4:25   **cum venerit:** fut. perf. in gen. temp. clause, "when he has come" (i.e. whenever that is)

The Disciples Rejoin Jesus

²⁷ καὶ ἐπὶ τούτῳ ἦλθαν οἱ μαθηταὶ αὐτοῦ, καὶ ἐθαύμαζον ὅτι μετὰ γυναικὸς ἐλάλει· οὐδεὶς μέντοι εἶπεν «Τί ζητεῖς; ἤ Τί λαλεῖς μετ’ αὐτῆς;»

²⁸ ἀφῆκεν οὖν τὴν ὑδρίαν αὐτῆς ἡ γυνὴ καὶ ἀπῆλθεν εἰς τὴν πόλιν καὶ λέγει τοῖς ἀνθρώποις ²⁹ «Δεῦτε ἴδετε ἄνθρωπον ὃς εἶπέ μοι πάντα ἃ ἐποίησα· μήτι οὗτός ἐστιν ὁ χριστός;» ³⁰ ἐξῆλθον ἐκ τῆς πόλεως καὶ ἤρχοντο πρὸς αὐτόν.

³¹ ἐν τῷ μεταξὺ ἠρώτων αὐτὸν οἱ μαθηταὶ λέγοντες «Ῥαββεί, φάγε.»

³² ὁ δὲ εἶπεν αὐτοῖς «Ἐγὼ βρῶσιν ἔχω φαγεῖν ἣν ὑμεῖς οὐκ οἴδατε.»

³³ ἔλεγον οὖν οἱ μαθηταὶ πρὸς ἀλλήλους «Μή τις ἤνεγκεν αὐτῷ φαγεῖν;»

ἀφίημι: to release, leave behind
βρῶσις, -εως, ἡ: meat
δεῦτε: hither! come here!
ἐρωτάω: to ask
ἔφαγον: to eat (aor.)
ἤνεγκον: to bear (aor.)

θαυμάζω: to wonder
μέντοι: nevertheless
μεταξύ: between
οἶδα: to know (perf.)
πόλις, -εως, ἡ: a city
ὑδρία, ἡ: a water-pot, pitcher, urn

4:27 ἐπὶ τούτῳ (sc. χρόνῳ): "at that moment"
ἦλθαν: aor. with weak aor. ending, "they came"
4:28 ἀφῆκεν: aor. of ἀπο-ίημι, "she left behind"
4:29 ἴδετε: aor. imper. of εἶδον, "behold"
μήτι: expressing doubt, "is this perhaps?"
4:30 ἐξῆλθον ...ἤρχοντο: aor. and impf., "they left and were coming"
4:31 ἐν τῷ μεταξὺ (sc. χρόνῳ): "in the meantime"
φάγε: aor. imper., "eat!"
4:32 φαγεῖν: aor. inf. expressing purpose, "I have food to eat"
4:33 μή τις ἤνεγκεν: aor. of φέρω, "did no one bring?"

The Disciples Rejoin Jesus

²⁷ Et continuo venerunt discipuli eius et mirabantur quia cum muliere loquebatur; nemo tamen dixit: "Quid quaeris aut quid loqueris cum ea?"

²⁸ Reliquit ergo hydriam suam mulier et abiit in civitatem et dicit illis hominibus: ²⁹ "Venite, videte hominem, qui dixit mihi omnia, quaecumque feci; numquid ipse est Christus?" ³⁰ Exierunt de civitate et veniebant ad eum.

³¹ Interea rogabant eum discipuli dicentes: "Rabbi, manduca."

³² Ille autem dixit eis: "Ego cibum habeo manducare, quem vos nescitis."

³³ Dicebant ergo discipuli ad invicem: "Numquid aliquis attulit ei manducare?"

---

abeo (4), **abii**: to depart, go forth
affero, afferre, attuli: to bring
aliquis, -quae, -quod: someone, something
cibus, -i *m*: food
civitas, -tatis *f*: city
continuo: immediately,
exeo, (4), **exii**: to leave
hydria, -ae *f*: water-pot
interea: meanwhile

invicem: in turn; mutually
loquor (3), **locutus sum**: to speak
manduco, (1): to eat
miro, (1): to wonder; marvel at
numquid: is it possible, can it be that?
relinquo, (3) **reliqui, relictus**: to leave
rogo, (1): to ask
tamen: yet, nevertheless
venio (4) **veni, ventus**: to come

4:29   **quaecumque:** n. pl. acc., "said to me *whatever* I did"
4:32   **manducare:** inf. expressing purpose, "I have food *to eat*"
4:33   **ad invicem:** "to each other alternately," with *ad redundant*

³⁴ λέγει αὐτοῖς ὁ Ἰησοῦς «Ἐμὸν βρῶμά ἐστιν ἵνα ποιήσω τὸ θέλημα τοῦ πέμψαντός με καὶ τελειώσω αὐτοῦ τὸ ἔργον. ³⁵ οὐχ ὑμεῖς λέγετε ὅτι Ἔτι τετράμηνός ἐστιν καὶ ὁ θερισμὸς ἔρχεται ; ἰδοὺ λέγω ὑμῖν, ἐπάρατε τοὺς ὀφθαλμοὺς ὑμῶν καὶ θεάσασθε τὰς χώρας ὅτι λευκαί εἰσιν πρὸς θερισμόν· ³⁶ ἤδη ὁ θερίζων μισθὸν λαμβάνει καὶ συνάγει καρπὸν εἰς ζωὴν αἰώνιον, ἵνα ὁ σπείρων ὁμοῦ χαίρῃ καὶ ὁ θερίζων. ³⁷ ἐν γὰρ τούτῳ ὁ λόγος ἐστὶν ἀληθινὸς ὅτι ἄλλος ἐστὶν ὁ σπείρων καὶ ἄλλος ὁ θερίζων· ³⁸ ἐγὼ ἀπέστειλα ὑμᾶς θερίζειν ὃ οὐχ ὑμεῖς κεκοπιάκατε· ἄλλοι κεκοπιάκασιν, καὶ ὑμεῖς εἰς τὸν κόπον αὐτῶν εἰσεληλύθατε.»

βρῶμα, -ατος, τό: food, meat
εἰσῆλονι: to go in or into, enter (aor.)
ἐπαίρω: to lift up and set on
ἔργον, τό: work, deed
ἤδη: now, already
θεάομαι: to look on, gaze at, view, behold
θέλημα, -ατος, τό: will
θερίζω: to mow, reap
θερισμός, ὁ: reaping-time, harvest
καρπός, ὁ: fruit
κοπιάω: to labor, grow weary
κόπος, ὁ: labor, toil

λευκός, -ή, -όν: light, white
μισθός, ὁ: wages, pay, hire
ὁμοῦ: at the same place, together
ὀφθαλμός, ὁ: the eye
πέμπω: to send, despatch
σπείρω: to sow
συνάγω: to collect
τελειόω: to make perfect, complete
τετράμηνος, -ον: lasting four months
χώρα, ἡ: a space, place
ὡς: when

4:34 ἵνα ποιήσω: aor. subj. in noun clause that is the predicate of βρῶμα, "my food is *that I should do*"
τοῦ πέμψαντός: aor. part. of πέμπω, "of the one who sent"
τελειώσω: aor. subj. of τελειόω also with ἵνα, "and that I complete"
4:35 ἰδοὺ: aor. imper. of εἶδον, "behold!"
ἐπάρατε: aor. imper. of ἐπι-αίρω, "*raise up* your eyes!"
πρὸς θερισμόν: "white *for harvest*" i.e. ripe for harvest
4:36 ἵνα ... χαίρῃ: pres. subj. of χαίρω in result clause, "so he rejoices"
4:37 ἄλλος ἐστὶν ... καὶ ἄλλος: one is the sower ... *one* is the harvester"
4:38 ἀπέστειλα: aor. of ἀπο-στέλλω, "I sent"
θερίζειν: inf. of purpose, "sent *to harvest*"
κεκοπιάκατε: perf. of κοπιάω, "you have become weary"
εἰσεληλύθατε: perf. of εἰς-ῆλθον, "*you have entered* their toil"

³⁴ Dicit eis Iesus: "Meus cibus est, ut faciam voluntatem eius, qui misit me, et ut perficiam opus eius. ³⁵ Nonne vos dicitis: 'Adhuc quattuor menses sunt, et messis venit'? Ecce dico vobis: Levate oculos vestros et videte regiones, quia albae sunt ad messem! ³⁶ Iam qui metit, mercedem accipit et congregat fructum in vitam aeternam, ut et qui seminat, simul gaudeat et qui metit. ³⁷ In hoc enim est verbum verum: 'Alius est qui seminat, et alius est qui metit.' ³⁸ Ego misi vos metere, quod vos non laborastis; alii laboraverunt, et vos in laborem eorum introistis."

---

accipio, (3): to receive, accept
adhuc: thus far, till now
aeternus, –a, -um: eternal, everlasting
albus, -a, -um: white, favorable
alius, alia, aliud: other, another
congrego, (1): to collect
fructus, -us *m*: crops, fruit, reward
gaudeo, (2): to be glad, rejoice
introeo, (4), **introii**: to enter, go in or into
labor, -oris, *m*. labor, toil
laboro, (1): to work, labor, produce
levo, (1): to lift, raise
mensis, mensis *m*: month
merces, mercedis *f*: pay

messis, messis *m/f*: harvest
meto, (3): to reap; harvest
mitto (3) **misi, missus**: to send
oculus, -i *m*: eye
opus, operis *n*: work
perficio, (3): to complete, finish
quattuor: four
regio, regionis *f*: area, region
semino, (1): to plant, sow
simul: likewise; also; simultaneously
verbum, -i *n*: word, proverb
verus, -a, -um: true
vita, -ae *f*: life
voluntas, voluntatis *f*: will, desire

4:34 **ut faciam ... perficiam**: pres. subj. in noun clauses that are predicates of *cibus*: "my food is *that I do ...that I complete*"

albae sunt ad messem: "they are white for the harvest," i.e. ripe

4:36 **ut... gaudeat**: pres. subj. result clause, "so he rejoices"

et qui ... et qui: "both he who sows... and he who reaps"

4:38 **metere**: pres. inf. of purpose., "I sent you *to reap*"

quod: "(that) *for which* you have not labored"

non laborastis: sync. perf. (= *laboravistis*), "you have not labored"

introistis: perf., "you have entered"

Many Samaritans Believe

³⁹ ἐκ δὲ τῆς πόλεως ἐκείνης πολλοὶ ἐπίστευσαν εἰς αὐτὸν τῶν Σαμαρειτῶν διὰ τὸν λόγον τῆς γυναικὸς μαρτυρούσης ὅτι «Εἶπέν μοι πάντα ἃ ἐποίησα.» ⁴⁰ ὡς οὖν ἦλθον πρὸς αὐτὸν οἱ Σαμαρεῖται, ἠρώτων αὐτὸν μεῖναι παρ’ αὐτοῖς· καὶ ἔμεινεν ἐκεῖ δύο ἡμέρας. ⁴¹ καὶ πολλῷ πλείους ἐπίστευσαν διὰ τὸν λόγον αὐτοῦ,

⁴² τῇ τε γυναικὶ ἔλεγον ὅτι «Οὐκέτι διὰ τὴν σὴν λαλιὰν πιστεύομεν· αὐτοὶ γὰρ ἀκηκόαμεν, καὶ οἴδαμεν ὅτι οὗτός ἐστιν ἀληθῶς ὁ σωτὴρ τοῦ κόσμου.»

ἀληθῶς: truly	λαλιά, ἡ: talking, talk, chat
γυνή, γυναικός, ἡ: a woman	οὐκέτι: no more, no longer, no further
ἐρωτάω: to ask	πλείων, -ον: more
ἡμέρα, ἡ: day	σωτήρ, -ῆρος, ὁ: a saviour, deliverer

4:39 μαρτυρούσης: pres. part. circum. modifying γυναικὸς, "the word of the woman *witnessing* that"

4:40 μεῖναι: aor. inf. in ind. quest. after ἠρώτων, "they asked him *to remain*"
δύο ἡμέρας: acc. of duration, "for two days"

4:41 πολλῷ: dat. of degree of difference with πλείους, "more *by much*"

4:42 αὐτοὶ γὰρ ἀκηκόαμεν: perf. of ἀκούω, "we ourselves have heard"

Many Samaritans Believe

³⁹ Ex civitate autem illa multi crediderunt in eum Samaritanorum propter verbum mulieris testimonium perhibentis: "Dixit mihi omnia, quaecumque feci!" ⁴⁰ Cum venissent ergo ad illum Samaritani, rogaverunt eum, ut apud ipsos maneret; et mansit ibi duos dies. ⁴¹ Et multo plures crediderunt propter sermonem eius;

⁴² et mulieri dicebant: "Iam non propter tuam loquelam credimus; ipsi enim audivimus et scimus quia hic est vere Salvator mundi"!

---

apud: at, by, near, among (+ *acc.*)
audio, (4), **audivi**, **auditus**: to hear
dies, diei *m/f.* day
duo, duae, duo: two
ibi: there, in that place
loquela, -ae *f.*: speech, utterance
maneo, (2): to remain, stay

multus, -a, -um: many, much
plus, pluris (*gen.*): more
salvator, salvatoris *m*: savior
Samaritanus, -a, -um: Samaritan
scio, (4): to know, understand
sermo, sermonis *m*: speech, word
vere: really, truly, actually

4:39   **Samaritanorum**: gen. partitive with *multi*, "many *of the Samaritans*"
    perhibentis: pres. part. gen. attributive, "word of the women *providing* testimony"
4:40   **cum venissent**: plupf. subj. *cum* circumstantial clause, "when they had come"
    ut... maneret: impf. subj. in indirect command, "they asked him *to stay*"
    duos dies: acc. of duration, "for two days"
4:41   **multo**: abl. of degree of difference with *plures*, "more *by much*"

57

The Healing of the Official's Son

⁴³ μετὰ δὲ τὰς δύο ἡμέρας ἐξῆλθεν ἐκεῖθεν εἰς τὴν Γαλι-
λαίαν· ⁴⁴ αὐτὸς γὰρ Ἰησοῦς ἐμαρτύρησεν ὅτι προφήτης ἐν
τῇ ἰδίᾳ πατρίδι τιμὴν οὐκ ἔχει. ⁴⁵ ὅτε οὖν ἦλθεν εἰς τὴν
Γαλιλαίαν, ἐδέξαντο αὐτὸν οἱ Γαλιλαῖοι, πάντα ἑωρακότες
ὅσα ἐποίησεν ἐν Ἱεροσολύμοις ἐν τῇ ἑορτῇ, καὶ αὐτοὶ γὰρ
ἦλθον εἰς τὴν ἑορτήν.

⁴⁶ ἦλθεν οὖν πάλιν εἰς τὴν Κανὰ τῆς Γαλιλαίας, ὅπου
ἐποίησεν τὸ ὕδωρ οἶνον. Καὶ ἦν τις βασιλικὸς οὗ ὁ υἱὸς
ἠσθένει ἐν Καφαρναούμ· ⁴⁷ οὗτος ἀκούσας ὅτι Ἰησοῦς ἥκει
ἐκ τῆς Ἰουδαίας εἰς τὴν Γαλιλαίαν ἀπῆλθεν πρὸς αὐτὸν καὶ
ἠρώτα ἵνα καταβῇ καὶ ἰάσηται αὐτοῦ τὸν υἱόν, ἤμελλεν γὰρ
ἀποθνήσκειν.

ἀποθνήσκω: to die	ἴδιος, -α, -ον: one's own
ἀσθενέω: to be ill	Ἰουδαῖα, ἡ: Judea
βασιλικός, -ή, -όν: royal, kingly	καταβαίνω: to go or come down
Γαλιλαῖοι, οἱ: the Galileans	μέλλω: to be about to do (+ inf.)
δέχομαι: to take, accept, receive	οἶνος, ὁ: wine
ἐκεῖθεν: from that place, thence	ὅσος, -η, -ον: how much
ἐξῆλθον: to go or come out of (aor.)	πατρίς, -ίδος, ἡ: fatherland
ἑορτή, ἡ: a feast or festival, holiday	τιμή, ἡ: honor, value
ἥκω: to have come, be present, be here	υἱός, ὁ: son
ἰάομαι: to heal, cure	

4:45 ἐδέξαντο: aor. of δέχομαι, "they received him"

ἑωρακότες: perf. part. of ὁράω, "the Galileans *having seen*"

4:46 ὅπου ἐποίησεν: aor. of ποιέω, "*where he made* the water wine" in Book 2 above

οὗ: relative pronoun gen., "*whose son*"

4:47 ἠρώτα: impf. of ἐρωτάω, "this one *was asking*"

ἵνα καταβῇ ... ἰάσηται: aor. subj. in a noun clause expressing ind. com., "asked him *to come down ...to heal*"

ἤμελλεν: impf., "he was about to" + inf.

The Healing of the Official's Son

⁴³ Post duos autem dies exiit inde in Galilaeam;   ⁴⁴ ipse enim Iesus testimonium perhibuit, quia propheta in sua patria honorem non habet.   ⁴⁵ Cum ergo venisset in Galilaeam, exceperunt eum Galilaei, cum omnia vidissent, quae fecerat Hierosolymis in die festo; et ipsi enim venerant in diem festum.

⁴⁶ Venit ergo iterum in Cana Galilaeae, ubi fecit aquam vinum. Et erat quidam regius, cuius filius infirmabatur Capharnaum;   ⁴⁷ hic, cum audisset quia Iesus advenerit a Iudaea in Galilaeam, abiit ad eum et rogabat, ut descenderet et sanaret filium eius; incipiebat enim mori.

---

abeo, (4), **abii**: depart
advenio, (4): to come to, arrive
aqua, -ae *f.*: water
Cana (*indecl.*): Cana
descendo, (3): to descend, come down
excipio, (3), **excepi, exceptus**: to receive
festus, festa, festum: festive, joyous
filius, fili *m*: son
honor, honoris *m*: honor
incipio, (3): to begin; start
inde: from that place

infirmor, (1): to be ill
Iudaea, -ae *f.*: Judea, Israel
morior, (3), **mortuus sum**: to die
omnis, -e: all
patria, -ae *f.*: native land, home, native city
perhibeo, (2), **perhibui, perhibitus**: to present, give
regius, regia, regium: royal, regal
sano, (1): to cure, heal; correct; quiet;
vinum, -i *n*: wine

4:45 **cum... venisset ... vidissent**: plupf. subj. *cum* circumstantial clauses, "when he had come ...when they had seen"
 in diem festum: "had come *to the feast day*"
4:46 **Galilaeae**: gen., "Cana (of the province) *of Galilaea*"
 quidam regius: nom. substantive, "there was a certain royal (person)"
 Capharnaum: locative, "in Capharnaum"
4:47 **cum audisset**: plupf. subj. *cum* circumstantial clause, "when he had heard"
 quia Iesus advenerit: perf. subj. in ind. st., "heard *that Jesus has come*," violating the sequence of tenses
 ut descenderet et sanaret: impf. subj. indirect question, "asked *that he come down and heal*"

⁴⁸ εἶπεν οὖν ὁ Ἰησοῦς πρὸς αὐτόν «Ἐὰν μὴ σημεῖα καὶ τέρατα ἴδητε, οὐ μὴ πιστεύσητε.»

⁴⁹ λέγει πρὸς αὐτὸν ὁ βασιλικός «Κύριε, κατάβηθι πρὶν ἀποθανεῖν τὸ παιδίον μου.»

⁵⁰ λέγει αὐτῷ ὁ Ἰησοῦς «Πορεύου· ὁ υἱός σου ζῇ.» ἐπίστευσεν ὁ ἄνθρωπος τῷ λόγῳ ὃν εἶπεν αὐτῷ ὁ Ἰησοῦς καὶ ἐπορεύετο. ⁵¹ ἤδη δὲ αὐτοῦ καταβαίνοντος οἱ δοῦλοι αὐτοῦ ὑπήντησαν αὐτῷ λέγοντες ὅτι ὁ παῖς αὐτοῦ ζῇ. ⁵² ἐπύθετο οὖν τὴν ὥραν παρ' αὐτῶν ἐν ᾗ κομψότερον ἔσχεν· εἶπαν οὖν αὐτῷ ὅτι «Ἐχθὲς ὥραν ἑβδόμην ἀφῆκεν αὐτὸν ὁ πυρετός.»

⁵³ ἔγνω οὖν ὁ πατὴρ ὅτι ἐκείνῃ τῇ ὥρᾳ ἐν ᾗ εἶπεν αὐτῷ ὁ Ἰησοῦς «Ὁ υἱός σου ζῇ,» καὶ ἐπίστευσεν αὐτὸς καὶ ἡ οἰκία αὐτοῦ ὅλη.

δοῦλος, ὁ: a slave
ἕβδομος, -η, -ον: seventh
ἐχθές: yesterday
καταβαίνω: to step down, go or come down
κομψός, -ή, -όν: good, sound
οἰκία, ἡ: a building, house, dwelling
ὅλος, -η, -ον: whole, entire
παιδίον, τό: little or young child
παῖς, παιδός, ὁ: a child

πιστεύω: to trust, believe in
πορεύω: to make to go, carry, convey
πρίν: before (+ *inf.*)
πυνθάνομαι: to learn by inquiry
πυρετός, ὁ: burning heat, fiery heat
σημεῖον, τό: a sign, a mark, token
τέρας, -εος, τό: a sign, wonder, marvel
ὑπαντάω: to come or go to meet

4:48 ἐὰν μὴ ... ἴδητε: aor. subj. of εἶδον in fut. more vivid protasis, "unless you see signs"

πιστεύσητε: aor. subj. with οὐ μὴ indicates a strong denial, "you certainly will never believe"

4:49 κατάβηθι: aor. imper. of κατα-βαίνω, "come down!"

πρὶν ἀποθανεῖν: aor. inf., "before he dies"

4:50 πορεύου: pres. mid. imper., "make your way"

4:51 καταβαίνοντος: pres. part. in gen. abs., "when he was *going down*"

ὑπήντησαν: aor. of ὑπο-αντάω, "they encountered"

4:52 ἐπύθετο: aor. of πυνθάνομαι, "he inquired"

ὥραν ἑβδόμην: acc., "at the seventh hour" where we would expect the dative

ἔσχεν: aor. of ἔχω, "the hour in which *he got* better"

ἀφῆκεν: aor. of ἀπο-ἵημι, "the fever *left* him"

4:53 ἔγνω: aor. of γινώσκω, "he realized"

⁴⁸ Dixit ergo Iesus ad eum: "Nisi signa et prodigia videritis, non credetis."

⁴⁹ Dicit ad eum regius: "Domine, descende priusquam moriatur puer meus."

⁵⁰ Dicit ei Iesus: "Vade. Filius tuus vivit."

Credidit homo sermoni, quem dixit ei Iesus, et ibat. ⁵¹ Iam autem eo descendente, servi eius occurrerunt ei dicentes quia puer eius vivit. ⁵² Interrogabat ergo horam ab eis, in qua melius habuerit. Dixerunt ergo ei: "Heri hora septima reliquit eum febris."

⁵³ Cognovit ergo pater quia illa hora erat, in qua dixit ei Iesus: "Filius tuus vivit," et credidit ipse et domus eius tota.

---

dominus, -i *m*: master; the Lord
domus, -us *f*: house
febris, febris *f*: fever
heri: yesterday
homo, hominis *m*:: a man
interrogo, (1): to ask, question
melior, -or, -us: better
morior (3): to die
occurro, (3), **occurri, occursus**: to run to meet
priusquam: before (+ *subj.*)

prodigium, -i *n*: wonder
puer, -i *m*: boy
regius, -a, -um: royal, officer
relinquo, (3), **reliqui, relictus**: to leave behind, abandon
septimus, -a, -um: seventh
servus, -i *m*: slave, servant
signum, -i *n*: sign
totus, -a, -um: whole, entire
video (2), **vidi**: to see
vivo, (3): to live; survive

4:48 **nisi…videritis**: fut. perf. in a fut. more vivid protasis, "unless you see"
4:49 **priusquam moriatur**: pres. subj. anticipatory, "before he dies"
4:51 **eo descendente**: abl. abs., "when he was going down"
4:52 **ab eis**: "he asked the hour *from them*," i.e. the servants
       melius: nom. pred., "when he became *better*"
       habuerit: perf. subj. in indirect question, "in what hour *he became* better," violating the sequence of tenses
       hora septima: abl. of time when, "at the seventh hour"

⁵⁴ τοῦτο δὲ πάλιν δεύτερον σημεῖον ἐποίησεν ὁ Ἰησοῦς ἐλθὼν ἐκ τῆς Ἰουδαίας εἰς τὴν Γαλιλαίαν.

Chapter 5

The Healing at the Pool

¹ μετὰ ταῦτα ἦν ἑορτὴ τῶν Ἰουδαίων, καὶ ἀνέβη Ἰησοῦς εἰς Ἱεροσόλυμα. ² ἔστιν δὲ ἐν τοῖς Ἱεροσολύμοις ἐπὶ τῇ προβατικῇ κολυμβήθρα ἡ ἐπιλεγομένη Ἑβραϊστὶ Βηθζαθά, πέντε στοὰς ἔχουσα· ³ ἐν ταύταις κατέκειτο πλῆθος τῶν ἀσθενούντων, τυφλῶν, χωλῶν, ξηρῶν. ⁵ ἦν δέ τις ἄνθρωπος ἐκεῖ τριάκοντα καὶ ὀκτὼ ἔτη ἔχων ἐν τῇ ἀσθενείᾳ αὐτοῦ· ⁶ τοῦτον ἰδὼν ὁ Ἰησοῦς κατακείμενον, καὶ γνοὺς ὅτι πολὺν ἤδη χρόνον ἔχει, λέγει αὐτῷ «Θέλεις ὑγιὴς γενέσθαι;»

ἀναβαίνω: to go up, mount, to go up to
ἀσθένεια, ἡ: feebleness, sickliness
ἀσθενέω: to weaken, to be ill
γινώσκω: to know, to perceive
δεύτερος, -α, -ον: second
ἑορτή, ἡ: a festival, feast
ἐπιλέγω: to name
ἔτος, -εος, τό: a year
ἔχω: : to be in a certain condition
θέλω: to will, wish, purpose
κατάκειμαι: to lie down, lie outstretched
κολυμβήθρα, ἡ: a swimming-bath

ξηρός, -ά, -όν: dry, withered
ὀκτώ (indecl.): eight
πέντε (indecl.): five
πλῆθος, -εος, τό: a great number, crowd
πολύς, πολλά, πολύ: many
προβατικός, -ή, -όν: of sheep or goats
στοά, -ᾶς, ἡ: a roofed colonnade
τριάκοντα (indecl.): thirty
τυφλός, -ή, -όν: blind
ὑγιής, -ές: sound, healthy
χρόνος, ὁ: time
χωλός, -ή, -όν: lame

4:54 ἐλθών: aor. part. temporal, "after he had come"
5:1 ἀνέβη: aor. of ἀνα-βαίνω, "he went up"
5:2 ἐπὶ τῇ προβατικῇ (sc. πύλη): "at the Sheep Gate"
ἡ ἐπιλεγομένη Ἑβραϊστὶ: attrib. phrase, "the one called in Hebrew"
5:3 τῶν ἀσθενούντων: pres. part. gen. pl., "a number *of those being ill*"
5:5 ἔχων: pres. part. circum., "a man *being* in his sickness"
5:6 κατακείμενον: pres. part. circum., "having seen him *lying*"
ἰδὼν ...γνοὺς: aor. part., "having seen ...realized"
πολὺν ἤδη χρόνον: acc. of duration of time, "already a long time"
γενέσθαι: aor. inf. complementing θέλεις, "do you wish *to become*"

⁵⁴ Hoc iterum secundum signum fecit Iesus, cum venisset a Iudaea in Galilaeam.

Chapter 5

The Healing at the Pool

¹ Post haec erat dies festus Iudaeorum, et ascendit Iesus Hierosolymam. ² Est autem Hierosolymis, super Probatica, piscina, quae cognominatur Hebraice Bethsatha, quinque porticus habens. ³ In his iacebat multitudo languentium, caecorum, claudorum, aridorum. (⁴⁻⁵) Erat autem quidam homo ibi triginta et octo annos habens in infirmitate sua. ⁶ Hunc cum vidisset Iesus iacentem, et cognovisset quia multum iam tempus habet, dicit ei: "Vis sanus fieri?"

---

annus, -i *m*: year
aridus, -a, -um: whithered; shriveled
ascendo, (3), ascendi, ascensus: to climb, go up
Bethsaida: Bethsaida (north of the Sea of Galilee)
caecus, -i *m*: blind person
claudus, -a, -um: limping, lame
cognominor, (1): to be named, called
Hebraicus, -a, -um: in Hebrew language
iaceo, (2): to lie, lie down
infirmitas, -tatis *f*: weakness; sickness
langueo, (2): to be unwell, ill
multitudo, -dinis *f*: multitude, crowd

multus, -a, -um: much, many
octo: eight
piscina, -ae *f*: pool
porticus, -us *m/f*: colonnade, covered walk
Probatica, -orum *n*: "sheep gate" a transliteration from Greek
quinque: five
sanus, -a, -um: sound, healthy
secundus, –a, -um,: second
signum, -i *n*: sign
tempus, temporis *n*: time
triginta: thrity
volo, velle: to be willing, wish

4:54 **cum venisset**: plupf. subj. *cum* circumstantial clause, "when he had come"
5:1-2 **Hierosolymam ...Hierosolymis:** note the variation in the number of this name, from singular to plural
5:4-5 **triginta et octo annos**: acc. duration of time, "for thrity eight years"
　　　habens: "a man *being* in his illness"
5:6 **cum vidisset ...cognovisset**: plupf. subj. *cum* circumstantial clauses, "when he had seen ...understood"
　　　multum iam tempus: acc. duration of time, "already for much time"

⁷ ἀπεκρίθη αὐτῷ ὁ ἀσθενῶν «Κύριε, ἄνθρωπον οὐκ ἔχω ἵνα ὅταν ταραχθῇ τὸ ὕδωρ βάλῃ με εἰς τὴν κολυμβήθραν· ἐν ᾧ δὲ ἔρχομαι ἐγὼ ἄλλος πρὸ ἐμοῦ καταβαίνει.»

⁸ λέγει αὐτῷ ὁ Ἰησοῦς «Ἔγειρε ἆρον τὸν κράβαττόν σου καὶ περιπάτει.» ⁹ καὶ εὐθέως ἐγένετο ὑγιὴς ὁ ἄνθρωπος, καὶ ἦρε τὸν κράβαττον αὐτοῦ καὶ περιεπάτει.

Ἦν δὲ σάββατον ἐν ἐκείνῃ τῇ ἡμέρᾳ. ¹⁰ ἔλεγον οὖν οἱ Ἰουδαῖοι τῷ τεθεραπευμένῳ Σάββατόν ἐστιν, καὶ οὐκ ἔξεστίν σοι ἆραι τὸν κράβαττον.

¹¹ ὃς δὲ ἀπεκρίθη αὐτοῖς «Ὁ ποιήσας με ὑγιῆ ἐκεῖνός μοι εἶπεν Ἆρον τὸν κράβαττόν σου καὶ περιπάτει .»

¹² ἠρώτησαν αὐτόν «Τίς ἐστιν ὁ ἄνθρωπος ὁ εἰπών σοι Ἆρον καὶ περιπάτει ;»

αἴρω: to take up, raise, lift up
βάλλω: to throw
ἐγείρω: to wake up, rouse
ἔξεστι: it is in one's power, is possible
εὐθέως: straightaway
θεραπεύω: to be an attendant, do service

κράβαττος, ὁ: litter
περιπατέω: to walk about
Σάββατον, τό: Sabbath
ταράσσω: to stir, stir up, trouble
ὑγιής, -ές: sound, healthy, hearty, sound in

5:7 ὅταν ταραχθῇ: aor. subj. of ταράσσω in general temporal clause, "whenever the water is stirred up"

ἵνα ... βάλῃ: aor. subj. in purpose clause, "I don't have a man *to throw me* in"

ἐν ᾧ (sc. χρόνῳ): "in which time" i.e. when

ἄλλος: "*someone else goes down*"

5:8 ἔγειρε: pres. imper., "arise!"

ἆρον: aor. imper. of αἴρω, "*take up* your cot!"

περιπάτει: pres. imper., "walk around!"

5:9 ἐγένετο: aor. of γίνομαι, "*he became* well"

ἦρεν: aor. of αἴρω, "*he took up* his cot"

περιεπάτει: impf. inceptive, "he started walking around"

5:10 τῷ τεθεραπευμένῳ: perf. part. pass. dat. s., "said *to the one who was healed*"

ἆραι: aor. inf. of αἴρω complementing ἔξεστίν, "it is not permitted *to pick up*"

5:11 ὃς δὲ: "*but that one* answered"

5:12 ἠρώτησαν: aor., "they asked"

⁷ Respondit ei languidus: "Domine, hominem non habeo, ut, cum turbata fuerit aqua, mittat me in piscinam; dum autem venio ego, alius ante me descendit."

⁸ Dicit ei Iesus: "Surge, tolle grabatum tuum et ambula." ⁹ Et statim sanus factus est homo et sustulit grabatum suum et ambulabat.

Erat autem sabbatum in illo die. ¹⁰ Dicebant ergo Iudaei illi, qui sanatus fuerat: "Sabbatum est, et non licet tibi tollere grabatum tuum."

¹¹ Ille autem respondit eis: "Qui me fecit sanum, ille mihi dixit: 'Tolle grabatum tuum et ambula'."

¹² Interrogaverunt eum: "Quis est ille homo, qui dixit tibi: 'Tolle et ambula'?"

---

alius, alia, aliud: other, another
ambulo, (1): to walk
aqua, -ae *f.*: water
dies, -ei *m/f.*: day
grabatus, -i *m*: cot, camp bed, pallet
languidus, -i *m*: an invalid
licet, (2): it is permitted (+ *inf.*)
mitto (3): to send

piscina, -ae *f.*: pool
Sabbatum, -i *n*: Sabbath
sano, (1): to cure, heal
statim: at once, immediately
surgo, (3): to rise
tollo, (3), sustuli, sublatus: to lift up, take
turbo, (1): to disturb, turn up

5:7 **ut... mittat**: pres. subj. purpose clause, "I do not have a man *to put me in*"
　　cum turbata fuerit: fut. perf. in general temporal clause, "*whenever* the water *is stirred up*"
5:10 **qui sanatus fuerat**: plupf. pass. periphrastic, "about that one *who had become healed*"

¹³ ὁ δὲ ἰαθεὶς οὐκ ᾔδει τίς ἐστιν, ὁ γὰρ Ἰησοῦς ἐξένευσεν ὄχλου ὄντος ἐν τῷ τόπῳ.

¹⁴ μετὰ ταῦτα εὑρίσκει αὐτὸν ὁ Ἰησοῦς ἐν τῷ ἱερῷ καὶ εἶπεν αὐτῷ «Ἴδε ὑγιὴς γέγονας· μηκέτι ἁμάρτανε, ἵνα μὴ χεῖρόν σοί τι γένηται,» ¹⁵ ἀπῆλθεν ὁ ἄνθρωπος καὶ εἶπεν τοῖς Ἰουδαίοις ὅτι Ἰησοῦς ἐστιν ὁ ποιήσας αὐτὸν ὑγιῆ.

The Authority of the Son

¹⁶ καὶ διὰ τοῦτο ἐδίωκον οἱ Ἰουδαῖοι τὸν Ἰησοῦν ὅτι ταῦτα ἐποίει ἐν σαββάτῳ. ¹⁷ ὁ δὲ ἀπεκρίνατο αὐτοῖς «Ὁ πατήρ μου ἕως ἄρτι ἐργάζεται, κἀγὼ ἐργάζομαι.» ¹⁸ διὰ τοῦτο οὖν μᾶλλον ἐζήτουν αὐτὸν οἱ Ἰουδαῖοι ἀποκτεῖναι ὅτι οὐ μόνον ἔλυε τὸ σάββατον ἀλλὰ καὶ πατέρα ἴδιον ἔλεγε τὸν θεόν, ἴσον ἑαυτὸν ποιῶν τῷ θεῷ.

ἁμαρτάνω: to miss, miss the mark	ἕως: until, till
ἀποκτείνω: to kill, slay	ἰάομαι: to heal
ἄρτι: just now	ἰδέ: lo, behold
διώκω: to pursue	ἱερόν, τό: temple
ἐκνεύω: to turn the head aside	λύω: to loose
ἐλύω: to roll round	ὄχλος, ὁ: a moving crowd, a throng, mob
ἐργάζομαι: to work, labour	ὑγιής, -ές: sound, healthy
εὑρίσκω: to find	χείρων, χεῖρον: worse, meaner, inferior

5:13   ἰαθεὶς: aor. part. pass., "the one *who had been cured*"
     οὐκ ᾔδει: plupf., "he did not know"
     ἐξένευσεν: aor. of ἐκ-νεύω, "he turned his head away" i.e. he avoided
     ὄντος: pres. part. circum., "from the crowd *which was* in the place"
5:14   γέγονας: perf. of γίνομαι, "*you have become* well"
     ἵνα μὴ ... γένηται: aor. subj. in purpose clause, "*lest something befall* you"
     χεῖρόν: acc. n. s. with τι, "lest something *worse*"
5:15   ὑγιῆ: pred. acc. after ποιήσας, "the one who made him *healthy*"
5:17   ἕως ἄρτι: "up to the just now," i.e. even now
5:18   ἀποκτεῖναι: aor. inf. of ἀπο-κτείνω of purpose, "seeking *to kill* him"
     οὐ μόνον ... ἀλλὰ καί: "not only ... but also"
     πατέρα ἴδιον ... τὸν θεόν (sc. εἶναι): ind. st.after ἔλεγε, "he was saying God (to be) his own father"
     ἴσον: "himself *equal to*" + dat.

¹³ Is autem, qui sanus fuerat effectus, nesciebat quis esset; Iesus enim declinavit a turba constituta in loco.

¹⁴ Postea invenit eum Iesus in templo et dixit illi: "Ecce sanus factus es; iam noli peccare, ne deterius tibi aliquid contingat." ¹⁵ Abiit ille homo et nuntiavit Iudaeis quia Iesus esset, qui fecit eum sanum.

The Authority of the Son

¹⁶ Et propterea persequebantur Iudaei Iesum, quia haec faciebat in sabbato. ¹⁷ Iesus autem respondit eis: "Pater meus usque modo operatur, et ego operor." ¹⁸ Propterea ergo magis quaerebant eum Iudaei interficere, quia non solum solvebat sabbatum, sed et Patrem suum dicebat Deum, aequalem se faciens Deo.

---

abeo, (4), **abii**, **abitum**: to depart, go away
aequalis, **aequale**,: equal to (+ *dat.*)
aliquis, -quid: someone, something
constitutus, -a, -um: constituted, gathered
contingo, (3), **contigi**, **contactus**: to touch, happen, befall
declino, (1): to avoid, stray, slip away
ecce: behold! see! look!
efficio, (3), **effeci**, **effectus**: to bring about
enim: indeed, in fact
homo, hominis *m*: man
interficio, (3): to kill, destroy
invenio, (4): to come upon; discover
locus, loci *m*: place

modo: presently
nolo, nolle: wish not to; refuse to
nuntio, (1): to announce, report, tell
operor, (1): to work
pecco, (1): to sin; do wrong
persequor, (3): to follow up, pursue, persecute
postea: afterwards
propterea: therefore, for this reason
solum: only, alone
solvo, (3): to loosen, release, break
templum, -i *n*: temple
turba, -ae *f*: crowd, mob, multitude
usque: always, continuously

5:13   **fuerat effectus**: plupf. periph., "who *had been made* well"
        quis essset: impf. subj. in indirect question, "did not know *who it was*"
5:14   **noli**: imperative, "do not!" + inf.
        ne... contingat: pres. subj. purpose clause, "*lest* something worse *befall you*"
5:15   **quia...esset**: impf. subj. in alleged ind. st., "announced *that it was* Jesus"
5:16   **in sabbato**: abl. of time when, "on the Sabbath"
5:18   **quia ... solvebat**: causal, "*because he was not keeping* the Sabbath"
        patrem suum: acc. predicate, "was saying God was *his father*"

¹⁹ ἀπεκρίνατο οὖν ὁ Ἰησοῦς καὶ ἔλεγεν αὐτοῖς «Ἀμὴν ἀμὴν λέγω ὑμῖν, οὐ δύναται ὁ υἱὸς ποιεῖν ἀφ᾽ ἑαυτοῦ οὐδὲν ἂν μή τι βλέπῃ τὸν πατέρα ποιοῦντα· ἃ γὰρ ἂν ἐκεῖνος ποιῇ, ταῦτα καὶ ὁ υἱὸς ὁμοίως ποιεῖ. ²⁰ ὁ γὰρ πατὴρ φιλεῖ τὸν υἱὸν καὶ πάντα δείκνυσιν αὐτῷ ἃ αὐτὸς ποιεῖ, καὶ μείζονα τούτων δείξει αὐτῷ ἔργα, ἵνα ὑμεῖς θαυμάζητε. ²¹ ὥσπερ γὰρ ὁ πατὴρ ἐγείρει τοὺς νεκροὺς καὶ ζωοποιεῖ, οὕτως καὶ ὁ υἱὸς οὓς θέλει ζωοποιεῖ. ²² οὐδὲ γὰρ ὁ πατὴρ κρίνει οὐδένα, ἀλλὰ τὴν κρίσιν πᾶσαν δέδωκεν τῷ υἱῷ, ²³ ἵνα πάντες τιμῶσι τὸν υἱὸν καθὼς τιμῶσι τὸν πατέρα. ὁ μὴ τιμῶν τὸν υἱὸν οὐ τιμᾷ τὸν πατέρα τὸν πέμψαντα αὐτόν.

βλέπω: to see, have the power of sight
δείκνυμι: to bring to light, display, exhibit
δύναμαι: to be able (+ *inf.*)
ζωοποιέω: to cause to live
θαυμάζω: to wonder, marvel, be astonied
κρίνω: to judge
κρίσις, ἡ: a judgement

νεκρός, ὁ: a dead body, corpse
ὅμοιος, -α, -ον: like, resembling
πέμπω: to send
τιμάω: to honor
υἱός, ὁ: a son
φιλέω: to love, regard with affection

5:19 ἀφ᾽ ἑαυτοῦ: "from himself" i.e. independent of the Father
   ἂν (=ἐὰν) μή τι βλέπῃ: pres. subj. in pres. general protasis, "except what he sees"
   ποιοῦντα: pres. part. circum., "sees the father *doing*"
   ἃ γὰρ ἂν ἐκεῖνος ποιῇ: pres. subj. in general relative clause, "whatever that one does"
5:20 τούτων: gen. of comparison after μείζονα, "greater *than these*"
   δείξει: fut. of δείκνυμι, "he will show"
   ἵνα ὑμεῖς θαυμάζητε: pres. subj. in result/purpose clause, "so that you will be amazed"
5:21 ὥσπερ ... οὕτως: "just as ... just so"
   οὓς θέλει: "whom he wishes"
5:22 οὐδὲ ... οὐδένα: the second negative is redundant
   δέδωκεν: perf. of δίδωμι, "he *has given* to the son"
5:23 ἵνα τιμῶσι: pres. subj. in result/purpose clause, "*so that all honor* the son"
   καθὼς (=κατα ὥς): "*just as* they honor the father"
   τὸν πέμψαντα: aor. part. attributive, "the father, *the one who sent*"

¹⁹ Respondit itaque Iesus et dixit eis: "Amen, amen dico vobis:

Non potest Filius a se facere quidquam, nisi quod viderit Patrem

facientem; quaecumque enim ille faciat, haec et Filius similiter facit.

²⁰ Pater enim diligit Filium et omnia demonstrat ei, quae ipse facit,

et maiora his demonstrabit ei opera, ut vos miremini. ²¹ Sicut enim

Pater suscitat mortuos et vivificat, sic et Filius, quos vult, vivificat.

²² Neque enim Pater iudicat quemquam, sed iudicium omne dedit

Filio, ²³ ut omnes honorificent Filium, sicut honorificant Patrem.

Qui non honorificat Filium, non honorificat Patrem, qui misit illum.

---

demonstro, (1): to point out, show
diligo, (3): to love
honorifico, (1): to honor
itaque: and so, therefore
iudicium, -i *n*: judgment, sentence
iudico, (1): to judge, give judgment
maior, -us: greater, larger

miror, (1): to be amazed, wonder at
mitto, (3), misi, missus: send
mortuus, -i *m*: the dead
possum, posse: be able, can
similiter: similarly
suscito, (1): to awaken, raise
vivifico, (1): to bring back to life, make live

5:19   **a se:** not the agency expression, but expressing origin, "from himself" i.e.
     independently

     quod viderit: perf. subj. in relative clause of characteristic, "except *what he has
     seen*"

     facientem: pres. part. circum., "what he has seen his father *doing*"

     faciat: pres. subj. in general relative clause, "whatever *he does*"

5:20   **his:** abl. of comparison after *maiora*, "greater than *these*"

     ut...miremini: pres. subj. in result clause, "will show *so that you will wonder*"

5:21   **vult:** 3 s. of *volo*, "whom *he wishes*"

5:23   **ut... honorificent:** pres. subj. in purpose clause, "*in order to honor* the son"

²⁴ ἀμὴν ἀμὴν λέγω ὑμῖν ὅτι ὁ τὸν λόγον μου ἀκούων καὶ πιστεύων τῷ πέμψαντί με ἔχει ζωὴν αἰώνιον, καὶ εἰς κρίσιν οὐκ ἔρχεται ἀλλὰ μεταβέβηκεν ἐκ τοῦ θανάτου εἰς τὴν ζωήν. ²⁵ ἀμὴν ἀμὴν λέγω ὑμῖν ὅτι ἔρχεται ὥρα καὶ νῦν ἐστιν ὅτε οἱ νεκροὶ ἀκούσουσιν τῆς φωνῆς τοῦ υἱοῦ τοῦ θεοῦ καὶ οἱ ἀκούσαντες ζήσουσιν. ²⁶ ὥσπερ γὰρ ὁ πατὴρ ἔχει ζωὴν ἐν ἑαυτῷ, οὕτως καὶ τῷ υἱῷ ἔδωκεν ζωὴν ἔχειν ἐν ἑαυτῷ· ²⁷ καὶ ἐξουσίαν ἔδωκεν αὐτῷ κρίσιν ποιεῖν, ὅτι υἱὸς ἀνθρώπου ἐστίν.

²⁸ μὴ θαυμάζετε τοῦτο, ὅτι ἔρχεται ὥρα ἐν ᾗ πάντες οἱ ἐν τοῖς μνημείοις ἀκούσουσιν τῆς φωνῆς αὐτοῦ ²⁹ καὶ ἐκπορεύσονται οἱ τὰ ἀγαθὰ ποιήσαντες εἰς ἀνάστασιν ζωῆς, οἱ τὰ φαῦλα πράξαντες εἰς ἀνάστασιν κρίσεως. ³⁰ οὐ δύναμαι ἐγὼ ποιεῖν ἀπ᾽ ἐμαυτοῦ οὐδέν· καθὼς ἀκούω κρίνω, καὶ ἡ κρίσις ἡ ἐμὴ δικαία ἐστίν, ὅτι οὐ ζητῶ τὸ θέλημα τὸ ἐμὸν ἀλλὰ τὸ θέλημα τοῦ πέμψαντός με.

ἀγαθός, -ή, -όν: good
ἀνάστασις, -εως, ἡ: a raising up
δίκαιος, -η, -ον: just
ἐκπορεύω: to go out
ἐμαυτοῦ: of me, of myself
ἐξουσία, ἡ: power or authority
ζωή, ἡ: life
θάνατος, ὁ: death

καθώς: just as
μεταβαίνω: to pass over from one place to another
μνημεῖον, τό: a monument, tomb
πράσσω: to do
φαῦλος, -η, -ον: evil
φωνή, ἡ: a sound, tone
ὥρα, ἡ: period of time, hour

5:24 μεταβέβηκεν: perf. of μετα-βαίνω, "he has passed from X to Y"
5:25 οἱ ἀκούσαντες: aor. part. attributive, "they who have heard"
5:26 ἔχειν: inf. of purpose after ἔδωκεν, "he granted the son *to have*"
5:27 υἱὸς ἀνθρώπου: this phrase usually occurs with the definite article
    ὅτι ... ἐστίν: causal, "*because he is* the son"
5:28 ὥρα ἐν ᾗ: "*the hour in which* all will hear" i.e. when
    τῆς φωνῆς: gen. of after ἀκούσισιν where acc. would be expected; see τὸν λόγον ἀκούων in verse 24 above
5:29 οἱ ... πράξαντες: aor. part. of πράττω, "*those having done* good ...evil'"
5:30 τοῦ πέμψαντός: aor. part. gen. of πέμπω, "the will *of the one who sent* me"

²⁴ Amen, amen dico vobis: Qui verbum meum audit et credit ei, qui misit me, habet vitam aeternam et in iudicium non venit, sed transiit a morte in vitam. ²⁵ Amen, amen dico vobis: Venit hora, et nunc est, quando mortui audient vocem Filii Dei et, qui audierint, vivent. ²⁶ Sicut enim Pater habet vitam in semetipso, sic dedit et Filio vitam habere in semetipso; ²⁷ et potestatem dedit ei iudicium facere, quia Filius hominis est.

²⁸ Nolite mirari hoc, quia venit hora, in qua omnes, qui in monumentis sunt, audient vocem eius; ²⁹ et procedent, qui bona fecerunt, in resurrectionem vitae, qui vero mala egerunt, in resurrectionem iudicii. ³⁰ Non possum ego a meipso facere quidquam; sicut audio, iudico, et iudicium meum iustum est, quia non quaero voluntatem meam, sed voluntatem eius, qui misit me.

---

aeternus, -a, -um: eternal, everlasting
ago, (3), egi, actus: to conduct, act
audio, 4): to hear
bonus, -a, -um: good
iudicium, -i n: a judgement
iustus, -a, -um: just
malus, –a, -um: bad, evil, wicked
miror, (1): to be amazed, wonder at
monumentum, -i n: memorial, grave, tomb
mors, mortis f: death
potestas, -tatis f: power to (+ inf.)
procedo, (3): to proceed; advance

quaero, (3), quaesivi, quaesitus: to search for, seek
quando: when
resurrectio, -onis f: resurrection, rising again
semetipse, -a, -um: one's self
testimonium, -i n: testimony
transeo, (4), transii: to go over, cross, transition
verbum, -i n: word
vero: but
voluntas, -tatis f: good will
vox, vocis f: voice

5:25 **venit**: pres. with future force, "the day is coming"
    qui audierint: perf. subj. in general relative clause, "those *who have heard*"
5:29 **bona ... mala**: n. pl., "good things ... bad things"
5:30 **a meipso**: "to do *by myself*" i.e. independently
    iustum: nom. predicate, "my judgement is *just*"

Witnesses to Jesus

³¹ ἐὰν ἐγὼ μαρτυρῶ περὶ ἐμαυτοῦ, ἡ μαρτυρία μου οὐκ ἔστιν ἀληθής· ³² ἄλλος ἐστὶν ὁ μαρτυρῶν περὶ ἐμοῦ, καὶ οἶδα ὅτι ἀληθής ἐστιν ἡ μαρτυρία ἣν μαρτυρεῖ περὶ ἐμοῦ.

³³ ὑμεῖς ἀπεστάλκατε πρὸς Ἰωάνην, καὶ μεμαρτύρηκε τῇ ἀληθείᾳ. ³⁴ ἐγὼ δὲ οὐ παρὰ ἀνθρώπου τὴν μαρτυρίαν λαμβάνω, ἀλλὰ ταῦτα λέγω ἵνα ὑμεῖς σωθῆτε. ³⁵ ἐκεῖνος ἦν ὁ λύχνος ὁ καιόμενος καὶ φαίνων, ὑμεῖς δὲ ἠθελήσατε ἀγαλλιαθῆναι πρὸς ὥραν ἐν τῷ φωτὶ αὐτοῦ·

³⁶ ἐγὼ δὲ ἔχω τὴν μαρτυρίαν μείζω τοῦ Ἰωάνου, τὰ γὰρ ἔργα ἃ δέδωκέν μοι ὁ πατὴρ ἵνα τελειώσω αὐτά, αὐτὰ τὰ ἔργα ἃ ποιῶ,

---

ἀγαλλιάω: to rejoice exceedingly
ἀποστέλλω: to send off
καίω: to burn
λαμβάνω: to take, receive
λύχνος, ὁ: a portable light, a lamp
μαρτυρέω: to bear witness

μαρτυρία, ἡ: witness, testimony
σῴζω: to save
τελειόω: to make perfect, complete
φαίνω: to bring to light, make to appear
φῶς, φωτός, τό: light, daylight
ὥρα, ἡ; hour, time

5:31 ἐὰν ἐγὼ μαρτυρῶ: pres. subj of μαρτυρέω in pres. gen protasis, "if (ever) I witness"

5:32 ἣν μαρτυρεῖ; cognate acc., "the testimony *which he gives*"

5:33 ἀπεστάλκατε: perf. of ἀπο-στέλλω, "*you have sent* to John"
μεμαρτύρηκεν: perf., "*you have witnessed* to" + dat.

5:34 παρὰ ἀνθρώπου: "testsimony not *from a human*"
ἵνα ὑμεῖς σωθῆτε: aor. pass. subj. of σῴζω in purpose/result clause, "I speak *so that you be saved*"

5:35 ἀγαλλιαθῆναι: aor. inf. pass. complementing ἠθελήσατε, "you wished *to rejoice*"
πρὸς ὥραν: idiomatic, "for an hour" i.e. for a while

5:36 τοῦ Ἰωάννου (sc. τῆς μαρτυρίας): "greater than *John's* (testimony)"
ἵνα τελειώσω: aor. subj. in purpose clause after δέδωκέν, "he granted *to accomplish*"
αὐτὰ τὰ ἔργα: "*these very works* witness"

Witnesses to Jesus

³¹ Si ego testimonium perhibeo de meipso, testimonium meum non est verum; ³² alius est, qui testimonium perhibet de me, et scio quia verum est testimonium, quod perhibet de me.

³³ Vos misistis ad Ioannem, et testimonium perhibuit veritati; ³⁴ ego autem non ab homine testimonium accipio, sed haec dico, ut vos salvi sitis. ³⁵ Ille erat lucerna ardens et lucens; vos autem voluistis exsultare ad horam in luce eius.

³⁶ Ego autem habeo testimonium maius Ioanne; opera enim, quae dedit mihi Pater, ut perficiam ea, ipsa opera, quae ego facio,

---

accipio, (3): to receive, accept
ardeo, (2): to burn, glow
exsulto, (1): to rejoice, enjoy
Ioannes, Ioannis *m*: John
luceo, (2), luxi: shine, emit light
lucerna, -ae *f*: oil lamp
lux, lucis *f*: light
opus, operis *n*: work

pater, patris *m*: father
perficio, (3): to complete, finish
perhibeo, (2), perhibui, perhibitus: to present
salvus, -a, -um: safe, saved
scio, (4): to know, understand
veritas, veritatis *f*: truth, fact
verus, -a, -um: true

5:32 **quia verum est**: ind. st., "know that the testimony *is true*"
5:33 **misistis**: perf., "*you sent* (a message) to John"
 veritati: dat. after compound verb, "you gave testimony *to the truth*"
5:34 **ut... sitis**: pres. subj. purpose clause, "*in order that you will be* saved"
5:35 **ad horam**: "for a time" with superfluous preposition
5:36 **Ioanne**: gen., "greater than (the testimony) *of John*"
 ut perficiam: pres. subj. purpose clause, "in order that I may finish"

μαρτυρεῖ περὶ ἐμοῦ ὅτι ὁ πατήρ με ἀπέσταλκεν, ³⁷ καὶ ὁ πέμψας με πατὴρ ἐκεῖνος μεμαρτύρηκεν περὶ ἐμοῦ. οὔτε φωνὴν αὐτοῦ πώποτε ἀκηκόατε οὔτε εἶδος αὐτοῦ ἑωράκατε, ³⁸ καὶ τὸν λόγον αὐτοῦ οὐκ ἔχετε ἐν ὑμῖν μένοντα, ὅτι ὃν ἀπέστειλεν ἐκεῖνος τούτῳ ὑμεῖς οὐ πιστεύετε. ³⁹ ἐραυνᾶτε τὰς γραφάς, ὅτι ὑμεῖς δοκεῖτε ἐν αὐταῖς ζωὴν αἰώνιον ἔχειν· καὶ ἐκεῖναί εἰσιν αἱ μαρτυροῦσαι περὶ ἐμοῦ· ⁴⁰ καὶ οὐ θέλετε ἐλθεῖν πρός με ἵνα ζωὴν ἔχητε.

⁴¹ δόξαν παρὰ ἀνθρώπων οὐ λαμβάνω, ⁴² ἀλλὰ ἔγνωκα ὑμᾶς ὅτι τὴν ἀγάπην τοῦ θεοῦ οὐκ ἔχετε ἐν ἑαυτοῖς. ⁴³ ἐγὼ ἐλήλυθα ἐν τῷ ὀνόματι τοῦ πατρός μου καὶ οὐ λαμβάνετέ με· ἐὰν ἄλλος ἔλθῃ ἐν τῷ ὀνόματι τῷ ἰδίῳ, ἐκεῖνον λήμψεσθε. ⁴⁴ πῶς δύνασθε ὑμεῖς πιστεῦσαι, δόξαν παρ᾽ ἀλλήλων λαμβάνοντες, καὶ τὴν δόξαν τὴν παρὰ τοῦ μόνου θεοῦ οὐ ζητεῖτε;

ἀγάπη, ἡ: love
ἀλλήλων: of one another
γινώσκω: to know
γραφή, ἡ: a writing, scripture
δόξα, ἡ: glory, opinion
εἶδος, τό: an appearance

ἐραυνάω: to search, explore
μόνος, -η, -ον: alone
ὄνομα, -ατος, τό: name
ὁράω: to see
πώποτε: ever yet

5:36   ἀπέσταλκεν: perf. of ἀπο-στέλλω in ind. st., "witness that *he has sent* me"

5:37   μεμαρτύρηκεν: perf. of μαρτυρέω, "that one has witnessed"
     ἀκηκόατε ... ἑωράκατε: perf., "you have heard ... you have seen"

5:38   ἄμενόντα: pres. part., acc. pred., "have his word *remaining* in you"
     ἀπέστειλεν: aor. of ἀπο-στέλλω, "whom that one *sent*"
     ἐκεῖνος: the subject of ἀπέστειλεν, "*that one* (the father) sent"
     τούτῳ: dat. after πιστεύετε, "believes in *this one*" whose antecedent is ὃν ἀπέστειλεν

5:39   ἔχειν pres. inf after δοκεῖτε: "because you expect *to have*"
     αἱ μαρτυροῦσαι: pres. part. pred., "they (the scriptures) are *the ones witnessing*"

5:40   ἵνα ζωὴν ἔχητε: pres. subj. in purpose clause, "come *in order to have life*"

5:42   ἔγνωκα ὑμᾶς ὅτι: perf. of γινώσκω, "I know you (I know) that"

5:43   ἐὰν ἄλλος ἔλθῃ: aor. subj. in fut. more vivid protasis, "if another comes"
     λήμψεσθε: fut. of λαμβάνω, "you will receive him"

5:44   πιστεῦσαι: aor. inf. complementing δύνασθε, "how are you able *to believe*"

testimonium perhibent de me, quia Pater me misit; ³⁷ et, qui misit
me, Pater, ipse testimonium perhibuit de me. Neque vocem eius
umquam audistis neque speciem eius vidistis; ³⁸ et verbum eius
non habetis in vobis manens, quia, quem misit ille, huic vos non
creditis. ³⁹ Scrutamini Scripturas, quia vos putatis in ipsis vitam
aeternam habere; et illae sunt, quae testimonium perhibent de me.
⁴⁰ Et non vultis venire ad me, ut vitam habeatis.

⁴¹ Gloriam ab hominibus non accipio, ⁴² sed cognovi vos,
quia dilectionem Dei non habetis in vobis. ⁴³ Ego veni in nomine
Patris mei, et non accipitis me; si alius venerit in nomine suo, illum
accipietis. ⁴⁴ Quomodo potestis vos credere, qui gloriam ab invicem
accipitis, et gloriam, quae a solo est Deo, non quaeritis?

---

accipio, (3): to receive, accept	**scriptura, -ae** *f.*: scripture
aeternus, -a, -um: eternal, everlasting	**scrutor**, (1): to search, examine carefully
dilectio, -onis *f.*: love	**solus, -a, -um**: alone, only
invicem: in turn, reciprocally, mutually	**species, -ei** *f.*: appearance, splendor
nomen, -inis *n*: name	**umquam**: ever, at any time
puto, (1): to think, expect (+ *inf.*)	**vado**, (3): to go
quomodo: how, in what way?	**vita, -ae** *f.*: life

5:37 **audistis**: syncopated perf (= *audivistis*), "*you have* not *heard*"

5:38 **huic**: dat. whose antecedent is *quem misit*, "whom he (i.e. the father) sent, you
do not believe in *him*"

5:40 **ut... habeatis**: pres. subj. purpose clause, "come *in order to have*"
non vultis: pres. 2 pl. of *volo*, "you do not *wish* to come"

5:42 **vos, quia ...non habetis**: both the pronoun and the clause are objects of
cognovi, "I know you ...I know that you do not have"

5:43 **si alius venerit**: fut. perf. in fut. more vivid protasis, "if another one comes"

⁴⁵ μὴ δοκεῖτε ὅτι ἐγὼ κατηγορήσω ὑμῶν πρὸς τὸν πατέρα·
ἔστιν ὁ κατηγορῶν ὑμῶν Μωυσῆς, εἰς ὃν ὑμεῖς ἠλπίκατε. ⁴⁶ εἰ
γὰρ ἐπιστεύετε Μωυσεῖ, ἐπιστεύετε ἂν ἐμοί, περὶ γὰρ ἐμοῦ
ἐκεῖνος ἔγραψεν. ⁴⁷ εἰ δὲ τοῖς ἐκείνου γράμμασιν οὐ πιστεύετε,
πῶς τοῖς ἐμοῖς ῥήμασιν πιστεύσετε;»

Chapter 6

Jesus Feeds the Five Thousand

¹ μετὰ ταῦτα ἀπῆλθεν ὁ Ἰησοῦς πέραν τῆς θαλάσσης
τῆς Γαλιλαίας τῆς Τιβεριάδος. ² ἠκολούθει δὲ αὐτῷ ὄχλος
πολύς, ὅτι ἐθεώρουν τὰ σημεῖα ἃ ἐποίει ἐπὶ τῶν ἀσθενούντων.
³ ἀνῆλθεν δὲ εἰς τὸ ὄρος Ἰησοῦς, καὶ ἐκεῖ ἐκάθητο μετὰ τῶν
μαθητῶν αὐτοῦ. ⁴ ἦν δὲ ἐγγὺς τὸ πάσχα, ἡ ἑορτὴ τῶν Ἰουδαίων.

ἀκολουθέω: to follow
Γαλιλαία, ἡ: Galileia
γράμμα, -ατος, τό: writing, scripture
γράφω: to write
ἐγγύς: near, at hand
ἐλπίζω: to hope for, look for, expect
ἑορτή, ἡ: a festival, feast
θάλασσα, ἡ: the sea

θεωρέω: to look at, view, behold
κάθημαι: to be seated
κατηγορέω: to speak against, to accuse
ὄρος, -εος, τό: a mountain, hill
πάσχα, τό (indecl.): Passover
πέραν: on the other side of (+ gen.)
ῥῆμα, -ατος, τό: a word, saying
Τιβεριάς, -άδος, ἡ: Tiberias

5:45   μὴ δοκεῖτε: in prohibition, "don't think!"

      Μωυσῆς: nom. pred., "the one accusing is *Moses*"

      εἰς ὅν: "Moses *in whom* you have hoped"

      ἠλπίκατε: perf. of ἐλπίζω

5:46   εἰ ἐπιστεύετε … ἐπιστεύετε ἂν: pres. contrafactual condition, "if you now
      believed Moses, you would believe"

5:47   εἰ οὐ πιστεύετε… πῶς πιστεύσετε: mixed condition, "if you do not believe …
      how will you believe"

      ἐκείνου: "believe the words *of that one*" i.e. Moses

6:1   πέραν: "to the other side of" + gen.

6:2   ἠκολούθει … ἐθεώρουν: impf., "the crowd *was following* because *they saw*"

      τῶν ἀσθενούντων: pres. part. attributive, "upon *those who were sick*"

6:3   ἐκάθητο: impf., "he seated himself"

⁴⁵ Nolite putare quia ego accusaturus sim vos apud Patrem; est qui accuset vos: Moyses, in quo vos speratis. ⁴⁶ Si enim crederetis Moysi, crederetis forsitan et mihi; de me enim ille scripsit. ⁴⁷ Si autem illius litteris non creditis, quomodo meis verbis credetis?"

Chapter 6

Jesus Feeds the Five Thousand

¹ Post haec abiit Iesus trans mare Galilaeae, quod est Tiberiadis. ² Et sequebatur eum multitudo magna, quia videbant signa, quae faciebat super his, qui infirmabantur. ³ Subiit autem in montem Iesus et ibi sedebat cum discipulis suis. ⁴ Erat autem proximum Pascha, dies festus Iudaeorum.

---

abeo, (4), **abii**, **abitum**: to depart, go away
accuso, (1): to accuse, blame, find fault
apud: before, in the presence of (+ *acc.*)
forsitan: perhaps
Galilaea, -ae *f*: Galilee
littera, -ae *f*: writing, scripture
magnus, -a, -um: great, large
mare, maris *n*: sea
mons, montis *m*: mountain
multitudo, -inis *f*: multitude, great number, crowd

Pascha, -atis *n*: Passover
proximus, -a, -um: near, close to
scribo, (3), **scripsi**, **scriptus**: to write
sedeo, (2): to sit, remain; settle
sequor, (3), **secutus sum**: follow
signum, -i *n*: sign
spero, (1): to trust
subeo, (4), **subii**, **subitum**: go up, climb, ascend
trans: across (+ *acc.*)

5:45 **quia... sim**: pres. subj. with fut. part. periphrastic in ind. st. after *putare*, "think *that I am about to accuse*" indicating an alleged statement

qui accuset: pres. subj. in relative clause of characteristic, "there is one *who would accuse you*"

5:46 **si... crederetis**: impf. subj. in pres. contrary to fact protasis, "*if you now believed in* Moses, you would believe in me"

6:1 **Tiberiadis**: "which is (the sea) *of Tiberias*"

6:4 **proximum**: predicate adj., "Passover was *near*"

⁵ ἐπάρας οὖν τοὺς ὀφθαλμοὺς ὁ Ἰησοῦς καὶ θεασάμενος ὅτι πολὺς ὄχλος ἔρχεται πρὸς αὐτὸν λέγει πρὸς Φίλιππον «Πόθεν ἀγοράσωμεν ἄρτους ἵνα φάγωσιν οὗτοι;» ⁶ τοῦτο δὲ ἔλεγεν πειράζων αὐτόν, αὐτὸς γὰρ ᾔδει τί ἔμελλεν ποιεῖν.

⁷ ἀπεκρίθη αὐτῷ Φίλιππος «Διακοσίων δηναρίων ἄρτοι οὐκ ἀρκοῦσιν αὐτοῖς ἵνα ἕκαστος βραχὺ λάβῃ.»

⁸ λέγει αὐτῷ εἷς ἐκ τῶν μαθητῶν αὐτοῦ, Ἀνδρέας ὁ ἀδελφὸς Σίμωνος Πέτρου ⁹ «Ἔστιν παιδάριον ὧδε ὃς ἔχει πέντε ἄρτους κριθίνους καὶ δύο ὀψάρια· ἀλλὰ ταῦτα τί ἐστιν εἰς τοσούτους;»

ἀγοράζω: to buy
ἀδελφός ὁ: brother
Ἀνδρέας, ὁ: Andrew
ἀρκέω: to suffice
ἄρτος, ὁ: a loaf of wheat-bread
βραχύς, -εῖα, -ύ: short
δηνάριον, τό: a denarius (coin)
διακόσιοι, -αι, -α: two hundred
εἷς, μία, ἕν: one
ἕκαστος, -η, -ον: every, every one
ἐπαίρω: to lift up and set on

θεάομαι: to look on, gaze at, view, behold
κρίθινος, -η, -ον: made of or from barley
μέλλω: to intend to do, to be about to do
ὀφθαλμός, ὁ: the eye
ὀψάριον, τό: food, fish
παιδάριον, τό: a young, little boy
πειράζω: to make trial of
πέντε (indecl): five
τοσοῦτος, -αύτη, -οῦτο: so large
Φίλιππος: Philip

6:5 **ἐπάρας**: aor. part. of **ἐπι-αίρω**, "Jesus, *having raised*"
πόθεν ἀγοράσωμεν: aor. subj. in deliberative quest., "whence should we buy?"
ἵνα φάγωσιν: aor. subj. of **ἐσθίω** in result clause, "so that these might eat"
6:6 **πειράζων**: pres. part. showing purpose, "he said this *in order to test*"
τί ἔμελλεν: ind. quest., "knew *what he was about to*" + inf.
6:7 **Διακοσίων δηναρίων**: gen. of value, "worth 200 denarii"
ἀρκοῦσιν: "are sufficient for" + dat.
ἵνα λάβῃ: aor. subj. of **λαμβάνω** in result, "so that each one have"
6:9 **ὧδε**: "there is a boy *here*"
εἰς τοσούτους: "*for so many* people"

⁵ Cum sublevasset ergo oculos Iesus et vidisset quia multitudo magna venit ad eum, dicit ad Philippum: "Unde ememus panes, ut manducent hi?" ⁶ Hoc autem dicebat tentans eum; ipse enim sciebat quid esset facturus.

⁷ Respondit ei Philippus: "Ducentorum denariorum panes non sufficiunt eis, ut unusquisque modicum quid accipiat!"

⁸ Dicit ei unus ex discipulis eius, Andreas frater Simonis Petri: ⁹ "Est puer hic, qui habet quinque panes hordeaceos et duos pisces; sed haec quid sunt propter tantos?"

---

accipio, (3): to receive, accept
Andreas *m*: Andrew
denarius, -i *m*: denarius (silver coin)
ducenti, --as, -a: two hundred
duo, duae, duo: two
emo, (3): to buy, gain, acquire
frater, fratris *m*: brother
hordeaceus, -a, -um: barley
magnus, –a, -um: large, great
manduco, (1): to eat
modicus, i: small amount
multitudo, -inis *f*: multitude, crowd
oculus, -i *m*: eye

panis, panis *m*: bread
Petrus, -i *m*: Peter
Philippus, -i *m*: Philip
piscis, -is *m*: fish
puer, -i *m*: boy
quinque: five
Simon, Simonis *m*: Simon
sublevo, (1): to lift up, raise
sufficio, (3): to be sufficient, suffice
tantus, -a, -um: of such size, so many
tento, (1): to test
unde: from where, whence
unusquisque: each one, everyone

6:5 **cum sublevasset... vidisset**: plupf. subj. *cum* circumstantial clause, "when he had raised ... when he had seen"

ut manducent: pres. subj. result clause, "buy bread *in order that they may eat*"

6:6 **quid esset facturus**: impf. subj. with fut. part. in periphrastic ind. quest., "knew *what he was about to do*"

6:7 **ducentorum denariorum**: gen. of price, "loaves *worth two hundred denaria* are not sufficient"

ut... accipiat: pres. subj. result clause, "suffice *in order that each receive*"

6:9 **haec quid sunt (sc. boni)**: "What (of good) are these?

¹⁰ εἶπεν ὁ Ἰησοῦς «Ποιήσατε τοὺς ἀνθρώπους ἀναπεσεῖν.» ἦν δὲ χόρτος πολὺς ἐν τῷ τόπῳ. ἀνέπεσαν οὖν οἱ ἄνδρες τὸν ἀριθμὸν ὡς πεντακισχίλιοι. ¹¹ ἔλαβεν οὖν τοὺς ἄρτους ὁ Ἰησοῦς καὶ εὐχαριστήσας διέδωκεν τοῖς ἀνακειμένοις, ὁμοίως καὶ ἐκ τῶν ὀψαρίων ὅσον ἤθελον.

¹² ὡς δὲ ἐνεπλήσθησαν λέγει τοῖς μαθηταῖς αὐτοῦ «Συνα-γάγετε τὰ περισσεύσαντα κλάσματα, ἵνα μή τι ἀπόληται.» ¹³ συνήγαγον οὖν, καὶ ἐγέμισαν δώδεκα κοφίνους κλασμά-των ἐκ τῶν πέντε ἄρτων τῶν κριθίνων ἃ ἐπερίσσευσαν τοῖς βεβρωκόσιν.

ἀνάκειμαι: to be laid up
ἀναπίπτω: to fall back
ἀπόλλυμι: to destroy utterly, lose
ἀριθμός: number
βιβρώσκω: to eat, eat up
γεμίζω: to fill
διαδίδωμι: to distribute
δώδεκα: twelve
ἐμπίμπλημι: to fill
εὐχαριστέω: to be thankful, return thanks

κλάσμα, -ατος, τό: a fragment, morsel
κόφινος, ὁ: a basket
κρίθινος, -η, -ον: made of or from barley
ὅμοιος, -α, -ον: like, resembling
ὅσος, -η, -ον: how much
πεντακισχίλιοι, -αι: five thousand
πέντε (indecl.): five
περισσεύω: to be left over
συνάγω: to gather together, collect
χόρτος, ὁ: an inclosed place

6:10 ἀναπεσεῖν: aor. inf. of ἀνα-πίπτω after ποιήσατε, "cause them *to fall back*"
ἀνέπεσαν: aor. 3 pl. of ἀνα-πίπτω with weak ending, "they fell back"
τὸν ἀριθμὸν: acc. of resp., "5000 *in number*"
ὡς: "*about* five thousand"

6:11 εὐχαριστήσας: aor. part., "Jesus *having blessed*"
διέδωκεν: aor. of δια-δίδωμι, "he distributed"
ὅσον ἤθελον: impf. of ἐθέλω, "as much as *they wished*"

6:12 ἐνεπλήσθησαν: aor. pass. of ἐμ-πίμπλημι, "they were filled"
τὰ περισσεύσαντα: aor. part. attributive, "*the remaining* morsels"
ἵνα μή τι ἀπόληται: aor. subj. of ἀπολλυμι in purpose clause, "lest anything be wasted"

6:13 συνήγαγον ... ἐγέμισαν: aor., "they gathered ...they filled"
ἃ ἐπερίσσευσαν: aor., "fragments *which remained*"
τοῖς βεβρωκόσιν: perf. part. dat. pl. of agent, "remained *from those who had eaten*"

¹⁰ Dixit Iesus: "Facite homines discumbere." Erat autem fenum multum in loco. Discubuerunt ergo viri numero quasi quinque milia. ¹¹ Accepit ergo panes Iesus et, cum gratias egisset, distribuit discumbentibus; similiter et ex piscibus, quantum volebant.

¹² Ut autem impleti sunt, dicit discipulis suis: "Colligite, quae superaverunt, fragmenta, ne quid pereat." ¹³ Collegerunt ergo et impleverunt duodecim cophinos fragmentorum ex quinque panibus hordeaceis, quae superfuerunt his, qui manducaverunt.

---

ago, (3), **egi, actus**: to thank (+ *gratias*)
colligo, (3): to collect, assemble
cophinus, -i *m*: basket
discumbo, (3), **discubui, discubitus**: to sit (to eat), recline
distribuo, (3), **distribui, distributus**: to divide, distribute
duodecim: twelve
fenum, -i *n*: hay, grass
fragmentum, -i *n*: fragment, piece
gratia, -ae *f*: thanks, appreciation
hordeaceus, -a, -um: barley
impleo, (2), **implevi, impletus**: to fill up, satisfy

locus, **loci** *m*: place
manduco, (1): to eat
mille, milis *n*: a thousand
multus, -a -um: much, many
numerus, -i *m*: number
pereo, (4): to go to waste
quantum: how much?
quasi: about
quinque: five
similiter: similarly
supero, (1): to remain
supersum, -esse, -fui: to be over and above
volo, velle: to wish, want, prefer

6:10   **discumbere**: pres. inf. after causative *facite*, "make them *sit down*"

6:11   **cum... egisset**: plupf. subj. *cum* circumstantial clause, "when he had given thanks"

      discumbientibus: pres. part. attributive dat., "he distributed *to those sitting*"

6:12   **ut**: translating ὡς, "*when* they were filled"

      ne quid (=quidquid) pereat: pres. subj. purpose clause, "lest any go to waste"

6:13   **qui manducaverunt**: perf. where plupf. would be expected, "from these *who had eaten*"

¹⁴ οἱ οὖν ἄνθρωποι ἰδόντες ἃ ἐποίησεν σημεῖα ἔλεγον ὅτι «Οὗτός ἐστιν ἀληθῶς ὁ προφήτης ὁ ἐρχόμενος εἰς τὸν κόσμον.» ¹⁵ Ἰησοῦς οὖν γνοὺς ὅτι μέλλουσιν ἔρχεσθαι καὶ ἁρπάζειν αὐτὸν ἵνα ποιήσωσιν βασιλέα ἀνεχώρησεν πάλιν εἰς τὸ ὄρος αὐτὸς μόνος.

Jesus Walks on the Water

¹⁶ ὡς δὲ ὀψία ἐγένετο κατέβησαν οἱ μαθηταὶ αὐτοῦ ἐπὶ τὴν θάλασσαν, ¹⁷ καὶ ἐμβάντες εἰς πλοῖον ἤρχοντο πέραν τῆς θαλάσσης εἰς Καφαρναούμ. καὶ σκοτία ¹⁸ ἤδη ἐγεγόνει καὶ οὔπω ἐληλύθει πρὸς αὐτοὺς ὁ Ἰησοῦς, ἥ τε θάλασσα ἀνέμου μεγάλου πνέοντος διεγείρετο. ¹⁹ ἐληλακότες οὖν ὡς

ἀναχωρέω: to go back
ἄνεμος, ὁ: wind
ἁρπάζω: to snatch away, carry off
βασιλεύς, -έως, ὁ: a king, chief
διεγείρω: to rise up
ἐμβαίνω: to step in
Καφαρναούμ: Capharnum
κόσμος, ὁ: world

μόνος, -η, -ον: alone
οὔπω: not yet
ὀψία, ἡ: the evening
πλοῖον, τό: a ship, vessel
πνέω: to blow
προφήτης, -ου, ὁ: a prophet
σκοτία, ἡ: darkness, gloom

6:14 ἰδόντες: aor. part. of εἶδον, "having seen"
 ἃ ... σημεῖα: *the signs which* he did"
6:15 γνοὺς: aor. part. of γινώσκω, "having realized"
 ἵνα ποιήσωσιν: aor. subj. of ποιέω in purpose clause, "*in order to make* him king"
 ἀνεχώρησεν: aor. of ἀνα-χωρέω, "he withdrew"
6:16 ἐγένετο: aor. of γίνομαι, "*it became* evening"
 κατέβησαν: aor. of κατα-βαίνω, "they went down"
6:17 ἐμβάντες: aor. of ἐν-βαίνω, "having stepped on" i.e. gone onboard
6:18 ἐγεγόνει: plupf. of γίνομαι, "*it had become* dark"
 ἐληλύθει: plupf. of ἔρχομαι, "he had gone"
 ἀνέμου μεγάλου πνέοντος: gen. abs., "a great wind blowing"
 διεγείρετο: impf. of δια-ἐγείρω, "the sea was rising"
6:19 ἐληλακότες: perf. part. of ἐλαύνω, "having driven out," i.e. having proceeded
 ὡς: "*about* 25 or 30 stades"

¹⁴ Illi ergo homines, cum vidissent quod fecerat signum, dicebant: "Hic est vere propheta, qui venit in mundum!" ¹⁵ Iesus ergo, cum cognovisset quia venturi essent, ut raperent eum et facerent eum regem, secessit iterum in montem ipse solus.

Jesus Walks on the Water

¹⁶ Ut autem sero factum est, descenderunt discipuli eius ad mare ¹⁷ et, cum ascendissent navem, veniebant trans mare in Capharnaum. Et tenebrae iam factae erant, et nondum venerat ad eos Iesus. ¹⁸ Mare autem, vento magno flante, exsurgebat. ¹⁹ Cum remigassent ergo quasi

---

ascendo, (3): to embark, climb on, board
exsurgo, (3): to swell, rise, rear
flo, (1): to blow
iterum: again
magnus, -a -um: large, great
mons, montis *m*: mountain
mundus, -i *m*: world
navis, navis *f*: ship
nondum: not yet
propheta, -ae *m*: prophet
quasi: about

rapio, (3), **rapui, raptus**: to seize, take
remigo, (1): to row, use oars
rex, regis *m*: king
secedo, (3), **secessi, secessus**: to withdraw
sero: late, evening
stadium, -i *n*: stade, Greek measure of distance (about 607 feet)
tenebrae, -arum *f*: darkness, night
trans: across, over (+ *acc.*)
ventus, venti *m*: wind
vere: really, truly

6:14 **cum vidissent**: plupf. subj. circumstantial clause., "when they had seen"
6:15 **cum cognovisset**: plupf. subj. circumstantial clause, "when he had understood"
    quia venturi essent: impf. subj. with fut. part. in periphrastic in ind. st., "knew *that they were about to come*"
    ut raperent ... facerent: impf. subj. purpose clause, "in order that they seize ...in order that they make"
6:16 **sero**: abl. time when as a predicate, "when it became *late*"
6:17 **cum ascendissent**: plupf. subj. *cum* circumstantial clause, "when they had boarded"
6:18 **vento magno flante**: abl. abs., "with a great wind blowing"
6:19 **cum remigassent (= remigavissent)**: plupf. subj. *cum* circumstantial clause, "when they had rowed"

σταδίους εἴκοσι πέντε ἢ τριάκοντα θεωροῦσιν τὸν Ἰησοῦν
περιπατοῦντα ἐπὶ τῆς θαλάσσης καὶ ἐγγὺς τοῦ πλοίου γινό-
μενον, καὶ ἐφοβήθησαν. ²⁰ ὁ δὲ λέγει αὐτοῖς «Ἐγώ εἰμι, μὴ
φοβεῖσθε.» ²¹ ἤθελον οὖν λαβεῖν αὐτὸν εἰς τὸ πλοῖον, καὶ
εὐθέως ἐγένετο τὸ πλοῖον ἐπὶ τῆς γῆς εἰς ἣν ὑπῆγον.

²² τῇ ἐπαύριον ὁ ὄχλος ὁ ἑστηκὼς πέραν τῆς θαλάσσης
εἶδον ὅτι πλοιάριον ἄλλο οὐκ ἦν ἐκεῖ εἰ μὴ ἕν, καὶ ὅτι οὐ
συνεισῆλθεν τοῖς μαθηταῖς αὐτοῦ ὁ Ἰησοῦς εἰς τὸ πλοῖον ἀλλὰ
μόνοι οἱ μαθηταὶ αὐτοῦ ἀπῆλθον· ²³ ἀλλὰ ἦλθεν πλοῖα ἐκ
Τιβεριάδος ἐγγὺς τοῦ τόπου ὅπου ἔφαγον τὸν ἄρτον εὐχαρι-
στήσαντος τοῦ κυρίου. ²⁴ ὅτε οὖν εἶδεν ὁ ὄχλος ὅτι Ἰησοῦς οὐκ

ἀπῆλθον: to go away, depart from (*aor.*)
ἐγγύς: near, at hand
εἴκοσι (*indecl.*): twenty
ἐλαύνω: to drive, drive on, set in motion
ἐπαύριον (*adv.*): on the morrow
εὐθέως (*adv.*): straightaway
εὐχαριστέω: to be thankful, return thanks
ἔφαγον: to eat (*aor.*)
ἵστημι: to make to stand
κύριος, ὁ: a lord, master
μόνος, -η, -ον: only

πέντε (*indecl.*): five
πλοιάριον, τό: a skiff, boat
πλοῖον, τό: a ship, vessel
στάδιον, τό: a stade
συνεισῆλθον: to enter along with (*aor.*)
Τιβεριάς, -άδος, ἡ: Tiberias (Sea)
τόπος, ὁ: a place
τριάκοντα (*indecl.*): thirty
ὑπάγω: to withdraw
φοβέομαι: to be afraid

6:19   περιπατοῦντα: pres. part. circum. after θεωροῦσιν, "saw him *walking around*"
      ἐφοβήθησαν: aor. pass. of φοβέομαι, "they became afraid"

6:21   λαβεῖν: aor. inf. after ἤθελον, "they wished *to grab*"
      ἐγένετο: aor. of γίνομαι, "the boat became"
      ὑπῆγον: impf., "towards which *they were heading*"

6:22   τῇ ἐπαύριον (sc. ἡμέρᾳ): dat. of time when, "on the morrow"
      ὁ ἑστηκὼς: perf. part. of ἵστημι, "the crowd *which was standing*"
      εἰ μὴ ἕν: "there was no other *except one*"
      οὐ συνεισῆλθεν: aor., "he had not entered with" + dat.

6:23   ἔφαγον: aor. of ἐσθίω, "where *they ate* the bread"
      εὐχαριστήσαντος: aor. part. in gen. abs., "the lord *having blessed*"

stadia viginti quinque aut triginta, vident Iesum ambulantem super

mare et proximum navi fieri, et timuerunt. ²⁰ Ille autem dicit eis:

"Ego sum, nolite timere!" ²¹ Volebant ergo accipere eum in navem,

et statim fuit navis ad terram, in quam ibant.

²² Altera die turba, quae stabat trans mare, vidit quia navicula

alia non erat ibi, nisi una, et quia non introisset cum discipulis

suis Iesus in navem, sed soli discipuli eius abiissent; ²³ aliae super-

venerunt naves a Tiberiade iuxta locum, ubi manducaverant panem,

gratias agente Domino. ²⁴ Cum ergo vidisset turba quia Iesus non

---

abeo, (4), **abii**: to depart, go away
accipio, (3): to receive, accept
ago, (3), **egi**, **actus**: to give thanks (w/*gratias*)
alius, alia, aliud: other, another
alter, -a, -um: one (of two); next
ambulo, (1): to walk
eo, (4), **ii, itus**: go, advance, sail
gratia, -ae *f*: thanks, gratefulness
introeo, (4), **introii**: enter, go into
iuxta: near, close to (+ *acc.*)
locus, loci *m*: place, location
navicula, -ae *f*: small ship

nolo, nolle: be unwilling; wish not to
proximus, -a, -um: near to + dat
quinque: five
statim: at once, immediately
sto, (1): to stand, remain
supervenio, (4): to come up, arrive
terra, -ae *f*: earth, land
timeo, (2), **timui**: to fear, dread, be afraid
trans: across (+ *acc.*)
triginta: thirty
viginti: twenty

6:19   **fieri**: pres. pass. inf. in ind. st., "they see Jesus *to have become*," i.e. "*to be* near"
       navi: dat. with *proximum*, "near *to the ship*"
6:21   **ad terram**: expressing place where instead of motion toward, "on the land"
6:22   **quia... introisset ... abiissent**: plupf. subj. in alleged ind. st., "saw *that he had not entered* ... *that they had left*" note the change from indicative (*quia non erat*) to subjunctive, contrasting what is actually seen with what is assumed
6:23   **gratias agente Domino**: abl. abs., "the lord giving thanks."
6:24   **cum vidisset**: plupf. subj. in *cum* circumstantial clause, "when they had seen"

ἔστιν ἐκεῖ οὐδὲ οἱ μαθηταὶ αὐτοῦ, ἐνέβησαν αὐτοὶ εἰς τὰ πλοιάρια καὶ ἦλθον εἰς Καφαρναοὺμ ζητοῦντες τὸν Ἰησοῦν.

Jesus the Bread of Life

²⁵ καὶ εὑρόντες αὐτὸν πέραν τῆς θαλάσσης εἶπον αὐτῷ «Ῥαββεί, πότε ὧδε γέγονας;»

²⁶ ἀπεκρίθη αὐτοῖς ὁ Ἰησοῦς καὶ εἶπεν «Ἀμὴν ἀμὴν λέγω ὑμῖν, ζητεῖτέ με οὐχ ὅτι εἴδετε σημεῖα ἀλλ' ὅτι ἐφάγετε ἐκ τῶν ἄρτων καὶ ἐχορτάσθητε. ²⁷ ἐργάζεσθε μὴ τὴν βρῶσιν τὴν ἀπολλυμένην ἀλλὰ τὴν βρῶσιν τὴν μένουσαν εἰς ζωὴν αἰώνιον, ἣν ὁ υἱὸς τοῦ ἀνθρώπου ὑμῖν δώσει, τοῦτον γὰρ ὁ πατὴρ ἐσφράγισεν ὁ θεός.»

αἰώνιος, -α, -ον: lasting for an age
ἀπόλλυμαι: to be destroyed
βρῶσις, -εως, ἡ: food
δίδωμι: to give
εἶπον: to say (aor.)
ἐμβαίνω: to step in
ἐργάζομαι: to labor
ζητέω: to seek, seek for
μαθητής, -οῦ, ὁ: a disciple

μένω: to remain
οἶδα: to know (perf.)
πλοιάριον, τό: a skiff, boat
Ῥαββεί (Hebr): teacher
σημεῖον, τό: a sign, a mark, token
σφραγίζω: to seal
υἱός, ὁ: a son
χορτάζω: to feed, fatten

6:24   ἐνέβησαν: aor. of ἐμ-βαίνω, "they boarded"
6:25   εὑρόντες: aor. part., "they *having found*"
       γέγονας: perf. of γίνομαι, "when *did you become* here?"
6:26   ὅτι εἴδετε: aor. in causal clause, "you seek not *because you saw* signs"
       ὅτι ἐφάγετε: aor., "but because *you ate*"
       ἐχορτάσθητε: aor. pass., "(because) you were fattened"
6:27   μὴ τὴν ... ἀλλὰ τὴν: acc. of goal after ἐργάζεσθε, "labor *not for this ... but for that*"
       τὴν ἀπολλυμένην ...τὴν μένουσαν: pres. part. attrib., "the food being destroyed ...the food remaining"
       τοῦτον: acc., "set his seal upon *this*," i.e. the everlasting bread"

esset ibi neque discipuli eius, ascenderunt ipsi naviculas et venerunt Capharnaum quaerentes Iesum.

Jesus the Bread of Life

²⁵ Et cum invenissent eum trans mare, dixerunt ei: "Rabbi, quando huc venisti?"

²⁶ Respondit eis Iesus et dixit: "Amen, amen dico vobis: Quaeritis me, non quia vidistis signa, sed quia manducastis ex panibus et saturati estis. ²⁷ Operamini non cibum, qui perit, sed cibum, qui permanet in vitam aeternam, quem Filius hominis vobis dabit; hunc enim Pater signavit Deus!"

---

cibus, -i *m*: food
huc: here, to this place
noster, -tra, -trum: our
operor, (1): to labor, work
pereo, (4): to be destroyed, go to waste, spoil
permaneo, (2): to last, continue, endure

quando: when, at what time
saturo, (1): to fill to repletion, satisfy
signo, (1): to signal, set a seal on
trans: across (+ *acc.*)
vita, -ae *f*: life

6:24   **quia non esset**: impf. subj. in ind. st., "had seen *that he was not*"
        Capharnaum: acc. place to which, "they went *to Capharnaum*"
6:25   **cum invenissent**: plupf. subj. *cum* circumstantial clause, "when they come upon"
6:26   **manducastis**: syncopated perf (=*manducavistis*), "because *you ate*"
6:27   **operamini**: imper. of *operor* with middle force, "exercise yourselves for" + acc.
        hunc: acc., "set his seal on *this*" i.e. the everlasting food

²⁸ εἶπον οὖν πρὸς αὐτόν «Τί ποιῶμεν ἵνα ἐργαζώμεθα τὰ ἔργα τοῦ θεοῦ;»

²⁹ ἀπεκρίθη ὁ Ἰησοῦς καὶ εἶπεν αὐτοῖς «Τοῦτό ἐστιν τὸ ἔργον τοῦ θεοῦ ἵνα πιστεύητε εἰς ὃν ἀπέστειλεν ἐκεῖνος.»

³⁰ εἶπον οὖν αὐτῷ «Τί οὖν ποιεῖς σὺ σημεῖον, ἵνα ἴδωμεν καὶ πιστεύσωμέν σοι; τί ἐργάζῃ; ³¹ οἱ πατέρες ἡμῶν τὸ μάννα ἔφαγον ἐν τῇ ἐρήμῳ, καθώς ἐστιν γεγραμμένον Ἄρτον ἐκ τοῦ οὐρανοῦ ἔδωκεν αὐτοῖς φαγεῖν .»

³² εἶπεν οὖν αὐτοῖς ὁ Ἰησοῦς «Ἀμὴν ἀμὴν λέγω ὑμῖν, οὐ Μωυσῆς ἔδωκεν ὑμῖν τὸν ἄρτον ἐκ τοῦ οὐρανοῦ, ἀλλ᾽ ὁ πατήρ μου δίδωσιν ὑμῖν τὸν ἄρτον ἐκ τοῦ οὐρανοῦ τὸν ἀληθινόν· ³³ ὁ γὰρ ἄρτος τοῦ θεοῦ ἐστὶν ὁ καταβαίνων ἐκ τοῦ οὐρανοῦ καὶ ζωὴν διδοὺς τῷ κόσμῳ.»

ἀληθινός, -ή, -όν: true
ἀποστέλλω: to send off, send to
ἄρτος, ὁ: bread
δίδωμι: to give
εἶδον: to see (aor.)
ἐρῆμος, ὁ: desert
ἔφαγον: to eat (aor.)

ζωή, ἡ: life
καθώς: just as
καταβαίνω: to go down
μάννα, τό: manna
οὐρανός, ὁ: heaven
πάντοτε: at all times, always

6:28-9 εἶπον πρὸς αὐτόν ... εἶπεν αὐτοῖς: note the variation for the indirect object

6:28　τί ποιῶμεν: pres. subj. in deliberative quest., "what should we do"

　　　ἵνα ἐργαζώμεθα: pres. subj. in result clause, "so that we may work"

6:29　ἵνα πιστεύητε: pres. subj. in subst. clause explaining ἔργον, "this is the work of God, namely, *that you believe*"

6:30　τί ... σημεῖον: "*what sign* do you do?"

　　　ἵνα ἴδωμεν καὶ πιστεύσωμέν: aor. subj. in result clause, "so that we see and believe"

6:31　ἐστιν γεγραμμένον: perf. periphrastic, "as it is written" (Ex. 16)

　　　φαγεῖν: aor. inf. showing purpose, "he gave *to eat*"

6:33　ὁ καταβαίνων ... διδοὺς: pres. part. attributive, "the one descending ... the one giving"

²⁸ Dixerunt ergo ad eum: "Quid faciemus, ut operemur opera Dei?"

²⁹ Respondit Iesus et dixit eis: "Hoc est opus Dei, ut credatis in eum, quem misit ille."

³⁰ Dixerunt ergo ei: "Quod ergo tu facis signum, ut videamus et credamus tibi? Quid operaris? ³¹ Patres nostri manna manducaverunt in deserto, sicut scriptum est: 'Panem de caelo dedit eis manducare'."

³² Dixit ergo eis Iesus: "Amen, amen dico vobis: Non Moyses dedit vobis panem de caelo, sed Pater meus dat vobis panem de caelo verum; ³³ panis enim Dei est, qui descendit de caelo et dat vitam mundo."

---

caelus, -i *m*: heaven
descendo, (3): to descend
desertum, -i *n*: desert
manna (*indecl.*) *n*: manna (food from God in the Exodus)
operor (1): to work, labor

opus, operis *n*: a work, labor
panis, -is *m*: bread
semper: always
signum, -i *n*: sign,
verus, -a, -um: true

6:28   **opera**: acc. cognate with *operemur*, "work the works" i.e. do works
     quid faciemus: fut. in deliberative question where one would expect a subj., "what should we do?"
     ut operemur: pres. subj. purpose clause, "in order that we may work"
6:28-9 **dixerunt ad eum ... dixit eis**: note the variation for indirect object
6:29   **ut credatis**: pres. subj. in noun clause explaining *opus*, "this is the work of God, namely, *that you believe*"
6:30   **ut videamus... credamus**: pres. subj. purpose clause, "what sign do you make *in order that we may see and believe?*"
6:31   **sicut scriptum est**: Exodus 16:4; Psalm 78:24-25; Nehemiah 9:15
     manducare: pres. inf. expressing purpose, "gave them *to eat*"
6:33   **mundo**: dat. ind. obj., "gives light *to the world*"

³⁴ εἶπον οὖν πρὸς αὐτόν «Κύριε, πάντοτε δὸς ἡμῖν τὸν ἄρτον τοῦτον.»

³⁵ εἶπεν αὐτοῖς ὁ Ἰησοῦς «Ἐγώ εἰμι ὁ ἄρτος τῆς ζωῆς· ὁ ἐρχόμενος πρὸς ἐμὲ οὐ μὴ πεινάσῃ, καὶ ὁ πιστεύων εἰς ἐμὲ οὐ μὴ διψήσει πώποτε. ³⁶ ἀλλ' εἶπον ὑμῖν ὅτι καὶ ἑωράκατε καὶ οὐ πιστεύετε. ³⁷ πᾶν ὃ δίδωσίν μοι ὁ πατὴρ πρὸς ἐμὲ ἥξει, καὶ τὸν ἐρχόμενον πρός με οὐ μὴ ἐκβάλω ἔξω, ³⁸ ὅτι καταβέβηκα ἀπὸ τοῦ οὐρανοῦ οὐχ ἵνα ποιῶ τὸ θέλημα τὸ ἐμὸν ἀλλὰ τὸ θέλημα τοῦ πέμψαντός με· ³⁹ τοῦτο δέ ἐστιν τὸ θέλημα τοῦ πέμψαντός με ἵνα πᾶν ὃ δέδωκέν μοι μὴ ἀπολέσω ἐξ αὐτοῦ ἀλλὰ ἀναστήσω αὐτὸ τῇ ἐσχάτῃ ἡμέρᾳ. ⁴⁰ τοῦτο γάρ ἐστιν τὸ θέλημα τοῦ πατρός μου ἵνα πᾶς ὁ θεωρῶν τὸν υἱὸν

ἀνίστημι: to raise up
ἀπόλλυμι: to destroy
διψάω: to be thirsty
ἐκβάλλω: to throw or cast out of
ἔξω (*adv.*): outside
ἔρχομαι: to come or go
ἔσχατος, -η, -ον: last
ζωή, ἡ: life
ἥκω: to have come, be present, be here
ἡμέρα, ἡ: day

θέλημα, -ατος, τό: will
θεωρέω: to see
καταβαίνω: to step down, go or come down
κύριος, ὁ; lord
οὐρανός, ὁ; heaven
πατήρ, πατρός, ὁ: a father
πεινάω: to be hungry, suffer hunger
πέμπω: to send, despatch
πώποτε: ever yet

6:34 **δός**: aor. imper. of **δίδωμι**, "give!"

6:35 **οὐ μὴ πεινάσῃ**: aor. subj. indicating strong denial, "he certainly shall not hunger"

οὐ μὴ διψήσει fut. indic. of **διψήσει** also in strong denial, "he shall not thirst"

6:36 **ἑωράκατε**: perf., "*you have seen* and do not believe"

6:37 **ἥξει**: fut. of **ἥκω**, "everything *will come*"

οὐ μὴ ἐκβάλω: aor. subj. in strong denial" I shall not cast out"

6:38 **καταβέβηκα**: perf., "I have descended"

ἵνα ποιῶ: pres. subj. in purpose clause, "descended *in order to do*"

τοῦ πέμψαντός: aor. part. attributive, gen. of **πέμπω**, "the will *of the one who sent* me"

6:39 **ἵνα ... μὴ ἀπολέσω ... ἀναστήσω**: aor. subj. in obj. clause explaining **θέλημα**, "his will, namely, *not to destroy* ...but *in order to raise it up*"

³⁴ Dixerunt ergo ad eum: "Domine, semper da nobis panem hunc."

³⁵ Dixit eis Iesus: "Ego sum panis vitae. Qui venit ad me, non esuriet; et, qui credit in me, non sitiet umquam. ³⁶ Sed dixi vobis, quia et vidistis me et non creditis. ³⁷ Omne, quod dat mihi Pater, ad me veniet; et eum, qui venit ad me, non eiciam foras, ³⁸ quia descendi de caelo, non ut faciam voluntatem meam sed voluntatem eius, qui misit me. ³⁹ Haec est autem voluntas eius, qui misit me, ut omne, quod dedit mihi, non perdam ex eo, sed resuscitem illud in novissimo die. ⁴⁰ Haec est enim voluntas Patris mei, ut omnis, qui videt Filium

---

caelus, -i *m*: heaven
eicio, (3): to drive out, expel
esurio, (4): to be hungry, hunger
foras (*adv.*): out of doors, out
murmuro, (1): to murmur, mutter
novissimus, -a, -um: last, rear

omnis, -e: all
perdo, (3): to ruin, destroy
resuscito, (1): to rouse again, reawaken, raise
sitio, (4), **sitivi**: to be thirsty
umquam: ever, at any time
video, (2) **vidi**: to see

6:35   **qui venit ...qui credit**: pres. with indefinite conditional force, "he who comes" or "whoever comes" or "if anyone comes"

6:36   **quia vidistis**: perf. in ind. st., "I say *that you have seen*"

6:38   **non ut faciam**: pres. subj. purpose clause, "I descended not *that I may do*" where *ne* would be expected

6:39   **ut non... perdam... resuscitem**: pres. subj. noun clause explaining *voluntas*, "this is his will, *namely that I destroy ... namely, that I resurrect*"

        in novissimo die: abl. of time when, "on the last day"

καὶ πιστεύων εἰς αὐτὸν ἔχῃ ζωὴν αἰώνιον, καὶ ἀναστήσω αὐτὸν ἐγὼ τῇ ἐσχάτῃ ἡμέρᾳ.»

⁴¹ ἐγόγγυζον οὖν οἱ Ἰουδαῖοι περὶ αὐτοῦ ὅτι εἶπεν «Ἐγώ εἰμι ὁ ἄρτος ὁ καταβὰς ἐκ τοῦ οὐρανοῦ,» καὶ ἔλεγον ⁴² «Οὐχὶ οὗτός ἐστιν Ἰησοῦς ὁ υἱὸς Ἰωσήφ, οὗ ἡμεῖς οἴδαμεν τὸν πατέρα καὶ τὴν μητέρα; πῶς νῦν λέγει ὅτι Ἐκ τοῦ οὐρανοῦ καταβέβηκα ;»

⁴³ ἀπεκρίθη Ἰησοῦς καὶ εἶπεν αὐτοῖς «Μὴ γογγύζετε μετ' ἀλλήλων. ⁴⁴ οὐδεὶς δύναται ἐλθεῖν πρός με ἐὰν μὴ ὁ πατὴρ ὁ πέμψας με ἑλκύσῃ αὐτόν, κἀγὼ ἀναστήσω αὐτὸν ἐν τῇ ἐσχάτῃ ἡμέρᾳ. ⁴⁵ ἔστιν γεγραμμένον ἐν τοῖς προφήταις Καὶ ἔσονται πάντες διδακτοὶ θεοῦ· πᾶς ὁ ἀκούσας παρὰ τοῦ πατρὸς καὶ μαθὼν ἔρχεται πρὸς ἐμέ. ⁴⁶ οὐχ ὅτι τὸν πατέρα ἑώρακέν τις

ἀκούω: to hear
ἀλλήλων: of one another
γογγύζω: to mutter, murmur
διδακτός, -η, -ον: taught, learnt

ἕλκω: to draw, drag
καταβαίνω: to go down
μανθάνω: to learn
μήτηρ, μητρός, ἡ: a mother

6:40 ἵνα ... ἔχῃ: pres. subj. explaining θέλημα, "his will, namely, *that everyone have*"
6:41 ὁ καταβὰς: aor. part. attributive, "the bread *descending*"
6:42 οὐχὶ οὗτός ἐστιν: anticipating a negative answer, "is this not?"
  οὗ οἴδαμεν: perf., "*whose* father *we know*" with relative attracted into the case of the antecedent
  καταβέβηκα: perf., "I have descended"
6:43 μὴ γογγύζετε: pres. imper., "don't murmur!"
6:44 ἐὰν μὴ ... ἑλκύσῃ: aor. subj. of ἕλκω in pres. general protasis, "unless the father draws"
  ἀναστήσω: fut. of ἀνα-ίστημι, "I will raise him up"
6:45 ἔστιν γεγραμμένον: perf. part. in pres. periphrastic, "it is written" (Is. 54:13)
  ἔσονται: fut. of εἰμί, "all *will be* taught"
  πᾶς ὁ ἀκούσας ... μαθὼν: aor. part., "everyone *who has heard ... and who has learned*"
  παρὰ τοῦ πατρὸς: "from the father" but the gen. of source without a preposition is normal after ἀκούω
6:46 οὐχ (sc. ἐστι) ὅτι: "it is not the case that"

et credit in eum, habeat vitam aeternam; et resuscitabo ego eum in novissimo die."

⁴¹ Murmurabant ergo Iudaei de illo, quia dixisset: "Ego sum panis, qui de caelo descendi," ⁴² et dicebant: "Nonne hic est Iesus filius Ioseph, cuius nos novimus patrem et matrem? Quomodo dicit nunc: 'De caelo descendi'?"

⁴³ Respondit Iesus et dixit eis: "Nolite murmurare in invicem. ⁴⁴ Nemo potest venire ad me, nisi Pater, qui misit me, traxerit eum; et ego resuscitabo eum in novissimo die. ⁴⁵ Est scriptum in Prophetis: 'Et erunt omnes docibiles Dei.' Omnis, qui audivit a Patre et didicit, venit ad me. ⁴⁶ Non quia Patrem vidit quisquam,

---

audio, (4), **audivi**, **auditus**: to hear
caelus, **caeli** *m*: heaven
desertum, **-i** *n*: desert
disco, (3), **didici**, **discitus**: to learn
docibilis, **-e**: teachable
invicem: in turn; reciprocally, mutually
Ioseph (*indecl.*): Joseph

mater, **matris** *f*: mother
mitto, (3), **misi**, **missus**: to send
nemo, **neminis** *m/f*: no one, nobody
nonne: not? (interrogative expecting the answer "Yes")
nosco, (3), **novi**, **notus**: to know, recognize
traho, (3), **traxi**, **tractus**: to draw, get

6:40 **ut... habeat**: pres. subj. noun clause, "his will is *that* everyone *have*"
6:41 **quia dixisset**: plupf. subj. in alleged causal clause, "murmured *because he had said*"
6:42 **Ioseph**: gen., "son *of Joseph*"
    cuius nos novimus patrem: "whose father we know" where the relative is attracted into the case (gen.) of the antecedent
6:43 **in invicem**: "don't murmuer *with each other*" the preposition is redundant
6:44 **nisi ... traxerit**: fut. perf. in pres. general protasis, "unless the father *has drawn*"
6:45 **in Prophetis**: Isaiah 54:13
6:46 **non quia**: "it is not the case that" where *quod* is normal

εἰ μὴ ὁ ὢν παρὰ [τοῦ] θεοῦ, οὗτος ἑώρακεν τὸν πατέρα. ⁴⁷ ἀμὴν ἀμὴν λέγω ὑμῖν, ὁ πιστεύων ἔχει ζωὴν αἰώνιον. ⁴⁸ ἐγώ εἰμι ὁ ἄρτος τῆς ζωῆς· ⁴⁹ οἱ πατέρες ὑμῶν ἔφαγον ἐν τῇ ἐρήμῳ τὸ μάννα καὶ ἀπέθανον· ⁵⁰ οὗτός ἐστιν ὁ ἄρτος ὁ ἐκ τοῦ οὐρανοῦ καταβαίνων ἵνα τις ἐξ αὐτοῦ φάγῃ καὶ μὴ ἀποθάνῃ. ⁵¹ ἐγώ εἰμι ὁ ἄρτος ὁ ζῶν ὁ ἐκ τοῦ οὐρανοῦ καταβάς· ἐάν τις φάγῃ ἐκ τούτου τοῦ ἄρτου ζήσει εἰς τὸν αἰῶνα, καὶ ὁ ἄρτος δὲ ὃν ἐγὼ δώσω ἡ σάρξ μου ἐστὶν ὑπὲρ τῆς τοῦ κόσμου ζωῆς.»

⁵² ἐμάχοντο οὖν πρὸς ἀλλήλους οἱ Ἰουδαῖοι λέγοντες «Πῶς δύναται οὗτος ἡμῖν δοῦναι τὴν σάρκα [αὐτοῦ] φαγεῖν;»

αἰών, -ῶνος, ὁ	ζωή, ἡ: life
αἰώνιος, -α, -ον	καταβαίνω: to go down
ἀποθνήσκω: to die off, die	κόσμος, ὁ
ἄρτος, ὁ: a loaf of wheat-bread	μάννα, τό: manna
ἔρημος, ὁ	μάχομαι: to fight, quarrel
ἔφαγον: to eat (aor.)	οὐρανός, ὁ
ζάω: to live	σάρξ, -κος, ἡ: flesh

6:46   **εἰ μὴ ὁ ὢν**: pres. part. conditional, "except the one being" i.e. the one who is from God

6:49   **ἔφαγον ... ἀπέθανον**: aor., "they ate ... they died"

6:50   **ὁ καταβαίνων**: pres. part. attributive, "this one is the bread *descending*"
      ἵνα τις φάγῃ ... καὶ μὴ ἀποθάνῃ: aor. subj. in result clause, "so that someone may eat ... and not die

6:51   **ὁ ζῶν**: pres. part. attrib., "*the living* bread"
      ὁ ... καταβάς: aor. part. attrib., "the bread *that descended*"
      ἐάν τις φάγῃ: aor. subj. in fut. more vivid protasis, "*if anyone eats*, he shall live"
      ἡ σάρξ: nom. pred., "the bread is *my flesh*"

6:52   **δοῦναι**: aor. inf. after **δύναται**, "how is he able *to give*"
      φαγεῖν: aor. inf. expressing purpose, "give to us *to eat*"

nisi is qui est a Deo, hic vidit Patrem. ⁴⁷ Amen, amen dico vobis:

Qui credit, habet vitam aeternam. ⁴⁸ Ego sum panis vitae. ⁴⁹ Patres

vestri manducaverunt in deserto manna et mortui sunt. ⁵⁰ Hic est

panis de caelo descendens, ut, si quis ex ipso manducaverit, non

moriatur. ⁵¹ Ego sum panis vivus, qui de caelo descendi. Si quis

manducaverit ex hoc pane, vivet in aeternum; panis autem, quem

ego dabo, caro mea est pro mundi vita."

⁵² Litigabant ergo Iudaei ad invicem dicentes: "Quomodo potest

hic nobis carnem suam dare ad manducandum?"

---

caelus, -i *m*: heaven
caro, carnis *f*: flesh, body
filius, fili *m*: son
invicem: in turn; reciprocally
litigo, (1): to quarrel
manduco, (1): to eat

manna (*indecl.*) *n*: manna
morior, (3), mortuus sum: to die, expire
panis, -is, *m*. bread
vivo, (3): to be alive, live, survive
vivus, -a, -um: alive, living

6:50 **si quis... manducaverit**: fut. perf. in future more vivid protasis with general force, "if anyone eats"

ut... non moriatur: pres. subj. result clause also serving as apodosis, "so that he does not die"

6:51 **pro mundi vita**: "my flesh is *for the life of the world*"

6:52 **ad invicem**: like *in invicem* above, "mutually" with redundant prepostion

ad manducandum: gerundive showing purpose, "to give *in order to be eaten*"

⁵³ εἶπεν οὖν αὐτοῖς ὁ Ἰησοῦς «Ἀμὴν ἀμὴν λέγω ὑμῖν, ἐὰν μὴ φάγητε τὴν σάρκα τοῦ υἱοῦ τοῦ ἀνθρώπου καὶ πίητε αὐτοῦ τὸ αἷμα, οὐκ ἔχετε ζωὴν ἐν ἑαυτοῖς. ⁵⁴ ὁ τρώγων μου τὴν σάρκα καὶ πίνων μου τὸ αἷμα ἔχει ζωὴν αἰώνιον, κἀγὼ ἀναστήσω αὐτὸν τῇ ἐσχάτῃ ἡμέρᾳ· ⁵⁵ ἡ γὰρ σάρξ μου ἀληθής ἐστι βρῶσις, καὶ τὸ αἷμά μου ἀληθής ἐστι πόσις. ⁵⁶ ὁ τρώγων μου τὴν σάρκα καὶ πίνων μου τὸ αἷμα ἐν ἐμοὶ μένει κἀγὼ ἐν αὐτῷ. ⁵⁷ καθὼς ἀπέστειλέν με ὁ ζῶν πατὴρ κἀγὼ ζῶ διὰ τὸν πατέρα, καὶ ὁ τρώγων με κἀκεῖνος ζήσει δι᾽ ἐμέ. ⁵⁸ οὗτός ἐστιν ὁ ἄρτος ὁ ἐξ οὐρανοῦ καταβάς, οὐ καθὼς ἔφαγον οἱ πατέρες καὶ ἀπέθανον· ὁ τρώγων τοῦτον τὸν ἄρτον ζήσει εἰς τὸν αἰῶνα.» ⁵⁹ ταῦτα εἶπεν ἐν συναγωγῇ διδάσκων ἐν Καφαρναούμ.

αἷμα, -ατος, τό: blood
αἰώνιος, -ον: lasting for an age
ἀληθής, -ές: unconcealed, true
ἄρτος, ὁ: bread
διδάσκω: to teach
ἔσχατος, -η, -ον: last
ζάω: to live
ζωή, ἡ: life

καταβαίνω: to descend
Καφαρναούμ: Capharnum
οὐρανός, ὁ: heaven
πίνω: to drink
πόσις, -ιος, ἡ: a drink, beverage
συναγωγή, ἡ: a synagogue
τρώγω: to gnaw, nibble, munch

6:53 ἐὰν μὴ φάγητε καὶ πίητε: aor. subj. in pres. general protasis, "unless you eat and drink"

οὐκ ἔχετε: apodosis of pres. general condition, "you do not have"

6:54 οὐκ ὁ τρώγων: pres. part. attrib. with conditional force like others in this verse, "if eating ...drinking, etc."

ἀναστήσω: fut. of ἀνα-ίστημι, "I will raise him up"

6:56 κἀγὼ (=καὶ ἐγώ) ἐν αὐτῷ: "and I (remain) in him"

6:57 ἀπέστειλέν: aor. of ἀπο-στέλλω, "just as *he sent*"

κἀκεῖνος: = καὶ ἐκεῖνος, "*that one too* shall seek"

⁵³ Dixit ergo eis Iesus: "Amen, amen dico vobis: Nisi manducaveritis carnem Filii hominis et biberitis eius sanguinem, non habetis vitam in vobismetipsis. ⁵⁴ Qui manducat meam carnem et bibit meum sanguinem, habet vitam aeternam; et ego resuscitabo eum in novissimo die. ⁵⁵ Caro enim mea verus est cibus, et sanguis meus verus est potus. ⁵⁶ Qui manducat meam carnem et bibit meum sanguinem, in me manet, et ego in illo. ⁵⁷ Sicut misit me vivens Pater, et ego vivo propter Patrem; et, qui manducat me, et ipse vivet propter me. ⁵⁸ Hic est panis, qui de caelo descendit, non sicut manducaverunt patres et mortui sunt; qui manducat hunc panem, vivet in aeternum." ⁵⁹ Haec dixit in synagoga docens in Capharnaum.

---

bibo, (3): to drink	**potus, potus** *m*: a drink
cibus, -i *m*: food	**resuscito**, (1): to raise up, revive
doceo, (2): to teach	**sanguis, -inis** *m*: blood
durus, -a, -um: hard, harsh, cruel	**synagoga, -ae** *f*: synagogue
novissimus, -a, -um: last	**verus, -a, -um**: true
panis, panis *m*: bread	**vivo**, (3): to live

6:53 **nisi manducaveritis ...biberitis**: fut. perf. in pres. general protasis, "unless you have eaten ...have drunk"

vobismetipsis: *vobis* + *met* + *ipsis* emphatic, "in you yourselves"

6:57 **propter patrem ...propter me**: translating διά, perhaps meaning "near"

6:59 **in Capharnaum**: "in Capharnaum" with redundant preposition

Many Disciples Desert Jesus

⁶⁰ πολλοὶ οὖν ἀκούσαντες ἐκ τῶν μαθητῶν αὐτοῦ εἶπαν «Σκληρός ἐστιν ὁ λόγος οὗτος· τίς δύναται αὐτοῦ ἀκούειν;» ⁶¹ εἰδὼς δὲ ὁ Ἰησοῦς ἐν ἑαυτῷ ὅτι γογγύζουσιν περὶ τούτου οἱ μαθηταὶ αὐτοῦ εἶπεν αὐτοῖς «Τοῦτο ὑμᾶς σκανδαλίζει; ⁶² ἐὰν οὖν θεωρῆτε τὸν υἱὸν τοῦ ἀνθρώπου ἀναβαίνοντα ὅπου ἦν τὸ πρότερον; ⁶³ τὸ πνεῦμά ἐστιν τὸ ζωοποιοῦν, ἡ σὰρξ οὐκ ὠφελεῖ οὐδέν· τὰ ῥήματα ἃ ἐγὼ λελάληκα ὑμῖν πνεῦμά ἐστιν καὶ ζωή ἐστιν. ⁶⁴ ἀλλὰ εἰσὶν ἐξ ὑμῶν τινες οἳ οὐ πιστεύουσιν.» ᾔδει γὰρ ἐξ ἀρχῆς ὁ Ἰησοῦς τίνες εἰσὶν οἱ μὴ πιστεύοντες καὶ τίς ἐστιν ὁ παραδώσων αὐτόν. ⁶⁵ καὶ ἔλεγεν «Διὰ τοῦτο εἴρηκα ὑμῖν ὅτι οὐδεὶς δύναται ἐλθεῖν πρός με ἐὰν μὴ ᾖ δεδομένον αὐτῷ ἐκ τοῦ πατρός.»

ἀναβαίνω: to go up
ἀρχή, ἡ: a beginning
δύναμαι: to be able, capable (+ *inf.*)
ἐρέω: to say (*fut.*)
ζωοποιέω: to make living
λαλέω: to talk
παραδίδωμι: to hand over to another, betray
πνεῦμα, -ατος, τό: spirit

πολύς, πολλά, πολύ: many
πρότερος, -α, -ον: prior
ῥῆμα, -ατος, τό: a word, saying
σάρξ, σαρκός, ἡ: flesh
σκανδαλίζω: to give offence to
σκληρός, -ά, -όν: hard
ὠφελέω: to help, aid, assist

6:61 εἰδὼς: perf. part., "Jesus *knowing*"

6:62 ἐὰν οὖν θεωρῆτε: pres. subj. in fut. more vivid protasis with apodosis suppressed, "*if you saw* (what would you say?)" i.e. what if you saw?

ὅπου ἦν: local relative clause, "going up *where he was*"

6:63 λελάληκα: perf., "which *I have spoken*"

6:64 τίνες εἰσὶν ... τίς ἐστιν: ind. quest., "he knows *who they are ... who is*"

ὁ παραδώσων: fut. part., attributive, "the one about to betray him"

6:65 εἴρηκα: perf., "I have spoken"

ἐὰν μὴ ᾖ δεδομένον: perf. subj. periphrastic of δίδωμι in a pres. general protasis, "unless it has been granted"

Many Disciples Desert Jesus

⁶⁰ Multi ergo audientes ex discipulis eius dixerunt: "Durus est hic sermo! Quis potest eum audire?"

⁶¹ Sciens autem Iesus apud semetipsum quia murmurarent de hoc discipuli eius, dixit eis: "Hoc vos scandalizat? ⁶² Si ergo videritis Filium hominis ascendentem ubi erat prius? ⁶³ Spiritus est, qui vivificat, caro non prodest quidquam; verba, quae ego locutus sum vobis, Spiritus sunt et vita sunt. ⁶⁴ Sed sunt quidam ex vobis, qui non credunt." Sciebat enim ab initio Iesus, qui essent non credentes, et quis traditurus esset eum. ⁶⁵ Et dicebat: "Propterea dixi vobis: Nemo potest venire ad me, nisi fuerit ei datum a Patre."

---

ascendo, (3): to rise, ascend
datum, -i *n*: present, gift
initium, -i *n*: beginning
loquor, (3), **locutus sum**: speak, tell
multus, -a, -um: much, many
murmuro, (1): to murmur, mutter
possum, posse, potui: be able, can
prior, prius: earlier, before
propterea: therefore, for this reason

prosum, prodesse: be useful, be advantageous
scandalizo, (1): to tempt to evil, offend
scio, (4): to know, understand
semetipse, -a, -um: one's self
sermo, sermonis *m*: diction, speech, teaching
spiritus, -us *m*: spirit
trado, (3), **tradidi, traditus**: to hand over, surrender
verbum, -i *n*: word
vivifico, (1): to bring back to life, make live

6:61 **quia murmurarent**: impf. subj. in ind. st. after *sciens*, "knowing *that they were murmuring*"

6:62 **si...videritis**: fut. perf. in fut. more vivid protasis with apodosis suppressed, "if you shall see (what then?)"

ubi erat prius: acc. adverbial, "ascending to (the place) *where he was before*"

6:64 **qui essent**: impf. subj. in ind. quest., "knew *who were* the ones"

quis traditurus esset: impf. subj. in future periphrastic in ind. quest., "knew *who was about to betray*"

6:65 **nisi fuerit datum**: fut. perf. periphrastic in pres. general protasis, "unless it has been given"

99

⁶⁶ Ἐκ τούτου πολλοὶ ἐκ τῶν μαθητῶν αὐτοῦ ἀπῆλθον εἰς τὰ ὀπίσω καὶ οὐκέτι μετ' αὐτοῦ περιεπάτουν.

⁶⁷ Εἶπεν οὖν ὁ Ἰησοῦς τοῖς δώδεκα «Μὴ καὶ ὑμεῖς θέλετε ὑπάγειν;»

⁶⁸ ἀπεκρίθη αὐτῷ Σίμων Πέτρος «Κύριε, πρὸς τίνα ἀπελευσόμεθα; ῥήματα ζωῆς αἰωνίου ἔχεις, ⁶⁹ καὶ ἡμεῖς πεπιστεύκαμεν καὶ ἐγνώκαμεν ὅτι σὺ εἶ ὁ ἅγιος τοῦ θεοῦ.»

⁷⁰ ἀπεκρίθη αὐτοῖς ὁ Ἰησοῦς «Οὐκ ἐγὼ ὑμᾶς τοὺς δώδεκα ἐξελεξάμην; καὶ ἐξ ὑμῶν εἷς διάβολός ἐστιν.» ⁷¹ ἔλεγεν δὲ τὸν Ἰούδαν Σίμωνος Ἰσκαριώτου· οὗτος γὰρ ἔμελλεν παραδιδόναι αὐτόν, εἷς ἐκ τῶν δώδεκα.

ἅγιος, -α, -ον: sacred, holy
γινώσκω: to know
διάβολος, ὁ: a devil
δώδεκα: twelve
ἐκλέγω: to pick or single out
Ἰσκαριώτης, -ου, ὁ: the Iscariot

ὀπίσω: backwards
οὐκέτι: no more, no longer, no further
παραδίδωμι: to give or hand over, betray
Σίμων, -ονος, ὁ: Simon
ὑπάγω: to withdraw

6:66   ἐκ τούτου (sc. χρόνου): "from this point in time"
     εἰς τὰ ὀπίσω: "they went *to the back* (of the crowd)"
     οὐκέτι περιεπάτουν: impf., "they no longer were walking around"
6:67   μὴ θέλετε: expecting a negative answer, "don't you wish to" + inf.
6:68   ἀπελευσόμεθα: fut., "to whom *shall we go*"
6:69   πεπιστεύκαμεν ... ἐγνώκαμεν: perf., "we have believed ...we have known"
6:70   οὐκ ἐξελεξάμην: aor. expecting a positive answer, "have I not chosen you?"
6:71   ἔλεγεν: impf., "he was talking about" + acc.
     παραδιδόναι: pres. inf. after ἔμελλεν, "he was about *to betray*"

⁶⁶ Ex hoc multi discipulorum eius abierunt retro et iam non cum illo ambulabant.

⁶⁷ Dixit ergo Iesus ad Duodecim: "Numquid et vos vultis abire?"

⁶⁸ Respondit ei Simon Petrus: "Domine, ad quem ibimus? Verba vitae aeternae habes; ⁶⁹ et nos credidimus et cognovimus quia tu es Sanctus Dei."

⁷⁰ Respondit eis Iesus: "Nonne ego vos Duodecim elegi? Et ex vobis unus Diabolus est." ⁷¹ Dicebat autem Iudam Simonis Iscariotis; hic enim erat traditurus eum, cum esset unus ex Duodecim.

---

abeo, (4), **abii**, **abitum**: to depart, go away	**Petrus**, **-i** *m*: Peter
ambulo, (1): to walk	**retro** (*adv*.): back
credo, (3), **credidi**, **creditus**: to trust, believe	**sanctus**, **-a**, **-um**: divine, holy
diabolus, **-i** *m*: devil	**Simon**, **Simonis** *m*: Simon
duodecim: twelve	**vado**, (3): to go
eligo, (3), **elegi**, **electus**: to pick out, choose	**volo**, **velle**: to wish, want

6:66   **ex hoc (sc. tempore)**: "from this moment"
      iam non: "they were *no longer* waling"
6:67   **vultis**: pres. of *volo*, "*don't you wish* to learn?"
6:71   **traditurus**: fut. part. in periphrasis with *erat*, "he was *about to betray*"
      cum esset: impf. subj. in concessive clause, "although he was one of the Twelve"

Chapter 7

Jesus Goes to the Festival of Tabernacles

¹ καί μετὰ ταῦτα περιεπάτει ὁ Ἰησοῦς ἐν τῇ Γαλιλαίᾳ, οὐ γὰρ ἤθελεν ἐν τῇ Ἰουδαίᾳ περιπατεῖν, ὅτι ἐζήτουν αὐτὸν οἱ Ἰουδαῖοι ἀποκτεῖναι. ² ἦν δὲ ἐγγὺς ἡ ἑορτὴ τῶν Ἰουδαίων ἡ σκηνοπηγία. ³ εἶπον οὖν πρὸς αὐτὸν οἱ ἀδελφοὶ αὐτοῦ «Μετάβηθι ἐντεῦθεν καὶ ὕπαγε εἰς τὴν Ἰουδαίαν, ἵνα καὶ οἱ μαθηταί σου θεωρήσουσιν [σοῦ] τὰ ἔργα ἃ ποιεῖς· ⁴ οὐδεὶς γάρ τι ἐν κρυπτῷ ποιεῖ καὶ ζητεῖ αὐτὸς ἐν παρρησίᾳ εἶναι· εἰ ταῦτα ποιεῖς, φανέρωσον σεαυτὸν τῷ κόσμῳ.» ⁵ οὐδὲ γὰρ οἱ ἀδελφοὶ αὐτοῦ ἐπίστευον εἰς αὐτόν.

⁶ λέγει οὖν αὐτοῖς ὁ Ἰησοῦς «Ὁ καιρὸς ὁ ἐμὸς οὔπω πάρεστιν, ὁ δὲ καιρὸς ὁ ὑμέτερος πάντοτέ ἐστιν ἕτοιμος. ⁷ οὐ δύναται ὁ κόσμος μισεῖν ὑμᾶς, ἐμὲ δὲ μισεῖ, ὅτι ἐγὼ μαρτυρῶ περὶ αὐτοῦ

ἀποκτείνω: to kill, slay
Γαλιλαία, ἡ: Galilea
ἐντεῦθεν: hence, from here
ἑορτή, ἡ: a feast, festival
ἕτοιμος, -ον: at hand, ready, prepared
θέλω: to will, wish
καιρός, ὁ: due measure, proper time
κρυπτός, -ή, -όν: hidden, secret
μαρτυρέω: to bear witness
μεταβαίνω: to go from one place to another

μισέω: to hate
οὔπω: not yet
πάντοτε: at all times, always
παρρησία, ἡ: freespokenness, openness
περιπατέω: to walk about
σκηνοπηγία, ἡ: the Feast of Tents or Tabernacles
ὑμέτερος, -α, -ον: your
ὑπάγω: to withdraw
φανερόω: to make manifest

7:1   ἀποκτεῖναι: aor. inf. of purpose after ἐζήτουν, "they were seeking *to kill* him"

7:2   σκηνοπηγία: the feast of the Tabernacles commemorated the wandering in the desert (Lev. 23: 39-43).

7:3   μετάβηθι: aor. imper. of μετα-βαίνω, "go elsewhere!"
     ἵνα θεωρήσουσιν: aor. subj. in purpose/result clause, "go *so they may see*"

7:4   ποιεῖ καὶ ζητεῖ: "no one *does and seeks*" i.e. no one does both
     φανέρωσον: aor. imper., "show yourself!"

7:7   μισεῖν: pres. inf. complementing δύναται, "not able *to hate*"
     περὶ αὐτοῦ: "I will witness *about it*" i.e. the world

Chapter 7

Jesus Goes to the Festival of Tabernacles

¹ Et post haec ambulabat Iesus in Galilaeam; non enim volebat in Iudaeam ambulare, quia quaerebant eum Iudaei interficere. ² Erat autem in proximo dies festus Iudaeorum, Scenopegia. ³ Dixerunt ergo ad eum fratres eius: "Transi hinc et vade in Iudaeam, ut et discipuli tui videant opera tua, quae facis. ⁴ Nemo quippe in occulto quid facit et quaerit ipse in palam esse. Si haec facis, manifesta teipsum mundo." ⁵ Neque enim fratres eius credebant in eum.

⁶ Dicit ergo eis Iesus: "Tempus meum nondum adest, tempus autem vestrum semper est paratum. ⁷ Non potest mundus odisse vos; me autem odit, quia ego testimonium perhibeo de illo,

---

assum, adesse: be near, be present
hinc: from here, henceforth
interficio, (3): to kill, destroy
Iudaea, -ae *f*: Judea, Israel
malus, -a, -um: bad, evil, wicked
manifesto, (1): to make visible, disclose
nondum: not yet
occultum, -i *n*: secrecy, hiding
odi, odisse: to hate (perf.)
opus, -eris *n*: work, deed

palam: openly, publicly
paratus, -a, -um: prepared, ready, equipped
perhibeo, (2): to present, give
proximus, -a, -um: close
quippe: of course; naturally
scenopegia, -ae *f*: Jewish Feast of Tabernacles
tempus, -oris *n*: time
testimonium, -i *n*: testimony
transeo, (4): to go over, cross
vado, (3): to go

7:1   **in Galilaeam, in Iudaeam**: acc. where one would expect the ablative to translate the Greek dat., "in Galilee, in Judaea"

7:2   **in proximo**: the prep. phrase is used as a predicate, "the day was *near*"

7:3   **transi**: pres. imper. of *transeo*, "cross over!"
    ut ... videant: pres. subj. purpose clause, "in order that they may see"

7:4   **quid = quidquid**: "nobody does *anything*"
    in palam: "in the open" with redundant preposition

7:7   **odisse**: perf. inf. with present meaning, "able *to hate* you"
    de illo: "give testimony *about that*" i.e. the world

ὅτι τὰ ἔργα αὐτοῦ πονηρά ἐστιν. ⁸ ὑμεῖς ἀνάβητε εἰς τὴν ἑορτήν· ἐγὼ οὔπω ἀναβαίνω εἰς τὴν ἑορτὴν ταύτην, ὅτι ὁ ἐμὸς καιρὸς οὔπω πεπλήρωται.» ⁹ ταῦτα δὲ εἰπὼν αὐτοῖς ἔμεινεν ἐν τῇ Γαλιλαίᾳ.

¹⁰ ὡς δὲ ἀνέβησαν οἱ ἀδελφοὶ αὐτοῦ εἰς τὴν ἑορτήν, τότε καὶ αὐτὸς ἀνέβη, οὐ φανερῶς ἀλλὰ ὡς ἐν κρυπτῷ. ¹¹ οἱ οὖν Ἰουδαῖοι ἐζήτουν αὐτὸν ἐν τῇ ἑορτῇ καὶ ἔλεγον «Ποῦ ἐστιν ἐκεῖνος;»

¹² καὶ γογγυσμὸς περὶ αὐτοῦ ἦν πολὺς ἐν τοῖς ὄχλοις· οἱ μὲν ἔλεγον ὅτι Ἀγαθός ἐστιν,

ἄλλοι δὲ ἔλεγον Οὔ, ἀλλὰ πλανᾷ τὸν ὄχλον. ¹³ οὐδεὶς μέντοι παρρησίᾳ ἐλάλει περὶ αὐτοῦ διὰ τὸν φόβον τῶν Ἰου-δαίων.

ἀγαθός, -ή, -όν: good
ἀναβαίνω: to go up, mount, to go up to
Γαλιλαία, -ας, ἡ: Galilee
γογγυσμός, ὁ: a murmuring
ἑορτή, ἡ: a festival, feast
καιρός, ὁ: due measure, proper time
κρυπτός, -ή, -όν: hidden, secret
ὄχλος, ὁ: a crowd, a throng

παρρησία, ἡ: openness, frankness
πλανάω: to cause to wander
πληρόω: to make full
πονηρός, -ά, -όν: toilsome, painful, grievous
τότε: at that time, then
φανερός, -ά, -όν: visible, manifest, evident
φόβος, ὁ: fear

7:8   ἀνάβητε: aor. imper. of ἀνα-βαίνω, "go up to the feast!"
       πεπλήρωται: perf., "my time is not yet *fulfilled*"
7:9   ἔμεινεν: aor., "he remained"
7:10 ἀνέβησαν ... ἀνέβη: aor. of ἀνα-βαίνω, "as *they went up* ...he himself *went up*"
7:12 πλανᾷ: pres., "*he is causing* the crowd *to wander*"

quia opera eius mala sunt. ⁸ Vos ascendite ad diem festum; ego non ascendo ad diem festum istum, quia meum tempus nondum impletum est." ⁹ Haec autem cum dixisset, ipse mansit in Galilaea.

¹⁰ Ut autem ascenderunt fratres eius ad diem festum, tunc et ipse ascendit, non manifeste sed quasi in occulto. ¹¹ Iudaei ergo quaerebant eum in die festo et dicebant: "Ubi est ille?"

¹² Et murmur multus de eo erat in turba. Alii quidem dicebant: "Bonus est!"

alii autem dicebant: "Non, sed seducit turbam!" ¹³ Nemo tamen palam loquebatur de illo propter metum Iudaeorum.

---

alius, -a, -ud: other, another
ascendo, (3), ascendi, ascensus: to climb, go up, rise
bonus, -a, -um *m*: good
festus, -a, -um: festive
impleo, (2), implevi, impletus: to fulfill, complete
maneo (2), mansi: to remain
manifestus, -a, -um: conspicuous, noticeable
medio, (1): to be in the middle
metus, metus *m*: fear, anxiety, dread

murmur, -is *n*: murmur
occultum, -i *n*: secrecy, hiding
opus, -eris *n*: work deed
palam: openly, publicly
quasi: as if, just as
seduco, (3): to lead astray
tamen: yet, nevertheless, still
tempus, -oris *n*: time
tunc: then, at that time
turba, -ae *f*: crowd, multitude

7:9   **cum dixisset**: plupf. subj. *cum* circumstantial clause, "when he had said"
7:12   **alii quidem ...alii autem**: translating οἱ μὲν ...ἀλλοὶ, "while some ...others"
7:13   **de illo**: "was speaking *about him*" i.e. Jesus
          Iudaeorum: objective gen. after *metum*, "fear *of the Jews*"

105

Jesus Teaches at the Festival

¹⁴ ἤδη δὲ τῆς ἑορτῆς μεσούσης ἀνέβη Ἰησοῦς εἰς τὸ ἱερὸν καὶ ἐδίδασκεν. ¹⁵ ἐθαύμαζον οὖν οἱ Ἰουδαῖοι λέγοντες «Πῶς οὗτος γράμματα οἶδεν μὴ μεμαθηκώς;»

¹⁶ ἀπεκρίθη οὖν αὐτοῖς Ἰησοῦς καὶ εἶπεν «Ἡ ἐμὴ διδαχὴ οὐκ ἔστιν ἐμὴ ἀλλὰ τοῦ πέμψαντός με· ¹⁷ ἐάν τις θέλῃ τὸ θέλημα αὐτοῦ ποιεῖν, γνώσεται περὶ τῆς διδαχῆς πότερον ἐκ τοῦ θεοῦ ἐστιν ἢ ἐγὼ ἀπ᾽ ἐμαυτοῦ λαλῶ. ¹⁸ ὁ ἀφ᾽ ἑαυτοῦ λαλῶν τὴν δόξαν τὴν ἰδίαν ζητεῖ· ὁ δὲ ζητῶν τὴν δόξαν τοῦ πέμψαντος αὐτὸν οὗτος ἀληθής ἐστιν καὶ ἀδικία ἐν αὐτῷ οὐκ ἔστιν. ¹⁹ οὐ Μωυσῆς ἔδωκεν ὑμῖν τὸν νόμον; καὶ οὐδεὶς ἐξ ὑμῶν ποιεῖ τὸν νόμον. τί με ζητεῖτε ἀποκτεῖναι;»

²⁰ ἀπεκρίθη ὁ ὄχλος «Δαιμόνιον ἔχεις· τίς σε ζητεῖ ἀποκτεῖναι;»

ἀδικία, ἡ: wrong-doing, injustice	θέλω: to will, wish (+ *inf.*)
γράμμα, -ατος, τό: a writing	ἴδιος, -α, -ον: one's own
δαιμόνιον, τό: a demon	ἱερόν, τό: temple
διδαχή, ἡ: teaching	μανθάνω: to learn
ἑορτή, ἡ: a festival, feast	μεσόω: to be in the middle
ἤδη: now, already	νόμος, ὁ: custom, law
θαυμάζω: to wonder, marvel	πότερος, -α, -ον: which of the two?

7:14 **μεσούσης**: pres. part. of **μεσόω** in gen. abs., "the festival *being in the middle*"
    ἐδίδασκεν: impf., "he started teaching"

7:15 **μὴ μεμαθηκώς**: perf. part. with **μὴ** indicating conditional force, "if not having learned"

7:16 **τοῦ πέμψαντός**: aor. part. gen., "the teaching *of the one who sent me*"

7:17 **ἐάν τις θέλῃ**: pres. subj. in fut. more vivid protasis, "if someone wishes"
    πότερον ἐστιν ἢ ... λαλῶ: ind. quest. after **γνώσεται**: "will know *whether it is ... or whether I speak*"

7:18 **ὁ ἀφ᾽ ἑαυτοῦ λαλῶν**: "the one speaking from himself" i.e. independently
    ὁ δὲ ζητῶν ... οὗτος: *the one seeking ... this one* is true"

7:19 **ἀποκτεῖναι**: aor. inf. of purpose, "why do you seek *to kill?*"

Jesus Teaches at the Festival

¹⁴ Iam autem die festo mediante, ascendit Iesus in templum et docebat. ¹⁵ Mirabantur ergo Iudaei dicentes: "Quomodo hic litteras scit, cum non didicerit?"

¹⁶ Respondit ergo eis Iesus et dixit: "Mea doctrina non est mea sed eius, qui misit me. ¹⁷ Si quis voluerit voluntatem eius facere, cognoscet de doctrina utrum ex Deo sit, an ego a meipso loquar. ¹⁸ Qui a semetipso loquitur, gloriam propriam quaerit; qui autem quaerit gloriam eius, qui misit illum, hic verax est, et iniustitia in illo non est. ¹⁹ Nonne Moyses dedit vobis legem? Et nemo ex vobis facit legem. Quid me quaeritis interficere?"

²⁰ Respondit turba: "Daemonium habes! Quis te quaerit interficere?"

---

ascendo, (3), **ascendi, ascensus**: to climb, go
daemonium, -i *n*: evil demon
disco, (3), **didici, discitus**: to learn
doctrina, -ae *f*: learning, teaching
iniustitia, -ae *f*: injustice, false
lex, legis *f*: law
littera, litterae *f*: literature, books
miro, (1): to wonder; marvel at
opus, operis *n*: deed

proprius, -a, -um: individual
quaero (3), **quaesivi, quaesitus**: to search for, seek
quomodo: how, in what way?
semetipse, -a, -um: one's self
templum, -i *n*: temple
utrum... an: whether... or
verax, -a, -um: speaking the truth, truthful
voluntas, voluntatis *f*: will, desire

7:14 **die festo mediante**: abl. abs., "the festival day being in the middle"

7:15 **cum... didicerit**: perf. subj. in *cum* concessive clause, "although he has not been taught"

7:17 **si quis voluerit**: fut. perf. indic. in fut. more vivid protasis, "if anyone wishes"+ inf.

   utrum... sit an... loquar: pres. subj. in indirect question, "know *whether it is* from God or *whether I speak* from myself"

7:18 Note the profusion of pronouns produced by the translation of Greek participles by relative clauses. The final three demonstratives (*illum, hic, illo*) all have the same antecedent, the subject of *qui autem quaerit*

107

²¹ ἀπεκρίθη Ἰησοῦς καὶ εἶπεν αὐτοῖς «Ἓν ἔργον ἐποίησα καὶ πάντες θαυμάζετε. ²² διὰ τοῦτο Μωυσῆς δέδωκεν ὑμῖν τὴν περιτομήν, — οὐχ ὅτι ἐκ τοῦ Μωυσέως ἐστὶν ἀλλ' ἐκ τῶν πατέρων, — καὶ [ἐν] σαββάτῳ περιτέμνετε ἄνθρωπον. ²³ εἰ περιτομὴν λαμβάνει ὁ ἄνθρωπος ἐν σαββάτῳ ἵνα μὴ λυθῇ ὁ νόμος Μωυσέως, ἐμοὶ χολᾶτε ὅτι ὅλον ἄνθρωπον ὑγιῆ ἐποίησα ἐν σαββάτῳ; ²⁴ μὴ κρίνετε κατ' ὄψιν, ἀλλὰ τὴν δικαίαν κρίσιν κρίνετε.»

Division Over Who Jesus Is

²⁵ ἔλεγον οὖν τινὲς ἐκ τῶν Ἱεροσολυμειτῶν «Οὐχ οὗτός ἐστιν ὃν ζητοῦσιν ἀποκτεῖναι; ²⁶ καὶ ἴδε παρρησίᾳ λαλεῖ καὶ οὐδὲν αὐτῷ λέγουσιν· μή ποτε ἀληθῶς ἔγνωσαν οἱ ἄρχοντες ὅτι οὗτός ἐστιν ὁ χριστός; ²⁷ ἀλλὰ τοῦτον οἴδαμεν πόθεν ἐστίν· ὁ δὲ χριστὸς ὅταν ἔρχηται οὐδεὶς γινώσκει πόθεν ἐστίν.»

ἄρχων, -οντος, ὁ: a commander, captain
γινώσκω: to know
δίκαιος, -η, -ον: just
ἰδέ: lo, behold
Ἱεροσολυμειτής, ὁ: an Israelite
κρίνω: to judge
κρίσις, ἡ: a judgement
λαμβάνω: to take
λύω: to loose

ὅλος, -η, -ον: whole, complete
ὄψις, -εως, ἡ: look, appearance, aspect
περιτέμνω: to circumcize
περιτομή, ἡ: circumcision
πόθεν: whence?
Σάββατον, τό: Sabbath
ὑγιής, -ές: sound, healthy, hearty, sound in
χολάω: to be angry
χριστός, -ή, -όν: annointed

7:21 ἓν ἔργον: "I have done *one deed*"
7:23 ἵνα μὴ λυθῇ: aor. subj. pass. of λύω in purpose clause, "*lest that* the law *is not loosed*"
    ὑγιῆ: acc. pred., "I made a whole man *well*"
7:24 κατ' ὄψιν: "don't judge *according to appearance*"
    κρίσιν: cognate accusative, "judge *a judgement*" i.e. make a judgement
7:25 οὐχ οὗτός ἐστιν: anticipating an affirmative answer, "is this not?"
7:26 μήποτε ἀληθῶς ἔγνωσαν: anticipating a negative answer, "surely they do not realize"
7:27 ὅταν ἔρχηται: pres. subj. in general temporal clause, "whenever he comes"

²¹ Respondit Iesus et dixit eis: "Unum opus feci, et omnes miramini. ²² Propterea Moyses dedit vobis circumcisionem -- non quia ex Moyse est sed ex patribus -- et in sabbato circumciditis hominem. ²³ Si circumcisionem accipit homo in sabbato, ut non solvatur lex Moysis, mihi indignamini, quia totum hominem sanum feci in sabbato? ²⁴ Nolite iudicare secundum faciem, sed iustum iudicium iudicate."

Division Over Who Jesus Is

²⁵ Dicebant ergo quidam ex Hierosolymitis: "Nonne hic est, quem quaerunt interficere? ²⁶ Et ecce palam loquitur, et nihil ei dicunt. Numquid vere cognoverunt principes quia hic est Christus? ²⁷ Sed hunc scimus unde sit, Christus autem cum venerit, nemo scit unde sit."

---

accipio, (3): to receive, accept
circumcido, (3): to circumcize
circumcisio, -onis f.: circumcision
clamo, (1): to proclaim, shout?
ecce: behold! see!
facies, faciei f.: presence, appearance
Hierosolymis, -itis, m./f.: a Jerusamelite
indignor, (1): to scorn, regard with indignation
iudicium, -i n.: judgment, decision
iudico, (1): to judge, give judgment
iustus, -a, -um: just, fair; right, lawful

miror, (1): to wonder at
nihil (*indecl.*): nothing
palam: openly, publicly, plainly
princeps, principis m.: leader
sabbatum, -i n.: Sabbath
sanus, -a, -um: sound, healthy
secundus, -a, -um: inferior
solvo, (3): to loosen, release, unbind
totus, -a, -um: whole, all, entire
unde: from where, whence
vere: truly, actually, indeed

7:22   **et in sabbato**: "even on the Sabbath" circumcision was required on the 8th day even if it fell on the Sabbath

7:23   **ut non solvatur**: pres. subj. in purpose clause, "*lest* the law *be loosed*"

     mihi indignamini: "are you indignant with me?" a rhetorical question that is also an apodosis

     totum ... sanum: predicate adjs., "I made a man *whole* and *sound*"

7:24   **nolite**: imper., "don't!" + inf.

     iustum iudicium: cognate acc. with *iudicate*, "judge a just judgement"

7:27   **unde sit**: pres. subj. indirect question after *scimus* and *scit*, "know *whence he is*"

     cum... venerit: fut. perf. in circumstantial clause, "when(ever) he has come"

²⁸ ἔκραξεν οὖν ἐν τῷ ἱερῷ διδάσκων ὁ Ἰησοῦς καὶ λέγων «Κἀμὲ οἴδατε καὶ οἴδατε πόθεν εἰμί· καὶ ἀπ᾽ ἐμαυτοῦ οὐκ ἐλήλυθα, ἀλλ᾽ ἔστιν ἀληθινὸς ὁ πέμψας με, ὃν ὑμεῖς οὐκ οἴδατε· ²⁹ ἐγὼ οἶδα αὐτόν, ὅτι παρ᾽ αὐτοῦ εἰμι κἀκεῖνός με ἀπέστειλεν.»

³⁰ ἐζήτουν οὖν αὐτὸν πιάσαι, καὶ οὐδεὶς ἐπέβαλεν ἐπ᾽ αὐτὸν τὴν χεῖρα, ὅτι οὔπω ἐληλύθει ἡ ὥρα αὐτοῦ. ³¹ ἐκ τοῦ ὄχλου δὲ πολλοὶ ἐπίστευσαν εἰς αὐτόν, καὶ ἔλεγον «Ὁ χριστὸς ὅταν ἔλθῃ μὴ πλείονα σημεῖα ποιήσει ὧν οὗτος ἐποίησεν;»

³² ἤκουσαν οἱ Φαρισαῖοι τοῦ ὄχλου γογγύζοντος περὶ αὐτοῦ ταῦτα, καὶ ἀπέστειλαν οἱ ἀρχιερεῖς καὶ οἱ Φαρισαῖοι ὑπηρέτας ἵνα πιάσωσιν αὐτόν.

ἀληθινός, -η, -ον: true	ὄχλος, ὁ: a crowd
ἀρχιερεύς, -έως, ὁ: a chief-priest	πιάζω: to arrest
ἐπιβάλλω: to throw or cast upon	πλείων, πλεῖον: more
ἦλθον: to go (aor.)	ὑπηρέτης, -ου, ὁ: a public slave
ἱερόν, τό: a temple	χείρ, χειρός, ἡ: the hand
κράζω: to cry out	ὥρα, ἡ: hour

7:28 ἔκραξεν: aor. of κράζω, "he cried out"
  κἀμὲ (=καὶ ἐμέ) οἴδατε: perf., "you know me also"
  οὐκ ἐλήλυθα: perf. of ἔρχομαι, "*I have not come* from my own authority"
7:29 κἀκεῖνός = καὶ ἐκεῖνος: "*and that one* sent me" i.e. the father
7:30 πιάσαι: aor. inf. of purpose after ἐζήτουν, "they were seeking *to arrest* him"
  ἐπέβαλεν: aor. of ἐπι-βάλλω, "no one *placed a hand on him*"
  ἐληλύθει: plupf. of ἔρχομαι, "his hour *had* not yet *come*"
7:31 ὅταν ἔλθῃ: aor. subj. in general temporal clause, "*when his hour comes*" (whenever that will be)
  ὧν: rel. pron. gen. attracted into the case of its unexpressed antecedent, which was a gen. of comparison after πλείονα (= τούτων ἃ ἐποίησεν), "will he do more things (than the ones) *which* this one did"
7:32 τοῦ ὄχλου γογγύζοντος: gen. after ἤκουσαν, "they heard *the crowd grumbling*"
  ἵνα πιάσωσιν: aor. subj. in purpose clause, "they sent servants *to arrest him*"

²⁸ Clamavit ergo docens in templo Iesus et dicens: "Et me scitis et unde sim scitis. Et a meipso non veni, sed est verus, qui misit me, quem vos non scitis. ²⁹ Ego scio eum, quia ab ipso sum, et ipse me misit."

³⁰ Quaerebant ergo eum apprehendere, et nemo misit in illum manus, quia nondum venerat hora eius. ³¹ De turba autem multi crediderunt in eum et dicebant: "Christus cum venerit, numquid plura signa faciet quam quae hic fecit?"

³² Audierunt pharisaei turbam murmurantem de illo haec et miserunt pontifices et pharisaei ministros, ut apprehenderent eum.

---

adhuc: thus far, till now
apprehendo, (3): to seize, apprehend
audio, (4): to hear
hora, **-ae** *f*: hour, time
manus, **-us** *f*: hand
minister, **ministri** *m*: guard, attendant

murmuro, (1): to murmur, mutter
pharisaeus, **-i** *m*: Pharisee
plus, **pluris** (*gen.*): more
pontifex, **-icis** *m*: high priest
signum, **-i** *n*: sign
verus, **-a**, **-um**: true

7:28   **unde sim**: pres. subj. in indirect question, "know *whence I am*"
7:30   **manus**: acc. pl. direct obj. of *misit*, "no one placed *their hands*"
7:31   **cum... venerit**: fut. perf. in gen. temporal clause, "when he has come" (whenever that will be)
        plura signa... quam: "does anyone make *more signs ... than* he?"
7:32   **haec**: acc. obj. of *murmurantem*, "murmuring *these things*"
        ut apprehenderent: impf. subj. purpose clause, "sent attendants *to arrest*"

³³ εἶπεν οὖν ὁ Ἰησοῦς «Ἔτι χρόνον μικρὸν μεθ᾿ ὑμῶν εἰμὶ καὶ ὑπάγω πρὸς τὸν πέμψαντά με. ³⁴ ζητήσετέ με καὶ οὐχ εὑρήσετέ με, καὶ ὅπου εἰμὶ ἐγὼ ὑμεῖς οὐ δύνασθε ἐλθεῖν.»

³⁵ εἶπον οὖν οἱ Ἰουδαῖοι πρὸς ἑαυτούς «Ποῦ οὗτος μέλλει πορεύεσθαι ὅτι ἡμεῖς οὐχ εὑρήσομεν αὐτόν; μὴ εἰς τὴν διασπορὰν τῶν Ἑλλήνων μέλλει πορεύεσθαι καὶ διδάσκειν τοὺς Ἕλληνας; ³⁶ τίς ἐστιν ὁ λόγος οὗτος ὃν εἶπε Ζητήσετέ με καὶ οὐχ εὑρήσετέ με καὶ ὅπου εἰμὶ ἐγὼ ὑμεῖς οὐ δύνασθε ἐλθεῖν ;»

³⁷ ἐν δὲ τῇ ἐσχάτῃ ἡμέρᾳ τῇ μεγάλῃ τῆς ἑορτῆς εἱστήκει ὁ Ἰησοῦς, καὶ ἔκραξεν λέγων «Ἐάν τις διψᾷ ἐρχέσθω πρός με καὶ πινέτω. ³⁸ ὁ πιστεύων εἰς ἐμέ, καθὼς εἶπεν ἡ γραφή, ποταμοὶ ἐκ τῆς κοιλίας αὐτοῦ ῥεύσουσιν ὕδατος ζῶντος.»

γραφή, ἡ: a writing, scripture
διασπορά, ἡ: dispersion
διψάω: to thirst
δύναμαι: to be able (+ *inf.*)
Ἕλλην, -ηνος, ὁ: a Greek
ἑορτή, ἡ: a festival, feast
εὑρίσκω: to find
ἵστημι: to set up
κοιλία, ἡ: belly

κράζω: to shout
μικρός, -ά, -όν: small, little
πίνω: to drink
πορεύω: to make to go
ποταμός, ὁ: a river, stream
ῥέω: to flow, run, stream, gush
ὕδωρ, ὕδατος, τό: water
ὑπάγω: to withdraw

7:33 ἔτι χρόνον μικρὸν: acc. of duration, "for a small time still"
7:34 εὑρήσετε: fut. of εὑρίσκω, "you will find"
ἐλθεῖν: aor. inf. complementing δύνασθε, "you will not be able *to go*"
7:35 ποῦ οὗτος: "*whither is this one* about to go?" expecting ποῖ
πορεύεσθαι: pres. inf. complementing μέλλει, "he intends *to go*"
ὅτι: epexegetic, "*with the effect that* we will not find him"
μὴ ... μέλλει: a rhet. quest., "surely he does not intend?"
7:37 εἱστήκει: plupf. of ἵστημι, "he was standing"
ἐάν τις διψᾷ: pres. subj. in fut. more vivid protasis, "if anyone thirsts"
ἐρχέσθω ... πινέτω: 3 s. pres. imper., "let him come! ... let him drink!"
7:38 ῥεύσουσιν: fut. of ῥέω, "they will flow"
ὕδατος ζῶντος: gen. of description, "rivers *of living water*" (Is. 58·11)

³³ Dixit ergo Iesus: "Adhuc modicum tempus vobiscum sum et vado ad eum, qui misit me. ³⁴ Quaeretis me et non invenietis; et ubi sum ego, vos non potestis venire."

³⁵ Dixerunt ergo Iudaei ad seipsos: "Quo hic iturus est, quia nos non inveniemus eum? Numquid in dispersionem Graecorum iturus est et docturus Graecos? ³⁶ Quis est hic sermo, quem dixit: 'Quaeretis me et non invenietis' et: 'Ubi sum ego, vos non potestis venire'?"

³⁷ In novissimo autem die magno festivitatis stabat Iesus et clamavit dicens: "Si quis sitit, veniat ad me et bibat, ³⁸ qui credit in me. Sicut dixit Scriptura, flumina de ventre eius fluent aquae vivae."

---

aqua, -ae *f*: water
bibo, (3): to drink
dispersio, -onis *f*: dispersion, diaspora
doceo, (2), **docui, doctus**: to teach
eo, (4), ii, itus: go
festivitas, -tatis *f*: festivity, feast
flumen, -inis *n*: river
fluo, (3): to flow, stream, emanate
Graecus, -i *m*: a Greek
invenio, (4): to come upon; find
magnus, -a, -um: great

modicus, -a, -um: short, small amount
novissimus, -a, -um: last
scriptura, -ae *f*: writing, scripture
seipse, seipsa, seipsum: one's self
sitio, (4): to be thirsty
sto, (1): to stand
tempus, temporis *n*: time
vado (3): to go
venter, ventris *m*: stomach, womb; belly
vivus, -a, -um: alive, living

7:33 **modicum tempus**: acc. of duration, "for a small amount of time"
7:35 **quo iturus est**: fut. part. in periphrastic "whither is he about to go?" i.e
        "whither will he go?"
      quia: epexegetic (= *quod*), "where will he go *with the effect that*"
      iturus est et docturus: fut. periph., "is he about to go and about to teach?"
7:37 **veniat... bibat**: pres. jussive subj., "let him come! ... let him drink!"
7:38 **aquae vivae**: gen. description, "rivers *of living water*"

³⁹ τοῦτο δὲ εἶπεν περὶ τοῦ πνεύματος οὗ ἔμελλον λαμβάνειν οἱ πιστεύσαντες εἰς αὐτόν· οὔπω γὰρ ἦν πνεῦμα, ὅτι Ἰησοῦς οὔπω ἐδοξάσθη.

⁴⁰ ἐκ τοῦ ὄχλου οὖν ἀκούσαντες τῶν λόγων τούτων ἔλεγον ὅτι «Οὗτός ἐστιν ἀληθῶς ὁ προφήτης·»

⁴¹ ἄλλοι ἔλεγον «Οὗτός ἐστιν ὁ χριστός·»

οἱ δὲ ἔλεγον «Μὴ γὰρ ἐκ τῆς Γαλιλαίας ὁ χριστὸς ἔρχεται; ⁴² οὐχ ἡ γραφὴ εἶπεν ὅτι ἐκ τοῦ σπέρματος Δαυεὶδ καὶ ἀπὸ Βηθλεὲμ τῆς κώμης, ὅπου ἦν Δαυείδ, ἔρχεται ὁ χριστός ;» ⁴³ σχίσμα οὖν ἐγένετο ἐν τῷ ὄχλῳ δι᾽ αὐτόν. ⁴⁴ τινὲς δὲ ἤθελον ἐξ αὐτῶν πιάσαι αὐτόν, ἀλλ᾽ οὐδεὶς ἔβαλεν ἐπ᾽ αὐτὸν τὰς χεῖρας.

Unbelief of the Jewish Leaders

⁴⁵ ἦλθον οὖν οἱ ὑπηρέται πρὸς τοὺς ἀρχιερεῖς καὶ Φαρισαίους, καὶ εἶπον αὐτοῖς ἐκεῖνοι «Διὰ τί οὐκ ἠγάγετε αὐτόν;»

ἄγω: to lead or carry
Βηθλεὲμ (indecl.): Bethlehem
Γαλιλαία, ἡ: Galileia
Δαυείδ (indecl.): David
δοξάζομαι: to be magnified, glorified
ἐπιβάλλω: to throw upon

κώμη, ἡ: country town, village
πιάζω: to arrest
σπέρμα, -ατος, τό: a seed
σχίσμα, -ατος, τό: a division
ὑπηρέτης, -ου, ὁ: a public official
χείρ, χειρός, ἡ: a hand

7:39 οὗ: rel. pron. gen. after λαμβάνειν, "which they were about to receive"
ἐδοξάσθη: aor. pass., "he had not yet been glorified"
7:40 ἀκούσαντες: aor. part., "having heard" + gen.
7:41 οἱ δὲ: "but they said"
μὴ ἔρχεται: "does he not come?" expecting a negative answer
7:42 οὐχ ἡ γραφὴ εἶπεν: expecting an affirmative answer, "does scripture not say?"
ὅπου ἦν Δαυίδ: ind. quest., "say whence David was"
7:43 ἐγένετο: aor. of γίνομαι, "there arose"
7:44 πιάσαι: aor. inf. after ἤθελον, "some wished to arrest him"
ἐπέβαλεν: aor. of ἐπι-βάλλω, "no one laid hands on"
7:45 οἱ ὑπηρέται: lit., "rowers," then "public servants," then "public officials"
ἠγάγετε: aor., "why did you not lead him?"

³⁹ Hoc autem dixit de Spiritu, quem accepturi erant qui crediderant in eum. Nondum enim erat Spiritus, quia Iesus nondum fuerat glorificatus.

⁴⁰ Ex illa ergo turba, cum audissent hos sermones, dicebant: "Hic est vere propheta!"

⁴¹ alii dicebant: "Hic est Christus!"

quidam autem dicebant: "Numquid a Galilaea Christus venit? ⁴² Nonne Scriptura dixit: 'Ex semine David et de Bethlehem castello, ubi erat David, venit Christus'?" ⁴³ Dissensio itaque facta est in turba propter eum. ⁴⁴ Quidam autem ex ipsis volebant apprehendere eum, sed nemo misit super illum manus.

Unbelief of the Jewish Leaders

⁴⁵ Venerunt ergo ministri ad pontifices et pharisaeos; et dixerunt eis illi: "Quare non adduxistis eum?"

---

accipio, (3) **accepi**, **acceptus**: to receive, accept
adduco, (3), **adduxi**, **adductus**: to lead away, arrest
alius, **alia**, **aliud**: other, another; different
apprehendo, (3): to seize, grasp, arrest
Bethlehem (*indecl.*): Bethlehem
castellum, -i *n*: town, village

David (*indecl.*) *m*: David
dissensio, -onis *f*: disagreement, conflict
glorifico, (1): to glorify, honor, worship
itaque: thus, therefore
nonne: is it not? (interog, expects the answer "Yes")
semen, **seminis** *n*: seed, line
vere: really, truly, actually

7:39   **accepturi**: fut. part. used peripharstically with *erant*, "they were *about to receive*"

   fuerat glorificatus (= erat glorificatus): plupf., "because *he had* not *been glorified*"

7:40   **cum audissent**: plupf. subj. in *cum* circumstantial clause, "when they had heard"

7:42   **David ...Bethlehem**: indecl., here both genitive, "seed *of David* ...village *of Bethlehem*"

7:44   **manus**: acc. pl. direct obj. of *misit*, "no one placed *their hands* on him"

⁴⁶ ἀπεκρίθησαν οἱ ὑπηρέται «Οὐδέποτε ἐλάλησεν οὕτως ἄνθρωπος.»

⁴⁷ ἀπεκρίθησαν οὖν αὐτοῖς οἱ Φαρισαῖοι «Μὴ καὶ ὑμεῖς πεπλάνησθε; ⁴⁸ μή τις ἐκ τῶν ἀρχόντων ἐπίστευσεν εἰς αὐτὸν ἢ ἐκ τῶν Φαρισαίων; ⁴⁹ ἀλλὰ ὁ ὄχλος οὗτος ὁ μὴ γινώσκων τὸν νόμον ἐπάρατοί εἰσιν.»

⁵⁰ λέγει Νικόδημος πρὸς αὐτούς, ὁ ἐλθὼν πρὸς αὐτὸν πρότερον, εἷς ὢν ἐξ αὐτῶν ⁵¹ «Μὴ ὁ νόμος ἡμῶν κρίνει τὸν ἄνθρωπον ἐὰν μὴ ἀκούσῃ πρῶτον παρ' αὐτοῦ καὶ γνῷ τί ποιεῖ;»

⁵² ἀπεκρίθησαν καὶ εἶπαν αὐτῷ «Μὴ καὶ σὺ ἐκ τῆς Γαλιλαίας εἶ; ἐραύνησον καὶ ἴδε ὅτι ἐκ τῆς Γαλιλαίας προφήτης οὐκ ἐγείρεται.»

⁵³ καὶ ἐπορεύθησαν ἕκαστος εἰς τὸν οἶκον αὐτοῦ,

ἄκουσις, ἡ: a hearing
ἐγείρω: to arise
ἕκαστος, -η, -ον: each, each one
ἐπάρατος, -ον: accursed, laid under a curse
ἐραυνάω: to search

οἶκος, -ου, ὁ: a house
οὐδέποτε: never
πλανάω: to make to wander, seduce
πορεύω: to go, convey
πρότερος, -α, ον: prior

7:46 ἐλάλησεν: aor. of λαλέω, "a man *has never spoken*"
7:47 πεπλάνησθε: perf. pass., "have you been led astray?"
7:48 μή τις ἐκ: "did not any of" + gen.
7:49 ὁ μὴ γινώσκων: μὴ with an attrib. part. has a conditional force, "if (the crowd) does not know"
      ἐπάρατοί εἰσιν: "they are cursed," pl. by sense of the word ὄχλος
7:50 ὁ ἐλθὼν: aor. part. attributive, "the one who came"
      εἷς ὢν: pres. part. circum., "being one of them (now)"
7:51 ἐὰν μὴ ἀκούσῃ ... γνῷ: aor. subj. in pres. general protasis, "if it (the law) does not first hear ... if it does not come to know"
7:52 ἐραύνησον: aor. imper. of ἐραυνάω, "search!"
7:53 ἐπορεύθησαν: aor. pass., "they made their way"
      αὐτοῦ: gen., "to *his own* house" where a reflexive would be expected

116

⁴⁶ Responderunt ministri: "Numquam sic locutus est homo."

⁴⁷ Responderunt ergo eis pharisaei: "Numquid et vos seducti estis? ⁴⁸ Numquid aliquis ex principibus credidit in eum aut ex pharisaeis? ⁴⁹ Sed turba haec, quae non novit legem, maledicti sunt!"

⁵⁰ Dicit Nicodemus ad eos, ille qui venit ad eum antea, qui unus erat ex ipsis: ⁵¹ "Numquid lex nostra iudicat hominem, nisi audierit ab ipso prius et cognoverit quid faciat?"

⁵² Responderunt et dixerunt ei: "Numquid et tu ex Galilaea es? Scrutare et vide quia propheta a Galilaea non surgit!"

⁵³ Et reversi sunt unusquisque in domum suam.

---

antea: before
domus, -us *f.*: house
Galilaea, -ae *f.*: Galilee
lex, legis, *f.* a law
maledico, (3), maledixi, maledictus: to curse
nosco, (3), novi, notus: to know, learn
noster, -tra, -trum: our
numquam: never

prior, prius: earlier, before
propheta, -ae *m*: prophet
revertor, (3), reversus sum: to go back, return
scruto, (1): to examine carefully
seduco, (3), seduxi, seductus: to lead astray, deceive
surgo, (3): to rise, come from
turba, -ae *f.*: crowd
unusquisque: each one

7:49 **maledicti sunt**: plural because of the meaning of *turba*
7:50 **ex ipsis**: "who was *from those very ones*" i.e. the Pharisees
7:51 **nisi audierit… cognoverit**: fut. perf. in gen. cond., "unless (our law) has first heard…has known"

    quid faciat: pres. subj. indirect question after *cognoverit*, "has known *what he does*"
7:52 **scrutare**: pres. imper. pl., "examine!"

    quia non surgit: ind. st., "know *that a prophet does not rise*"
7:53 Many manuscripts do not have John 7:53–8:11. Its earlierst witness is a Latin manuscript

Chapter 8

¹ Ἰησοῦς δὲ ἐπορεύθη εἰς τὸ Ὄρος τῶν Ἐλαιῶν.

² ὄρθρου δὲ πάλιν παρεγένετο εἰς τὸ ἱερόν, καὶ πᾶς ὁ λαὸς ἤρχετο πρὸς αὐτόν, καὶ καθίσας ἐδίδασκεν αὐτούς. ³ ἄγουσιν δὲ οἱ γραμματεῖς καὶ οἱ Φαρισαῖοι γυναῖκα ἐπὶ μοιχείᾳ κατειλημ-μένην, καὶ στήσαντες αὐτὴν ἐν μέσῳ ⁴ λέγουσιν αὐτῷ «Διδά-σκαλε, αὕτη ἡ γυνὴ κατείληπται ἐπ' αὐτοφώρῳ μοιχευομένη· ⁵ ἐν δὲ τῷ νόμῳ ἡμῖν Μωυσῆς ἐνετείλατο τὰς τοιαύτας λιθάζειν·

ἄγω: to lead or carry
αὐτόφωρος, -ον: caught in the act
γραμματεύς, -έως, ὁ: a secretary, clerk
διδάσκαλος, ὁ: a teacher, master
ἐντέλλω: to enjoin, command
ἵστημι: to make to stand
καθίζω: to make to sit down, seat
καταλαμβάνω: to seize
λαός, ὁ: the people

λιθάζω: to fling stones
μέσος, -η, -ον: middle
μοιχεία, ἡ: adultery
μοιχεύω: to commit adultery
ὄρθρος, ὁ: dawn
ὄρος, -εος, τό: a mountain, hill
παραγίγνομαι: to be near
πορεύω: to make one's way
τοιοῦτος, -αύτη, -οῦτο: such as this

8:1   τὸ Ὄρος τῶν Ἐλαιῶν: "the mount of Olives," beyond the city walls of Jerusalem

8:2   ὄρθρου: gen., "at dawn" instead of dative of time when
   παρεγένετο: aor. of παρα-γίνομαι, "he was present"
   ἤρχετο: impf., "all the people *were going*"
   καθίσας: aor. part., "*having sat down* he began teaching"

8:3   ἄγουσιν etc. The story of the adulteress is absent from many manuscripts and may not belong here.
   κατειλημμένην: perf. part. circum. of κατα-λαμβάνω, "led a woman *having been caught*"
   στήσαντες: aor. transitive of ἵστημι, "having set her up"

8:4   κατείληπται: perf. of κατα-λαμβάνω, "she has been caught"
   ἐπ' αὐτοφώρῳ: "very clearly"
   μοιχεθμένη: pres. part. supplementary, "has been caught *committing adultery*"

8:5   ἐνετείλατο: aor. of ἐν-τέλλω, "Moses *enjoined* us"
   λιθάζειν: pres. inf. after ἐνετείλατο, "enjoined us *to stone*"

Chapter 8

¹ Iesus autem perrexit in montem Oliveti.

² Diluculo autem iterum venit in templum, et omnis populus veniebat ad eum, et sedens docebat eos. ³ Adducunt autem scribae et pharisaei mulierem in adulterio deprehensam et statuerunt eam in medio ⁴ et dicunt ei: "Magister, haec mulier manifesto deprehensa est in adulterio. ⁵ In lege autem Moyses mandavit nobis huiusmodi lapidare;

---

adduco, (3): to lead, bring
adulterium, **-i** *n*: adultery
deprehendo, (3), **deprehendi, deprehensus**: to catch, discover
diluculum, **-i** *n*: dawn, daybreak
iterum: again; a second time
lapido, (1): to throw stones at; stone
magister, **-tri** *m*: teacher, master
mando, (1): to order, command
manifesto (*adv.*): openly, clearly

medium, **-i** *n*: middle, center
mons, montis *m*: mountain
mulier, mulieris *f*: woman
olivetum, **-i** *n*: olive-yard
pergo, (3), **perrexi**: to go on, proceed
populus, **-i** *m*: people
scriba, **-ae** *m*: scribe, clerk
sedeo, (2): to sit, remain
statuo, (3): to set up, place

8:1 **in montem Oliveti**: "to the Mount of Olives" just east of Jerusalem
8:2 **diliculo**: abl., "at daybreak"
docebat: impf. inceptive, "he began teaching"
8:3 **deprehensam**: perf. part. circum., "a woman *caught* in adultery"
8:5 **lapidare**: pres. inf. indirect command, "commands us *to stone*"
huiusmodi: gen., "someone *of this kind*"

σὺ οὖν τί λέγεις;» ⁶ τοῦτο δὲ ἔλεγον πειράζοντες αὐτόν, ἵνα ἔχωσιν κατηγορεῖν αὐτοῦ.

ὁ δὲ Ἰησοῦς κάτω κύψας τῷ δακτύλῳ κατέγραφεν εἰς τὴν γῆν. ⁷ ὡς δὲ ἐπέμενον ἐρωτῶντες αὐτόν, ἀνέκυψεν καὶ εἶπεν «Ὁ ἀναμάρτητος ὑμῶν πρῶτος ἐπ᾽ αὐτὴν βαλέτω λίθον·» ⁸ καὶ πάλιν κατακύψας ἔγραφεν εἰς τὴν γῆν.

⁹ οἱ δὲ ἀκούσαντες ἐξήρχοντο εἷς καθ᾽ εἷς ἀρξάμενοι ἀπὸ τῶν πρεσβυτέρων, καὶ κατελείφθη μόνος, καὶ ἡ γυνὴ ἐν μέσῳ οὖσα. ¹⁰ ἀνακύψας δὲ ὁ Ἰησοῦς εἶπεν αὐτῇ «Γύναι, ποῦ εἰσίν; οὐδείς σε κατέκρινεν;»

ἀνακύπτω: to lift up the head
ἀναμάρτητος, -ον: without sin
ἄρχομαι: to be first, begin
βάλλω: to throw
γῆ, ἡ: earth
γράφω: to write
γυνή, ἡ: a woman
δάκτυλος, ὁ: a finger
ἐξέρχομαι: to go or come out of
ἐπιμένω: to stay on, persist
ἐρωτάω: to question
καταγράφω: to scratch, write down

κατακρίνω: to condemn
κατακύπτω: to bend down, stoop
καταλείπω: to leave behind
κατηγορέω: to speak against, to accuse
κάτω (adv.): down, downwards
κύπτω: to bend forward, stoop down
λίθος, ὁ: a stone
μέσος, -η, -ον: middle
μόνος, -η, -ον: alone
πειράζω: to make proof or trial of
πρεσβύτερος, -α, -ον: older
πρῶτος, -η, -ον: first

8:6 πειράζοντες: pres. part. expressing purpose, "spoke *in order to test* him"
ἵνα ἔχωσιν: pres. subj. of ἔχω expressing purpose and result, "test him *so that they could*" + inf.
κύψας: aor. part. of κύπτω, "having stooped"
κατέγραφεν: impf., "he began writing down"
8:7 ἐπέμενον: impf. of ἐπι-μένω, "when they persisted" + part.
ἐρωτῶντες: pres. part. supplementary, "persisted *asking*"
ἀνέκυψεν: aor. of ἀνα-κύπτω, "he lifted his head"
βαλέτω: aor. imper. 3. s. of βάλλω, "let him throw!"
8:8 ἔγραφεν: impf., "he kept writing;" in some later manuscripts it is added that he was writing "the sins of each of them"
8:9 ἐξήρχοντο: impf. of ἐξ-ἔρχομαι, "they began leaving"
εἷς καθ᾽ εἷς: nom. subject, "one by one"
κατελείφθη: aor. pass. of κατα-λαμβάνω, "he was left behind"
8:10 ἀνακύψας: aor., "having raised his head"
κατέκρινεν: aor. of κατα-κρίνω, "*did* no one *condemn* you?"

tu ergo quid dicis?" ⁶ Hoc autem dicebant tentantes eum, ut possent accusare eum.

Iesus autem inclinans se deorsum digito scribebat in terra. ⁷ Cum autem perseverarent interrogantes eum, erexit se et dixit eis: "Qui sine peccato est vestrum, primus in illam lapidem mittat"; ⁸ et iterum se inclinans scribebat in terra.

⁹ Audientes autem unus post unum exibant, incipientes a senioribus, et remansit solus, et mulier in medio stans. ¹⁰ Erigens autem se Iesus dixit ei: "Mulier, ubi sunt? Nemo te condemnavit?"

---

accuso, (1): to accuse, blame, find fault
autem: but
condemno, (1): to condemn, convict
deorsum (*adv.*): down, downwards
digitus, -i *m*: finger
erigo, (3), **erexi, erectus**: raise
exeo, (4): to go
incipio, (3): to begin, start
inclino, (1): to lower
interrogo, (1): to ask, question, interrogate
lapis, lapidis *m*: stone
medium, -i *n*: middle, center

mitto, (3): to send
nemo, neminis *m/f*: no one
peccatum, -i *n*: sin
persevero, (1): to persist
primus, -a, -um: first
remaneo, (2), **remansi, remansus**: stay behind, remain
scribo, (3): to write
senior, senioris *m*: senior, elderly
solus, -a, -um: only, alone
tento, (1): to test, try
terra, -ae *f*: earth, ground

8:6 **tentantes**: pres. part. expressing purpose, "were saying *in order to test*"
  ut possent: impf. subj. purpose clause, "testing *so that they would be able*" + inf.
  digito: abl. of means, "writing *with his finger*"
8:7 **cum... perseverarent**: impf. subj. in *cum* causal clause, "*since they persisted questioning him*"
  interrogantes: supplementary part. after *perseverarent*
  vestrum: partitive gen., "who *of you*"
  mittat: pres. subj. jussive, "let him throw"
8:9 **unus post unum exibant**: construction according to sense rather than agreement, "one after another they left"
  solus: "Jesus *alone* remained"

121

¹¹ ἡ δὲ εἶπεν «Οὐδείς, κύριε.»

εἶπεν δὲ ὁ Ἰησοῦς «Οὐδὲ ἐγώ σε κατακρίνω· πορεύου, ἀπὸ τοῦ νῦν μηκέτι ἁμάρτανε.»

Dispute Over Jesus' Testimony

¹² πάλιν οὖν αὐτοῖς ἐλάλησεν ὁ Ἰησοῦς λέγων «Ἐγώ εἰμι τὸ φῶς τοῦ κόσμου· ὁ ἀκολουθῶν μοι οὐ μὴ περιπατήσῃ ἐν τῇ σκοτίᾳ, ἀλλ᾽ ἕξει τὸ φῶς τῆς ζωῆς.»

¹³ εἶπον οὖν αὐτῷ οἱ Φαρισαῖοι «Σὺ περὶ σεαυτοῦ μαρτυρεῖς· ἡ μαρτυρία σου οὐκ ἔστιν ἀληθής.»

¹⁴ ἀπεκρίθη Ἰησοῦς καὶ εἶπεν αὐτοῖς «Κἂν ἐγὼ μαρτυρῶ περὶ ἐμαυτοῦ, ἀληθής ἐστιν ἡ μαρτυρία μου, ὅτι οἶδα πόθεν ἦλθον καὶ ποῦ ὑπάγω· ὑμεῖς δὲ οὐκ οἴδατε πόθεν ἔρχομαι ἢ ποῦ ὑπάγω. ¹⁵ ὑμεῖς κατὰ τὴν σάρκα κρίνετε, ἐγὼ οὐ κρίνω οὐδένα. ¹⁶ καὶ ἐὰν κρίνω δὲ ἐγώ, ἡ κρίσις ἡ ἐμὴ ἀληθινή ἐστιν, ὅτι μόνος οὐκ εἰμί, ἀλλ᾽ ἐγὼ

ἀκολουθέω: to follow
ἁμαρτάνω: to sin
κόσμος, ὁ: world
μαρτυρία, ἡ: witness, testimony, evidence
μηκέτι: no more, no longer
μόνος, -η, -ον: alone

πάλιν: again
πέμπω: to send, despatch
σάρξ, -κος, ἡ: flesh
σκοτία, ἡ: darkness, gloom
ὑπάγω: to withdraw, go
φῶς, φωτός, τό: light, daylight

8:11　ἡ δὲ: "*but she* said"
　　　ἀπὸ τοῦ νῦν: "from the present" i.e. from now on
8:12　οὐ μὴ περιπατήσῃ: aor. subj. of περι-πατέω expressing strong denial, "he will surely not walk around"
　　　ἕξει: fut. of ἔχω, "*he will have* the light"
8:14　κἂν (=καὶ ἐὰν) μαρτυρῶ: pres. subj. in pres. general protasis, "even if I am witnessing"
　　　πόθεν ἦλθον ... ποῦ ὑπάγω: ind. quest., "I know *whence I came ...where I go*"
8:15　οὐ κρίνω οὐδένα: οὐδένα is emphatic, "I judge *no one*"
8:16　ἐὰν κρίνω: pres. subj. of κρίνω in pres. general protasis, "if ever I judge"

¹¹ Quae dixit: "Nemo, Domine."

Dixit autem Iesus: "Nec ego te condemno; vade et amplius iam noli peccare."

Dispute Over Jesus' Testimony

¹² Iterum ergo locutus est eis Iesus dicens: "Ego sum lux mundi; qui sequitur me, non ambulabit in tenebris, sed habebit lucem vitae."

¹³ Dixerunt ergo ei pharisaei: "Tu de teipso testimonium perhibes; testimonium tuum non est verum."

¹⁴ Respondit Iesus et dixit eis: "Et si ego testimonium perhibeo de meipso, verum est testimonium meum, quia scio unde veni et quo vado; vos autem nescitis unde venio aut quo vado. ¹⁵ Vos secundum carnem iudicatis, ego non iudico quemquam. ¹⁶ Et si iudico ego, iudicium meum verum est, quia solus non sum, sed ego

---

ambulo, (1): to walk
amplior, amplius: further, more
iudico (1): to judge
loquor, (3) **locutus sum**: to speak
lux, lucis *f.* light
nescio, (4): to not know, be ignorant
nolo, nolle: to wish not to (+ *inf.*)
pecco, (1): to sin

perhibeo, (2): to present, give, bestow
secundum: according to (+ *acc.*)
sequor, (3), **secutus sum**: follow
tenebrae, -arum *f.* darkness
vado (3): to go
verus, -a, -um: true
vita, -ae *f.* life

8:14 **si ... perhibeo**: an instance in which a presesnt general condition is translated with a pres. indic. instead of a fut. perf., "if (ever) I bear witness"
unde veni et quo vado: vivid ind. quest., "know *whence I came and whither I go*"
8:16 **ego et Pater**: (sc. *iudicamus*), "*both I and the father* judge"
si iudico: pres. indicative in general condition instead of a fut. perf., "if I judge"

καὶ ὁ πέμψας με. ¹⁷ καὶ ἐν τῷ νόμῳ δὲ τῷ ὑμετέρῳ γέγραπται ὅτι δύο ἀνθρώπων ἡ μαρτυρία ἀληθής ἐστιν. ¹⁸ ἐγώ εἰμι ὁ μαρτυρῶν περὶ ἐμαυτοῦ καὶ μαρτυρεῖ περὶ ἐμοῦ ὁ πέμψας με πατήρ.»

¹⁹ ἔλεγον οὖν αὐτῷ «Ποῦ ἐστὶν ὁ πατήρ σου;»

ἀπεκρίθη Ἰησοῦς «Οὔτε ἐμὲ οἴδατε οὔτε τὸν πατέρα μου· εἰ ἐμὲ ᾔδειτε, καὶ τὸν πατέρα μου ἂν ᾔδειτε.» ²⁰ ταῦτα τὰ ῥήματα ἐλάλησεν ἐν τῷ γαζοφυλακίῳ διδάσκων ἐν τῷ ἱερῷ· καὶ οὐδεὶς ἐπίασεν αὐτόν, ὅτι οὔπω ἐληλύθει ἡ ὥρα αὐτοῦ.

Dispute Over Who Jesus Is

²¹ εἶπεν οὖν πάλιν αὐτοῖς «Ἐγὼ ὑπάγω καὶ ζητήσετέ με, καὶ ἐν τῇ ἁμαρτίᾳ ὑμῶν ἀποθανεῖσθε· ὅπου ἐγὼ ὑπάγω ὑμεῖς οὐ δύνασθε ἐλθεῖν.»

²² ἔλεγον οὖν οἱ Ἰουδαῖοι «Μήτι ἀποκτενεῖ ἑαυτὸν ὅτι λέγει Ὅπου ἐγὼ ὑπάγω ὑμεῖς οὐ δύνασθε ἐλθεῖν ;»

ἀληθής, -ές: unconcealed, true
ἁμαρτία, ἡ: a failure, fault, sin
γαζοφυλάκιον, τό: a treasury
διδάσκω: to teach

ζητέω: to seek, seek for
νόμος, ὁ: custom, law
ῥῆμα, -ατος, τό: a word, saying
ὑμέτερος, -α, -ον: your, yours

8:17 γέγραπται: perf., "it is written" (Deut. 19:15)
8:19 εἰ ἐμὲ ᾔδειτε : plupf. in pres. contrafactual protasis, "*if you knew me,* you would know my father"
8:20 ἐληλύθει: plupf., "his hour *had not yet come*"
8:21 ζητήσετε: fut., "*you will seek* me"
    ἀποθανεῖσθε: fut. of ἀποθνήσκω, "*you will die* in sin"
    ὅπου ...ὑπάγω: local relaative clause where we expect ποῖ, "whither I go"
8:22 μήτι ἀποκτενεῖ: expecting a neg. answer, "he won't kill himself, will he?"

et, qui me misit, Pater. ¹⁷ Sed et in lege vestra scriptum est, quia duorum hominum testimonium verum est. ¹⁸ Ego sum, qui testimonium perhibeo de meipso, et testimonium perhibet de me, qui misit me, Pater."

¹⁹ Dicebant ergo ei: "Ubi est Pater tuus?"

Respondit Iesus: "Neque me scitis neque Patrem meum; si me sciretis, forsitan et Patrem meum sciretis." ²⁰ Haec verba locutus est in gazophylacio docens in templo; et nemo apprehendit eum, quia necdum venerat hora eius.

Dispute Over Who Jesus Is

²¹ Dixit ergo iterum eis: "Ego vado, et quaeretis me et in peccato vestro moriemini! Quo ego vado, vos non potestis venire."

²² Dicebant ergo Iudaei: "Numquid interficiet semetipsum, quia dicit: 'Quo ego vado, vos non potestis venire'?"

---

apprehendo, (3), **apprehendi, apprehensus**: to seize, grasp, arrest	**interficio**, (3): to kill
duo, duae, duo: two	**morior** (3): to die
forsitan: perhaps	**necdum**: not yet
gazophylachium, -i *n*: offertory box, treasury	**semetipse, -a, -um**: one's self
homo, hominis *m*: man	**testimonium, -i** *n*: testimony
	verbum, -i *n*: word

8:17   **quia verum est:** ind. st., "it is written *that it is true*"
8:19   **si... sciretis... sciretis:** impf. subj. in pres. contrary to fact cond., "*If you knew* me... *then you would know* my father"
8:21   **quaeretis ...moriemini:** fut., "you will seek ...you will die"
8:22   **numquid interficiet:** fut., "surely he won't kill himself?"

²³ καὶ ἔλεγεν αὐτοῖς «Ὑμεῖς ἐκ τῶν κάτω ἐστέ, ἐγὼ ἐκ τῶν ἄνω εἰμί· ὑμεῖς ἐκ τούτου τοῦ κόσμου ἐστέ, ἐγὼ οὐκ εἰμὶ ἐκ τοῦ κόσμου τούτου. ²⁴ εἶπον οὖν ὑμῖν ὅτι ἀποθανεῖσθε ἐν ταῖς ἁμαρτίαις ὑμῶν· ἐὰν γὰρ μὴ πιστεύσητε ὅτι ἐγώ εἰμι, ἀποθανεῖσθε ἐν ταῖς ἁμαρτίαις ὑμῶν.»

²⁵ ἔλεγον οὖν αὐτῷ «Σὺ τίς εἶ;» εἶπεν αὐτοῖς ὁ Ἰησοῦς «Τὴν ἀρχὴν ὅτι καὶ λαλῶ ὑμῖν. ²⁶ πολλὰ ἔχω περὶ ὑμῶν λαλεῖν καὶ κρίνειν· ἀλλ' ὁ πέμψας με ἀληθής ἐστιν, κἀγὼ ἃ ἤκουσα παρ' αὐτοῦ ταῦτα λαλῶ εἰς τὸν κόσμον.»

²⁷ οὐκ ἔγνωσαν ὅτι τὸν πατέρα αὐτοῖς ἔλεγεν. ²⁸ εἶπεν οὖν ὁ Ἰησοῦς «Ὅταν ὑψώσητε τὸν υἱὸν τοῦ ἀνθρώπου, τότε γνώσεσθε ὅτι ἐγώ εἰμι, καὶ ἀπ' ἐμαυτοῦ ποιῶ οὐδέν, ἀλλὰ καθὼς ἐδίδαξέν με ὁ πατὴρ ταῦτα λαλῶ. ²⁹ καὶ ὁ πέμψας με μετ' ἐμοῦ ἐστίν· οὐκ ἀφῆκέν με μόνον, ὅτι ἐγὼ

ἁμαρτία, ἡ: sin
ἄνω (adv.): upwards
ἀφίημι: to send forth, discharge
γινώσκω: to know
κάτω (adv.): down, downwards

κόσμος, ὁ: the world
λαλέω: to talk, say
πατήρ, πατρός, ὁ: a father
τότε: at that time, then
ὑψόω: to lift high, exalt

8:23 ἐκ τῶν κάτω/ἄνω : "from the things below/above"
8:24 ἀποθανεῖσθε: fut. in apodosis, "you will die"
    ἐὰν γὰρ μὴ πιστεύσητε: aor. subj. of πιστεύω in fut. more vivid protasis, "for unless you believe"
8:25 τὴν ἀρχὴν: acc. adverbial, "from the beginning"
    ὅτι καὶ λαλῶ: noun phrase as pred., "(I am) what I am saying"
8:26 ἔχω: "I am able" + inf.
8:27 οὐκ ἔγνωσαν: aor., "they did not realize"
8:28 ὅταν ὑψώσητε: aor. subj. in general temporal clause linked to a future more vivid protasis, "when(ever) you exalt"
    γνώσεσθε: fut. of γινώσκω, "then you will realize"
    καθὼς ἐδίδαξέν: aor., "just as he taught me"
8:29 οὐκ ἀφῆκέν: aor. of ἀπο-ίημι, *"he has not left* me alone"

²³ Et dicebat eis: "Vos de deorsum estis, ego de supernis sum; vos de mundo hoc estis, ego non sum de hoc mundo. ²⁴ Dixi ergo vobis quia moriemini in peccatis vestris; si enim non credideritis quia ego sum, moriemini in peccatis vestris."

²⁵ Dicebant ergo ei: "Tu quis es?" Dixit eis Iesus: "In principio id quod et loquor vobis! ²⁶ Multa habeo de vobis loqui et iudicare; sed, qui misit me, verax est, et ego, quae audivi ab eo, haec loquor ad mundum."

²⁷ Non cognoverunt quia Patrem eis dicebat. ²⁸ Dixit ergo eis Iesus: "Cum exaltaveritis Filium hominis, tunc cognoscetis quia ego sum et a meipso facio nihil, sed, sicut docuit me Pater, haec loquor. ²⁹ Et qui me misit, mecum est; non reliquit me solum, quia ego,

---

audio, (4), audivi, auditus: to hear
deorsum: down, downwards, below
enim: indeed, in fact
exalto, (1): to exalt, elevate, praise
filius, fili *m*: son
mitto, (3), misi, missus: to send

mundus, -i *m*: world
nihil: nothing
principium, -i *n*: beginning
supernus, -a, -um: heaven, above
verax, -a, -um: speaking the truth, truthful
relinquo, (3), reliqui, relictus: to leave
    behind, abandon

8:23 **de deorsum**: adv. as object of prep., "from below"
8:24 **quia moriemini**" ind. st., "I said *that you will die*"
 si... credideritis: fut. perf. in future more vivid protasis, "if you will not have believed"
 habeo: "I am able to" + inf. translating ἔχω
8:27 **patrem**: acc. without preposition, "that he was speaking *about the father*"
8:28 **cum exaltaveritis**: fut. perf. in temporal clause with conditional force, "*when you exalt* (i.e. if you exalt) then you will know"

τὰ ἀρεστὰ αὐτῷ ποιῶ πάντοτε.» ³⁰ ταῦτα αὐτοῦ λαλοῦντος πολλοὶ ἐπίστευσαν εἰς αὐτόν.

Dispute Over Whose Children Jesus' Opponents Are

³¹ ἔλεγεν οὖν ὁ Ἰησοῦς πρὸς τοὺς πεπιστευκότας αὐτῷ Ἰουδαίους «Ἐὰν ὑμεῖς μείνητε ἐν τῷ λόγῳ τῷ ἐμῷ, ἀληθῶς μαθηταί μού ἐστε, ³² καὶ γνώσεσθε τὴν ἀλήθειαν, καὶ ἡ ἀλήθεια ἐλευθερώσει ὑμᾶς.»

³³ ἀπεκρίθησαν πρὸς αὐτόν «Σπέρμα Ἀβραάμ ἐσμεν καὶ οὐδενὶ δεδουλεύκαμεν πώποτε· πῶς σὺ λέγεις ὅτι Ἐλεύθεροι γενήσεσθε ;»

³⁴ ἀπεκρίθη αὐτοῖς ὁ Ἰησοῦς «Ἀμὴν ἀμὴν λέγω ὑμῖν ὅτι πᾶς ὁ ποιῶν τὴν ἁμαρτίαν δοῦλός ἐστιν [τῆς ἁμαρτίας]· ³⁵ ὁ δὲ δοῦλος οὐ μένει ἐν τῇ οἰκίᾳ εἰς τὸν αἰῶνα· ὁ υἱὸς μένει εἰς τὸν αἰῶνα. ³⁶ ἐὰν οὖν ὁ υἱὸς ὑμᾶς ἐλευθερώσῃ,

Ἀβραάμ (*indecl.*): Abraham	ἐλευθερόω: to free, set free
αἰών, -ῶνος, ὁ: age	μαθητής, -οῦ, ὁ: a disciple
ἀλήθεια, ἡ: the truth	μένω: to remain
ἀληθῶς: truly	οἰκία, ἡ: a building, house, dwelling
ἀρεστός, -η, -ον: pleasing to (+ *dat.*)	οὐδείς, οὐδεμία, οὐδέν: no one, nothing
γινώσκω: to know	πάντοτε: at all times, always
δουλεύω: to be a slave	πώποτε: ever yet
δοῦλος, ὁ: a slave	σπέρμα, -ατος, τό: a seed

8:30 λαλοῦντος: pres. part. in gen. abs., "him (Jesus) *speaking* these things"
8:31 πρὸς τοὺς πεπιστευκότας: perf. part. attrib., "to those who believed"
    ἐὰν ὑμεῖς μείνητε: aor. subj. in pres. general protasis, "*if you remain*, then you are"
8:32 γνώσεσθε ... ἐλευθερώσει: fut., switching to a future more vivid apodosis, "and you will know ... and the truth *will set you free*"
8:33 δεδουλεύκαμεν: perf., "we have not been enslaved to" + *dat.*
    ὅτι: here introducing the last verse (although not the exact words) in direct speech, "how do you know *that?*"
    γενήσεσθε: fut. of γίνομαι, "that *you will become*"
8:34 ὁ ποιῶν: pres. part. attrib. with general force, "every (i.e. any) man *doing*"
8:35 εἰς τὸν αἰῶνα: "forever"
8:36 ἐὰν ἐλευθερώσῃ: aor. subj. of ἐλευθερόω in fut. more vivid protasis, "if he frees you"

quae placita sunt ei, facio semper." ³⁰ Haec illo loquente, multi crediderunt in eum.

Dispute Over Whose Children Jesus' Opponents Are

³¹ Dicebat ergo Iesus ad eos, qui crediderunt ei, Iudaeos: "Si vos manseritis in sermone meo, vere discipuli mei estis ³² et cognoscetis veritatem, et veritas liberabit vos."

³³ Responderunt ei: "Semen Abrahae sumus et nemini servivimus umquam! Quomodo tu dicis: 'Liberi fietis'?"

³⁴ Respondit eis Iesus: "Amen, amen dico vobis: Omnis, qui facit peccatum, servus est peccati. ³⁵ Servus autem non manet in domo in aeternum; filius manet in aeternum. ³⁶ Si ergo Filius vos liberaverit,

---

Abraham, -ae *m*: Abraham
aeternus, -a, -um: eternal, everlasting
fio, (3): to become
liber, -a, -um: free
libero, (1): to free
maneo, (2), **mansi, mansus**: to remain, stay
nemo, neminis *m/f*: no one
placeo, (2), **placui, placitus**: to please, give pleasure to (+ *dat.*)

semen, -inis *n*: seed, line
semper: always
sermo, sermonis *m*: diction, speech
servio, (4), **servivi, servitus**: to serve (+ *dat.*)
servus, -i *m*: slave, servant
umquam: ever, at any time
vere: really, truly
veritas, veritatis *f*: truth, fact

8:29   **quae placita sunt**: "because I do (those things) *which are pleasing*"
8:30   **illo loquente**: abl. abs., *"with him speaking* these things"
8:31   **si… manseritis**: fut. perf. in pres. gen. protasis, "if you have abided"
8:32   **cognoscetis… liberabit**: fut. more vivid apodosis, "then you will learn… it will free you"
8:33   **fietis**: fut. pass., *"you will become* free"
8:36   **si… liberaverit**: fut. perf. in future more vivid protasis: "if he frees"

ὄντως ἐλεύθεροι ἔσεσθε. ³⁷ οἶδα ὅτι σπέρμα Ἀβραάμ ἐστε·
ἀλλὰ ζητεῖτέ με ἀποκτεῖναι, ὅτι ὁ λόγος ὁ ἐμὸς οὐ χωρεῖ ἐν
ὑμῖν. ³⁸ ἃ ἐγὼ ἑώρακα παρὰ τῷ πατρὶ λαλῶ· καὶ ὑμεῖς οὖν
ἃ ἠκούσατε παρὰ τοῦ πατρὸς ποιεῖτε.»

³⁹ ἀπεκρίθησαν καὶ εἶπαν αὐτῷ ‘Ο «πατὴρ ἡμῶν Ἀβραάμ
ἐστιν.»

λέγει αὐτοῖς ὁ Ἰησοῦς «Εἰ τέκνα τοῦ Ἀβραάμ ἐστε, τὰ
ἔργα τοῦ Ἀβραάμ ποιεῖτε· ⁴⁰ νῦν δὲ ζητεῖτέ με ἀποκτεῖναι,
ἄνθρωπον ὃς τὴν ἀλήθειαν ὑμῖν λελάληκα ἣν ἤκουσα παρὰ
τοῦ θεοῦ· τοῦτο Ἀβραὰμ οὐκ ἐποίησεν. ⁴¹ ὑμεῖς ποιεῖτε τὰ
ἔργα τοῦ πατρὸς ὑμῶν.»

εἶπαν αὐτῷ «Ἡμεῖς ἐκ πορνείας οὐκ ἐγεννήθημεν· ἕνα
πατέρα ἔχομεν τὸν θεόν.»

ἀκούω: to hear
ἀποκτείνω: to kill, slay
γεννάω: to beget, engender
εἷς, μία, ἕν: one
ἔργον, τό: work

πορνεία, ἡ: fornication, prostitution
σπέρμα, -ατος, τό: a seed
τέκνον, τό: a child
χωρέω: to find a place

8:36 ὄντως: adv. form of pres. part., "really"
     ἔσεσθε: fut. of εἰμί, "you will be"
8:37 ἀποκτεῖναι: fut. inf. after ζητεῖτέ, "you seek *to kill*"
8:38 ἑώρακα: perf., "what *I have seen*"
     παρὰ τοῦ πατρὸς: "what you hear *from your father*"
8:39 εἰ ἐστε ... ποιεῖτε: the form is a simple condition, but the following verse
     implies that this one is contrafactual, which would require the impf. ind.
     with ἄν in the apodosis "if you were ... then you would be doing" vs. "if you
     are ... then you are doing;" see the Latin translation.
8:40 ὃς ... λελάληκα: perf., "I *who have spoken*"
8:41 οὐκ ἐγεννήθημεν: aor. pass. of γεννάω, "we were not born"
     τὸν θεόν: "one father, namely, *God*"

vere liberi eritis. ³⁷ Scio quia semen Abrahae estis; sed quaeritis me interficere, quia sermo meus non capit in vobis. ³⁸ Ego, quae vidi apud Patrem, loquor; et vos ergo, quae audivistis a patre, facitis."

³⁹ Responderunt et dixerunt ei: "Pater noster Abraham est."

Dicit eis Iesus: "Si filii Abrahae essetis, opera Abrahae faceretis. ⁴⁰ Nunc autem quaeritis me interficere, hominem, qui veritatem vobis locutus sum, quam audivi a Deo; hoc Abraham non fecit. ⁴¹ Vos facitis opera patris vestri."

Dixerunt itaque ei: "Nos ex fornicatione non sumus nati; unum patrem habemus Deum!"

---

apud: among, with (+ *acc.*)
capio, (3): to take hold
fornicatio, -onis *f.*: fornication
interficio, (3): to kill, destroy
itaque: and so, therefore
liber, -a, -um: free
loquor, (3) **locutus sum**: to speak

nascor, (3), **natus sum**: to be born, begotten
nunc: now, today, at present
opus, operis *n*: need, work
quaero, (3): to search for, seek to (+ *inf.*)
semen, seminis *n*: seed, line
vere: really, truly

8:37   **non capit**: "because it *does not take hold*," i.e., does not find a space in
8:39   **si essetis… faceretis**: impf. subj. in pres. contrary to fact condition, "if you
          were… than you would do"

131

⁴² εἶπεν αὐτοῖς ὁ Ἰησοῦς «Εἰ ὁ θεὸς πατὴρ ὑμῶν ἦν ἠγαπᾶτε ἂν ἐμέ, ἐγὼ γὰρ ἐκ τοῦ θεοῦ ἐξῆλθον καὶ ἥκω· οὐδὲ γὰρ ἀπ' ἐμαυτοῦ ἐλήλυθα, ἀλλ' ἐκεῖνός με ἀπέστειλεν. ⁴³ διὰ τί τὴν λαλιὰν τὴν ἐμήν οὐ γινώσκετε; ὅτι οὐ δύνασθε ἀκούειν τὸν λόγον τὸν ἐμόν. ⁴⁴ ὑμεῖς ἐκ τοῦ πατρὸς τοῦ διαβόλου ἐστὲ καὶ τὰς ἐπιθυμίας τοῦ πατρὸς ὑμῶν θέλετε ποιεῖν. ἐκεῖνος ἀνθρωποκτόνος ἦν ἀπ' ἀρχῆς, καὶ ἐν τῇ ἀληθείᾳ οὐκ ἔστηκεν, ὅτι οὐκ ἔστιν ἀλήθεια ἐν αὐτῷ. ὅταν λαλῇ τὸ ψεῦδος, ἐκ τῶν ἰδίων λαλεῖ, ὅτι ψεύστης ἐστὶν καὶ ὁ πατὴρ αὐτοῦ. ⁴⁵ ἐγὼ δὲ ὅτι τὴν ἀλήθειαν λέγω, οὐ πιστεύετέ μοι. ⁴⁶ τίς ἐξ ὑμῶν ἐλέγχει με περὶ ἁμαρτίας; εἰ ἀλήθειαν λέγω, διὰ τί ὑμεῖς οὐ πιστεύετέ μοι; ⁴⁷ ὁ ὢν ἐκ τοῦ θεοῦ τὰ ῥήματα τοῦ θεοῦ ἀκούει· διὰ τοῦτο ὑμεῖς οὐκ ἀκούετε ὅτι ἐκ τοῦ θεοῦ οὐκ ἐστέ.»

ἀγαπάω: to love, be fond of
ἀνθρωποκτόνος, -ον: homicidal
ἀποστέλλω: to send off
ἀρχή, ἡ: a beginning
διάβολος, ὁ: a devil
ἐλέγχω: to accuse
ἐπιθυμία, ἡ: desire, yearning, longing

ἥκω: to have come, be present, be here
θέλω: to will, wish, purpose
λαλιά, ἡ: talking, talk, chat
στήκω: to stand
ψεῦδος, -εος, τό: a falsehood, untruth, lie
ψεύστης, -ου, ὁ: a liar, cheat

8:42 **εἰ ὁ θεὸς ἦν ... ἠγαπᾶτε ἂν ἐμέ**: impf. tenses in pres. contrafactual condition, "if God were your father, you would love me"

    ἐλήλυθα: perf., "I did not come"

8:44 **ἀπ' ἀρχῆς**: "from the start"

    ἔστηκεν: impf. of **στήκω**, a collateral form of **ἵστημι**, "was not standing"

    ὅταν λαλῇ: pres. subj. in general temp. clause, "whenever he speaks"

    ὁ πατὴρ αὐτοῦ: not "and so is his father," but "and the father of this (i.e. of falsehood)"

8:47 **ὅτι ... οὐκ ἐστέ**: causal, "because you are not"

⁴² Dixit eis Iesus: "Si Deus pater vester esset, diligeretis me; ego enim ex Deo processi et veni; neque enim a meipso veni, sed ille me misit. ⁴³ Quare loquelam meam non cognoscitis? Quia non potestis audire sermonem meum. ⁴⁴ Vos ex patre Diabolo estis et desideria patris vestri vultis facere. Ille homicida erat ab initio et in veritate non stabat, quia non est veritas in eo. Cum loquitur mendacium, ex propriis loquitur, quia mendax est et pater eius. ⁴⁵ Ego autem quia veritatem dico, non creditis mihi. ⁴⁶ Quis ex vobis arguit me de peccato? Si veritatem dico, quare vos non creditis mihi? ⁴⁷ Qui est ex Deo, verba Dei audit; propterea vos non auditis, quia ex Deo non estis."

---

arguo, (3), **argui, argutus**: to prove, accuse
desiderium, -i *n*: desire
diabolus, -i *m*: devil, Satan
diligo, (3): to love, hold dear
homicida, -ae *m/f*: murderer, homicide
initium, -i *n*: beginning
loquela, -ae *f*: speech
loquor, (3), **locutus sum**: speak
mendacium, -i *n*: falsehood, untruth

possum, posse, potui: be able, can
procedo, (3), **processi, processus**: to proceed, advance
proprius, -a, -um: own, very own
quare: in what way? how?
sto, (1): to stand
vado, (3): to go
vester, -tra, -trum: your
volo, velle, volui: to be willing, wish

8:42 **si... esset...diligeretis**: impf. subj. pres. contrary to fact condition, "*if he were* your father ...*then you would love*"
8:44 **pater**: predicate nom., "and he is *the father* of it (i.e. of the lie)"
vultis: pres. of *volo*, "you wish to" + inf.

133

Jesus' Claims About Himself

⁴⁸ ἀπεκρίθησαν οἱ Ἰουδαῖοι καὶ εἶπαν αὐτῷ «Οὐ καλῶς λέγομεν ἡμεῖς ὅτι Σαμαρείτης εἶ σὺ καὶ δαιμόνιον ἔχεις;»

⁴⁹ ἀπεκρίθη Ἰησοῦς «Ἐγὼ δαιμόνιον οὐκ ἔχω, ἀλλὰ τιμῶ τὸν πατέρα μου, καὶ ὑμεῖς ἀτιμάζετέ με. ⁵⁰ ἐγὼ δὲ οὐ ζητῶ τὴν δόξαν μου· ἔστιν ὁ ζητῶν καὶ κρίνων. ⁵¹ ἀμὴν ἀμὴν λέγω ὑμῖν, ἐάν τις τὸν ἐμὸν λόγον τηρήσῃ, θάνατον οὐ μὴ θεωρήσῃ εἰς τὸν αἰῶνα.»

⁵² εἶπαν αὐτῷ οἱ Ἰουδαῖοι «Νῦν ἐγνώκαμεν ὅτι δαιμόνιον ἔχεις. Ἀβραὰμ ἀπέθανεν καὶ οἱ προφῆται, καὶ σὺ λέγεις Ἐάν τις τὸν λόγον μου τηρήσῃ, οὐ μὴ γεύσηται θανάτου εἰς τὸν αἰῶνα· ⁵³ μὴ σὺ μείζων εἶ τοῦ πατρὸς ἡμῶν Ἀβραάμ, ὅστις ἀπέθανεν; καὶ οἱ προφῆται ἀπέθανον· τίνα σεαυτὸν ποιεῖς;»

ἀποθνήσκω: to die off, die
ἀτιμάζω: to dishonour, slight
γεύω: to give a taste of
δαιμόνιον, τό: an evil spirit
δόξα, ἡ: glory, opinion

θάνατος, ὁ: death
θεωρέω: to look at, view, behold
προφήτης, -ου, ὁ: a prophet
τηρέω: to watch over, protect, keep
τιμάω: to honor

8:48 οὐ καλῶς λέγομεν: expecting an affirmative answer, "do we not speak correctly?"
8:50 ἔστιν: note the accent, "*there is* one who seeks and judges"
8:51 ἐάν τις τηρήσῃ: aor. subj. in fut. more vivid protasis, "*if someone keeps* my word"
οὐ μὴ θεωρήσῃ: aor. subj. in strong denial, "he will surely not see"
8:52 ἐγνώκαμεν: perf. of γινώσκω, "we have realized"
ἀπέθανεν: aor., "Abraham and the prophets died"
οὐ μὴ γεύσηται: aor. subj. in strong denial, "you surely will not taste;" again, having the form of a direct quote, but changing the wording slightly
8:53 μὴ σὺ μείζων εἶ: expecting a negative answer, "surely you are not greater"
τίνα σεαυτὸν ποιεῖς: "whom do you fashion yourself (to be)?"

Jesus' Claims About Himself

⁴⁸ Responderunt Iudaei et dixerunt ei: "Nonne bene dicimus nos, quia Samaritanus es tu et daemonium habes?"

⁴⁹ Respondit Iesus: "Ego daemonium non habeo, sed honorifico Patrem meum, et vos inhonoratis me.   ⁵⁰ Ego autem non quaero gloriam meam; est qui quaerit et iudicat.   ⁵¹ Amen, amen dico vobis: Si quis sermonem meum servaverit, mortem non videbit in aeternum."

⁵² Dixerunt ergo ei Iudaei: "Nunc cognovimus quia daemonium habes. Abraham mortuus est et prophetae, et tu dicis: 'Si quis sermonem meum servaverit, non gustabit mortem in aeternum.' ⁵³ Numquid tu maior es patre nostro Abraham, qui mortuus est? Et prophetae mortui sunt! Quem teipsum facis?"

---

bene: well
daemonium, -i *n*: a demon
glorifico, (1): to glorify, honor
gusto, (1): to taste
honorifico, (1): to honor
inhonoro, (1): to dishonor
maior, -us: greater, larger

morior, (3), **mortuus sum**: to die
mors, mortis *f*: death
nihil: nothing
nosco, (3), **novi, notus**: to know
servo, (1): to watch over; protect, serve
similis, -e : like, similar

8:51   **si... servaverit**: fut. perf. in future more vivid protasis, "if you will obey"
         mortuus est: s. but the subj. is both *Abraham* and *prophetae*, "they are dead"
8:53   **Abraham**: abl. in apposition to *patre*, "greater than our father, *Abraham*"
         quem: predicate acc., "*whom* do you fashion yourself to be?"

⁵⁴ ἀπεκρίθη Ἰησοῦς «Ἐὰν ἐγὼ δοξάσω ἐμαυτόν, ἡ δόξα μου οὐδέν ἐστιν· ἔστιν ὁ πατήρ μου ὁ δοξάζων με, ὃν ὑμεῖς λέγετε ὅτι θεὸς ὑμῶν ἐστίν, ⁵⁵ καὶ οὐκ ἐγνώκατε αὐτόν, ἐγὼ δὲ οἶδα αὐτόν· κἂν εἴπω ὅτι οὐκ οἶδα αὐτόν, ἔσομαι ὅμοιος ὑμῖν ψεύστης· ἀλλὰ οἶδα αὐτὸν καὶ τὸν λόγον αὐτοῦ τηρῶ. ⁵⁶ Ἀβραὰμ ὁ πατὴρ ὑμῶν ἠγαλλιάσατο ἵνα ἴδῃ τὴν ἡμέραν τὴν ἐμήν, καὶ εἶδεν καὶ ἐχάρη.»

⁵⁷ εἶπαν οὖν οἱ Ἰουδαῖοι πρὸς αὐτόν «Πεντήκοντα ἔτη οὔπω ἔχεις καὶ Ἀβραὰμ ἑώρακας;»

⁵⁸ εἶπεν αὐτοῖς Ἰησοῦς «Ἀμὴν ἀμὴν λέγω ὑμῖν, πρὶν Ἀβραὰμ γενέσθαι ἐγὼ εἰμί.» ⁵⁹ ἦραν οὖν λίθους ἵνα βάλωσιν ἐπ᾽ αὐτόν· Ἰησοῦς δὲ ἐκρύβη καὶ ἐξῆλθεν ἐκ τοῦ ἱεροῦ.

ἀγαλλιάω: to rejoice exceedingly
αἴρω: to take up, raise, lift up
δοξάζομαι: to be magnified, glorified
δοξάζω: to magnify, glorify
ἔτος, -εος, τό: a year
κρύπτω: to hide, cover, cloak
οἶδα: to know (perf.)

ὅμοιος, -α, -ον: like, resembling (+ dat.)
οὔπω: not yet
πεντήκοντα (indecl.): fifty
πρίν: before (+ inf.)
τηρέω: to keep, preserve
χαίρω: to rejoice, be glad, be delighted
ψεύστης, -ου, ὁ: a liar, cheat

8:54 ἐὰν ἐγὼ δοξάσω: aor. subj. in pres. general protasis, "if ever I glorify"
8:55 ἐγνώκατε: perf., "you have not known"
      κἂν εἴπω: aor. subj. in fut. more vivid protasis, "even if I say"
      ἔσομαι: fut., "I shall be"
8:56 ἠγαλλιάσατο: aor., "he rejoiced"
      ἵνα ἴδῃ: aor. subj. complementing ἠγαλλιάσατο, "he rejoiced *to see*"
      ἐχάρη: aor. pass. of χαίρω, "he rejoiced"
8:57 πεντήκοντα ἔτη οὔπς ἔχεις: "you don't yet have 50 years"
8:58 πρὶν Ἀβραὰμ γενέσθαι: aor. inf. of γίνομαι, "before A. was born"
8:59 ἦραν: aor. of αἴρω, "they took up"
      ἵνα βάλωσιν: aor. subj. in purpose clause, "tghey took up stones in order to cast"
      ἐκρύβη: aor.pass. of κρύπτω, "he became hidden"

⁵⁴ Respondit Iesus: "Si ego glorifico meipsum, gloria mea nihil est; est Pater meus, qui glorificat me, quem vos dicitis: 'Deus noster est!' ⁵⁵ et non cognovistis eum. Ego autem novi eum. Et si dixero: 'Non scio eum,' ero similis vobis, mendax; sed scio eum et sermonem eius servo. ⁵⁶ Abraham pater vester exsultavit, ut videret diem meum; et vidit et gavisus est."

⁵⁷ Dixerunt ergo Iudaei ad eum: "Quinquaginta annos nondum habes et Abraham vidisti?"

⁵⁸ Dixit eis Iesus: "Amen, amen dico vobis: Antequam Abraham fieret, ego sum." ⁵⁹ Tulerunt ergo lapides, ut iacerent in eum; Iesus autem abscondit se et exivit de templo.

---

abscondo, (3), abscondi: to hide, conceal
annus, -i *m*: year
antequam: before
cognosco, (3) cognovi, cognitus: to know
dies, diei *m/f*: day
exeo, (4), exivi: to go, exit, leave
exsulto, (1): to rejoice, exalt
fero, ferre, tuli: to carry, picked up

gaudeo, (2), gavisus sum: to be glad, rejoice
gloria, -ae *f*: glory
iacio, (3): to throw
mendax, mendacis (*gen.*): lying, false
nondum: not yet
quinquaginta: fifty
similis, -e: similar to (+ *dat.*)
templum, -i *n*: temple

8:54 **si ... glorifico**: pres. indic. in general condition, instead of a fut. perf., "if ever I glorify"

8:56 **si dixero**: fut. perf. in fut. more vivid protasis, "If I say"
    mendax (sc. erit): "then it will be false"
    ut videret: impf. subj. complementing *exsultavit*, "he rejoiced *to see*"

8:58 **antequam ... fieret**: impf. subj. translating the Greek expression πρίν + inf. which is not indefinite, "before Abraham came into being"

8:59 **ut iacerent**: impf. subj. purpose clause, "they took up rocks *in order to throw* them"

Chapter 9

Jesus Heals a Man Born Blind

¹ καὶ παράγων εἶδεν ἄνθρωπον τυφλὸν ἐκ γενετῆς. ² καὶ ἠρώτησαν αὐτὸν οἱ μαθηταὶ αὐτοῦ λέγοντες «Ῥαββεί, τίς ἥμαρτεν, οὗτος ἢ οἱ γονεῖς αὐτοῦ, ἵνα τυφλὸς γεννηθῇ;»

³ ἀπεκρίθη Ἰησοῦς «Οὔτε οὗτος ἥμαρτεν οὔτε οἱ γονεῖς αὐτοῦ, ἀλλ' ἵνα φανερωθῇ τὰ ἔργα τοῦ θεοῦ ἐν αὐτῷ. ⁴ ἡμᾶς δεῖ ἐργάζεσθαι τὰ ἔργα τοῦ πέμψαντός με ἕως ἡμέρα ἐστίν· ἔρχεται νὺξ ὅτε οὐδεὶς δύναται ἐργάζεσθαι. ⁵ ὅταν ἐν τῷ κόσμῳ ὦ, φῶς εἰμὶ τοῦ κόσμου.»

ἁμαρτάνω: to miss, sin
γενετή, ἡ: the hour of birth
γονεύς, -έως, ὁ: a parent
δεῖ: it is necessary
ἐργάζομαι: to work, labour
ἔρχομαι: to come or go
ἐρωτάω: to ask
ἕως: until, while
ἡμέρα, ἡ: day

κόσμος, ὁ: the world
νύξ, νυκτός, ἡ: a night
παράγω: to lead by or past
πέμπω: to send
Ῥαββεί: (Hebr.) teacher
τυφλός, -ή, -όν: blind
φανερόω: to make manifest
φῶς, φωτός, ὁ: a light

9:1   παράγων: pres. part. circum., "as he was passing by"
9:2   ἵνα γεννηθῇ: aor. subj. pass. of γεννάω in result clause, "who sinned *so that he was born* blind"
9:3   ἵνα φανερωθῇ: aor. subj. pass. in purpose clause, "in order to make manifest"
9:4   ἐργάζεσθαι: pres. inf. after δεῖ, "it is necessary *to do*"
9:5   ὅταν ... ὦ: pres. subj. of εἰμι in general temporal clause, "as long as I am"

Chapter 9

Jesus Heals a Man Born Blind

¹ Et praeteriens vidit hominem caecum a nativitate.   ² Et interrogaverunt eum discipuli sui dicentes: "Rabbi, quis peccavit, hic aut parentes eius, ut caecus nasceretur?"

³ Respondit Iesus: "Neque hic peccavit neque parentes eius, sed ut manifestentur opera Dei in illo.   ⁴ Nos oportet operari opera eius, qui misit me, donec dies est; venit nox, quando nemo potest operari.   ⁵ Quamdiu in mundo sum, lux sum mundi."

---

caecus, –a, -um: blind, unseeing	**nox, noctis** *f*: night
dies, -ei m/*f*: day	**operor**, (1): to labor, toil, work
donec: while, until	**oportet**, (2): it is necessary + inf.
lux, lucis *f*: light	**opus, -eris** *n*: work, deed
manifesto, (1): to reveal, make known	**parens, parentis**, m/*f*: parent
mundus, -i, *m.* world	**pecco**, (1): to sin
nascor, (3) **natus sum**: to be born	**praetereo**, (4): pass, go by, proceed
nativitas, -tatis *f*: birth	**quamdiu**: for how long, however long
nemo, neminis m/*f*: no one, nobody	**quando**: when, at what time

---

9:2 **discipuli sui:** instead of *discipuli eius*, "his disciples"

ut... nasceretur: impf. subj. in result clause, "who sinned *so that he was born blind*?"

9:3 **ut... manifestentur:** pres. subj. purpose clause, "so that they may be manifest"

9:4 **operari:** dep. inf. after impersonal *oportet*: "it is necessary *that we work*"

opera: cognate acc. after *operari*, "do the works"

venit: pres. with fut. sense, "night *will come*"

⁶ ταῦτα εἰπὼν ἔπτυσεν χαμαὶ καὶ ἐποίησεν πηλὸν ἐκ τοῦ πτύσματος, καὶ ἐπέθηκεν αὐτοῦ τὸν πηλὸν ἐπὶ τοὺς ὀφθαλμούς, ⁷ καὶ εἶπεν αὐτῷ «Ὕπαγε νίψαι εἰς τὴν κολυμβήθραν τοῦ Σιλωάμ» (ὃ ἑρμηνεύεται Ἀπεσταλμένος). ἀπῆλθεν οὖν καὶ ἐνίψατο, καὶ ἦλθεν βλέπων.

⁸ οἱ οὖν γείτονες καὶ οἱ θεωροῦντες αὐτὸν τὸ πρότερον ὅτι προσαίτης ἦν ἔλεγον «Οὐχ οὗτός ἐστιν ὁ καθήμενος καὶ προσαιτῶν;»

⁹ ἄλλοι ἔλεγον ὅτι «Οὗτός ἐστιν·»

ἄλλοι ἔλεγον Οὐχί, ἀλλὰ ὅμοιος αὐτῷ ἐστίν.

ἐκεῖνος ἔλεγεν ὅτι «Ἐγώ εἰμι.»

ἀνοίγνυμι: to open
ἀπῆλθον: to go away, depart from (*aor.*)
βλέπω: to see, have the power of sight
γείτων, -ονος, ὁ: a neighbour
ἐπιτίθημι: to lay, put or place upon
ἑρμηνεύω: to translate»
κάθημαι: to be seated
κολυμβήθρα, ἡ: a swimming-bath
νίζω: to wash the hands or feet
ὅμοιος, -α, -ον: like, resembling + dat

ὀφθαλμός, ὁ: the eye
πηλός, ὁ: clay, earth
προσαιτέω: to beg
προσαίτης, -ου, ὁ: a beggar
πρότερος, -α, -ον: prior
πτύσμα, -ατος, τό: sputum
πτύω: to spit out or up
Σιλωάμ (*indecl.*): Siloa
ὑπάγω: to go, withdraw
χαμαί (*adv.*): on the earth, on the ground

9:6   ἔπτυσεν ... ἐπέθηκεν: aor., "he spit ...he placed upon"
      αὐτοῦ: "the eyes *of him*" i.e. the blind man

9:7   νίψαι: aor. imper. of νίζω, "go, *wash!*"
      ἀπεσταλμένος: perf. part., "which means 'having been sent forth'"
      ἐνίψατο: aor. mid. of νίζω, "he washed himself"

9:8   οἱ οὖν γείτονες καὶ οἱ θεωροῦντες: although joined by καὶ, the second is
      virtually attributive, "the neighbors who saw," a common feature of biblical
      Greek (Granville Sharp's rule)
      τὸ πρότερον: acc. adverbial, "earlier"
      ὅτι προσαίτης ἦν: ind. st. with impf. tense retained, "those seeing him, *that he
      had been a beggar*"

9:9   ὅτι Ἐγώ εἰμι: ὅτι introducing direct speech, "he said 'I am'"

⁶ Haec cum dixisset, exspuit in terram et fecit lutum ex sputo et linivit lutum super oculos eius ⁷ et dixit ei: "Vade, lava in natatoria 'Siloae!'" quod interpretatur "Missus." Abiit ergo et lavit et venit videns.

⁸ Itaque vicini et, qui videbant eum prius quia mendicus erat, dicebant: "Nonne hic est, qui sedebat et mendicabat?"

⁹ alii dicebant: "Hic est!" ;

alii dicebant: "Nequaquam, sed similis est eius!"

Ille dicebat: "Ego sum!"

---

abeo, (4), **abii, abitum**: to depart, go away
alii ... alii some ... others
exspuo, (3), **exspui, exsputus**: to spit
interpretor, (3), **interpretatus sum**: to translate
lavo, (1): to wash, bathe
linio, (4), **linivi, linitus**: to smear, rub over, cover
lutum, -i *n*: mud
mendico, (1): to be a beggar

mendicus, -i *m*: beggar
natatoria, -ae *f*: swimming, pool
nequaquam: by no means
oculus, -i *m*: eye
prior, prius: earlier, previously
Siloa, -ae *f*: Siloa
similis, -e: like, similar, resembling
sputum, -i *n*: spittle
vado (3): to go
vicinus, -i *m*: neighbor

9:6 **cum dixisset**: plupf. subj. in *cum* circumstantial clause, "when he had spoken"
9:7 **missus**: perf. part., "Siloa, which is translated 'having been sent'"
videns: pres. part. circum., "he went *seeing*," i.e., able to see
9:9 **similis est eius**: "similar to him" where we would expect the dative

¹⁰ ἔλεγον οὖν αὐτῷ «Πῶς [οὖν] ἠνεῴχθησάν σου οἱ ὀφθαλμοί;»

¹¹ ἀπεκρίθη ἐκεῖνος «Ὁ ἄνθρωπος ὁ λεγόμενος Ἰησοῦς πηλὸν ἐποίησεν καὶ ἐπέχρισέν μου τοὺς ὀφθαλμοὺς καὶ εἶπέν μοι ὅτι Ὕπαγε εἰς τὸν Σιλωὰμ καὶ νίψαι· ἀπελθὼν οὖν καὶ νιψάμενος ἀνέβλεψα.»

¹² καὶ εἶπαν αὐτῷ «Ποῦ ἐστιν ἐκεῖνος;»

λέγει «Οὐκ οἶδα.»

The Pharisees Investigate the Healing

¹³ ἄγουσιν αὐτὸν πρὸς τοὺς Φαρισαίους τόν ποτε τυφλόν. ¹⁴ ἦν δὲ σάββατον ἐν ᾗ ἡμέρᾳ τὸν πηλὸν ἐποίησεν ὁ Ἰησοῦς καὶ ἀνέῳξεν αὐτοῦ τοὺς ὀφθαλμούς. ¹⁵ πάλιν οὖν ἠρώτων αὐτὸν καὶ οἱ Φαρισαῖοι πῶς ἀνέβλεψεν. ὁ δὲ εἶπεν αὐτοῖς «Πηλὸν ἐπέθηκέν μου ἐπὶ τοὺς ὀφθαλμούς, καὶ ἐνιψάμην, καὶ βλέπω.»

¹⁶ ἔλεγον οὖν ἐκ τῶν Φαρισαίων τινές «Οὐκ ἔστιν οὗτος παρὰ θεοῦ ὁ ἄνθρωπος, ὅτι τὸ σάββατον οὐ τηρεῖ.»

ἄγω: to lead, bring
ἀναβλέπω: to see again
ἀπῆλθον: to go away (*aor.*)
δύναμαι: to be able, capable, strong enough
ἐπιτίθημι: to lay, put or place upon

ἐπιχρίω: to anoint, besmear
ἐρωτάω: to ask
νίζω: to wash
τηρέω: to keep

9:10   ἠνεῴχθησάν: aor. pass. of ἀνα-οίγνυμι, "how have your eyes *been opened?*"
9:11   νιψάμενος: aor. part. mid., "having washed myself"
9:13   τόν ποτε τυφλόν: in apposition to αὐτὸν, "the one formerly blind"
9:14   ἐν ᾗ ἡμέρᾳ: "on which day"
       ἀνέῳξεν: aor. of ἀνα-οίγνυμι, "he opened"
9:15   πῶς ἀνέβλεψεν: aor. in ind. quest., "they were asking *how he saw again*"
       ἐπέθηκέν: aor. of ἐπι-τίθημι, "he placed upon"

[10] Dicebant ergo ei: "Quomodo igitur aperti sunt oculi tibi?"

[11] Respondit ille: "Homo, qui dicitur Iesus, lutum fecit et unxit oculos meos et dixit mihi: 'Vade ad Siloam et lava!' Abii ergo et lavi et vidi."

[12] Et dixerunt ei: "Ubi est ille?"

Ait: "Nescio."

The Pharisees Investigate the Healing

[13] Adducunt eum ad pharisaeos, qui caecus fuerat.   [14] Erat autem sabbatum, in qua die lutum fecit Iesus et aperuit oculos eius. [15] Iterum ergo interrogabant et eum pharisaei quomodo vidisset. Ille autem dixit eis: "Lutum posuit super oculos meos, et lavi et video."

[16] Dicebant ergo ex pharisaeis quidam: "Non est hic homo a Deo, quia sabbatum non custodit!"

---

adduco, (3): to lead, bring	**nescio** (**4**): to not know
alius, **alia**, **aliud**: other, another	**pecco**, (1): to sin
aperio, (4), **aperui**, **apertus**: to open	**pono**, (3), **posui**, **positus**: to put, place
custodio, (4): to observe, heed	**Sabbatum, -i** *n*: the Sabbath
lavo, (1)**, lavi**: to wash	**ungo**, (2), **unxi**, **unctum**: to smear, anoint, rub
lutum, -i *n*: mud	

9:15   **quomodo vidisset**: plupf. subj. indirect question, "asked *how he had seen*" i.e. how he had come to see

143

ἄλλοι [δὲ] ἔλεγον «Πῶς δύναται ἄνθρωπος ἁμαρτωλὸς τοιαῦτα σημεῖα ποιεῖν;» καὶ σχίσμα ἦν ἐν αὐτοῖς.

¹⁷ λέγουσιν οὖν τῷ τυφλῷ πάλιν «Τί σὺ λέγεις περὶ αὐτοῦ, ὅτι ἠνέῳξέν σου τοὺς ὀφθαλμούς;»

ὁ δὲ εἶπεν ὅτι «Προφήτης ἐστίν.»

¹⁸ οὐκ ἐπίστευσαν οὖν οἱ Ἰουδαῖοι περὶ αὐτοῦ ὅτι ἦν τυφλὸς καὶ ἀνέβλεψεν, ἕως ὅτου ἐφώνησαν τοὺς γονεῖς αὐτοῦ τοῦ ἀναβλέψαντος ¹⁹ καὶ ἠρώτησαν αὐτοὺς λέγοντες «Οὗτός ἐστιν ὁ υἱὸς ὑμῶν, ὃν ὑμεῖς λέγετε ὅτι τυφλὸς ἐγεννήθη; πῶς οὖν βλέπει ἄρτι;»

²⁰ ἀπεκρίθησαν οὖν οἱ γονεῖς αὐτοῦ καὶ εἶπαν «Οἴδαμεν ὅτι οὗτός ἐστιν ὁ υἱὸς ἡμῶν καὶ ὅτι τυφλὸς ἐγεννήθη· ²¹ πῶς δὲ νῦν βλέπει οὐκ οἴδαμεν, ἢ τίς ἤνοιξεν αὐτοῦ τοὺς ὀφθαλμοὺς ἡμεῖς οὐκ οἴδαμεν· αὐτὸν ἐρωτήσατε, ἡλικίαν ἔχει, αὐτὸς περὶ ἑαυτοῦ λαλήσει.» ²² ταῦτα εἶπαν οἱ γονεῖς

ἁμαρτωλός, -όν: sinful
ἀναβλέπω: to see again
ἄρτι: just now
ἕως: until, till
ἡλικία, ἡ: time of life, age
ἠρωτάω: to ask

σημεῖον, τό: a sign, a mark, token
σχίσμα, -ατος, τό: a division
τοιοῦτος, -αύτη, -οῦτο: such as this
υἱός, ὁ: a son
φωνέω: to speak

9:17 ὅτι ἠνέῳξέν: aor. of ἀνοίγνυμι, "how do you say *that he opened*"
ὁ δὲ: "*but he* said"
9:18 ἕως ὅτου (sc. χρόνου): gen., "until such time"
τοῦ ἀναβλέψαντος: aor. part. attrib. gen. s., "parents *of the man recovering*"
9:19 ἐγεννήθη: aor. pass. of γεννάω, "you say that *he was born*"
9:21 τὶς ἤνοιξεν: aor. of ἀνοίγνυμι, "we do not know *who opened*"
ἡλικίαν ἔχει: "he has the age" i.e. he is of age
αὐτὸς λαλήσει: fut., "he himself will speak"

alii autem dicebant: "Quomodo potest homo peccator haec signa facere?" Et schisma erat in eis.

¹⁷ Dicunt ergo caeco iterum: "Tu quid dicis de eo quia aperuit oculos tuos?"

Ille autem dixit: "Propheta est!"

¹⁸ Non crediderunt ergo Iudaei de illo quia caecus fuisset et vidisset, donec vocaverunt parentes eius, qui viderat. ¹⁹ Et interrogaverunt eos dicentes: "Hic est filius vester, quem vos dicitis quia caecus natus est? Quomodo ergo nunc videt?"

²⁰ Responderunt ergo parentes eius et dixerunt: "Scimus quia hic est filius noster et quia caecus natus est. ²¹ Quomodo autem nunc videat nescimus, aut quis eius aperuit oculos nos nescimus; ipsum interrogate. Aetatem habet; ipse de se loquetur!" ²² Haec dixerunt parentes

---

aetas, aetatis *f*: age
aperio, (4), aperui: to uncover, open
donec: until
peccator, peccatoris *m*: sinner, transgressor
propheta, -ae *m*: prophet

schisma, -matis *n*: schism, divide, split
scio, (4): to know, understand
signum, -i *n*: sign
voco, (1): to call, summon

9:16 **peccator:** nom. appositive, "for a man *who is a sinner*"
9:18 **quia fuisset et vidisset:** plupf. subj. in indirect statement, "believed *that he had been blind and had seen*"
    qui viderat: "the parents of him *who had seen*" (i.e. gained his sight)
9:19 **quia natus est:** ind. st., "you say *that he was born* blind"
9:21 **quomodo ... videat:** pres. subj. indirect question, "we don't know *how he can see*"
    aetatem habet: "he is of age"

αὐτοῦ ὅτι ἐφοβοῦντο τοὺς Ἰουδαίους, ἤδη γὰρ συνετέθειντο οἱ
Ἰουδαῖοι ἵνα ἐάν τις αὐτὸν ὁμολογήσῃ Χριστόν, ἀποσυνάγωγος
γένηται. ²³ διὰ τοῦτο οἱ γονεῖς αὐτοῦ εἶπαν ὅτι «Ἡλικίαν ἔχει,
αὐτὸν ἐπερωτήσατε.»

²⁴ ἐφώνησαν οὖν τὸν ἄνθρωπον ἐκ δευτέρου ὃς ἦν τυφλὸς
καὶ εἶπαν αὐτῷ «Δὸς δόξαν τῷ θεῷ· ἡμεῖς οἴδαμεν ὅτι οὗτος
ὁ ἄνθρωπος ἁμαρτωλός ἐστιν.»

²⁵ ἀπεκρίθη οὖν ἐκεῖνος «Εἰ ἁμαρτωλός ἐστιν οὐκ οἶδα·
ἓν οἶδα ὅτι τυφλὸς ὢν ἄρτι βλέπω.»

²⁶ εἶπαν οὖν αὐτῷ «Τί ἐποίησέν σοι; πῶς ἤνοιξέν σου
τοὺς ὀφθαλμούς;»

²⁷ ἀπεκρίθη αὐτοῖς «Εἶπον ὑμῖν ἤδη καὶ οὐκ ἠκούσατε·
τί πάλιν θέλετε ἀκούειν; μὴ καὶ ὑμεῖς θέλετε αὐτοῦ μαθηταὶ
γενέσθαι;»

ἁμαρτωλός, -όν: sinful
ἀποσυνάγωγος, -ον: put out of the
    synagogue
δεύτερος, -α, -ον: second
δίδωμι: to give
ἐπερωτάω: to inquire of, question, consult

ἡλικία, ἡ: time of life, age
ὁμολογέω: to agree, confirm
συντίθημι: to put together, decide
φοβέομαι: to fear
χριστός, -ή, -όν: annointed

9:22   ὅτι ἐφοβοῦντο: impf. causal, "they spoke thus *because they were afraid*"
       συνετέθειντο: plupf. of συν-τίθημι, "they had decided"
       ἵνα ... γένηται: aor. subj. of γίνομαι in noun clause complementing
         συνετέθειντο, "decided *that he would be*"
       ἐάν τις αὐτὸν ὁμολογήσῃ: aor. subj. in pres. general protasis, "if anyone
         confirms"
       Χριστόν: pred. acc., "confirms him (to be) *the Christ*"
9:23   ἐπερωτήσατε: aor. imper., "ask him!"
9:24   ἐφώνησαν: aor., "they summoned"
       ἐκ δευτέρου: for a second time"
       δὸς: aor. imper. of δίδωμι, "*give* glory to God!"
9:25   εἰ ... ἐστιν: ind. quest., "know *whether he is*"
       ὅτι ... βλέπω: explaining ἓν, "one thing I know, *namely, that I see*"
9:27   γενέσθαι: aor. inf. after θέλετε, "do you wish *to become*"

eius, quia timebant Iudaeos; iam enim conspiraverant Iudaei, ut, si quis eum confiteretur Christum, extra synagogam fieret. ²³ Propterea parentes eius dixerunt: "Aetatem habet; ipsum interrogate!"

²⁴ Vocaverunt ergo rursum hominem, qui fuerat caecus, et dixerunt ei: "Da gloriam Deo! Nos scimus quia hic homo peccator est."

²⁵ Respondit ergo ille: "Si peccator est nescio; unum scio quia, caecus cum essem, modo video."

²⁶ Dixerunt ergo illi: "Quid fecit tibi? Quomodo aperuit oculos tuos?"

²⁷ Respondit eis: "Dixi vobis iam, et non audistis; quid iterum vultis audire? Numquid et vos vultis discipuli eius fieri?"

---

aetas, aetatis *f.*: age	**peccator, -oris** *m*: sinner, transgressor
audio, (4): to hear	**propterea**: therefore, for this reason
confiteor, (2): to confess, acknowledge	**rursum** (*adv.*): back, again
conspiro, (1): to plot, conspire	**synagoga, -ae** *f.*: synagogue
extra: outside (+ *acc.*)	**timeo**, (2), **timui**: to fear, dread
modo: just now, lately, presently	

9:22 **ut ... fieret**: impf. subj. in noun clause supplementing *conspiraverant* and
serving as an apodosis, "conspired *that he would become*"

si quis confiteretur: protasis of a pres. general condition changed in secondary
sequence to the impf. subj., "conspired *that if anyone acknowledges*"

Christum: predicate acc., "acknowledges him to be *the Christ*"

9:25 **si peccator est**: vivid ind. quest., "know *whether he is a sinner*"

cum essem: impf.. act. subj. concessive clause, "*although I was blind*, now I see"

9:27 **audire ...fieri**: pres. inf. complementing *vultis*, "wish *to hear* ... wish *to become*"

147

²⁸ καὶ ἐλοιδόρησαν αὐτὸν καὶ εἶπαν «Σὺ μαθητὴς εἶ ἐκείνου, ἡμεῖς δὲ τοῦ Μωυσέως ἐσμὲν μαθηταί· ²⁹ ἡμεῖς οἴδαμεν
ὅτι Μωυσεῖ λελάληκεν ὁ θεός, τοῦτον δὲ οὐκ οἴδαμεν πόθεν
ἐστίν.»

³⁰ ἀπεκρίθη ὁ ἄνθρωπος καὶ εἶπεν αὐτοῖς «Ἐν τούτῳ
γὰρ τὸ θαυμαστόν ἐστιν ὅτι ὑμεῖς οὐκ οἴδατε πόθεν ἐστίν, καὶ
ἤνοιξέν μου τοὺς ὀφθαλμούς. ³¹ οἴδαμεν ὅτι ὁ θεὸς ἁμαρτωλῶν
οὐκ ἀκούει, ἀλλ᾽ ἐάν τις θεοσεβὴς ᾖ καὶ τὸ θέλημα αὐτοῦ ποιῇ
τούτου ἀκούει. ³² ἐκ τοῦ αἰῶνος οὐκ ἠκούσθη ὅτι ἠνέῳξέν τις
ὀφθαλμοὺς τυφλοῦ γεγεννημένου· ³³ εἰ μὴ ἦν οὗτος παρὰ θεοῦ,
οὐκ ἠδύνατο ποιεῖν οὐδέν.»

³⁴ ἀπεκρίθησαν καὶ εἶπαν αὐτῷ «Ἐν ἁμαρτίαις σὺ ἐγεννήθης ὅλος, καὶ σὺ διδάσκεις ἡμᾶς;» καὶ ἐξέβαλον αὐτὸν ἔξω.

αἰών, -ῶνος, ὁ: time, age
ἁμαρτία, ἡ: sin
ἁμαρτωλός, -όν: sinful
ἀνοίγνυμι: to open
ἐκβάλλω: to throw or cast out of
ἔξω (adv.): out
θαυμαστός, -ή, -όν: wondrous

θέλημα, -ατος, τό: will
θεοσεβής, -ές: fearing God, religious
λοιδορέω: to abuse, revile
μαθητής, ὁ: follower, disciple
ὅλος, -η, -ον: whole, complete
τύφλος, -η, -ον: blind

9:29 λελάληκεν: perf. of λαλέω, "that God *has spoken*"
9:30 ἐν τούτῳ: "in this matter"
    πόθεν ἐστίν: ind. quest. know *whence he is*"
9:31 ἁμαρτωλῶν: gen. pl. after ἀκούει, "does not listen to *the sinful*"
    ἐάν τις θεοσεβὴς ᾖ ...ποιῇ: pres. subj. in pres. general protasis, "*if anyone is reverent and does* his will"
9:32 ἐκ τοῦ αἰῶνος: "from time immemorial"
    οὐκ ἠκούσθη: aor. pass. of ἀκούω, "it has not been heard"
    γεγεννημένου: perf. part. gen. of γεννάω, "the eyes of a man *born* blind"
9:33 εἰ μὴ ἦν ... οὐκ ἠδύνατο: impf. ind. in pres. contrafactual condition (without the usual ἄν in the apodosis), "*if he were not* from God, *he would not be able*"
9:34 ἐγεννήθης: aor. pass. of γεννάω, "*you were born* completely in sin"
    ἐξέβαλον: aor. of ἐκ-βάλλω, "they cast him out›

²⁸ Et maledixerunt ei et dixerunt: "Tu discipulus illius es, nos autem Moysis discipuli sumus. ²⁹ Nos scimus quia Moysi locutus est Deus; hunc autem nescimus unde sit."

³⁰ Respondit homo et dixit eis: "In hoc enim mirabile est, quia vos nescitis unde sit, et aperuit meos oculos! ³¹ Scimus quia peccatores Deus non audit; sed, si quis Dei cultor est et voluntatem eius facit, hunc exaudit. ³² A saeculo non est auditum quia aperuit quis oculos caeci nati; ³³ nisi esset hic a Deo, non poterat facere quidquam."

³⁴ Responderunt et dixerunt ei: "In peccatis tu natus es totus et tu doces nos?" Et eiecerunt eum foras.

---

cultor, -oris *m*: worshiper
eicio, (3), **eieci, eiectus**: to throw out, eject
enim: certainly
exaudio, (4): to hear clearly
foras (*adv.*): out of doors
maledico, (3), **maledixi, maledictus**: to speak ill of, slander (+ *dat.*)
mirabile, -is *n*: miracle, wondrous deed

Moysis, -is, *m*. Moses
peccator, -oris *m*: sinner
possum, posse: be able
saeculum, -i *n*: age, time
totus, -a. –um: whole, all, entire
unde: from where, whence
voluntas, -tatis *f*: will, desire

9:28 **Moysi**: dat., "God spoke *to Moses*"
9:29 **unde sit**: pres. subj. in indirect question, "know *where he is from*"
9:31 **si quis ... est ... facit**: pres. indic. in a present general condition instead of a fut. perf., "if (ever) someone is ... if someone does"
9:32 **est auditum**: impersonal, "*it has not been heard* that"
      quis = quisque, "that *anyone* opens the eyes"
9:33 **nisi esset**: impf. subj. in pres. contrary to fact protasis, "if he were not"
      non poterat: the indic. is used in the contrafactual apodosis rather than the subj. for emphasis, "then he was not able"

Spiritual Blindness

³⁵ ἤκουσεν Ἰησοῦς ὅτι ἐξέβαλον αὐτὸν ἔξω, καὶ εὑρὼν αὐτὸν εἶπεν. «Σὺ πιστεύεις εἰς τὸν υἱὸν τοῦ ἀνθρώπου;»

³⁶ ἀπεκρίθη ἐκεῖνος καὶ εἶπεν «Καὶ τίς ἐστιν, κύριε, ἵνα πιστεύσω εἰς αὐτόν;»

³⁷ εἶπεν αὐτῷ ὁ Ἰησοῦς «Καὶ ἑώρακας αὐτὸν καὶ ὁ λαλῶν μετὰ σοῦ ἐκεῖνός ἐστιν.»

³⁸ ὁ δὲ ἔφη «Πιστεύω, κύριε· καὶ προσεκύνησεν αὐτῷ.»

³⁹ καὶ εἶπεν ὁ Ἰησοῦς «Εἰς κρίμα ἐγὼ εἰς τὸν κόσμον τοῦτον ἦλθον, ἵνα οἱ μὴ βλέποντες βλέπωσιν καὶ οἱ βλέποντες τυφλοὶ γένωνται.»

⁴⁰ ἤκουσαν ἐκ τῶν Φαρισαίων ταῦτα οἱ μετ᾽ αὐτοῦ ὄντες, καὶ εἶπαν αὐτῷ «Μὴ καὶ ἡμεῖς τυφλοί ἐσμεν;»

⁴¹ εἶπεν αὐτοῖς ὁ Ἰησοῦς «Εἰ τυφλοὶ ἦτε, οὐκ ἂν εἴχετε ἁμαρτίαν· νῦν δὲ λέγετε ὅτι Βλέπομεν · ἡ ἁμαρτία ὑμῶν μένει.»

βλέπω: to see	κρίμα, -ατος, τό: decision, judgement
ἐκβάλλω: to cast out	κύριος, ὁ: a lord, master
εὑρίσκω: to find	προσκυνέω: to worship
κόσμος, ὁ: the world	τυφλός, -η, -ον

9:35 ὅτι ἐξέβαλον: aor. in ind. st. after ἤκουσεν, "heard *that they cast out*"
    εὑρὼν: aor., "having found him"

9:36 ἵνα πιστεύσω: aor. subj. in purpose and result clause, "who is he so that I may believe?"

9:37 ἑώρακας: perf., "you have seen"
    ἐκεῖνός: nom. pred., "the one speaking is *that one*"

9:39 εἰς κρίμα: "for the purpose of judgement"
    ἵνα ... βλέπωσιν ... γένωνται: subj. in result/purpose clause, "*so that* those not seeing *will see* ...so those seeing *will become* blind"

9:40 οἱ ὄντες: "*those being* with him" i.e. being with Jesus
    μὴ ... ἐσμεν: anticipating a negative answer, "surely we are not blind?"

9:41 εἰ τυφλοὶ ἦτε, οὐκ ἂν εἴχετε: impf. ind. in contrafactual condition, "if you were blind, you would not have sin"
    ὅτι Βλέπομεν: ὅτι introducing direct speech, "you say that 'we see'"

Spiritual Blindness

³⁵ Audivit Iesus quia eiecerunt eum foras et, cum invenisset eum, dixit ei: "Tu credis in Filium hominis?"

³⁶ Respondit ille et dixit: "Et quis est, Domine, ut credam in eum?"

³⁷ Dixit ei Iesus: "Et vidisti eum; et, qui loquitur tecum, ipse est."

³⁸ At ille ait: "Credo, Domine!" et adoravit eum.

³⁹ Et dixit Iesus: "In iudicium ego in hunc mundum veni, ut, qui non vident, videant, et, qui vident, caeci fiant."

⁴⁰ Audierunt haec ex pharisaeis, qui cum ipso erant, et dixerunt ei: "Numquid et nos caeci sumus?"

⁴¹ Dixit eis Iesus: "Si caeci essetis, non haberetis peccatum. Nunc vero dicitis: 'Videmus!'; peccatum vestrum manet."

---

adoro, (1): to honor, worship	**iudicium**, -i *n*: judgement
aio, (1): to say	**ostium**, -i *n*: gate, entrance
intro, (1): to enter, go into	**peccaatum**, -i *n*: sin
invenio, (4): to discover, find	**video (2)**: to see

9:35   **cum invenisset**: plupf. subj. *cum* circumstantial clause, "when he had found"

9:36   **ut credam**: pres. act. subj. result clause, "who is he *so I may believe?*"

9:39   **ut ... videant ... fiant**: pres. subj. in purpose clause, "I have come *in order that they may see ...in order that they become*"

9:39   **qui cum ipso**: "who were *with him*" although the Greek αὐτοῦ is not intensive in this case, so *cum eo* would be expected

9:41   **si...essetis ...haberetis**: impf. subj. in pres. contrary to fact condition, "*if you were* blind ...then you would not have sin"

      nunc vero: translating νῦν δὲ, "but now"

151

Chapter 10

The Good Shepherd and His Sheep

¹ «ἀμὴν ἀμὴν λέγω ὑμῖν, ὁ μὴ εἰσερχόμενος διὰ τῆς θύρας εἰς τὴν αὐλὴν τῶν προβάτων ἀλλὰ ἀναβαίνων ἀλλαχόθεν ἐκεῖνος κλέπτης ἐστὶν καὶ λῃστής· ² ὁ δὲ εἰσερχόμενος διὰ τῆς θύρας ποιμήν ἐστιν τῶν προβάτων. ³ τούτῳ ὁ θυρωρὸς ἀνοίγει, καὶ τὰ πρόβατα τῆς φωνῆς αὐτοῦ ἀκούει, καὶ τὰ ἴδια πρόβατα φωνεῖ κατ᾽ ὄνομα καὶ ἐξάγει αὐτά. ⁴ ὅταν τὰ ἴδια πάντα ἐκβάλῃ, ἔμπροσθεν αὐτῶν πορεύεται, καὶ τὰ πρόβατα αὐτῷ ἀκολουθεῖ, ὅτι οἴδασιν τὴν φωνὴν αὐτοῦ· ⁵ ἀλλοτρίῳ δὲ οὐ μὴ ἀκολουθήσουσιν ἀλλὰ φεύξονται ἀπ᾽ αὐτοῦ, ὅτι οὐκ οἴδασι τῶν ἀλλοτρίων τὴν φωνήν.»

ἀκολουθέω: to follow
ἀλλαχόθεν: from another place
ἀλλότριος, -α, -ον: belonging to another
ἀναβαίνω: to go up, mount, to go up to
ἀνοίγω: to open
αὐλή, ἡ: an open court
εἰσέρχομαι: to go in or into, enter
ἐκβάλλω: to bring out
ἔμπροσθεν: before, in front
ἐξάγω: to lead out
θύρα, ἡ: door

θυρωρός, ὁ: a door-keeper, porter
ἴδιος, -α, -ον: one's own
κλέπτης, -ου, ὁ: a thief
λῃστής, -οῦ, ὁ: a robber, plunderer
ὄνομα, -ατος, τό: name
ποιμήν, -ένος, ὁ: a shepherd
πορεύομαι: to make his way
πρόβατον, τό: sheep
φεύγω: to flee, take flight, run away
φωνέω: to call
φωνή, ἡ: a sound, tone

10:1 ὁ μὴ εἰσερχόμενος: pres. part. with conditional force, "if not coming"

10:3 τούτῳ: dat. of advantage, "opens *for this one*"
    κατ᾽ ὄνομα: "he calls them *by name*"

10:4 ὅταν ... ἐκβάλῃ: aor. subj. of ἐκ-βάλλω in general temporal clause, "whenever he brings out"
    ὅτι οἴδασιν: perf. (=ἴσασι), "because they know"

10:5 οὐ μὴ ἀκολουθήσουσιν: fut. in strong denial, where the subjunctive is more normal, "they certainly will not follow" + dat.
    φεύξονται: fut. of φεύγω, "they will flee"

Chapter 10

The Good Shepherd and His Sheep

¹ "Amen, amen dico vobis: Qui non intrat per ostium in ovile ovium, sed ascendit aliunde, ille fur est et latro; ² qui autem intrat per ostium, pastor est ovium. ³ Huic ostiarius aperit, et oves vocem eius audiunt, et proprias oves vocat nominatim et educit eas. ⁴ Cum proprias omnes emiserit, ante eas vadit, et oves illum sequuntur, quia sciunt vocem eius; ⁵ alienum autem non sequentur, sed fugient ab eo, quia non noverunt vocem alienorum."

---

alienus, -i *m*: outsider, stranger
aliunde: from elsewhere
aperio, (4): to open
ascendo, (3), **ascendi, ascensus**: to climb
educo, (3): to lead out
emitto, (3), **emisi, emissus**: to send out, drive
fugio, (3): to flee, run away
fur, furis *m/f*: thief, robber
latro, latronis *m*: robber, bandit

nominatim (*adv.*): by name
nosco, (3), **novi, notus**: to recall, recognize
ostiarius, -i *m*: doorkeeper
ovile, ovilis *n*: sheepfold
ovis, ovis *f*: sheep
pastor, pastoris *m*: shepherd, herdsman
proprius, -a, -um: one's own
sequor, (3), **secutus sum**: follow
vox, vocis *f*: voice, tone

10:3 **huic:** dat. of advantage, "*to this one* he opens"
10:4 **cum... emiserit:** fut. perf. in temporal clause, "when(ever) he sends out"

⁶ Ταύτην τὴν παροιμίαν εἶπεν αὐτοῖς ὁ Ἰησοῦς· ἐκεῖνοι δὲ οὐκ ἔγνωσαν τίνα ἦν ἃ ἐλάλει αὐτοῖς.

⁷ εἶπεν οὖν πάλιν ὁ Ἰησοῦς «Ἀμὴν ἀμὴν λέγω ὑμῖν, ἐγώ εἰμι ἡ θύρα τῶν προβάτων. ⁸ πάντες ὅσοι ἦλθον πρὸ ἐμοῦ κλέπται εἰσὶν καὶ λῃσταί· ἀλλ' οὐκ ἤκουσαν αὐτῶν τὰ πρόβατα. ἐγώ εἰμι ἡ θύρα· ⁹ δι' ἐμοῦ ἐάν τις εἰσέλθῃ σωθήσεται καὶ εἰσελεύσεται καὶ ἐξελεύσεται καὶ νομὴν εὑρήσει. ¹⁰ ὁ κλέπτης οὐκ ἔρχεται εἰ μὴ ἵνα κλέψῃ καὶ θύσῃ καὶ ἀπολέσῃ· ἐγὼ ἦλθον ἵνα ζωὴν ἔχωσιν καὶ περισσὸν ἔχωσιν.

¹¹ Ἐγώ εἰμι ὁ ποιμὴν ὁ καλός· ὁ ποιμὴν ὁ καλὸς τὴν ψυχὴν αὐτοῦ τίθησιν ὑπὲρ τῶν προβάτων· ¹² ὁ μισθωτὸς καὶ οὐκ ὢν ποιμήν, οὗ οὐκ ἔστιν τὰ πρόβατα ἴδια, θεωρεῖ τὸν λύκον ἐρχόμενον καὶ ἀφίησιν τὰ πρόβατα καὶ φεύγει, — καὶ

ἀπόλλυμι: to destroy utterly, kill, slay
ἀφίημι: to send forth, release
ζωή, ἡ: life
θύρα, ἡ: a door
θύω: sacrifice, slay
καλός, -η, -ον: good
κλέπτης, -ου, ὁ: a thief
κλέπτω: to steal, filch
λῃστής, -οῦ, ὁ: a robber, plunderer
λύκος, ὁ: a wolf

μισθωτός, ὁ: a hired hand
νομή, ἡ: a pasture, pasturage
ὅσος, -η, -ον: how many
παροιμία, ἡ: a proverb, parable
περισσός, -ή, -όν: abundant
ποιμήν, -ένος, ὁ: a shepherd
σῴζω: to save
τίθημι: to set, put, place
φεύγω: to flee, take flight, run away
ψυχή, ἡ: life

10:6 οὐκ ἔγνωσαν: aor., "they did not know"
    τίνα ἦν: ind. quest., "know *what the things were*"
10:9 ἐάν τις εἰσέλθῃ: aor. subj. in fut. more vivid protasis, "if someone enters"
    σωθήσεται: fut. pass. of σῴζω, "he will be saved"
    εἰσελεύσεται καὶ ἐξελεύσεται: fut., "he will enter and will exit"
    εὑρήσει: fut. of εὑρίσκω, "he will find"
10:10 ἵνα κλέψῃ καὶ θύσῃ καὶ ἀπολέσῃ: aor. subj. in purpose clause, "does not enter except *in order to steal, and slay and destroy*"
    ἵνα ἔχωσιν: pres. subj. in purpose clause, "I came *so that they may have*"
    περισσὸν: adverbial acc., "and have it *abundantly*"
10:12 ἴδια: pred., "the sheep are not *his own*"
    ἐρχόμενον: pres. part. circum., "sees the wolf *coming*"
    ἀφίησιν: pres. of ἀπο-ίημι, "he releases"

⁶ Hoc proverbium dixit eis Iesus; illi autem non cognoverunt quid esse, quod loquebatur eis.

⁷ Dixit ergo iterum Iesus: "Amen, amen dico vobis: Ego sum ostium ovium. ⁸ Omnes, quotquot venerunt ante me, fures sunt et latrones, sed non audierunt eos oves. ⁹ Ego sum ostium; per me, si quis introierit, salvabitur et ingredietur et egredietur et pascua inveniet. ¹⁰ Fur non venit, nisi ut furetur et mactet et perdat; ego veni, ut vitam habeant et abundantius habeant.

¹¹ Ego sum pastor bonus; bonus pastor animam suam ponit pro ovibus; ¹² mercennarius et, qui non est pastor, cuius non sunt oves propriae, videt lupum venientem et dimittit oves et fugit — et

---

abundantior, -us: more abundantly
anima, -ae *f.*: soul, spirit
bonus, –a, -um: good
dimitto, (3): to abandon, forsake
egredior, (3): to go, go beyond
fugio, (3): to flee
furor, (1): to steal, plunder
ingredior, (3): to advance, walk, enter
introeo, (4): to enter, go in
latro, latronis *m.*: bandit, plunderer
lupus, -i *m.*: wolf

macto, (1): to slaughter, destroy
mercennarius, -i *m.*: hired worker
ostium, -i *n.*: doorway, gate
pascuum, -i *n.*: pasture
perdo, (3): to ruin, destroy
proprius, -a, -um: own, very own
proverbium, -i *n.*: proverb, saying
quotquot: however many
salvo, (1): to save
vita, -ae *f.*: life

10:6   **quid esset**: impf. subj. in indirect question, "they did not know *what it was*"
10:9   **si... introierit**: fut. perf. in fut. more vivid conditional, "if he enters"
10:10   **ut furetur et mactet et perdat**: pres. subj. in purpose clauses, "except *in order that he may steal and slaughter and destroy*"
        ut ... habeant: pres. subj. in purpose clause, "I came *in order that they have*"
10:12   **et qui non est**: "a hired worker *and who is not* the shepherd"
        propriae: nom, pred., "when the sheep are not *his own*"
        venientem: pres. part. circum., "sees the wolf *coming*"

ὁ λύκος ἁρπάζει αὐτὰ καὶ σκορπίζει,— ¹³ ὅτι μισθωτός ἐστιν καὶ οὐ μέλει αὐτῷ περὶ τῶν προβάτων.

¹⁴ ἐγώ εἰμι ὁ ποιμὴν ὁ καλός, καὶ γινώσκω τὰ ἐμὰ καὶ γινώσκουσί με τὰ ἐμά, καθὼς γινώσκει με ὁ πατὴρ κἀγὼ γινώσκω τὸν πατέρα, ¹⁵ καὶ τὴν ψυχήν μου τίθημι ὑπὲρ τῶν προβάτων. ¹⁶ καὶ ἄλλα πρόβατα ἔχω ἃ οὐκ ἔστιν ἐκ τῆς αὐλῆς ταύτης· κἀκεῖνα δεῖ με ἀγαγεῖν, καὶ τῆς φωνῆς μου ἀκούσουσιν, καὶ γενήσονται μία ποίμνη, εἷς ποιμήν. ¹⁷ διὰ τοῦτό με ὁ πατὴρ ἀγαπᾷ ὅτι ἐγὼ τίθημι τὴν ψυχήν μου, ἵνα πάλιν λάβω αὐτήν. ¹⁸ οὐδεὶς ἦρεν αὐτὴν ἀπ' ἐμοῦ, ἀλλ' ἐγὼ τίθημι αὐτὴν ἀπ' ἐμαυτοῦ. ἐξουσίαν ἔχω θεῖναι αὐτήν, καὶ ἐξουσίαν ἔχω πάλιν λαβεῖν αὐτήν· ταύτην τὴν ἐντολὴν ἔλαβον παρὰ τοῦ πατρός μου.»

ἀγαπάω: love, be fond of
ἄγω: to lead or carry
αἴρω: to take up, raise, lift up
ἁρπάζω: to snatch away, carry off
αὐλή, ἡ: a forecourt, sheepstead
γινώσκω: to know
δεῖ: it is necessary (+ inf.)
ἐμαυτοῦ: of me, of myself
ἐντολή, ἡ: an order, command, behest
ἐξουσία, ἡ: power, authority

καθώς: just as
καλός, -ή, -όν: good
λαμβάνω: to take
μέλω: to be a care to (+ dat.)
μισθωτός, -ή, -όν: hired
πάλιν (adv.): again, back
ποίμνη, ἡ: a flock
σκορπίζω: to cause to disperse
ψυχή, ἡ: life

10:13 οὐ μέλει: impers., "*there is no care* to him"
10:16 κἀκεῖνα (=καὶ ἐκεῖνα) obj. of ἀγαγεῖν, "to lead *those also*"
    ἀγαγεῖν: aor. inf. with δεῖ, "it is necessary for me *to lead*"
    γενήσονται: fut., "*they will become* one flock"
10:17 ἵνα λάβω: aor. subj. in result/purpose clause, "I lay down my life *so that I may take it*"
10:18 ἦρεν: aor. of αἴρω, "no one *takes* it." The aorist is gnomic, not referring to any particular time.
    αὐτὴν = ψυχήν
    θεῖναι ... λαβεῖν: aor. inf. epexegetic after ἐξουσίαν, "power *to lay it down* ...*to take it back*"

lupus rapit eas et dispergit — ¹³ quia mercennarius est et non pertinet ad eum de ovibus.

¹⁴ Ego sum pastor bonus et cognosco meas, et cognoscunt me meae, ¹⁵ sicut cognoscit me Pater, et ego cognosco Patrem; et animam meam pono pro ovibus. ¹⁶ Et alias oves habeo, quae non sunt ex hoc ovili, et illas oportet me adducere, et vocem meam audient et fient unus grex, unus pastor. ¹⁷ Propterea me Pater diligit, quia ego pono animam meam, ut iterum sumam eam. ¹⁸ Nemo tollit eam a me, sed ego pono eam a meipso. Potestatem habeo ponendi eam et potestatem habeo iterum sumendi eam. Hoc mandatum accepi a Patre meo."

---

accipio, (3) **accepi, acceptus**: to receive, accept
adduco, (3): to lead
alius, alia, -aliud: other, different
dispergo, (3): to scatter, disperse
dissensio, -onis *f.* disagreement, quarrel
fio, (3): to become
grex, gregis *m/f.* flock, herd
mandatum, -i *n*: order, command

oportet, (2), **oportuit**: it is necessary, ought
ovile, ovilis *n*: sheepfold
pertineo, (2): to be a concern to
potestas, -tatis *f.* power
propterea: therefore, for this reason
rapio, (3): to snatch, destroy
sumo, (3): to take up, begin
tollo, (3): to remove, steal

10:13 **pertinet**: impersonal verb, "*it is not a concern*"
   ad eum: "a concern *to him*," where we would expect the dative
10:16 **unus grex**: "one flock;" this is the Old Latin translation, which has now replaced Jerome's erroneous *unum ovile* ("one fold").
10:17 **ut ... sumam**: pres. subj. in purpose clause, "I lay down my life *in order that I take up*"
10:18 **ponendi ...sumendi**: gen. gerund, "power *of placing it down ...of taking it up*" where a gerundive would be more common (*ponendi eius*)

¹⁹ σχίσμα πάλιν ἐγένετο ἐν τοῖς Ἰουδαίοις διὰ τοὺς λόγους τούτους. ²⁰ ἔλεγον δὲ πολλοὶ ἐξ αὐτῶν «Δαιμόνιον ἔχει καὶ μαίνεται· τί αὐτοῦ ἀκούετε;»

²¹ ἄλλοι ἔλεγον Ταῦτα τὰ ῥήματα οὐκ ἔστιν δαιμονιζομέ-νου· μὴ δαιμόνιον δύναται τυφλῶν ὀφθαλμοὺς ἀνοῖξαι;

Further Conflict Over Jesus' Claims

²² ἐγένετο τότε τὰ ἐνκαίνια ἐν τοῖς Ἱεροσολύμοις· χειμὼν ἦν, ²³ καὶ περιεπάτει ὁ Ἰησοῦς ἐν τῷ ἱερῷ ἐν τῇ στοᾷ τοῦ Σολομῶνος. ²⁴ ἐκύκλωσαν οὖν αὐτὸν οἱ Ἰουδαῖοι καὶ ἔλεγον αὐτῷ «Ἕως πότε τὴν ψυχὴν ἡμῶν αἴρεις; εἰ σὺ εἶ ὁ χριστός, εἰπὸν ἡμῖν παρρησίᾳ.»

δαιμονίζομαι: to be possessed by an evil spirit
δαιμόνιον, τό: evil spirit
ἕως: until, till
ἱερόν, τό: temple
κυκλόω: to encircle, surround
μαίνομαι: to rage, be furious
πάλιν: again (*adv.*)
παρρησία, ἡ: freespokenness, openness

περιπατέω: to walk about
ῥῆμα, -ατος, τό: a word, saying
Σολομῶν, ῶνος, ὁ: Solomon
στοά, -ᾶς, ἡ: a roofed colonnade
σχίσμα, -ατος, τό: a division
τὰ ἐνκαίνια: The Feast of the Dedication
τότε: at that time, then
χειμών, -ῶνος, ὁ: winter

10:19 ἐγένετο: aor., "a division *arose*"

10:20 αὐτοῦ: gen. of source after ἀκούετε, "why do you listen *to him?*"

10:21 δαιμονιζομένου: pres. part. gen., "words *of a possessed man*"
    μὴ δύναται: expecting a negative answer, "is a possessed man *able to* open?"
    ἀνοῖξαι: aor. inf. of ἀνοίγνυμι after δύναται, "able *to open*"

10:22 τὰ ἐνκαίνια: the feast commemorating the rededication of the temple in 164 BCE.

10:24 ἕως πότε: "until when?" i.e. how long? for ἕως οὗ
    εἰπὸν: aor. imper., "*speak* to us openly!"
    παρρησίᾳ: dat. of manner, "openly"

¹⁹ Dissensio iterum facta est inter Iudaeos propter sermones hos.

²⁰ Dicebant autem multi ex ipsis: "Daemonium habet et insanit! Quid eum auditis?"

²¹ Alii dicebant: "Haec verba non sunt daemonium habentis! Numquid daemonium potest caecorum oculos aperire?"

Further Conflict Over Jesus' Claims

²² Facta sunt tunc Encaenia in Hierosolymis. Hiems erat;   ²³ et ambulabat Iesus in templo in porticu Salomonis.   ²⁴ Circumdederunt ergo eum Iudaei et dicebant ei: "Quousque animam nostram tollis? Si tu es Christus, dic nobis palam!"

---

ambulo, (1): to walk
anima, -ae, *f.* spirit
aperio (4): to open
caecus, -a, -um: blind
circumdo, (1), **circumdedi**: to surround
daemonium, -i *n*: an evil spirit
Encaenium, -i *n*: Feast of the Dedication of the Temple (i.e. Hanukkah)
hiems, hiemis *f.* winter
Hierosolyma, -orum *n*: Jerusalem
insanio, (4): to be mad, act crazily

multus, -a, -um: much, many
noster, nostra, nostrum: our
palam: openly, plainly
porticus, porticus *m/f.* colonnade
quousque: how long?
Salomon, is *m*: Solomon
sermo, -onis *m*: conversation, speech
templum, -i *n*: temple
tollo (3): to raise up
verbum, -i *n*: word, proverb

10:21 **habentis**: pres. part., "the words *of one having* a dream"
   numquid potest: "is an evil spirit able?" expecting negative answer
10:24 **animam nostram tollis**: "how long *will you raise up our spirit?*" i.e. keep us in suspense

²⁵ ἀπεκρίθη αὐτοῖς ὁ Ἰησοῦς «Εἶπον ὑμῖν καὶ οὐ πιστεύετε·
τὰ ἔργα ἃ ἐγὼ ποιῶ ἐν τῷ ὀνόματι τοῦ πατρός μου ταῦτα
μαρτυρεῖ περὶ ἐμοῦ· ²⁶ ἀλλὰ ὑμεῖς οὐ πιστεύετε, ὅτι οὐκ ἐστὲ
ἐκ τῶν προβάτων τῶν ἐμῶν. ²⁷ τὰ πρόβατα τὰ ἐμὰ τῆς φωνῆς
μου ἀκούουσιν, κἀγὼ γινώσκω αὐτά, καὶ ἀκολουθοῦσίν μοι,
²⁸ κἀγὼ δίδωμι αὐτοῖς ζωὴν αἰώνιον, καὶ οὐ μὴ ἀπόλωνται
εἰς τὸν αἰῶνα, καὶ οὐχ ἁρπάσει τις αὐτὰ ἐκ τῆς χειρός μου.
²⁹ ὁ πατήρ μου ὃ δέδωκέν μοι πάντων μεῖζόν ἐστιν, καὶ οὐδεὶς
δύναται ἁρπάζειν ἐκ τῆς χειρὸς τοῦ πατρός. ³⁰ ἐγὼ καὶ ὁ
πατὴρ ἕν ἐσμεν.»

³¹ ἐβάστασαν πάλιν λίθους οἱ Ἰουδαῖοι ἵνα λιθάσωσιν
αὐτόν. ³² ἀπεκρίθη αὐτοῖς ὁ Ἰησοῦς «Πολλὰ ἔργα ἔδειξα ὑμῖν
καλὰ ἐκ τοῦ πατρός· διὰ ποῖον αὐτῶν ἔργον ἐμὲ λιθάζετε;»

αἰώνιος, -ον: lasting for an age	μαρτυρέω: to bear witness
βαστάζω: to lift	μείζων, μεῖζον: greater
δείκνυμι: to bring to light, display, exhibit	πάλιν: again
ἔργον, τό: deed, work	ποῖος, -α, -ον: of which?
καλός, -η, -ον: good	πολύς, πολλά, πολύ: many
λιθάζω: to fling stones	χείρ, χειρός, ἡ: the hand
λίθος, ὁ: a stone	

10:25 ταῦτα μαρτυρεῖ:"these works witness"

10:26 ὅτι οὐκ ἐστὲ: causal, "because you are not"

10:27 τῆς φωνῆς: gen. of source after ἀκούουσιν, "they hear my *voice*"

10:28 οὐ μὴ ἀπόλωνται: aor. subj. in strong denial, "they certainly won't die"

10:29 μεῖζον: n. nom. pred. agreeing with ὅ, "what he has given me is *greater*"
    πάντων: gen. of comparison after μεῖζόν, "greater than *all things*"

10:30 ἕν: nom. pred.,"we are *one*"

10:31 ἵνα λιθάσωσιν: aor. subj. in purpose clause, "they picked up stones *in order to
    stone him*"

10:32 διὰ ποῖον ... ἔργον: "on account of which work?"

²⁵ Respondit eis Iesus: "Dixi vobis, et non creditis; opera, quae ego facio in nomine Patris mei, haec testimonium perhibent de me. ²⁶ Sed vos non creditis, quia non estis ex ovibus meis. ²⁷ Oves meae vocem meam audiunt, et ego cognosco eas, et sequuntur me; ²⁸ et ego vitam aeternam do eis, et non peribunt in aeternum, et non rapiet eas quisquam de manu mea. ²⁹ Pater meus quod dedit mihi, maius omnibus est, et nemo potest rapere de manu Patris. ³⁰ Ego et Pater unum sumus."

³¹ Sustulerunt iterum lapides Iudaei, ut lapidarent eum. ³² Respondit eis Iesus: "Multa opera bona ostendi vobis ex Patre; propter quod eorum opus me lapidatis?"

---

aeternus, -a, -um: eternal, everlasting
Iudaeus, -i *m*: a Jew
lapido, (1): to throw stones at, stone
lapis, lapidis *m*: stone
maior, –us: greater
manus, manus *f*: hand
nomen, nominis *n*: name
opus, operis *n*: work

ostendeo, (2) **ostendi**: to show, reveal
pater, patris *m*: father
pereo, (4): to die
perhibeo, (2): to present, give
rapio, (3): to snatch, carry off
sequor, (3) to follow
testimonium, -i *n*: testimony

10:28 **non ... quisquam**: "*no one* will take them"
10:29 **maius**: n. nom. pred. agreeing with *quod*, "what he gave is *greater*"
　　　omnibus: dat. of comparison after *maius*, "greater than *all things*"
10:31 **ut... lapidarent**: impf. subj. purpose clause, "they took up stones *in order to stone* him"
10:32 **propter quod eorum opus**: "on account of which work of these (many good works)?

161

³³ ἀπεκρίθησαν αὐτῷ οἱ Ἰουδαῖοι «Περὶ καλοῦ ἔργου οὐ

λιθάζομέν σε ἀλλὰ περὶ βλασφημίας, καὶ ὅτι σὺ ἄνθρωπος

ὢν ποιεῖς σεαυτὸν θεόν.»

³⁴ ἀπεκρίθη αὐτοῖς ὁ Ἰησοῦς «Οὐκ ἔστιν γεγραμμένον

ἐν τῷ νόμῳ ὑμῶν ὅτι Ἐγὼ εἶπα Θεοί ἐστε; ³⁵ εἰ ἐκεί-

νους εἶπεν θεοὺς πρὸς οὓς ὁ λόγος τοῦ θεοῦ ἐγένετο, καὶ

οὐ δύναται λυθῆναι ἡ γραφή, ³⁶ ὃν ὁ πατὴρ ἡγίασεν καὶ

ἀπέστειλεν εἰς τὸν κόσμον ὑμεῖς λέγετε ὅτι Βλασφημεῖς, ὅτι

εἶπον Υἱὸς τοῦ θεοῦ εἰμί; ³⁷ εἰ οὐ ποιῶ τὰ ἔργα τοῦ πατρός

μου, μὴ πιστεύετέ μοι· ³⁸ εἰ δὲ ποιῶ, κἂν ἐμοὶ μὴ πιστεύητε

ἁγιάζω: to make holy	δύναμαι: to be able, capable
ἀποστέλλω: to send off	κόσμος, ὁ: world
βλασφημέω: to blaspheme	λύω: to loose
βλασφημία, ἡ: a profane speech	νόμος, ὁ: custom, law
γραφή, ἡ: a writing, scripture	υἱός, ὁ: a son
γράφω: to write	

10:33 ὤν: pres. part. concessive, "*although being* a man"
10:34 ἔστιν γεγραμμένον: periphrastic perf. of γράφω, "it has been written"
    εἶπα: aor. with weak ending (= εἶπον), "I said"
    Θεοί ἐστε: Ps. 82:6
10:35 θεούς: acc. pred., "if he called those *gods*"
    ἐκείνους ... πρὸς οὕς: "*those ... for whom* the speech was made"
    λυθῆναι: aor. pass. inf. after δύναται, "able *to be loosed*"
10:36 ὅν ... ἡγίασεν: aor., "(the one) *whom* the father *made holy*"
    ἀπέστειλεν: aor. of ἀπο-στέλλω, "whom *he sent*"
    λέγετε; the apodosis of εἰ ἐκείνους εἶπεν above, "then do you say?"
    ὅτι βλασφημεῖς: note the direct speech, "you say (that) 'you blaspheme'"
10:37 μὴ πιστεύετε: pres. imper. in prohibition (where the aor. subj. is normal),
      "don't believe!"
10:38 κἂν ἐμοὶ μὴ πιστεύητε: pres. subj. in fut. more vivid protasis, "even if you
      don't believe in me"

³³ Responderunt ei Iudaei: "De bono opere non lapidamus te

sed de blasphemia, et quia tu, homo cum sis, facis teipsum Deum."

³⁴ Respondit eis Iesus: "Nonne scriptum est in lege vestra:

'Ego dixi: Dii estis?'   ³⁵ Si illos dixit deos, ad quos sermo

Dei factus est, et non potest solvi Scriptura,   ³⁶ quem Pater

sanctificavit et misit in mundum, vos dicitis: 'Blasphemas!' quia

dixi: 'Filius Dei sum?'   ³⁷ Si non facio opera Patris mei, nolite

credere mihi;   ³⁸ si autem facio, et si mihi non vultis credere,

---

blasphemia, -ae *f.* blasphemy
blasphemo, (1): to blaspheme
filius, -i, *m.* son
lex, legis *f.* law
nolo, nolle: be unwilling, wish not to

sanctifico, (1): to sanctify, treat as holy
scribo, (3), scripsi, scriptus: to write
scriptura, -ae *f.* scripture
solvo, (3): to loosen, release, unbind

10:33 **cum sis**: pres. subj. *cum* concessive clause, "*although you are* a man"
10:35 **deos**: predicate acc., "if he called them *gods*"
    ad quos: where a dative of advantage is expected, "those *for whom* the speech
    was made"
    solvi: pass. inf. after *potest*, "able *to be dissolved*"
10:37 **nolite**: imper., "don't" + inf.
10:38 **et si:** "*even if* you do not wish"
    mihi ...operibus: dat. after *credite*, "believe in *me ...in my works*"

τοῖς ἔργοις πιστεύετε, ἵνα γνῶτε καὶ γινώσκητε ὅτι ἐν ἐμοὶ ὁ πατὴρ κἀγὼ ἐν τῷ πατρί.» ³⁹ ἐζήτουν οὖν αὐτὸν πάλιν πιάσαι· καὶ ἐξῆλθεν ἐκ τῆς χειρὸς αὐτῶν.

⁴⁰ καὶ ἀπῆλθεν πάλιν πέραν τοῦ Ἰορδάνου εἰς τὸν τόπον ὅπου ἦν Ἰωάνης τὸ πρῶτον βαπτίζων, καὶ ἔμενεν ἐκεῖ. ⁴¹ καὶ πολλοὶ ἦλθον πρὸς αὐτὸν καὶ ἔλεγον ὅτι «Ἰωάνης μὲν σημεῖον ἐποίησεν οὐδέν, πάντα δὲ ὅσα εἶπεν Ἰωάνης περὶ τούτου ἀληθῆ ἦν.» ⁴² καὶ πολλοὶ ἐπίστευσαν εἰς αὐτὸν ἐκεῖ.

ἀληθής, -ές: unconcealed, true
βαπτίζω: to baptize
γινώσκω: to know
ἔργον, τό: a deed
ζητέω: to seek
Ἰορδάνος, ὁ: Jordan River
μένω: to remain
πάλιν (adv.): again

πατήρ, πατρός, ὁ: a father
πέραν: on the other side (+ gen.)
πιάζω: to arrest
πιστεύω: to believe in
σημεῖον, τό: a sign
τόπος, ὁ: a place
χείρ, χειρός, ἡ: the hand

10:38 πιστεύετε: imper. serving as apodosis, "then believe in my works!"
    ἵνα γνῶτε καὶ γινώσκητε: aor. and pres. subj. in purpose clause, "so that you realize and continue to know"
10:39 πιάσαι: aor. inf. of purpose after ἐζήτουν, "they sought *to arrest* him"
10:40 τὸ πρῶτον: adverbial acc., "baptizing *at first*"
    ἦν ... βαπτίζων: periphrastic impf., "where John *was baptizing*"
10:41 πάντα δὲ ὅσα: "*everything that* he said was true"

operibus credite, ut cognoscatis et sciatis quia in me est Pater, et ego in Patre." 39 Quaerebant ergo iterum eum prehendere; et exivit de manibus eorum.

40 Et abiit iterum trans Iordanem in eum locum, ubi erat Ioannes baptizans primum, et mansit illic. 41 Et multi venerunt ad eum et dicebant: "Ioannes quidem signum fecit nullum; omnia autem, quaecumque dixit Ioannes de hoc, vera erant." 42 Et multi crediderunt in eum illic.

---

abeo, (4), **abii, abitum**: to depart, go away
autem: but (=δέ)
credo, (3) **credidi, creditus**: to believe in
exeo (4): **exii, exitus**: to depart
illic: there, in that place
Ioannes, Ioannis *m*: John
iterum (*adv.*): again
locus, -i *m*: place

maneo, (2), **mansi, mansus**: to remain, stay
nullus, -a, -um: no, none
omnis, -e: all
prehendo, (3): to catch, capture
primum (*adv.*): at first, before
quidem: indeed, while (=μὲν)
verus, -a, -um: true

10:38 **ut cognoscatis et sciatis**: pres. subj. result clause, "so that you understand and know"

10:40 **erat ... baptizans**: periphrastic impf. following the Greek (= *baptizabat*)

Chapter 11

The Death of Lazarus

¹ ἦν δέ τις ἀσθενῶν, Λάζαρος ἀπὸ Βηθανίας ἐκ τῆς κώμης Μαρίας καὶ Μάρθας τῆς ἀδελφῆς αὐτῆς. ² ἦν δὲ Μαριὰμ ἡ ἀλείψασα τὸν κύριον μύρῳ καὶ ἐκμάξασα τοὺς πόδας αὐτοῦ ταῖς θριξὶν αὐτῆς, ἧς ὁ ἀδελφὸς Λάζαρος ἠσθένει. ³ ἀπέστειλαν οὖν αἱ ἀδελφαὶ πρὸς αὐτὸν λέγουσαι «Κύριε, ἴδε ὃν φιλεῖς ἀσθενεῖ.»

⁴ ἀκούσας δὲ ὁ Ἰησοῦς εἶπεν «Αὕτη ἡ ἀσθένεια οὐκ ἔστιν πρὸς θάνατον ἀλλ᾽ ὑπὲρ τῆς δόξης τοῦ θεοῦ ἵνα δοξασθῇ ὁ υἱὸς τοῦ θεοῦ δι᾽ αὐτῆς.» ⁵ ἠγάπα δὲ ὁ Ἰησοῦς τὴν Μάρθαν καὶ τὴν ἀδελφὴν αὐτῆς καὶ τὸν Λάζαρον. ⁶ ὡς οὖν ἤκουσεν

ἀγαπάω: to love, be fond of	θάνατος, ὁ: death
ἀδελφή, -ης, ἡ: a sister	θρίξ, -κός, ἡ: the hair of the head
ἀδελφός, ὁ: a brother	κώμη, ἡ: country town
ἀκούω: to hear	Λάζαρος, ὁ: Lazarus
ἀλείφω: to anoint with oil, oil	Μάρθα, -ας, ἡ: Martha
ἀσθένεια, ἡ: illness	Μαρίαμ, -ας, ἡ: Mary
ἀσθενέω: to weaken, be ill	μύρον, τό: perfume
δοξάζομαι: to be magnified, glorified	πούς, ποδός, ὁ: a foot
ἐκμάσσω: to wipe off, wipe away	φιλέω: to love, regard with affection

---

11:1 τις ἀσθενῶν: pres. part. attrib. indef., "a certain man who was ill"

11:2 ἡ ἀλείψασα ... ἐκμάξασα: aor. part. used as a pred., "M. was *the one who annointed* ...*the one who wiped*"

  ταῖς θριξὶν: dat. of means, "wiped *with her hair*"

  ἧς: rel. pron. gen., "*whose* brother was ill"

11:3 ὅν: rel. pron. acc., "(he)*whom* you love is ill"

11:4 ἵνα δοξασθῇ: aor. subj. pass. in purpose clause, "for teh glory of God *in order for the son to be glorified*"

11:5 ἠγάπα: impf. of ἀγαπάω, "he (continuously) loved them"

  δι᾽ αὐτῆς: "glorified *by it*" (i.e the sickness) expressing means instead of the ablative

Chapter 11

The Death of Lazarus

¹ Erat autem quidam languens Lazarus a Bethania, de castello Mariae et Marthae sororis eius. ² Maria autem erat, quae unxit Dominum unguento et extersit pedes eius capillis suis, cuius frater Lazarus infirmabatur. ³ Miserunt ergo sorores ad eum dicentes: "Domine, ecce, quem amas, infirmatur."

⁴ Audiens autem Iesus dixit: "Infirmitas haec non est ad mortem sed pro gloria Dei, ut glorificetur Filius Dei per eam." ⁵ Diligebat autem Iesus Martham et sororem eius et Lazarum. ⁶ Ut ergo audivit

---

amo, (1): to love
autem: but, however
capillus, -i *m*: hair
castellum, -i *n*: town, village
diligo, (1): to love
dominus, -i *m*: lord
extergeo, (2), **extersi, extersum**: to wipe away, dry
filius, fili *m*: son
frater, fratris *m*: brother
glorifico, (1): to glorify

infirmitas, -tatis *f*: weakness, sickness
infirmo, (1): to be sick
langueo, (2): to be faint, be weak
Lazarus, -i *m*: Lazarus
Maria, -ae *f*: Mary
Martha, -ae *f*: Martha
mitto, (3), **misi, missus**: to send
mors, mortis *f*: death
pes, pedis *m*: foot
soror, sororis *f*: sister
ungo, (3), **unxi, unctum**: to anoint

11:2 **unguento ... capillis suis**: abl. means, "washed *with oil* ... dried *with her hair*"
11:4 **ut glorificetur**: pres. subj. purpose clause, "in order that he may be glorified"
per eam: "glorified *by it*" (the sickeness) expressing means instead of the ablative

ὅτι ἀσθενεῖ, τότε μὲν ἔμεινεν ἐν ᾧ ἦν τόπῳ δύο ἡμέρας·
⁷ ἔπειτα μετὰ τοῦτο λέγει τοῖς μαθηταῖς «Ἄγωμεν εἰς τὴν
Ἰουδαίαν πάλιν.»

⁸ λέγουσιν αὐτῷ οἱ μαθηταί «Ῥαββεί, νῦν ἐζήτουν σε
λιθάσαι οἱ Ἰουδαῖοι, καὶ πάλιν ὑπάγεις ἐκεῖ;»

⁹ ἀπεκρίθη Ἰησοῦς «Οὐχὶ δώδεκα ὧραί εἰσιν τῆς ἡμέρας;
ἐάν τις περιπατῇ ἐν τῇ ἡμέρᾳ, οὐ προσκόπτει, ὅτι τὸ φῶς τοῦ
κόσμου τούτου βλέπει· ¹⁰ ἐὰν δέ τις περιπατῇ ἐν τῇ νυκτί,
προσκόπτει, ὅτι τὸ φῶς οὐκ ἔστιν ἐν αὐτῷ.»

¹¹ ταῦτα εἶπεν, καὶ μετὰ τοῦτο λέγει αὐτοῖς «Λάζαρος ὁ
φίλος ἡμῶν κεκοίμηται, ἀλλὰ πορεύομαι ἵνα ἐξυπνίσω αὐτόν.»

¹² εἶπαν οὖν οἱ μαθηταὶ αὐτῷ «Κύριε, εἰ κεκοίμηται σωθήσεται.» ¹³ εἰρήκει δὲ ὁ Ἰησοῦς περὶ τοῦ θανάτου αὐτοῦ. ἐκεῖνοι
δὲ ἔδοξαν ὅτι περὶ τῆς κοιμήσεως τοῦ ὕπνου λέγει.

ἄγω: to lead or go	πάλιν: back
βλέπω: to see	πορεύομαι: to go, make one's way
δώδεκα: twelve	προσκόπτω: to stumble
ἐξυπνίζω: to awaken from sleep	Ῥαββεί: (Hebr.) teacher
ἐρῶ: to say or speak (*fut.*)	σώζω: to save
ἡμέρα, ἡ: day	τόπος, ὁ: a place
κοιμάω: to put to sleep	ὑπάγω: to withdraw
κοίμησις, -εως, ἡ: a lying down to sleep	ὕπνος, ὁ: sleep, slumber
Λάζαρος, ὁ: Lazarus	φίλος, -η, -ον: loved, beloved, dear
λιθάζω: to cast stones	φῶς, φωτός, τό: light, daylight
μένω: to remain	ὥρα, ἡ: hour
νύξ, νυκτός, ἡ: the night	

11:6 δύο ἡμέρας: acc. of duration, "stayed *for two days*"

11:7 ἄγωμεν: pres. subj. hortatory, "let us go"

11:8 λιθάσαι: aor. inf. of purpose, "they were seeking *to stone* you"

11:9 ἐάν τις περιπατῇ: pres. subj. in pres. general protasis, "if anyone one walks
around"

11:11 κεκοίμηται: perf. of κοιμάω, "he has fallen asleep"

ἵνα ἐξυπνίσω: aor. subj. in purpose clause, "I am going *in order to wake* him"

11:12 σωθήσεται: fut. pass., "he will be saved"

11:13 εἰρήκει: plupf., "Jesus *had spoken*"

περὶ τοῦ θανάτου αὐτοῦ: either "about his death" or "about death itself"

quia infirmabatur, tunc quidem mansit in loco, in quo erat, duobus diebus; ⁷ deinde post hoc dicit discipulis: "Eamus in Iudaeam iterum."

⁸ Dicunt ei discipuli: "Rabbi, nunc quaerebant te Iudaei lapidare, et iterum vadis illuc?"

⁹ Respondit Iesus: "Nonne duodecim horae sunt diei? Si quis ambulaverit in die, non offendit, quia lucem huius mundi videt; ¹⁰ si quis autem ambulaverit in nocte, offendit, quia lux non est in eo."

¹¹ Haec ait et post hoc dicit eis: "Lazarus amicus noster dormit, sed vado, ut a somno exsuscitem eum."

¹² Dixerunt ergo ei discipuli: "Domine, si dormit, salvus erit." ¹³ Dixerat autem Iesus de morte eius, illi autem putaverunt quia de dormitione somni diceret.

---

aio, (1): to say
ambulo, (1): to walk
amicus, -i *m*: friend
deinde: then
dies, -ei *m/f*: day
dormio, (4), **dormivi, dormitus**: to sleep
dormitio, -onis *f*: sleep, act of sleeping
duodecim: twelve
exsuscito, (1): to awaken
iterum: again
Iudaea, -ae: Judea
locus, -i *n*: place, position

lux, lucis *f*: light
maneo, (2) mansi: to remain
mors, mortis *m*: death
mundus, -i *m*: world
nox, noctis *f*: night
offendo, (3), **offendi, offensus**: to stumble
puto, (1): to think, suppose
quaero, (3): to search for, seek
salvus, -a, -um: well
somnus, -i *m*: sleep
vado, (3) to go

11:6 **duobus diebus**: dat. duration of time where one would expect the acc., "for two days"
11:7 **eamus**: pres. subj. hortatory, "let us go"
11:9-10 **si quis... ambulaverit**: fut. perf. in present general condition, "if anyone walks"
   in die ...in nocte: abl. of time with redundant *in*, "in the day...in the night"
   non est in eo: "the light is not *in him*" i.e. the one out at night
11:11 **ut... exsuscitem**: pres. subj. in purpose clause, "I go *in order to waken*"
11:13 **quia... diceret**: impf. subj. in alleged ind. st., "they supposed *that he was speaking*"

¹⁴ τότε οὖν εἶπεν αὐτοῖς ὁ Ἰησοῦς παρρησίᾳ «Λάζαρος ἀπέθανεν, ¹⁵ καὶ χαίρω δι᾿ ὑμᾶς, ἵνα πιστεύσητε, ὅτι οὐκ ἤμην ἐκεῖ· ἀλλὰ ἄγωμεν πρὸς αὐτόν.»

¹⁶ εἶπεν οὖν Θωμᾶς ὁ λεγόμενος Δίδυμος τοῖς συνμαθηταῖς «Ἄγωμεν καὶ ἡμεῖς ἵνα ἀποθάνωμεν μετ᾿ αὐτοῦ.»

Jesus Comforts the Sisters of Lazarus

¹⁷ ἐλθὼν οὖν ὁ Ἰησοῦς εὗρεν αὐτὸν τέσσαρας ἤδη ἡμέρας ἔχοντα ἐν τῷ μνημείῳ. ¹⁸ ἦν δὲ Βηθανία ἐγγὺς τῶν Ἱεροσολύμων ὡς ἀπὸ σταδίων δεκαπέντε. ¹⁹ πολλοὶ δὲ ἐκ τῶν Ἰουδαίων ἐληλύθεισαν πρὸς τὴν Μάρθαν καὶ Μαριὰμ ἵνα παραμυθήσωνται αὐτὰς περὶ τοῦ ἀδελφοῦ. ²⁰ ἡ οὖν Μάρθα ὡς ἤκουσεν ὅτι Ἰησοῦς ἔρχεται ὑπήντησεν αὐτῷ· Μαριὰμ δὲ ἐν τῷ οἴκῳ ἐκαθέζετο.

ἄγω: to lead, go	μνημεῖον, τό: a monument
ἀποθνήσκω: to die off, die	οἶκος, ὁ: a house, abode, dwelling
δεκαπέντε: fifteen	παραμυθέομαι: to encourage, console
δίδυμος, -ον: double, twin	παρρησία, ἡ; openness
ἐγγύς: near (+ gen.)	στάδιον, τό: a stade
εὑρίσκω: to find	συνμαθητής, -οῦ, ὁ: fellow disciple
ἤμερα, -ας, ἡ: day	τέσσαρες, -ων, οἱ: four
Θωμᾶς, ὁ: Thomas	ὑπαντάω: to go to meet
καθέζομαι: to remain sitting	χαίρω: to rejoice, be glad, be delighted

---

11:14 ἀπέθανεν: aor., "he has died"

11:15 ἵνα πιστεύσητε: aor. subj. in noun clause, complementing χαίρω, where a participle would be normal, "I rejoice *that you believe*"

ὅτι οὐκ ἤμην (=ἦ): causal, "*because I was not* there"

ἄγωμεν: pres. subj. hortatory, "let us go"

11:16 ἵνα ἀποθάνωμεν: aor. subj. in purpose clause, "in order to die"

11:17 τέσσαρας ἤδη ἡμέρας: acc. of duration of time, "for four days"

αὐτὸν ... ἔχοντα: pres. part. circum., "he found *him being* in the tomb"

11:18 ὡς δεκαπέντε: "*about fifteen* stades away"

11:19 ἐληλύθεισαν: plupf., "many *had come*"

ἵνα παραμυθήσωνται: aor. subj. in purpose clause, "in order to console them"

11:20 ὑπήντησεν: aor. of ὑπο-αντάω, "she went out to meet him"

¹⁴ Tunc ergo dixit eis Iesus manifeste: "Lazarus mortuus est, ¹⁵ et gaudeo propter vos, ut credatis, quoniam non eram ibi; sed eamus ad eum."

¹⁶ Dixit ergo Thomas, qui dicitur Didymus, ad condiscipulos: "Eamus et nos, ut moriamur cum eo!"

Jesus Comforts the Sisters of Lazarus

¹⁷ Venit itaque Iesus et invenit eum quattuor dies iam in monumento habentem. ¹⁸ Erat autem Bethania iuxta Hierosolymam quasi stadiis quindecim. ¹⁹ Multi autem ex Iudaeis venerant ad Martham et Mariam, ut consolarentur eas de fratre. ²⁰ Martha ergo ut audivit quia Iesus venit, occurrit illi; Maria autem domi sedebat.

Bethania, -ae *f*: Bethany
condiscipulus, -i *m*: fellow disciple
consolor, (1): to console
didymus, -a, -um: twin, double
gaudeo, (2), **gavisus sum**: to rejoice
Hierosolyma, -ae *f*: Jerusalem
itaque: and so, thus, therefore
iuxta: near, close to (+ *acc.*)
manifestus, -a, -um: open, openly
monumentum, -i *n*: tomb

morior, (3), **mortuus sum**: to die
occurro, (3) **occurri**: to run to meet (+ *dat.*)
quasi: about
quattuor: four
quindecim: fifteen
quoniam: because, since
sedeo, (2): to sit, remain
stadium, -i *n*: stade, Greek measure of distance, (607 feet)
Thomas (*indecl.*): Thomas

11:15 **ut credatis**: pres. subj. in noun clause, complementing *gaudeo*, where an infinitive would be normal, "I rejoice *that you believe*"

    quoniam non eram: causal, "seeing that I was not there"

    eamus: pres. subj. hortatory, "let us go"

11:16 **ut moriamur**: pres. subj. in purpose clause, "go *in order that we may die*"

11:17 **eum ...habentem**: pres. part. circum., "he found *him already being*"

    quattuor dies: acc. duration of time, "in the tomb *for four days*"

11:19 **ut consolarentur**: impf. subj. in purpose clause, "many had come in order to console"

11:20 **quia Iesus venit**: pres. indicative in vivid ind. quest., "she knew *that Jesus is coming*"

11:20 **domi**: locative, "Mary was sitting *at home*"

171

²¹ εἶπεν οὖν ἡ Μάρθα πρὸς Ἰησοῦν «Κύριε, εἰ ἦς ὧδε οὐκ ἂν ἀπέθανεν ὁ ἀδελφός μου· ²² καὶ νῦν οἶδα ὅτι ὅσα ἂν αἰτήσῃ τὸν θεὸν δώσει σοι ὁ θεός.»

²³ λέγει αὐτῇ ὁ Ἰησοῦς «Ἀναστήσεται ὁ ἀδελφός σου.»

²⁴ λέγει αὐτῷ ἡ Μάρθα «Οἶδα ὅτι ἀναστήσεται ἐν τῇ ἀναστάσει ἐν τῇ ἐσχάτῃ ἡμέρᾳ.»

²⁵ εἶπεν αὐτῇ ὁ Ἰησοῦς «Ἐγώ εἰμι ἡ ἀνάστασις καὶ ἡ ζωή· ²⁶ ὁ πιστεύων εἰς ἐμὲ κἂν ἀποθάνῃ ζήσεται, καὶ πᾶς ὁ ζῶν καὶ πιστεύων εἰς ἐμὲ οὐ μὴ ἀποθάνῃ εἰς τὸν αἰῶνα· πιστεύεις τοῦτο;»

²⁷ λέγει αὐτῷ «Ναί, κύριε· ἐγὼ πεπίστευκα ὅτι σὺ εἶ ὁ χριστὸς ὁ υἱὸς τοῦ θεοῦ ὁ εἰς τὸν κόσμον ἐρχόμενος.»

ἀδελφός, ὁ: brother
αἰτέω: to ask, beg
αἰών, -ῶνος, ὁ: age
ἀνάστασις, -εως, ἡ: a raising up, resurrection
ἀνίστημι: to make to stand up, raise up
ἀποθνῄσκω: to die
ἔρχομαι: to come or go
ἔσχατος, -η, -ον: last

ζάω: to live
ζωή, ἡ: life
κόσμος, ὁ: the world
ναί: yea, verily
οἶδα: to know (perf.)
πιστεύω: to believe in
φωνέω: to speak
χριστός, -ή, -όν: annointed

11:21 εἰ ἦς ὧδε: impf. in past contrafactual protasis, "if you had been here"

οὐκ ἂν ἀπέθανεν: aor. in past contrafactual apodosis, "if you had been here, *he would not have died*"

11:22 ὅσα ἂν αἰτήσῃ: aor. subj. in general relative protasis, "whatever you seek"

δώσει: fut. of δίδωμι, "God *will give*"

11:23 ἀναστήσεται: fut. of ἀνα-ίστημι, "he will rise again"

11:26 κἂν ἀποθάνῃ: aor. subj. in fut. more vivid protasis, "even if he dies"

οὐ μὴ ἀποθάνῃ: aor. subj. in strong denial, "anyone believing, *he shall certainly not die*"

11:27 πεπίστευκα: perf. of πιστεύω, "I have come to believe"

ὁ χριστὸς ...ἐρχόμενος: nom. pred. phrases, "you are *the annointed one*, etc."

²¹ Dixit ergo Martha ad Iesum: "Domine, si fuisses hic, frater meus non esset mortuus! ²² Sed et nunc scio quia, quaecumque poposceris a Deo, dabit tibi Deus."

²³ Dicit illi Iesus: "Resurget frater tuus."

²⁴ Dicit ei Martha: "Scio quia resurget in resurrectione in novissimo die."

²⁵ Dixit ei Iesus: "Ego sum resurrectio et vita. Qui credit in me, etsi mortuus fuerit, vivet; ²⁶ et omnis, qui vivit et credit in me, non morietur in aeternum. Credis hoc?"

²⁷ Ait illi: "Utique, Domine; ego credidi quia tu es Christus Filius Dei, qui in mundum venisti."

---

aeternus, -a, -um: eternal
credo, (3), credidi, creditus: to trust, believe
dies, diei *m/f.* day
do (1): to give
etsi: although, though, even if
aio (1): to say
morior (3): to die
novissimus, -a, -um: last

nunc: now
posco, (3), poposci: to ask, demand
resurgo, (3): to rise, lift up
resurrectio, -onis *f.* resurrection
utique: certainly, by all means
vita, -ae, *f.* : life
vivo, (3): to be alive, live

11:21 **si fuisses**: plupf. subj. in past contrary to fact protasis, "if you had been"
    esset: impf. subj. in pres. contrary to fact apodosis, "*he would* not now *be* dead"
11:22 **poposceris**: fut. perf. in fut. more vivid protasis, "whatever *you demand*"
11:25 **etsi ...mortui fuerit**: fut. perf. in fut. more vivid protasis, "even if he dies"
11:27 **qui... venisti**: relative clause with second person, "you who have come"

²⁸ καὶ τοῦτο εἰποῦσα ἀπῆλθεν καὶ ἐφώνησεν Μαριὰμ τὴν ἀδελφὴν αὐτῆς λάθρα εἴπασα «Ὁ διδάσκαλος πάρεστιν καὶ φωνεῖ σε.» ²⁹ ἐκείνη δὲ ὡς ἤκουσεν ἠγέρθη ταχὺ καὶ ἤρχετο πρὸς αὐτόν· ³⁰ οὔπω δὲ ἐληλύθει ὁ Ἰησοῦς εἰς τὴν κώμην, ἀλλ' ἦν ἔτι ἐν τῷ τόπῳ ὅπου ὑπήντησεν αὐτῷ ἡ Μάρθα. ³¹ οἱ οὖν Ἰουδαῖοι οἱ ὄντες μετ' αὐτῆς ἐν τῇ οἰκίᾳ καὶ παραμυθούμενοι αὐτήν, ἰδόντες τὴν Μαριὰμ ὅτι ταχέως ἀνέστη καὶ ἐξῆλθεν, ἠκολούθησαν αὐτῇ δόξαντες ὅτι «ὑπάγει εἰς τὸ μνημεῖον ἵνα κλαύσῃ ἐκεῖ.»

³² ἡ οὖν Μαριὰμ ὡς ἦλθεν ὅπου ἦν Ἰησοῦς ἰδοῦσα αὐτὸν ἔπεσεν αὐτοῦ πρὸς τοὺς πόδας, λέγουσα αὐτῷ «Κύριε, εἰ ἦς ὧδε οὐκ ἄν μου ἀπέθανεν ὁ ἀδελφός.»

ἀκολουθέω: to follow
ἀνίστημι: to rise up
διδάσκαλος, ὁ: a teacher, master
δοκέω: to think, suppose
ἐγείρω: to awaken, wake up, rouse
εἶπον: to say (aor.)
ἦλθον: to come or go (aor.)
κλαίω: to weep, lament, wail
κώμη, ἡ: country town
λάθρα: secretly

οἰκία, ἡ: a building, house, dwelling
οὔπω: not yet
παραμυθέομαι: to encourage, console
πάρειμι: to be present
πίπτω: to fall, fall down
πούς, ποδός, ὁ: foot
ταχέως: quickly
ταχύς, -εῖα, -ύ: quick, swift, fleet
τόπος, ὁ: a place
ὑπαντάω: to come or go to meet

11:28 εἰποῦσα ...εἴπασα: aor. part., note the variation between weak and strong forms, both meaning "*having said this*"
11:29 ἠγέρθη: aor. pass. of ἐγείρω, "she got up"
  ἤρχετο: impf. of ἔρχομαι, "she started going"
11:30 ἐληλύθει: plupf. of ἔρχομαι, "he had not yet come"
  ὅπου ὑπήντησεν: local relative clause, "to the place *where she met* him"
11:31 ὅτι ἀνέστη: aor. of ἀνα-ἵστημι, "seeing Mariam, *that she got up*"
  δόξαντες: aor. part. of δοκέω, "*having supposed* that" with ὅτι introducing direct speech
  ἵνα κλαύσῃ: aor. subj. of κλαίω in purpose clause, "she goes *in order to mourn*"
11:32 ἰδοῦσα: aor. part. of εἶδον, "having seen"
  ἔπεσεν: aor. of πίπτω, "she fell upon" + gen.
  εἰ ἦς ὧδε: past contrafactual protasis, "if you had been here"
  οὐκ ἄν ἀπέθανεν: aor. in past contrafactual apodosis, "he would not have died"

²⁸ Et cum haec dixisset, abiit et vocavit Mariam sororem suam silentio dicens: "Magister adest et vocat te." ²⁹ Illa autem ut audivit, surrexit cito et venit ad eum; ³⁰ nondum enim venerat Iesus in castellum, sed erat adhuc in illo loco, ubi occurrerat ei Martha. ³¹ Iudaei igitur, qui erant cum ea in domo et consolabantur eam, cum vidissent Mariam quia cito surrexit et exiit, secuti sunt eam putantes: "Vadit ad monumentum, ut ploret ibi."

³² Maria ergo, cum venisset ubi erat Iesus, videns eum cecidit ad pedes eius dicens ei: "Domine, si fuisses hic, non esset mortuus frater meus!"

---

abeo, (4), **abii, abitum**: to depart, go away
adhuc: thus far, till now
assum, adesse: be near, be present
cado, (3), **cecidi, casus**: to fall, sink, drop
castellum, -i *n*: town, village
cito: quickly
consolor, (1): to console
domus, -i *f.*: home, house
locus, -i *m*: place
magister, -**tri** *m*: teacher

nondum: not yet
occurro, (3): to run to meet
pes, pedis, *m.* foot
ploro, (1): to lament, weep
puto, (1): to think, believe
sequor (3) **secutus sum**: to follow
silentium, -i *n*: silence, quiet
surgo, (3), **surrexi, surrectus**: to rise
voco, (1): to call, summon

11:28 **cum... dixisset**: plupf. subj. *cum* circumstantial clause, "when she had said"
    silentio: abl. of manner, "quietly"
11:31 **in domo**: prep. phrase for locative (*domi*)
    cum vidissent: plupf. subj. in *cum* circumstantial clause, "when they had seen Mary, that she""
    ut ploret: pres. subj. purpose clause, "she is going *in order to lament*"
11:32 **cum venisset**: plupf. subj. in *cum* circumstantial clause, "when he had come"
    si fuisses: plupf. subj. in past contrary to fact protasis, "if you had been"
    esset: impf. subj. in pres. contrary to fact apodosis, "he would not be"

³³ Ἰησοῦς οὖν ὡς εἶδεν αὐτὴν κλαίουσαν καὶ τοὺς συνελ-
θόντας αὐτῇ Ἰουδαίους κλαίοντας ἐνεβριμήσατο τῷ πνεύματι
καὶ ἐτάραξεν ἑαυτόν, ³⁴ καὶ εἶπεν «Ποῦ τεθείκατε αὐτόν;»
λέγουσιν αὐτῷ «Κύριε, ἔρχου καὶ ἴδε.»

³⁵ ἐδάκρυσεν ὁ Ἰησοῦς.

³⁶ ἔλεγον οὖν οἱ Ἰουδαῖοι «Ἴδε πῶς ἐφίλει αὐτόν.»

³⁷ τινὲς δὲ ἐξ αὐτῶν εἶπαν «Οὐκ ἐδύνατο οὗτος ὁ ἀνοί-
ξας τοὺς ὀφθαλμοὺς τοῦ τυφλοῦ ποιῆσαι ἵνα καὶ οὗτος μὴ
ἀποθάνη;»

Jesus Raises Lazarus From the Dead

³⁸ Ἰησοῦς οὖν πάλιν ἐμβριμώμενος ἐν ἑαυτῷ ἔρχεται εἰς
τὸ μνημεῖον· ἦν δὲ σπήλαιον, καὶ λίθος ἐπέκειτο ἐπ᾽ αὐτῷ.
³⁹ λέγει ὁ Ἰησοῦς «Ἄρατε τὸν λίθον.»

αἴρω: to lift, take away	μνημεῖον, τό: the monument
ἀνοίγνυμι: to open	ὀφθαλμός, ὁ: the eye
δακρύω: to shed tears	πνεῦμα, -ατος, τό: spirit
δύναμαι: to be able, capable (+ *inf.*)	σπήλαιον, τό: a grotto, cave, cavern
ἐμβριμάομαι: to sigh	συνῆλθον: to go with (+ *dat.*) (*aor.*)
ἐπίκειμαι: to be placed upon	ταράσσω: to stir, stir up, trouble
ἴδέ: lo, behold	τίθημι: to put, place
κλαίω: to weep	τυφλός, -ή, -όν: blind
κύριος, ὁ: a lord, master	φιλέω: to love
λίθος, ὁ: a stone	

11:33 κλαίουσαν ...κλαίοντας: pres. part. circum., "saw her *weeping* ... them *weeping*"
  τοὺς συνελθόντας: aor. attrib., "Jesus saw *those going with* her"
  ἐνεβριμήσατο: aor. of ἐν-βριμάομαι, "he breathed deeply" i.e. "he sighed"
  ἐτάραξεν: aor. of ταράσσω, "he troubled himself" i.e. was troubled
11:34 τεθείκατε: perf. of τίθημι, "where *have you laid* him?"
  ἔρχου καὶ ἴδε: imper., "come and look!" where a particple is typical
11:36 πῶς ἐφίλει: impf. in ind. quest., "see *how he loved him*"
11:37 οὗτος ὁ ἀνοίξας: aor. part. of ἀνοίγνυμι, "this one who opened"
  ποιῆσαι: aor. inf. complementing ἐδύνατο, "is he not able *to make it*"
  ἵνα καὶ οὗτος μὴ ἀποθάνη: aor. subj. of ἀποθνήσκω in noun clause of result
    after ποιῆσαι, "to make it *that he does not die*"
11:38 ἐπέκειτο: impf. of ἐπι-κείμαι, "it had been placed"
11:39 ἄρατε: aor. imper. of αἴρω, "*remove* the stone!"

³³ Iesus ergo, ut vidit eam plorantem et Iudaeos, qui venerant cum ea, plorantes, fremuit spiritu et turbavit seipsum ³⁴ et dixit: "Ubi posuistis eum?"

Dicunt ei: "Domine, veni et vide."

³⁵ Lacrimatus est Iesus.

³⁶ Dicebant ergo Iudaei: "Ecce quomodo amabat eum!"

³⁷ Quidam autem dixerunt ex ipsis: "Non poterat hic, qui aperuit oculos caeci, facere, ut et hic non moreretur?"

Jesus Raises Lazarus From the Dead

³⁸ Iesus ergo rursum fremens in semetipso, venit ad monumentum; erat autem spelunca, et lapis superpositus erat ei. ³⁹ Ait Iesus: "Tollite lapidem!"

---

aio, (1): to say
amo, (1): to love
aperio, (4), **aperui, apertus**: to open
caecus, -a, -um: blind
foeteo, (2): to stink; have bad odor
fremo, (3), **fremui, fremitus**: to groan
lacrimor, (1): to shed tears, weep
lapis, -idis *m*: a stone
oculus, -i *m*: eye
ploro (1): to weep
pono, (3), **posui, positus**: to place, put

possum, posse: be able, can
quomodo: how
rursum: again
seipse, -a, -um: one's self
semetipse, -a, -um: one's self (emphatic)
spelunca, -ae *f*.: a cave
spiritus, -us *m*: spirit
superpono, (3), **superposui, superpositus**: to place over
tollo (3): to raise, take away
turbo, (1): to disturb, agitate

11:37 **ut ... non moreretur**: impf. subj. in noun clause after *facere*, "make it *so that he does not die*"

    et hic: "couldn't he make it so that *this one too* does not die" i.e. to save Lazarus in addition to the blind man

λέγει αὐτῷ ἡ ἀδελφὴ τοῦ τετελευτηκότος Μάρθα
«Κύριε, ἤδη ὄζει, τεταρταῖος γάρ ἐστιν.»

⁴⁰ λέγει αὐτῇ ὁ Ἰησοῦς «Οὐκ εἶπόν σοι ὅτι ἐὰν πιστεύσῃς
ὄψῃ τὴν δόξαν τοῦ θεοῦ;»

⁴¹ ἦραν οὖν τὸν λίθον. ὁ δὲ Ἰησοῦς ἦρεν τοὺς ὀφθαλμοὺς
ἄνω καὶ εἶπεν «Πάτερ, εὐχαριστῶ σοι ὅτι ἤκουσάς μου, ⁴² ἐγὼ
δὲ ᾔδειν ὅτι πάντοτέ μου ἀκούεις· ἀλλὰ διὰ τὸν ὄχλον τὸν
περιεστῶτα εἶπον ἵνα πιστεύσωσιν ὅτι σύ με ἀπέστειλας.»

⁴³ καὶ ταῦτα εἰπὼν φωνῇ μεγάλῃ ἐκραύγασεν «Λάζαρε,
δεῦρο ἔξω.» ⁴⁴ ἐξῆλθεν ὁ τεθνηκὼς δεδεμένος τοὺς πόδας καὶ
τὰς χεῖρας κειρίαις, καὶ ἡ ὄψις αὐτοῦ σουδαρίῳ περιεδέδετο.

ἄνω (adv.): upwards
ἀποστέλλω: to send off or away from
δεῦρο (adv.): hither
δέω: to bind
δόξα, ἡ: glory, opinion
ἔξω (adv.): out
εὐχαριστέω: to be grateful
ἤδη: now, already
κειρία, ἡ: the cord or girth of a bedstead
κραυγάζω: to shout
ὄζω: to smell

ὄχλος, ὁ: a crowd
ὄψις, -εως, ἡ: look, appearance, aspect
ὄψομαι: to see (fut.)
πάντοτε: at all times, always
περιδέω: to bind, tie round or on
περιίστημι: to place round
σουδάριον, τό: cloth, death-clothing
τελευτάω: to complete, finish, decease
τεταρταῖος, -α, -ον: on the fourth day
φωνή, ἡ: a sound, tone

11:39 τοῦ τετελευτηκότος: perf. part. gen. s. of τελευτάω, "sister *of the deceased man*"

11:40 ἐὰν πιστεύσῃς: aor. subj. of πιστεύω in fut. more vivid protasis, "if you believe"
  ὄψῃ: fut., "you will see"

11:41 ἦραν: aor. of αἴρω, "*they removed* the stone"
  ἦρεν: aor. of αἴρω, "*he lifted* his eyes"

11:42 ᾔδειν: plupf. of οἶδα, "I already knew"
  τὸν περιεστῶτα: perf. part. attrib. of περι-ίστημι, "because of the crowd *which was standing around*"
  ἵνα πιστεύσωσιν: aor. subj. in purpose clause, "I said this *in order that they believe*"

11:43 φωνῇ μεγάλῃ: dative of manner, "he shouted *in a loud voice*"

11:44 ὁ τεθνηκὼς: perf. part. of θνήσκω, "the dead man"
  δεδεμένος: perf. part. of δέω, "having been bound"
  κειρίαις ...σουδαρίῳ: dat. of means, "bound *with bandages ...with cloth*"
  τοὺς πόδας καὶ τὰς χεῖρας: acc. of resp., bound with respect to hands and feet
  περιεδέδετο: plupf. of περι-δέω, "his face *had been bound*"

Dicit ei Martha, soror eius, qui mortuus fuerat: "Domine, iam foetet; quatriduanus enim est!"

⁴⁰ Dicit ei Iesus: "Nonne dixi tibi quoniam, si credideris, videbis gloriam Dei?"

⁴¹ Tulerunt ergo lapidem. Iesus autem, elevatis sursum oculis, dixit: "Pater, gratias ago tibi quoniam audisti me.   ⁴² Ego autem sciebam quia semper me audis, sed propter populum, qui circumstat, dixi, ut credant quia tu me misisti."

⁴³ Et haec cum dixisset, voce magna clamavit: "Lazare, veni foras!"   ⁴⁴ Prodiit, qui fuerat mortuus, ligatus pedes et manus institis; et facies illius sudario erat ligata.

---

ago, (3): to thank (with *gratias*)
circumsto, (1): to gather, circle
clamo, (1): to proclaim, shout
elevo, (1): to lift up, raise
enim: indeed, in fact
facies, faciei *f*: face
fero, ferre, tuli, latus: to carry off
foras: out of doors, forth, out
gratia, -ae *f*: grace
instita, -ae *f*: strips of cloth
ligo, (1): to bind, tie, fasten

magnus, -a, -um: large, great
populus, -i *m*: people
prodio, (4), **prodii, proditus**: to go, come forth
quatriduanus, -a, -um: lasting four days
quoniam: because, that
scio, (4): to know, understand
semper (*adv.*): always
sudarium, -i *n*: cloth, shroud
sursum (*adv.*): up
vox, vocis *f*: voice

11:40 **quoniam**: introducing ind. st. instead of *quia*, "I said *that* you will see"
    si credideris: fut. perf. in fut. more vivid protasis, "if you believe"
11:41 **elevatis ... oculis**: abl. abs., "his eyes having been raised"
    quoniam audisiti: causal, "because you heard"
11:42 **ut credant**: pres. subj. purpose clause, "I spoke *in order that they may believe*"
11:43 **cum dixisset**: plupf. subj. in *cum* circumstantial clause, "when he had said"
    voce magna: abl. of manner, "shouted *in a loud voice*"
11:44 **fuerat mortuus**: plupf. (= *erat mortuus*), "he had been dead"
    pedes et manus: acc. of respect instead of ablative, "bound *with respect to his feet and hands*" following Greek usage (the so-called Greek accusative)
    institis ...sudario: abl. of means, "bound *with bandages ...with cloth*"

λέγει ὁ Ἰησοῦς αὐτοῖς «Λύσατε αὐτὸν καὶ ἄφετε αὐτὸν
ὑπάγειν.»

The Plot to Kill Jesus

⁴⁵ πολλοὶ οὖν ἐκ τῶν Ἰουδαίων, οἱ ἐλθόντες πρὸς τὴν
Μαριὰμ καὶ θεασάμενοι ὃ ἐποίησεν, ⁴⁶ ἐπίστευσαν εἰς αὐτόν·
τινὲς δὲ ἐξ αὐτῶν ἀπῆλθον πρὸς τοὺς Φαρισαίους καὶ εἶπαν
αὐτοῖς ἃ ἐποίησεν Ἰησοῦς.

⁴⁷ συνήγαγον οὖν οἱ ἀρχιερεῖς καὶ οἱ Φαρισαῖοι συνέδριον,
καὶ ἔλεγον «Τί ποιοῦμεν ὅτι οὗτος ὁ ἄνθρωπος πολλὰ ποιεῖ
σημεῖα; ⁴⁸ ἐὰν ἀφῶμεν αὐτὸν οὕτως, πάντες πιστεύσουσιν
εἰς αὐτόν, καὶ ἐλεύσονται οἱ Ῥωμαῖοι καὶ ἀροῦσιν ἡμῶν καὶ
τὸν τόπον καὶ τὸ ἔθνος.»

αἴρω: to raise, take away
ἀρχιερεύς, -έως, ὁ: a chief-priest
ἀφίημι: to send forth, discharge
ἔθνος, -εος, τό: a nation
θεάομαι: to look on, gaze at, view, behold
λύω: to loose

πιστεύω: to believe in
Ῥωμαῖοι, οἱ: the Romans
σημεῖον, τό: a sign, a mark, token
συνάγω: to gather together, convene
συνέδριον, τό: a council
τόπος, ὁ: place (perhaps the temple)
ὑπάγω: to withdraw

11:44 ἄφετε: aor. imper. of ἀπο-ίημι, "allow him to go!"
11:45 οἱ ἐλθόντες ... θεασάμενοι: aor. part., "the ones who went ...and who saw"
11:45-6 ὃ ἐποίησεν ...ἃ ἐποίησεν: note the variation in the number of the pronouns, both of which are translated the same by Jerome
11:47 συνήγαγον: aor. of συν-άγω, "they gathered"
    τί ποιοῦμεν: indic. in delib. quest. (= τί ποιῶμεν), "what should we do?"
11:48 ἐὰν ἀφῶμεν: aor. subj. of ἀπο-ίημι in fut. more vivid protasis, "if we release him"
    πιστεύσουσιν ... καὶ ἐλεύσονται ... καὶ ἀροῦσιν: futures connected simply with καὶ and a good example of the additive style of *koine*, "then all *will believe and the Romans will come and they will take away*"

180

Dicit Iesus eis: "Solvite eum et sinite eum abire."

The Plot to Kill Jesus

⁴⁵ Multi ergo ex Iudaeis, qui venerant ad Mariam et viderant, quae fecit, crediderunt in eum;   ⁴⁶ quidam autem ex ipsis abierunt ad pharisaeos et dixerunt eis, quae fecit Iesus.

⁴⁷ Collegerunt ergo pontifices et pharisaei concilium et dicebant: "Quid facimus, quia hic homo multa signa facit?   ⁴⁸ Si dimittimus eum sic, omnes credent in eum, et venient Romani et tollent nostrum et locum et gentem!"

---

abeo, (4), **abii, abitum**: to depart, go off
colligo, (3), **collegi, collectus**: to collect, assemble
concilium, -i *n*: assembly, council
dimitto, (3): to send away, dismiss
facio, (3) **fecit, factus**: to do, make
gens, gentis *f*: nation
locus, -i *m*: place, land

Pharisaeus, -i *m*: Pharisee
pontifex, pontificis *m*: high priest
Romanus, -i *m*: a Roman
sic: thus, so, in such a way
signum, -i *n*: sign
sino, (3): to allow, permit (+ *inf.*)
solvo, (3), : to loosen, unbind, untie
tollo, (3), : to carry off, take away

11:45-6 **quae fecit:** Jerome translates both ὅ and ἅ with the plural *quae*
11:47 **quid facimus:** deliberative question in the indicative where one would expect the subj., "what should we do?"
11:48 **si dimittimus:** present indicative instead of future translating the future more vivid protasis, "*if we allow*, they will believe"
   et locum et gentem: "they will take away *both our place and nation*"

⁴⁹ εἷς δέ τις ἐξ αὐτῶν Καιάφας, ἀρχιερεὺς ὢν τοῦ ἐνιαυ-

τοῦ ἐκείνου, εἶπεν αὐτοῖς «Ὑμεῖς οὐκ οἴδατε οὐδέν, ⁵⁰ οὐδὲ

λογίζεσθε ὅτι συμφέρει ὑμῖν ἵνα εἷς ἄνθρωπος ἀποθάνῃ ὑπὲρ

τοῦ λαοῦ καὶ μὴ ὅλον τὸ ἔθνος ἀπόληται.»

⁵¹ τοῦτο δὲ ἀφ᾽ ἑαυτοῦ οὐκ εἶπεν, ἀλλὰ ἀρχιερεὺς ὢν τοῦ

ἐνιαυτοῦ ἐκείνου ἐπροφήτευσεν ὅτι ἔμελλεν Ἰησοῦς ἀποθνῄσκειν

ὑπὲρ τοῦ ἔθνους, ⁵² καὶ οὐχ ὑπὲρ τοῦ ἔθνους μόνον, ἀλλ᾽ ἵνα καὶ

τὰ τέκνα τοῦ θεοῦ τὰ διεσκορπισμένα συναγάγῃ εἰς ἕν. ⁵³ ἀπ᾽

ἐκείνης οὖν τῆς ἡμέρας ἐβουλεύσαντο ἵνα ἀποκτείνωσιν αὐτόν.

ἀποκτείνω: to kill, slay	Καιάφας: Caiaphas
ἀπόλλυμι: to destroy	λαός, λαοῦ, ὁ: the people
ἀρχιερεύς, ὁ: a priest	λογίζομαι: to reckon, consider
βουλεύω: to deliberate, plan	μέλλω: to intend to do, to be about to do
διασκορπίζω: to scatter abroad	ὅλος, -η, -ον: whole, entire
ἔθνος, -εος, τό: the nation	προφητεύω: to prophecy
εἷς, μία, ἕν: one	συμφέρω: to be expedient
ἐνιαυτός, ὁ: year	συνάγω: to gather together
ἡμέρα, ἡ: a day	τέκνον, τό: a child

11:48 ἀροῦσιν: fut. of αἴρω, "*they will take* from us"
11:49 εἷς δέ τις: "*a certain one* of them"
  τοῦ ἐνιαυτοῦ ἐκείνου: gen. of time, "*during that year*"
  οὐκ οἴδατε οὐδέν: "he said '*you know nothing*'"
11:50 ἵνα εἷς ἄνθρωπος ἀποθάνῃ: aor. subj. of ἀποθνῄσκω in noun clause serving as
    subject of συμφέρει, "*that one man die* is expedient"
  μὴ ὅλον τὸ ἔθνος ἀπόληται: aor. subj. of ἀπόλλυμι also the subject of
    συμφέρει, "*that the whole nation not die* is expedient"
11:51 ἀφ᾽ ἑαυτοῦ: "of his own accord" i.e. independently
  ὤν: pres. part. causal, "*since he was high priest*"
  ἀποθνῄσκειν: pres. inf. after ἔμελλεν, "predicted that Jesus was about *to die*"
11:52 ἵνα ... συναγάγῃ: aor. subj. of συν-άγω in purpose clause, "in order to gather"
  τὰ διεσκορπισμένα: perf. part. attrib. of δια-σκορπίζω, "in order to gather the
    children *who have been scattered*"
11:53 ἵνα ἀποκτείνωσιν: aor. subj. in noun clause after ἐβουλεύσαντο instead of an
    infinitive, "they decided *to kill him*"

⁴⁹ Unus autem ex ipsis, Caiphas, cum esset pontifex anni illius, dixit eis: "Vos nescitis quidquam ⁵⁰ nec cogitatis quia expedit vobis, ut unus moriatur homo pro populo, et non tota gens pereat!"

⁵¹ Hoc autem a semetipso non dixit; sed, cum esset pontifex anni illius, prophetavit quia Iesus moriturus erat pro gente ⁵² et non tantum pro gente, sed et ut filios Dei, qui erant dispersi, congregaret in unum. ⁵³ Ab illo ergo die cogitaverunt, ut interficerent eum.

---

annus, -i *m*: year
Caiphas *m*: Caiphas
cogito, (1): to think, intend
congrego, (1): to collect, gather
dies, -ei *m/f*: day
dispergo, (3), **dispersi, dispersus**: to scatter, disperse
expedio, (4): to be profitable, advantageous
gens, gentis *f*: nation, people

homo, hominis *m*: man
interficio, (3): to kill, destroy
nescio, (4): to not know
pereo, (2): to die, pass away, be ruined
pontifex, -icis *m*: a high priest
populus, -i *m*: people, nation
propheto, (1): to foretell, predict
semetipse, -a, -um: one's self
totus, -a, -um: whole, all, entire

11:49 **cum esset**: impf. subj. *cum* causal clause, "*since he was* chief priest" repeated in verse 51 below

11:50 **ut...moriatur...pereat**: pres. subj. noun clause, subject of *expedit*, "it is expedient *that one die and* not the whole race *die*"

11:51 **moriturus**: fut. part. in periphrastic with *erat*, "predicted that he was *about to die*"

11:52 **non tantum ... sed et**: "not only ... but also"

   ut... congregaret: impf. subj. purpose clause after prophetavit, "prophesied that he would die *in order to gather* them into one"

11:53 **ut interficerent**: impf. subj. in noun clause, "they decided *that they would kill* him"

⁵⁴ ὁ οὖν Ἰησοῦς οὐκέτι παρρησίᾳ περιεπάτει ἐν τοῖς Ἰουδαίοις, ἀλλὰ ἀπῆλθεν ἐκεῖθεν εἰς τὴν χώραν ἐγγὺς τῆς ἐρήμου,
εἰς Ἐφραὶμ λεγομένην πόλιν, κἀκεῖ ἔμεινεν μετὰ τῶν μαθητῶν.

⁵⁵ ἦν δὲ ἐγγὺς τὸ πάσχα τῶν Ἰουδαίων, καὶ ἀνέβησαν
πολλοὶ εἰς Ἱεροσόλυμα ἐκ τῆς χώρας πρὸ τοῦ πάσχα ἵνα
ἁγνίσωσιν ἑαυτούς. ⁵⁶ ἐζήτουν οὖν τὸν Ἰησοῦν καὶ ἔλεγον
μετ᾿ ἀλλήλων ἐν τῷ ἱερῷ ἑστηκότες «Τί δοκεῖ ὑμῖν; ὅτι οὐ
μὴ ἔλθῃ εἰς τὴν ἑορτήν;» ⁵⁷ δεδώκεισαν δὲ οἱ ἀρχιερεῖς καὶ οἱ
Φαρισαῖοι ἐντολὰς ἵνα ἐάν τις γνῷ ποῦ ἐστιν μηνύσῃ, ὅπως
πιάσωσιν αὐτόν.

ἀγνίζω: to cleanse away, purify
ἀλλήλων: of one another
ἀναβαίνω: to go up, to go up to
δίδωμι: to give
ἐγγύς: near (+ gen.)
ἐκεῖθεν: from that place, thence
ἐντολή, ἡ: a command
ἑορτή, ἡ: a festival, feast
ἔρημος, ὁ: desert
Ἐφραὶμ: Ephraim
ζητέω: to seek, seek for
ἱερόν, τό: a temple

ἵστημι: to make to stand
μαθητής, -οῦ, ὁ: a disciple
μένω: to remain
μηνύω: to reveal, betray
οὐκέτι: no more, no longer
παρρησία, ἡ: freespokenness, openness
πάσχα, τό (indecl.): Passover
περιπατέω: to walk about
πιάζω: to arrest
πόλις, πόλεως, ἡ : a city
χώρα, ἡ: the place

11:54 Ἐφραὶμ: about 15 miles north of Jerusalem
    κἀκεῖ: = καὶ ἐκεῖ, "and there"
11:55 τὸ πάσχα: the feast of the passover
    ἀνέβησαν: aor. of ἀνα-βαίνω, "many went up"
    ἵνα ἁγνίσωσιν: aor. subj. in purpose cl., "went up *in order to purify* themselves"
11:56 ἑστηκότες: perf. part. circum. of ἵστημι, "while they were standing"
    οὐ μὴ ἔλθῃ: aor. subj. of ἔρχομαι in strong denial, "surely he will not come!"
11:57 δεδώκεισαν: plupf. 3 pl. of δίδωμι, "*they had given* orders"
    ἵνα ... μηνύσῃ: aor. subj. of μηνύω in noun clause expressing ind. com., "had
        given the order *to reveal*"
    ἐάν τις γνῷ: aor. subj. of γινώσκω in present general protasis, "if anyone knows"
    ποῦ ἐστιν: ind. quest., "knows *where he is*"
    ὅπως πιάσωσιν: aor. subj. of in a result clause, "*so that they can arrest* him"

⁵⁴ Iesus ergo iam non in palam ambulabat apud Iudaeos, sed abiit inde in regionem iuxta desertum, in civitatem, quae dicitur Ephraim, et ibi morabatur cum discipulis.

⁵⁵ Proximum autem erat Pascha Iudaeorum, et ascenderunt multi Hierosolymam de regione ante Pascha, ut sanctificarent seipsos. ⁵⁶ Quaerebant ergo Iesum et colloquebantur ad invicem in templo stantes: "Quid videtur vobis? Numquid veniet ad diem festum?" ⁵⁷ Dederant autem pontifices et pharisaei mandatum, ut, si quis cognoverit, ubi sit, indicet, ut apprehendant eum.

---

abeo, (4), **abii, abitum**: to depart, go off
ambulo, (1): to walk
apprehendo, (3): to seize, lay hold of
apud: among (+ *acc.*)
ascendo, (3): to embark, ascend
civitas, civitatis *f.*: community, city
cognosco, (3) **cognovi, cognitus**: to know
colloquor, (3), **collocutus sum**: to converse, discuss, confer
desertum, -i *n*: desert
Hierosolyma, -ae *f.*: Jerusalem
inde: thence, thenceforth
indico, (1): to point out, show, indicate
invicem: in turn, reciprocally, mutually
iuxta: near (+ *acc.*)
mandatum, -i *n*: order, command
moror, (1): to stay
palam: openly, publicly
Pascha, -atis *n*: Passover
pontifex, -icis, *m.* a priest
proximus, -a, -um: near, close
quaero, (3): to ask, seek
regio, regionis *f.*: area, region
sanctifico, (1): to sanctify, treat as holy
seipse, -a, -um: one's self
sto, (1): to stand
templum, -i *n*: temple

11:55 **ut sanctificarent**: impf. subj., "ascended *in order that they may cleanse*"
11:57 **ut ... indicet**: pres. subj. in indirect com., "had ordered *that he show*" and also the apodosis of the condition
    si quis ...cognoverit: fut. perf. in present general protasis, "if anyone knows"
    ubi sit: pres. subj. indirect question, "knows *where he is*"
    ut ...indicet: pres. subj. in ind. com., "gave the order *to show*"
    ut apprehendant: pres. subj. in purpose clause, "show *so they can arrest*"

Chapter 12

Jesus Anointed at Bethany

¹ ὁ οὖν Ἰησοῦς πρὸ ἓξ ἡμερῶν τοῦ πάσχα ἦλθεν εἰς Βηθανί-
αν, ὅπου ἦν Λάζαρος, ὃν ἤγειρεν ἐκ νεκρῶν Ἰησοῦς. ² ἐποίησαν
οὖν αὐτῷ δεῖπνον ἐκεῖ, καὶ ἡ Μάρθα διηκόνει, ὁ δὲ Λάζαρος εἷς
ἦν ἐκ τῶν ἀνακειμένων σὺν αὐτῷ· ³ ἡ οὖν Μαριὰμ λαβοῦσα
λίτραν μύρου νάρδου πιστικῆς πολυτίμου ἤλειψεν τοὺς πόδας
[τοῦ] Ἰησοῦ καὶ ἐξέμαξεν ταῖς θριξὶν αὐτῆς τοὺς πόδας αὐτοῦ·
ἡ δὲ οἰκία ἐπληρώθη ἐκ τῆς ὀσμῆς τοῦ μύρου.

⁴ λέγει δὲ Ἰούδας ὁ Ἰσκαριώτης εἷς τῶν μαθητῶν αὐτοῦ, ὁ
μέλλων αὐτὸν παραδιδόναι, ⁵ «Διὰ τί τοῦτο τὸ μύρον οὐκ ἐπράθη

ἀλείφω: to anoint with oil
ἀνάκειμαι: to recline
Βηθανία, ἡ: Bethany
δεῖπνον, τό: the principal meal
διακονέω: to minister, serve
ἐγείρω: to raise
ἐκμάσσω: to wipe off, wipe away
ἥμερα, -ας, ἡ: a day
θρίξ, ἡ: the hair of the head
Ἰούδας, ὁ: Judas
Ἰσκαριώτης, -ου, ὁ: the Iscariot
Λάζαρος, ὁ: Lazarus

λίτρα, ἡ: a pint
μύρον, τό: perfume
νάρδος, ἡ: nard-oil
νεκρός, ὁ: a dead body, corpse
ὀσμή, ἡ: a smell, scent, odor
παραδίδωμι: to hand over, betray
πιπράσκω: to sell
πιστικός, -ή, -όν: liquid
πληρόω: to make full
πολύτιμος, -ον: very costly
πούς, ποδός, ὁ: a foot

12:1 πρὸ τοῦ πάσχα: "six days *before the feast*"
      ὃν ἤγειρεν: aor., "Lazarus *whom he raised*"
12:2 ὁ Λάζαρος εἷς ἦν: *Lazarus was one* of the those reclining"
12:3 λαβοῦσα: aor. part. of λαμβάνω, "Mary *having taken*"
      ἤλειψεν ... ἐξέμαξεν: aor., "she annointed ... she wiped off"
      ταῖς θριξὶν: dat. of means, "wiped *with her hair*"
      ἐπληρώθη: aor. pass., "the house *was filled*"
      ἐκ τῆς ὀσμῆς: using a preposition instead of the genitive after ἐπληρώθη,
         "filled *with the smell*"
12:4 ὁ μέλλων: pres. part. attributive, "the one about to" + inf.
12:5 ἐπράθη: aor. pass. of πιπράσκω, "why was this not sold?"

Chapter 12

Jesus Anointed at Bethany

¹ Iesus ergo ante sex dies Paschae venit Bethaniam, ubi erat Lazarus, quem suscitavit a mortuis Iesus. ² Fecerunt ergo ei cenam ibi, et Martha ministrabat, Lazarus vero unus erat ex discumbentibus cum eo. ³ Maria ergo accepit libram unguenti nardi puri, pretiosi, et unxit pedes Iesu et extersit capillis suis pedes eius; domus autem impleta est ex odore unguenti.

⁴ Dicit autem Iudas Iscariotes, unus ex discipulis eius, qui erat eum traditurus: ⁵ "Quare hoc unguentum non veniit

---

accipio, (3) **accepi**, **acceptus**: to receive, accept
Bethania, -ae *f*: Bethany
capillus, -i *m*: hair
cena, -ae *f*: dinner, supper
discumbens, -entis *m*: guest
domus, -i *f*: home
extergeo, (3), **extersi**, **extersum**: to wipe, wipe dry
impleo, (2), **implevi**, **impletus**: to fill up
libra, -ae *f*: unit of measure equal to about twelve ounces
Maria, -ae *f*: Mary
Martha, -ae *f*: Martha
ministro, (1): to attend, serve

mortuus, -i *m*: corpse, the dead
nardus, -i *m*: the ointment nard
odor, odoris *m*: scent, odor
Pascha, -ae, *f*: Passover
pes, pedis *m*: a foot
pretiosus, -a, -um: expensive, precious
purus, -a, -um: pure, clean
sex: six
suscito, (1): to raise, awaken
trado, (3), **tradidi**, **traditus**: to hand over, surrender
ungo, (3), **unxi**, **unctus**: to anoint, rub
unguentum, -i *n*: oil, perfume
veneo, (4), **venii**, **venitus**: to sell

12:3 **capillis suis:** abl. of means, "wiped *with her hair*"

ex odore: after *impleta est* where the ablative would be normal, "filled *with the odor*"

12:4 **traditurus:** fut. part. periphrasitic, "who was *about to betray*"

12:5 **non veniit:** perf., "why *did we not sell?*"

187

τριακοσίων δηναρίων καὶ ἐδόθη πτωχοῖς;» ⁶ εἶπεν δὲ τοῦτο
οὐχ ὅτι περὶ τῶν πτωχῶν ἔμελεν αὐτῷ ἀλλ᾽ ὅτι κλέπτης ἦν
καὶ τὸ γλωσσόκομον ἔχων τὰ βαλλόμενα ἐβάσταζεν.

⁷ εἶπεν οὖν ὁ Ἰησοῦς «Ἄφες αὐτήν, ἵνα εἰς τὴν ἡμέραν τοῦ
ἐνταφιασμοῦ μου τηρήσῃ αὐτό· ⁸ τοὺς πτωχοὺς γὰρ πάντοτε
ἔχετε μεθ᾽ ἑαυτῶν, ἐμὲ δὲ οὐ πάντοτε ἔχετε.»

⁹ ἔγνω οὖν ὁ ὄχλος πολὺς ἐκ τῶν Ἰουδαίων ὅτι ἐκεῖ ἐστίν,
καὶ ἦλθαν οὐ διὰ τὸν Ἰησοῦν μόνον ἀλλ᾽ ἵνα καὶ τὸν Λάζαρον
ἴδωσιν ὃν ἤγειρεν ἐκ νεκρῶν. ¹⁰ ἐβουλεύσαντο δὲ οἱ ἀρχιερεῖς
ἵνα καὶ τὸν Λάζαρον ἀποκτείνωσιν, ¹¹ ὅτι πολλοὶ δι᾽ αὐτὸν
ὑπῆγον τῶν Ἰουδαίων καὶ ἐπίστευον εἰς τὸν Ἰησοῦν.

ἀφίημι: to release, let go
βάλλω: to throw
βαστάζω: to carry off, steal
βουλεύω: to deliberate, plan
γλωσσόκομος, ὁ: a case, box
δηνάριον, τό: a denarius (a coin)
ἐνταφιασμός, ὁ: burial

κλέπτης, -ου, ὁ: a thief
μέλω: to be an object of care or thought
πιστεύω: to believe in
πτωχός, ὁ: a beggar, a poor person
τηρέω: to watch over, protect, keep
τριακόσιοι, -αι, -α: three hundred

τριακοσίων δηναρίων: gen. of price, "sold *for 300 denarii*"
ἐδόθη: aor. pass. of δίδωμι, "and why *was it not given?*"
12:6 οὐχ ὅτι ... ἔμελεν: impf. of μελω, "*not because there was a care* to him"
ἔχων: pres. part. with causal force, "*since he had* the moneybox"
τὰ βαλλόμενα: pres. part. attrib., "carry off *the things cast* into it"
12:7 ἄφες: aor. imper. of ἀπο-ίημι, "*leave* her!"
ἵνα ... τηρήσῃ: aor. subj. in result clause, "so that she can keep it"
αὐτό: i.e. the perfume
12:9 ἔγνω: aor. of γινώσκω, "the crowd *knew*"
ἵνα ... ἴδωσιν: aor. subj. of εἶδον in purpose clause, "went *to see* Lazarus"
12:10 ἵνα ... ἀποκτείνωσιν: aor. subj. in noun clause after ἐβουλεύσαντο instead of
an inf., "they planned *to kill*"
12:11 ὑπῆγον: impf. of ὑπο-ἄγω, "many *were withdrawing*"

trecentis denariis et datum est egenis?" ⁶ Dixit autem hoc, non quia de egenis pertinebat ad eum, sed quia fur erat et, loculos habens, ea, quae mittebantur, portabat.

⁷ Dixit ergo Iesus: "Sine illam, ut in diem sepulturae meae servet illud. ⁸ Pauperes enim semper habetis vobiscum, me autem non semper habetis."

⁹ Cognovit ergo turba multa ex Iudaeis quia illic est, et venerunt non propter Iesum tantum, sed ut et Lazarum viderent, quem suscitavit a mortuis. ¹⁰ Cogitaverunt autem principes sacerdotum, ut et Lazarum interficerent, ¹¹ quia multi propter illum abibant ex Iudaeis et credebant in Iesum.

---

abeo, (4): to depart, go away, go off
denarius, -i *m*: denarius (silver coin)
egenus, -a, -**um**: needy, poor
fur, furis *m/f*: thief, robber
loculus, -i *m*: money-box
pauper, -eris *m*: poor man
pertineo, (2): to concern, pertain to
porto, (1): to carry, bring
semper: always
sepultura, -ae *f*: burial, grave
servo, (1): to preserve, save

sino, (3): to allow, permit
trecentus, -a, -**um**: three hundred
multus, -a, -**um**: much, many
illic: in that place, there
tantum: so much, so far, only
suscito, (1): to awaken, rouse
cogito, (1): to know, intend, decide
princeps, -**ipis** *m*: leader, chief
sacerdos, -**dotis** *m/f*: priest
turba, -ae *f*: crowd, multitude

12:5   **trecentis denariis**: abl. of price, "worth three hundred denarii"
12:6   **pertinebat**: impersonal, "not because *there was a concern*"
12:7   **ut...servet**: pres. subj. in purpose clause, "allow her *to serve*"
12:9   **non propter Iesum tantum**: "not only because of Jesus"
      ut ... viderent: impf. subj. in purpose clause, "they went *in order to see*"
12:10 **ut... interficerent**: impf. subj. in noun clause of purpose after *cogitaverunt*,
      "they decided *that they would kill*"

Jesus Comes to Jerusalem as King

¹² τῇ ἐπαύριον ὁ ὄχλος πολὺς ὁ ἐλθὼν εἰς τὴν ἑορτήν, ἀκούσαντες ὅτι ἔρχεται Ἰησοῦς εἰς Ἱεροσόλυμα, ¹³ ἔλαβον τὰ βαΐα τῶν φοινίκων καὶ ἐξῆλθον εἰς ὑπάντησιν αὐτῷ, καὶ ἐκραύγαζον « Ὡσαννά, εὐλογημένος ὁ ἐρχόμενος ἐν ὀνόματι Κυρίου, καὶ ὁ βασιλεὺς τοῦ Ἰσραήλ.»

¹⁴ εὑρὼν δὲ ὁ Ἰησοῦς ὀνάριον ἐκάθισεν ἐπ᾽ αὐτό, καθώς ἐστιν γεγραμμένον

¹⁵ «Μὴ φοβοῦ, θυγάτηρ Σιών·

ἰδοὺ ὁ βασιλεύς σου ἔρχεται,

καθήμενος ἐπὶ πῶλον ὄνου.»

βαΐον, τό: a branch
βασιλεύς, -έως, ὁ: a king, chief
ἐπαύριον: on the morrow
εὐλογέω: to speak well, bless
εὑρίσκω: to find
θυγάτηρ, -τήρος, ἡ: a daughter
Ἰσραήλ (indecl.): Israel
κάθημαι: to be seated
καθίζω: to make to sit down
καθώς: just as

λαμβάνω: to take
ὀνάριον, τό: an ass
ὄνομα, -ατος, τό: name
ὄνος, ὁ: an ass
πῶλος, ὁ: a foal
Σιών (indecl.): Sion
ὑπάντησις, ἡ: coming to meet
φοβέομαι: to be afraid
φοῖνιξ, -ικος, ὁ: a palm leaf
Ὡσαννά: a cry of jubilation

12:12 τῇ ἐπαύριον (sc. ἡμέρᾳ): dat. of time when, "on the next day"
    ἀκούσαντες: aor. part., "having heard" agreeing with ὁ ὄχλος according to sense, not form
12:13 ἔλαβον: aor., "they *took* branches"
    εὐλογημένος: perf. part. pred., "*blessed* is the one"
12:14 εὑρὼν: aor. part. of εὑρίσκω, "Jesus *having found*"
    ἐστιν γεγραμμένον: perf. periphrastic, "just as *it is written*" (Zech. 9:9)
12:15 μὴ φοβοῦ: pres. imper. mid., "don't fear!"
    ἰδοὺ: aor. imper. mid. of εἶδον, "behold!"

Jesus Comes to Jerusalem as King

[12] In crastinum turba multa, quae venerat ad diem festum, cum audissent quia venit Iesus Hierosolymam, [13] acceperunt ramos palmarum et processerunt obviam ei et clamabant: "Hosanna! Benedictus, qui venit in nomine Domini, et rex Israel!"

[14] Invenit autem Iesus asellum et sedit super eum, sicut scriptum est:

[15] "Noli timere, filia Sion.

Ecce rex tuus venit

sedens super pullum asinae."

---

accipio, (3) **accepi, acceptus**: to receive
asellus, -i *m*: ass, donkey
asina, -ae *f*: she-ass
audio, (4): to hear
benedictus, -a, -um: blessed
clamo, (1): to cry out
crastinum, -i *n*: tomorrow
filia, -ae *f*: daughter
Hierosolyma, -ae *f*: Jerusalem
Israel: (indecl) Israel, people of Israel
nolo, nolle, nolui: wish not to (+ *inf.*)
nomen, -inis *n*: name

obviam: in the way (+ *dat.*)
palma, -ae *f*: palm
procedo, (3), **processi, processus**: to proceed, advance
pullus, -i, *m*. a foal
ramus, -i *m*: branch
rex, regis *m*: king
scribo, (3), **scripsi, scriptus**: to write
sedeo, (2), **sedi, sessus**: to sit, settle
Sion (*indecl.*): Zion
timeo, (2), **timui**: to fear

12:12 **in crastinum**: "on the next day" where the ablative would be normal
   cum audissent: plupf. subj. *cum* circumstantial clause, "when they had heard"
12:15 **Sion**: gen., "daughter *of Zion*"

¹⁶ ταῦτα οὐκ ἔγνωσαν αὐτοῦ οἱ μαθηταὶ τὸ πρῶτον, ἀλλ᾽ ὅτε ἐδοξάσθη Ἰησοῦς τότε ἐμνήσθησαν ὅτι ταῦτα ἦν ἐπ᾽ αὐτῷ γεγραμμένα καὶ ταῦτα ἐποίησαν αὐτῷ. ¹⁷ ἐμαρτύρει οὖν ὁ ὄχλος ὁ ὢν μετ᾽ αὐτοῦ ὅτε τὸν Λάζαρον ἐφώνησεν ἐκ τοῦ μνημείου καὶ ἤγειρεν αὐτὸν ἐκ νεκρῶν. ¹⁸ διὰ τοῦτο καὶ ὑπήντησεν αὐτῷ ὁ ὄχλος ὅτι ἤκουσαν τοῦτο αὐτὸν πεποιηκέναι τὸ σημεῖον. ¹⁹ οἱ οὖν Φαρισαῖοι εἶπαν πρὸς ἑαυτούς «Θεωρεῖτε ὅτι οὐκ ὠφελεῖτε οὐδέν· ἴδε ὁ κόσμος ὀπίσω αὐτοῦ ἀπῆλθεν.»

Jesus Predicts His Death

²⁰ ἦσαν δὲ Ἕλληνές τινες ἐκ τῶν ἀναβαινόντων ἵνα προσκυνήσωσιν ἐν τῇ ἑορτῇ· ²¹ οὗτοι οὖν προσῆλθαν Φιλίππῳ τῷ ἀπὸ Βηθσαϊδὰ τῆς Γαλιλαίας, καὶ ἠρώτων αὐτὸν λέγοντες «Κύριε,

---

ἀναβαίνω: to go up, ascend
γράφω: to write
ἐγείρω: to raise
Ἕλλην, -ηνος, ὁ: a Greek
ἑορτή, ἡ: a feast day
ἐρωτάω: to ask
θεωρέω: to look at, view, behold
κόσμος, ὁ: the world
κύριος, ὁ: a lord
μιμνήσκω: to remind

μνημεῖον, τό: a monument
νεκρός, ὁ: a corpse, a dead man
ὀπίσω: backwards, behind
ὄχλος, ὁ: a crowd
προσῆλθον: to come or go to (aor.)
προσκυνέω: to worship
σημεῖον, τό; a sign
ὑπαντάω: to go to meet
ὠφελέω: to serve, benefit

12:16 οὐκ ἔγνωσαν : aor., "they did not realize"
  τὸ πρῶτον: adverbial acc.,"at first"
  ἐδοξάσθη: aor.pass., "after *he was glorified*"
  ἐμνήσθησαν: aor. pass. of μιμνήσκω, "they remembered"
  ἦν γεγραμμένα: plupf. periphrastic in ind. st., "remembered that these things *had been written*"
12:17 ὁ ὢν μετ᾽ αὐτοῦ: "the crowd *who was with him*"
12:18 ὑπήντησεν: aor., "the crowd met him"
  πεποιηκέναι: perf. inf. in ind. st. after ἤκουσαν, "they heard *that he had made this sign*"
12:19 ὅτι οὐκ ὠφελεῖτε: impf., "do you see that *you do not benefit* at all"
12:20 ἵνα προσκυνήσωσιν: aor. subj. in purpose clause, "going up *in order to worship*"

¹⁶ Haec non cognoverunt discipuli eius primum, sed quando glorificatus est Iesus, tunc recordati sunt quia haec erant scripta de eo, et haec fecerunt ei.

¹⁷ Testimonium ergo perhibebat turba, quae erat cum eo, quando Lazarum vocavit de monumento et suscitavit eum a mortuis. ¹⁸ Propterea et obviam venit ei turba, quia audierunt eum fecisse hoc signum. ¹⁹ Pharisaei ergo dixerunt ad semetipsos: "Videtis quia nihil proficitis? Ecce mundus post eum abiit!"

Jesus Predicts His Death

²⁰ Erant autem Graeci quidam ex his, qui ascenderant, ut adorarent in die festo; ²¹ hi ergo accesserunt ad Philippum, qui erat a Bethsaida Galilaeae, et rogabant eum dicentes: "Domine,

---

abeo, (4), **abii, abitum**: to depart, go away
accedo, (3) **accessi**: to come near, approach
adoro, (1): to honor, worship
audio, (4) **audivi, auditus**: to hear
Bethsaida: Bethsaida (north of the Sea of Galilee)
festus, -a, -um: festive
Galilaea, -ae *f*: Galilee
glorifico, (1): to glorify; magnify
Graecus, -i *m*: a Greek
monumentum, -i *n*: tomb
mundus, -i, *m*. the world
nihil: nothing
obviam: in the way (+ *dat.*)

perhibeo, (2): to present, give
Philippus, -i *m*: Philip
primum: at first; in the first place
proficio, (3): to make, accomplish, effect
propterea: therefore, for this reason
quando: when
recordor, (1): to think over; remember
rogo, (1): to ask
semetipse, -a, -um: one's self
suscito, (1): to awaken, rouse
testimonium, -i *n*: testimony
tunc: then, thereupon
voco, (1): to call, summon

12:16 **erant scripta:** plupf. in ind. st., "remembered that these things *had been written*"

12:18 **fecisse:** perf. inf. in ind. st., "because they heard *that he had done*"

12:20 **ut adorarent:** impf. subj. purpose clause, "had gone up *in order to worship*"

193

θέλομεν τὸν Ἰησοῦν ἰδεῖν.» ²² ἔρχεται ὁ Φίλιππος καὶ λέγει τῷ Ἀνδρέᾳ· ἔρχεται Ἀνδρέας καὶ Φίλιππος καὶ λέγουσιν τῷ Ἰησοῦ.

²³ ὁ δὲ Ἰησοῦς ἀποκρίνεται αὐτοῖς λέγων «Ἐλήλυθεν ἡ ὥρα ἵνα δοξασθῇ ὁ υἱὸς τοῦ ἀνθρώπου. ²⁴ ἀμὴν ἀμὴν λέγω ὑμῖν, ἐὰν μὴ ὁ κόκκος τοῦ σίτου πεσὼν εἰς τὴν γῆν ἀποθάνῃ, αὐτὸς μόνος μένει· ἐὰν δὲ ἀποθάνῃ, πολὺν καρπὸν φέρει. ²⁵ ὁ φιλῶν τὴν ψυχὴν αὐτοῦ ἀπολλύει αὐτήν, καὶ ὁ μισῶν τὴν ψυχὴν αὐτοῦ ἐν τῷ κόσμῳ τούτῳ εἰς ζωὴν αἰώνιον φυλάξει αὐτήν. ²⁶ ἐὰν ἐμοί τις διακονῇ ἐμοὶ ἀκολουθείτω, καὶ ὅπου εἰμὶ ἐγὼ ἐκεῖ καὶ ὁ διάκονος ὁ ἐμὸς ἔσται· ἐάν τις ἐμοὶ διακονῇ τιμήσει αὐτὸν ὁ πατήρ.

αἰώνιος, -α, -ον: lasting for an age
Ἀνδρέας, ὁ: Andrew
ἀπολύω: to loose from
γῆ, ἡ: earth
διακονέω: to minister, serve
διάκονος, ὁ: a servant, waiting-man
ζωή, ἡ: life
θέλω: to will, wish, purpose
καρπός, ὁ: fruit
κόκκος, ὁ: a grain, seed
κόσμος, ὁ: the world
μισέω: to hate

μόνος, -η, -ον: alone, only
πίπτω: to fall, fall down
πολύς, πολλά, πολύ: many
σῖτος, ὁ: corn, grain
τιμάω: to honor
υἱός, ὁ: a son
φέρω: to bear
φιλέω: to love
φυλάσσω: to keep, guard
ψυχή, ἡ: soul, life
ὥρα, ἡ: hour, period of time

12:21 ἰδεῖν: aor. inf. of εἶδον complementing θέλομεν, "we wish *to see*"
12:22 ἔρχεται ... καὶ λέγουσιν: note the casual shift from singular to plural
12:23 ἐλήλυθεν: perf., "the hour *has come*"
  ἵνα δοξασθῇ: aor. pass. subj. in clause of purpose and result, "the hour has come *for the son to be glorified*"
12:24 ἐὰν μὴ ... ἀποθάνῃ: aor. subj. in present general protasis, "unless a grain of wheat dies"
  πεσὼν: aor. part. of πίπτω, "a seed *having fallen*"
  ἐὰν δὲ ἀποθάνῃ: aor. subj. in pres. general protasis, "but if it dies"
12:25 φυλάξει: fut. of φυλάσσω, "he will keep it"
12:26 ἐὰν ἐμοί τις διακονῇ: pres. subj. in fut. more vivid protasis, "if anyone serves me"
  ἀκολουθείτω: pres. imper. 3 s. of ἀκολουθέω, "let him follow!"
  τιμήσει: fut. of τιμάω, "the father *will honor* him"

volumus Iesum videre." ²² Venit Philippus et dicit Andreae; venit Andreas et Philippus et dicunt Iesu.

²³ Iesus autem respondet eis dicens: "Venit hora, ut glorificetur Filius hominis. ²⁴ Amen, amen dico vobis: Nisi granum frumenti cadens in terram mortuum fuerit, ipsum solum manet; si autem mortuum fuerit, multum fructum affert. ²⁵ Qui amat animam suam, perdit eam; et, qui odit animam suam in hoc mundo, in vitam aeternam custodiet eam. ²⁶ Si quis mihi ministrat, me sequatur, et ubi sum ego, illic et minister meus erit; si quis mihi ministraverit, honorificabit eum Pater.

---

aeternus, -a, -um: eternal, everlasting
affero, afferre: to bring forth
amo, (1): to love
Andreas *m*: Andrew
anima, -ae *f*: soul, spirit
cado, (3): to fall, sink, drop
custodio, (4): to preserve, keep
fructus, -us *m*: crops, fruit
frumentum, -i *n*: grain
glorifico, (1): to glorify
granum, -i *n*: seed
honorifico, (1): to honor
hora, -ae *f*: hour, time

illic: in that place, there
maneo, (2): to remain
minister, -tri *m*. minister, servant
ministro, (1): to attend, serve
morior, (3), **mortuus sum**: to die
multus, -a, -um: much many
odi, odisse: to hate (*perf.*)
perdo, (3): to lose
sequor, (3), **secutus sum**: to follow
solus, -a, -um: only, single
terra, -ae *f*: land, ground
vita, -ae *f*: life
volo, velle: to wish, want

12:22 **venit Andreas et Philippus**: Jerome preserves the inconsistency in number between subject and verb from the Greek

12:23 **ut glorificetur**: pres. subj. in purpose/result clause, "the hour has come *for the son to be glorified*"

12:24 **nisi... mortuum fuerit**: fut. perf. in pres. general condition, "*unless* a grain *becomes dead*"

12:26 **si quis ministrat ... si quis ministraverit**: note the variation in translating the Greek διακονῇ because of the different apodoses, one an imperative, one a future

²⁷ νῦν ἡ ψυχή μου τετάρακται, καὶ τί εἴπω; πάτερ, σῶσόν με ἐκ τῆς ὥρας ταύτης. ἀλλὰ διὰ τοῦτο ἦλθον εἰς τὴν ὥραν ταύτην. ²⁸ πάτερ, δόξασόν σου τὸ ὄνομα.»

ἦλθεν οὖν φωνὴ ἐκ τοῦ οὐρανοῦ «Καὶ ἐδόξασα καὶ πάλιν δοξάσω.» ²⁹ ὁ οὖν ὄχλος ὁ ἑστὼς καὶ ἀκούσας ἔλεγεν βροντὴν γεγονέναι· ἄλλοι ἔλεγον «Ἄγγελος αὐτῷ λελάληκεν.»

³⁰ ἀπεκρίθη καὶ εἶπεν Ἰησοῦς «Οὐ δι' ἐμὲ ἡ φωνὴ αὕτη γέγονεν ἀλλὰ δι' ὑμᾶς. ³¹ νῦν κρίσις ἐστὶν τοῦ κόσμου τούτου, νῦν ὁ ἄρχων τοῦ κόσμου τούτου ἐκβληθήσεται ἔξω· ³² κἀγὼ ἂν ὑψωθῶ ἐκ τῆς γῆς, πάντας ἑλκύσω πρὸς ἐμαυτόν.» ³³ τοῦτο δὲ ἔλεγεν σημαίνων ποίῳ θανάτῳ ἤμελλεν ἀποθνήσκειν.

ἄγγελος, ὁ: angel, messenger	μέλλω: to to be about to (+ *inf.*)
ἄρχων, -οντος, ὁ: commander, chief, captain	ὄνομα, -ατος, τό: a name
βροντή, ἡ: thunder	οὐρανός, ὁ: heaven
δοξάζω: to glorify	ὄχλος, ὁ: a crowd
ἐκβάλλω: to throw or cast out of	πατήρ, πατρός, ὁ: a father
ἕλκω: to draw, drag	ποῖος, -α, -ον: of what nature? of what sort?
ἐμαυτοῦ: of me, of myself	σημαίνω: to indicate, make known
ἔξω (*adv.*): outside	σώζω: to save
θάνατος, ὁ: death	ταράσσω: to trouble
κόσμος, ὁ: the world	ὑψόω: to lift high, exalt
κρίσις, ἡ: a judgement	φωνή, ἡ: a voice
λαλέω: to speak	ψυχή, ἡ: soul, life

12:27 τετάρακται: perf. of ταράσσω, "my soul is troubled"

τί εἴπω; aor. subj. of λέγω in delib. quest., "What should I say?"

σῶσόν: aor. imper. answering deliberative question, "(should I say) *save* me?"

12:29 ὁ ἑστὼς: perf. part. of ἵστημι, "the crowd *which was standing*"

γεγονέναι: perf. inf. in ind. st. after ἔλεγεν, "said that thunder *happened*"

12:30 γέγονεν: perf., "this voice *has happened*"

12:31 ἐκβληθήσεται: fut. pass. of ἐκ-βάλλω, "he shall be cast out"

12:32 ἂν ὑψωθῶ: aor. pass. subj. in fut. more vivid protasis,"if I am exalted"

ἑλκύσω: fut. of ἕλκω, "*I will draw* with me"

12:33 ποίῳ θανάτῳ: dat., "signalling *by what sort of death*"

ἤμελλεν: impf. + pres. inf., "*was destined to die*"

12:34 ὑψωθῆναι: aor. pass. inf. after δεῖ, "it is necessary for the son to be exalted"

²⁷ Nunc anima mea turbata est. Et quid dicam? Pater, salvifica me ex hora hac? Sed propterea veni in horam hanc. ²⁸ Pater, glorifica tuum nomen!"

Venit ergo vox de caelo: "Et glorificavi et iterum glorificabo." ²⁹ Turba ergo, quae stabat et audierat, dicebat tonitruum factum esse; alii dicebant: "Angelus ei locutus est."

³⁰ Respondit Iesus et dixit: "Non propter me vox haec facta est sed propter vos. ³¹ Nunc iudicium est huius mundi, nunc princeps huius mundi eicietur foras; ³² et ego, si exaltatus fuero a terra, omnes traham ad meipsum." ³³ Hoc autem dicebat significans, qua morte esset moriturus.

---

alius, alia, aliud: other
angelus, -i *m*: angel
caelus, -i *m*: heaven
eicio, (3), **eieci, eiectus**: to cast out, expel, discharge
exalto, (1): to exalt, elevate
foras (*adv*.): outside
glorifico, (1): to glorify
hora, -ae *f*: hour
iudicium, -i *n*: judgement
loquor, (3), **locutus sum**: to speak
mors, mortis *f*: death

mundus, -i *m*: world
nomen, -inis *n*: name
nunc: now, today
pater, patris *m*: father
princeps, -cipis *m*: lord
salvifico, (1): to save, deliver
significo, (1): to signify, indicate, show
tonitrus, -us: thunder
traho, (3): to draw, drag
turba, -ae *f*: crowd
vox, vocis, *f*: voice

12:27 **quid dicam**: pres. subj. deliberative, "what should I say?"
　　　salvifica: pres. imper. answering deliberative question, "(should I say) *save* me?"
12:28 **factum esse**: perf. inf. in ind. st., "were saying that thunder *had been made*"
12:32 **si exaltatus fuero**: fut. perf. periphrastic in future more vivid protasis, "if I am exalted"
12:33 **qua... esset moriturus**: impf. subj. with fut. act. part. periphrastic in ind. quest., "signifying by what death *he would die*"

³⁴ ἀπεκρίθη οὖν αὐτῷ ὁ ὄχλος «Ἡμεῖς ἠκούσαμεν ἐκ τοῦ νόμου ὅτι ὁ χριστὸς μένει εἰς τὸν αἰῶνα, καὶ πῶς λέγεις σὺ ὅτι δεῖ ὑψωθῆναι τὸν υἱὸν τοῦ ἀνθρώπου ; τίς ἐστιν οὗτος ὁ υἱὸς τοῦ ἀνθρώπου;»

³⁵ εἶπεν οὖν αὐτοῖς ὁ Ἰησοῦς «Ἔτι μικρὸν χρόνον τὸ φῶς ἐν ὑμῖν ἐστίν. περιπατεῖτε ὡς τὸ φῶς ἔχετε, ἵνα μὴ σκοτία ὑμᾶς καταλάβῃ, καὶ ὁ περιπατῶν ἐν τῇ σκοτίᾳ οὐκ οἶδεν ποῦ ὑπάγει. ³⁶ ὡς τὸ φῶς ἔχετε, πιστεύετε εἰς τὸ φῶς, ἵνα υἱοὶ φωτὸς γένησθε.» Ταῦτα ἐλάλησεν Ἰησοῦς, καὶ ἀπελθὼν ἐκρύβη ἀπ' αὐτῶν.

Belief and Unbelief Among the Jews

³⁷ τοσαῦτα δὲ αὐτοῦ σημεῖα πεποιηκότος ἔμπροσθεν αὐτῶν οὐκ ἐπίστευον εἰς αὐτόν, ³⁸ ἵνα ὁ λόγος Ἡσαίου τοῦ προφήτου πληρωθῇ ὃν εἶπεν

δεῖ: it is necessary
ἔμπροσθεν (adv.): before, in front
καταλαμβάνω: to seize upon, overtake
κρύπτω: to hide, cover, cloak
μικρός, -ά, -όν: small, little
νόμος, ὁ: custom, law
ὄχλος, ὁ: a crowd

περιπατέω: to walk about
πληρόω: to fulfill
σκοτία, ἡ: darkness, gloom
τοσοῦτος, -αύτη, -οῦτο: so large, so tall
ὑψόω: to lift high, raise up
φῶς, φωτός, τό: light, daylight
χριστός, -ή, -όν: annointed

12:35 ἔτι μικρὸν χρόνον: acc. of duration of time, "for a short time more"
  περιπατεῖτε: imper., "walk!"
  ὡς τὸ φῶς ἔχετε: "so long as you have the light"
  ἵνα μὴ ... καταλάβῃ: aor. subj. in result/purpose clause," so that the darkness does not overtake"
12:36 ἵνα ... γένησθε: aor. subj. in clause of purpose/result, "so that *you become* sons"
  ἐκρύβη: aor. pass. of κρύπτω, "he became hidden"
12:37 πεποιηκότος: perf. part. in gen. abs. with concessive force, "despite him having done"
12:38 ἵνα ... πληρωθῇ: aor. pass. subj. in result clause, "so that the word of Isaiah was fulfilled" (Is. 6:9-10)

198

³⁴ Respondit ergo ei turba: "Nos audivimus ex Lege, quia Christus manet in aeternum; et quomodo tu dicis: 'Oportet exaltari Filium hominis'? Quis est iste Filius hominis?"

³⁵ Dixit ergo eis Iesus: "Adhuc modicum tempus lumen in vobis est. Ambulate, dum lucem habetis, ut non tenebrae vos comprehendant; et, qui ambulat in tenebris, nescit quo vadat. ³⁶ Dum lucem habetis, credite in lucem, ut filii lucis fiatis." Haec locutus est Iesus et abiit et abscondit se ab eis.

Belief and Unbelief Among the Jews

³⁷ Cum autem tanta signa fecisset coram eis, non credebant in eum, ³⁸ ut sermo Isaiae prophetae impleretur, quem dixit:

---

abeo, (4), **abii, abitum**: to depart, go away
abscondo, (3): to hide, conceal
adhuc: thus far, still
aeternus, -a, -um: eternal
ambulo, (1): to walk
comprehendo, (3): to grasp, overtake
coram: in person, in the presence of (+ *dat.*)
impleo (2): to fill, fulfill
Isaia, -ae *m*: Isaiah
iste, ista, istud: that one
lex, legis *f*: law
loquor, (3), **locutus sum**: to speak
lumen, luminis *n*: light
lux, lucis *f*: light
maneo (2): to remain
modicus, -a, -um: small
oportet, (2): it is right, ought
propheta, -ae *m*: prophet
quomodo: how, in what way
sermo, sermonis *m*: diction, word
signum, -i *n*: a sign
tantus, -a, -um: so great
tempus, temporis *n*: time
tenebrae, -arum *f*: darkness
vado, (3), **vasi**: to go

12:35 **ut non ... comprehendant**: pres. subj. mixing result and purpose, "walk around *lest* the darkness *overtake*"
quo vadat: pres. subj. indirect question, "he does not know *where he goes*"
12:36 **ut... fiatis**: pres. subj. clause mixing purpose and result, "believe *so that you become*"
12:37 **cum... fecisset**: plupf. subj. *cum* concessive clause, "although he had done"
12:38 **ut... impleretur**: impf. subj. purpose clause, "they did not believe *in order to fufill*"

«Κύριε, τίς ἐπίστευσεν τῇ ἀκοῇ ἡμῶν;
καὶ ὁ βραχίων Κυρίου τίνι ἀπεκαλύφθη;»

³⁹ διὰ τοῦτο οὐκ ἠδύναντο πιστεύειν, ὅτι πάλιν εἶπεν Ἡσαΐας

⁴⁰ «Τετύφλωκεν αὐτῶν τοὺς ὀφθαλμοὺς
καὶ ἐπώρωσεν αὐτῶν τὴν καρδίαν,
ἵνα μὴ ἴδωσιν τοις ὀφθαλμοῖς
καὶ νοήσωσιν τῇ καρδίᾳ
καὶ στραφῶσιν, καὶ ἰάσωμαι αὐτούς.»

⁴¹ ταῦτα εἶπεν Ἡσαΐας ὅτι εἶδεν τὴν δόξαν αὐτοῦ, καὶ ἐλάλησεν περὶ αὐτοῦ.

ἀκοή, ἡ: a hearing, the sound heard
ἀποκαλύπτω: to uncover
βραχίων, -ονος, ὁ: the arm
δόξα, ἡ: glory
ἰάομαι: to heal, cure
καρδία, ἡ: the heart
κύριος, ὁ: lord

λαλέω: to speak
νοέω: to perceive by the eyes, observe
ὀφθαλμός, ὁ: the eye
πάλιν: again
πωρόω: to petrify, turn into stone
στρέφω: to turn about or aside, turn
τυφλόω: to blind, make blind

12:38 ἀπεκαλύφθη: aor. pass. of ἀπο-καλύπτω, "to whom has it been revealed?"
12:39 ἠδύναντο: aor., "they were unable to" + inf.
12:40 τετύφλωκεν: perf. of τυφλόω, "he has blinded these eyes"
    ἐπώρωσεν: aor. of πωρόω, "he has hardened their hearts"
    ἵνα μὴ ἴδωσιν ... νοήσωσιν ... στραφῶσιν ... ἰάσωμαι: aor. subj. expressing purpose and result, "so that they do not see ...so that they do not understand ... so that they are not converted ... so that I do not heal them"
12:41 περὶ αὐτοῦ: "about him" i.e. Jesus

"Domine, quis credidit auditui nostro,

et brachium Domini cui revelatum est?"

³⁹ Propterea non poterant credere, quia iterum dixit Isaias:

⁴⁰ "Excaecavit oculos eorum

et induravit eorum cor,

ut non videant oculis

et intellegant corde

et convertantur, et sanem eos."

⁴¹ Haec dixit Isaias, quia vidit gloriam eius et locutus est de eo.

---

auditus, -us *m*: hearing, listening
brachium, -i *n*: the arm
convertor, (3), **conversus sum**: to change, convert
cor, cordis *n*: heart
credo, (3): to believe in
excaeco, (1): to blind
induro, (1): to make hard

intellego, (3): to understand
iterum: again; a second time
loquor, (3) **locutus sum**: to speak
noster, -a, -um: our
oculus, -i *m*: the eye
possum, posse: be able, can (+ *inf.*)
revelo, (1): to show, reveal
sano, (1): to cure, heal

12:40 **ut non videant... intellegant... convertantur ...sanem**: pres. subj. mixing result and purpose, "so that they do not see ... do not understand ... are not converted ...and I do not heal them"

201

⁴² ὅμως μέντοι καὶ ἐκ τῶν ἀρχόντων πολλοὶ ἐπίστευσαν εἰς αὐτόν, ἀλλὰ διὰ τοὺς Φαρισαίους οὐχ ὡμολόγουν ἵνα μὴ ἀποσυνάγωγοι γένωνται, ⁴³ ἠγάπησαν γὰρ τὴν δόξαν τῶν ἀνθρώπων μᾶλλον ἤπερ τὴν δόξαν τοῦ θεοῦ.

⁴⁴ Ἰησοῦς δὲ ἔκραξεν καὶ εἶπεν «Ὁ πιστεύων εἰς ἐμὲ οὐ πιστεύει εἰς ἐμὲ ἀλλὰ εἰς τὸν πέμψαντά με, ⁴⁵ καὶ ὁ θεωρῶν ἐμὲ θεωρεῖ τὸν πέμψαντά με. ⁴⁶ ἐγὼ φῶς εἰς τὸν κόσμον ἐλήλυθα, ἵνα πᾶς ὁ πιστεύων εἰς ἐμὲ ἐν τῇ σκοτίᾳ μὴ μείνῃ.

⁴⁷ καὶ ἐάν τίς μου ἀκούσῃ τῶν ῥημάτων καὶ μὴ φυλάξῃ, ἐγὼ οὐ κρίνω αὐτόν, οὐ γὰρ ἦλθον ἵνα κρίνω τὸν κόσμον ἀλλ' ἵνα σώσω τὸν κόσμον. ⁴⁸ ὁ ἀθετῶν ἐμὲ καὶ μὴ λαμβάνων τὰ ῥήματά μου ἔχει τὸν κρίνοντα αὐτόν· ὁ λόγος ὃν ἐλάλησα ἐκεῖνος κρινεῖ αὐτὸν ἐν τῇ ἐσχάτῃ ἡμέρᾳ·

ἀγαπάω: to love, be fond of	κρίνω: to judge
ἀθετέω: to set aside	ὁμολογέω: to agree
ἀποσυνάγωγος, -ον: put out of the synagogue	ὁμῶς: equally, nevertheless
ἄρχων, -οντος, ὁ: a leader	πέμπω: to send, despatch
ἔσχατος, -η, -ον: last	ῥῆμα, -ατος, τό: a word, saying
ἡμέρα, ἡ: day	φυλάσσω: to keep watch, keep guard
κράζω: to cry out	φῶς, φωτός, τό: a light

12:42 οὐχ ὡμολόγουν: impf. of ὁμολογέω, "they were not agreeing"

> ἵνα μὴ ... γένωνται: aor. subj. in purp/result clause, "not agreeing *lest they become* ejected from the synagogue"

12:43 μᾶλλον ἤπερ: "loved X (acc.) *more than* Y (acc.)"

12:44 τὸν πέμψαντά: aor. part. attributive, "believes in *the one who sent* me"

12:46 ἵνα ... μὴ μείνῃ: aor. subj. in purpose clause, "lest the believer remain"

12:47 ἐάν τίς μου ἀκούσῃ ... μὴ φυλάξῃ: aor. subj. in pres. general protasis, "if anyone hears ... and does not keep"

> ἵνα κρίνω ... ἵνα σώσω: aor. subj. in purpose clause, "I did not come *in order to judge* ...but *in order to save*"

12:48 ὁ ἀθετῶν ...μὴ λαμβάνων: pres. part. conditional, "he who (if) rejecting ...if not receiving"

> τὸν κρίνοντα: pres. part. attributive, "he has *one who is judging him*"

> κρινεῖ: fut. of κρίνω, "the word which he spoke *will judge* him"

⁴² Verumtamen et ex principibus multi crediderunt in eum, sed propter pharisaeos non confitebantur, ut de synagoga non eicerentur; ⁴³ dilexerunt enim gloriam hominum magis quam gloriam Dei.

⁴⁴ Iesus autem clamavit et dixit: "Qui credit in me, non credit in me sed in eum, qui misit me; ⁴⁵ et, qui videt me, videt eum, qui misit me. ⁴⁶ Ego lux in mundum veni, ut omnis, qui credit in me, in tenebris non maneat.

⁴⁷ Et si quis audierit verba mea et non custodierit, ego non iudico eum; non enim veni, ut iudicem mundum, sed ut salvificem mundum. ⁴⁸ Qui spernit me et non accipit verba mea, habet, qui iudicet eum: sermo, quem locutus sum, ille iudicabit eum in novissimo die,

---

accipio, (3): to accept	**novissimus, -a, -um**: last
audio, (4): to hear	**perno**, (3): to scorn, despise
clamo, (1): to proclaim, declare	**princeps, -cipis** *m*: leader, chief
confiteor, (2), **confessus sum**: to confess	**salvifico**, (1): to save, deliver
diligo, (3), **dilexi, dilectus**: love	**sermo, -onis** *m*: word, speech
iudico, (1): to judge	**synagoga, -ae** *f.*: synagogue
lux, lucis *f.*: a light	**tenebrae, -arum** *f.*: darkness
mitto, (3), **misi, missus**: to send	**verbum, -i** *n*: word, proverb
mundus, -i *m*: world	**verumtamen**: but yet, nevertheless

12:42 **ut... non eicerentur**: impf. subj. in purpose clause, "*in order that they not be thrown out*" where we would expect *ne*.

12:43 **magis quam**: "*loved X (acc.) more than Y (acc.)*"

12:46 **ut... non maneat**: pres. subj. purpose clause, "come *in order that* all *do not remain*" where we would expect *ne*

12:47 **si quis ... audierit... custodierit**: fut. perf. in pres. general protasis, "*if anyone has heard and has not preserved*"

    ut iudicem ... ut salvificem: pres. subj. in purpose clause, "have not come *to judge ...but to save*"

12:48 **qui iudicet**: pres. subj. in relative clause of characteristic whose antecedent is the object of *habet*, "has (one) *who would judge*"

⁴⁹ ὅτι ἐγὼ ἐξ ἐμαυτοῦ οὐκ ἐλάλησα, ἀλλ᾽ ὁ πέμψας με πατὴρ αὐτός μοι ἐντολὴν δέδωκεν τί εἴπω καὶ τί λαλήσω. ⁵⁰ καὶ οἶδα ὅτι ἡ ἐντολὴ αὐτοῦ ζωὴ αἰώνιός ἐστιν. ἃ οὖν ἐγὼ λαλῶ, καθὼς εἴρηκέν μοι ὁ πατήρ, οὕτως λαλῶ.»

Chapter 13

Jesus Washes His Disciples' Feet

¹ πρὸ δέ τῆς ἑορτῆς τοῦ πάσχα εἰδὼς ὁ Ἰησοῦς ὅτι ἦλθεν αὐτοῦ ἡ ὥρα ἵνα μεταβῇ ἐκ τοῦ κόσμου τούτου πρὸς τὸν πατέρα ἀγαπήσας τοὺς ἰδίους τοὺς ἐν τῷ κόσμῳ εἰς τέλος ἠγάπησεν αὐτούς.

² καὶ δείπνου γινομένου, τοῦ διαβόλου ἤδη βεβληκό-τος εἰς τὴν καρδίαν ἵνα παραδῷ αὐτὸν Ἰούδας Σίμωνος Ἰσκαριώτης, ³ εἰδὼς ὅτι πάντα ἔδωκεν αὐτῷ ὁ πατὴρ εἰς

ἀγαπάω: to love	καρδία, ἡ: heart
αἰώνιος, -α, -ον: eternal	κόσμος, ὁ: the world
δεῖπνον, τό: the principal meal, dinner	λαλέω: to talk
διάβολος, -ον: the devil	μεταβαίνω: to pass from one place to another
ἑορτή, ἡ: a feast	παραδίδωμι: to betray
ζωή, ἡ: life	πέμπω: to send
ἴδιος, -α, -ον: one's own	τέλος, -εος, τό: the end

12:49 **πατὴρ αὐτός**: "the father himself"

    τί εἴπω καὶ τί λαλήσω: aor. subj. in ind. delib. quest., "commanded *what I should say and what should I speak*"

12:50 **εἴρηκέν**: perf., "just as *he has spoken*"

13:1 **εἰδὼς**: perf. part. of **εἶδον**, "Jesus, *knowing*"

    ἵνα μεταβῇ: aor. subj. of **μετα-βαίνω** in purpose clause, "the hour has arrived *for him to depart*"

    ἀγαπήσας: aor. part. circum., "*as he had loved* them"

13:2 **δείπνου γινομένου**: gen. abs., "while dinner was happening"

    βεβληκότος: perf. part. of **βάλλω** in gen. abs., "the devil *having already cast* into his heart"

    ἵνα παραδῷ: aor. subj. in noun clause serving as direct object of **βεβληκότος**, "having cast into his heart *to betray*"

    Σίμωνος: gen., "Judas, (the son) *of Simon*, the Isacariot," with the toponym here agreeing with Judas, not Simon

⁴⁹ quia ego ex meipso non sum locutus, sed, qui misit me, Pater, ipse mihi mandatum dedit quid dicam et quid loquar. ⁵⁰ Et scio quia mandatum eius vita aeterna est. Quae ergo ego loquor, sicut dixit mihi Pater, sic loquor."

Chapter 13

Jesus Washes His Disciples' Feet

¹ Ante diem autem festum Paschae, sciens Iesus quia venit eius hora, ut transeat ex hoc mundo ad Patrem, cum dilexisset suos, qui erant in mundo, in finem dilexit eos.

² Et in cena, cum Diabolus iam misisset in corde, ut traderet eum Iudas Simonis Iscariotis, ³ sciens quia omnia dedit ei Pater in

---

cena, cenae *f.*: dinner, supper	**mandatum, -i** *n*: command
cor, cordis *n*: the heart	**mundus, -i** *m*: the world
diabolus, -i *m*: devil	**scio**, (4): to know, understand
festus, -a, -um: festive	**sicut**: just as
finis, finis *m/f.*: limit, end	**Simon, Simonis** *m*: Simon
Iscariotes, -tis *m*: the Iscariot	**trado**, (3): to hand over
loquor, (3) **locutus sum**: to speak	**transeo**, (2): to go over, cross

12:49 **quid dicam et quid loquar**: pres. subj. in indirect deliberative question, "commanded *what I should say and what I should speak*"

13:1 **ut transeat**: pres. subj. in noun clause of purpose, "the hour arrived *for him to go over*"

    cum dilexisset: plupf. subj. *cum* circum. clause, "*as he had loved* his own"

13:2 **cum misisset**: plupf. subj. *cum* circumstantial clause, "when he had sent"

    in corde: "sent *into his heart*," where the acc. would be expected

    ut traderet: impf. subj. purpose clause, "sent into his heart *to betray*"

    Simonis Iscariotis: gen., "Judas (the son) *of Simon Iscariot* with the toponym agreeing with Simon, not Judas

τὰς χεῖρας, καὶ ὅτι ἀπὸ θεοῦ ἐξῆλθεν καὶ πρὸς τὸν θεὸν ὑπάγει,
⁴ ἐγείρεται ἐκ τοῦ δείπνου καὶ τίθησιν τὰ ἱμάτια, καὶ λαβὼν
λέντιον διέζωσεν ἑαυτόν· ⁵ εἶτα βάλλει ὕδωρ εἰς τὸν νιπτῆρα,
καὶ ἤρξατο νίπτειν τοὺς πόδας τῶν μαθητῶν καὶ ἐκμάσσειν
τῷ λεντίῳ ᾧ ἦν διεζωσμένος.

⁶ ἔρχεται οὖν πρὸς Σίμωνα Πέτρον. λέγει αὐτῷ «Κύριε,
σύ μου νίπτεις τοὺς πόδας;»

⁷ ἀπεκρίθη Ἰησοῦς καὶ εἶπεν αὐτῷ «Ὃ ἐγὼ ποιῶ σὺ οὐκ
οἶδας ἄρτι, γνώσῃ δὲ μετὰ ταῦτα.»

⁸ λέγει αὐτῷ Πέτρος «Οὐ μὴ νίψῃς μου τοὺς πόδας εἰς
τὸν αἰῶνα.»

ἀπεκρίθη Ἰησοῦς αὐτῷ «Ἐὰν μὴ νίψω σε, οὐκ ἔχεις
μέρος μετ' ἐμοῦ.»

αἰών, αἰῶνος, ὁ: age, eternity
ἄρτι: just now
ἄρχομαι: to begin
δεῖπνος, ὁ: the principal mean, dinner
διαζώννυμι: to gird round the middle
ἐγείρω: to awaken, wake up, rouse
ἐκμάσσω: to wipe off, wipe away
ἱμάτιον, τό: an outer garment, a cloak
λέντιον, τό: cloth, towel

μαθητής, ὁ: a disciple
μέρος, -εος, τό: a part, share
νιπτήρ, -ῆρος, ὁ: a washing vessel, basin
νίπτω: to wash the hands or feet
πούς, ποδός, ὁ: a foot
τίθημι: to set, put, place
ὕδωρ, ὕδατος, τό: water
ὑπάγω: to withdraw, go
χείρ, χειρός, ἡ: the hand

13:3   ἐξῆλθεν: aor., "knowing that *he had departed* from God"
13:4   λαβών: aor. part. circum., "having taken"
       διέζωσεν: aor. of δια-ζώννυμι, "*he girded* himself"
13:5   βάλλει: note the vivid presents interspersed in the account, "*he throws* water"
       ἤρξατο: aor. of ἄρχω, "he began" + inf.
       ᾧ ἦν διεζωσμένος: perf. periphrastic of δια-ζώννυμι, "the towel *with which he had girded* himself"
13:6   λέγει: "he (Peter) speaks." Note the lack of an indication of change of subject.
13:7   ὃ ἐγὼ ποιῶ: "what I do"
       γνώσῃ: fut., "you will know"
13:8   οὐ μὴ νίψῃς: aor. subj. in strong denial, "surely you do not wash!"
       ἐὰν μὴ νίψω: aor. subj. in pres. general protasis, "unless I wash"

manus, et quia a Deo exivit et ad Deum vadit, ⁴ surgit a cena et ponit vestimenta sua et, cum accepisset linteum, praecinxit se. ⁵ Deinde mittit aquam in pelvem et coepit lavare pedes discipulorum et extergere linteo, quo erat praecinctus.

⁶ Venit ergo ad Simonem Petrum. Dicit ei: "Domine, tu mihi lavas pedes?"

⁷ Respondit Iesus et dixit ei: "Quod ego facio, tu nescis modo, scies autem postea."

⁸ Dicit ei Petrus: "Non lavabis mihi pedes in aeternum!"

Respondit Iesus ei: "Si non lavero te, non habes partem mecum."

---

aeternus, -a, -um: eternal, everlasting
aqua, -ae f.: water
coepio, (3): to begin
deinde: then, next, afterward
dilego (3) dilexi, dilectum: to love
discipulus, -i m.: disciple
exeo, (2), exii: to come, go, leave
extergeo, (2): to wipe, wipe dry
lavo, (1), lavi, lotus: to wash, bathe
linteum, -i n.: cloth, towel
manus, -us f.: hand

modo: just now, presently
pelvis, pelvis f.: shallow bowl or basin
pes, pedis m.: foot
Petrus, -i m.: Peter
pono, (3): to put, place
postea: afterwards
praecingo, (3), praecinxi, praecinctus: to surround, encircle
Simon, Simonis m.: Simon
surgo, (3), surrexi, surrectus: to rise, lift
vestimentum, -i n.: garment, clothes

13:4 **cum accepisset**: plupf. subj. cum circumstantial clause, "when he had received"
praecinxit se: perf., "he girded himself" i.e. tied up his robe
13:4 **linteo, quo**: abl. of means, "wiped dry *with the towel with which* he was girded"
13:6 **mihi**: dat. of possession translating the gen. *μου*
13:8 **si... lavero**: fut. perf. in pres. general protasis, "unless I wash"

⁹ λέγει αὐτῷ Σίμων Πέτρος «Κύριε, μὴ τοὺς πόδας μου

μόνον ἀλλὰ καὶ τὰς χεῖρας καὶ τὴν κεφαλήν.»

¹⁰ λέγει αὐτῷ Ἰησοῦς «Ὁ λελουμένος οὐκ ἔχει χρείαν [εἰ

μὴ τοὺς πόδας] νίψασθαι, ἀλλ' ἔστιν καθαρὸς ὅλος· καὶ ὑμεῖς

καθαροί ἐστε, ἀλλ' οὐχὶ πάντες.» ¹¹ ᾔδει γὰρ τὸν παραδιδόντα

αὐτόν· διὰ τοῦτο εἶπεν ὅτι Οὐχὶ πάντες καθαροί ἐστε.

¹² ὅτε οὖν ἔνιψεν τοὺς πόδας αὐτῶν καὶ ἔλαβεν τὰ ἱμάτια

αὐτοῦ καὶ ἀνέπεσεν, πάλιν εἶπεν αὐτοῖς «Γινώσκετε τί πεποί-

ηκα ὑμῖν; ¹³ ὑμεῖς φωνεῖτέ με Ὁ διδάσκαλος καί Ὁ κύριος ,

καὶ καλῶς λέγετε, εἰμὶ γάρ. ¹⁴ εἰ οὖν ἐγὼ ἔνιψα ὑμῶν τοὺς

πόδας ὁ κύριος καὶ ὁ διδάσκαλος, καὶ ὑμεῖς ὀφείλετε ἀλλήλων

ἀλλήλων: of one another
ἀναπίπτω: to lie down
γινώσκω: to know
διδάσκαλος, ὁ: a teacher, master
ἱμάτια, τά: outer garments, clothing
καθαρός, -α, -ον: clean, spotless, pure
καλός, -η, -ον: good
κεφαλή, ἡ: the head
κύριος, ὁ: lord

λούω: to wash
νίπτω: to wash
ὅλος, -η, -ον: whole, entire
ὀφείλω: to owe, ought to
πάλιν (adv.): again
παραδίδωμι: to betray
φωνέω: to speak, call
χείρ, χειρός, ἡ: the hand
χρεία, ἡ: use, advantage, service

13:9 μὴ ... μόνον ἀλλὰ καὶ: "wash not only, but also"

13:10 ὁ λελουμένος: perf. part. of λούω, "the one who has bathed"

εἰ μὴ τοὺς πόδας: "no need to wash except his feet"

νίψασθαι: aor. mid. inf. explaining χρείαν, "has no need to wash himself"

13:11 ᾔδει: plupf. of εἶδον, "he knew"

εἶπεν ὅτι: here introducing direct speech, "he said: 'not all...'"

13:12 ἔλαβεν ... ἀνέπεσεν: aor., "he took up his garments ... he lay down"

τί πεποίηκα: perf. in ind. quest., "know what I have done"

13:14 ὁ κύριος καὶ ὁ διδάσκαλος: appositives to ἐγώ, "I, the lord and teacher, washed"

καὶ ὑμεῖς ὀφείλετε: pres., "you too ought to" + inf.

⁹ Dicit ei Simon Petrus: "Domine, non tantum pedes meos sed et manus et caput!"

¹⁰ Dicit ei Iesus: "Qui lotus est, non indiget nisi ut pedes lavet, sed est mundus totus; et vos mundi estis sed non omnes." ¹¹ Sciebat enim quisnam esset, qui traderet eum; propterea dixit: "Non estis mundi omnes."

¹² Postquam ergo lavit pedes eorum et accepit vestimenta sua, cum recubuisset iterum, dixit eis: "Scitis quid fecerim vobis? ¹³ Vos vocatis me 'Magister' et 'Domine', et bene dicitis; sum etenim. ¹⁴ Si ergo ego lavi vestros pedes, Dominus et Magister, et vos debetis alter

---

accipio, (3) accepi, acceptus: to receive, accept
bene: well, rightly
caput, capitis *n*: head
debeo, (2): ought, must (+ *inf.*)
etenim: and indeed, since
indigeo, (2): to need
lavo, (1) lavi, lotus: to wash

magister, magistri *m*: teacher
mundus, -a, -um: clean, pure
pars, partis *f*: part, share
quisnam, quaenam, quidnam: who?
recumbo, (3), recubui: to recline
totus, -a, -um: whole, all, entire
trado, (3) : to betray
voco, (1): to call

13:9   **non tantum … sed et**: "not only… but also"
13:10 **nisi ut lavet**: pres. subj. noun clause taking the place of an infinitive after *indiget*, "no need *except to wash*"
       mundus totus: adj. with adverbial force, "he is *completely clean*"
13:11 **quisnam esset**: impf. subj. in indirect question, "knew *who he was*"
       qui traderet: impf. subj. in relative clause of characteristic, "knew he was *who would betray him*"
13:12 **cum recubuisset**: plupf. subj. *cum* circumstantial clause, "when he had reclined"
       quid fecerim: perf. subj. in indirect question, "do you know *what I have done*"
13:14 **Dominus et Magister**: in apposition to *ego*, "I, your Lord and Teacher"

νίπτειν τοὺς πόδας· ¹⁵ ὑπόδειγμα γὰρ ἔδωκα ὑμῖν ἵνα καθὼς

ἐγὼ ἐποίησα ὑμῖν καὶ ὑμεῖς ποιῆτε. ¹⁶ ἀμὴν ἀμὴν λέγω ὑμῖν,

οὐκ ἔστιν δοῦλος μείζων τοῦ κυρίου αὐτοῦ οὐδὲ ἀπόστολος

μείζων τοῦ πέμψαντος αὐτόν. ¹⁷ εἰ ταῦτα οἴδατε, μακάριοί

ἐστε ἐὰν ποιῆτε αὐτά.

Jesus Predicts His Betrayal

¹⁸ οὐ περὶ πάντων ὑμῶν λέγω· ἐγὼ οἶδα τίνας ἐξελεξάμην·

ἀλλ᾽ ἵνα ἡ γραφὴ πληρωθῇ Ὁ τρώγων μου τὸν ἄρτον ἐπῆρεν

ἐπ᾽ ἐμὲ τὴν πτέρναν αὐτοῦ.

ἀπόστολος, ὁ: a messenger
ἄρτος, ὁ: a loaf of wheat-bread
γραφή, ἡ: a writing, scripture
δοῦλος, ὁ: a slave
ἐκλέγω: to pick out, choose
ἐπαίρω: to lift up and set on
καθώς: just as

κύριος, ὁ: a lord, master
μακάριος: blessed, happy
μείζων, μεῖζον: greater (+ gen.)
νίπτω: to wash
πτέρνη, ἡ: heel
τρώγω: to gnaw, eat
ὑπόδειγμα, -ατος, τό: a token, example

13:15 ἵνα ... ποιῆτε: pres. subj. in purpose clause, "I gave *in order that you do*"
   καθὼς ἐποίησα: aor., "*just as I did* to you"
13:16 μείζων: nom. pred., "servant is *greater than*" + gen.
   κυρίου ... τοῦ πεμψάντος: gen. after μείζων, "greater *than the master ... than
   the one who sent*"
13:17 μακάριοί ἐστε: pres. serves as apodosis of both protases, "then you are blessed"
   ἐὰν ποιῆτε: pres. subj. in pres. general protasis, "if you do these things"
13:18 τίνας ἐξελεξάμην: weak aor. of ἐκ-λέγω in ind. quest., "know *whom I have
   chosen*"
   ἵνα ἡ γραφὴ πληρωθῇ: aor. subj. in clause of purpose and result, "so that the
   scripture be fulfilled" (Ps. 41:9)
   ὁ τρώγων: pres. part. attrib., "*he who eats* my bread"
   ἐπῆρεν: aor. of ἐπι-αίρω, "*he has lifted* his heel against me" i .e. turned against
   me

alterius lavare pedes. ¹⁵ Exemplum enim dedi vobis, ut, quemadmodum ego feci vobis, et vos faciatis. ¹⁶ Amen, amen dico vobis: Non est servus maior domino suo, neque apostolus maior eo, qui misit illum. ¹⁷ Si haec scitis, beati estis, si facitis ea.

Jesus Predicts His Betrayal

¹⁸ Non de omnibus vobis dico, ego scio, quos elegerim, sed ut impleatur Scriptura: 'Qui manducat meum panem, levavit contra me calcaneum suum.'

---

alter, -a, -um: other, another
apostolus, -i *m*: apostle
beatus, -a, -um: blessed
calcaneum, -i *n*: heel
contra: against (+ *acc.*)
eligo, (3), elegi: to pick out, choose
exemplum, -i *n*: example
impleo, (2): to satisfy, fulfill

lavo, (1) lavi, lotus: to wash
levo, (1): to lift, raise
maior, -us: more, greater
manduco, (1): to eat
panis, panis *m*: bread, loaf
quemadmodum: how, just as
scriptura, -ae *f*: scripture
servus, -i *m*: slave, servant

13:14 **alterius**: gen., "the feet *of each other*"

13:15 **ut... faciatis**: pres. subj. purpose clause, "I gave the example *so that you do*"

13:16 **domino suo ...eo**: abl. of comparison after *maior*, "greater than *the master* ...than *the one* who sent"

13:17 **beati estis**: pres. serves as apodosis of both protases, "then you are blessed"
　　　si facitis: an instance in which a pres. general condition is translated with a pres. indic. instead of a fut. perf., "if you do"

13:18 **quos elegerim**: perf. subj. in relative clause of characteristic, "I know the ones *whom I have chosen*"
　　　ut impleatur: pres. subj. purpose clause, "so that it may be fulfilled"
　　　levavit ... calcaneum suum: "he has raised his heel," i.e. "he has turned against"

¹⁹ ἀπ᾽ ἄρτι λέγω ὑμῖν πρὸ τοῦ γενέσθαι, ἵνα πιστεύητε ὅταν

γένηται ὅτι ἐγώ εἰμι. ²⁰ ἀμὴν ἀμὴν λέγω ὑμῖν, ὁ λαμβάνων

ἄν τινα πέμψω ἐμὲ λαμβάνει, ὁ δὲ ἐμὲ λαμβάνων λαμβάνει

τὸν πέμψαντά με.»

²¹ ταῦτα εἰπὼν Ἰησοῦς ἐταράχθη τῷ πνεύματι καὶ ἐμαρ-

τύρησεν καὶ εἶπεν «Ἀμὴν ἀμὴν λέγω ὑμῖν ὅτι εἷς ἐξ ὑμῶν

παραδώσει με.»

²² ἔβλεπον εἰς ἀλλήλους οἱ μαθηταὶ ἀπορούμενοι περὶ

τίνος λέγει. ²³ ἦν ἀνακείμενος εἷς ἐκ τῶν μαθητῶν αὐτοῦ ἐν

τῷ κόλπῳ τοῦ Ἰησοῦ, ὃν ἠγάπα ὁ Ἰησοῦς· ²⁴ νεύει οὖν τούτῳ

Σίμων Πέτρος καὶ λέγει αὐτῷ «Εἰπὲ τίς ἐστιν περὶ οὗ λέγει.»

²⁵ ἀναπεσὼν ἐκεῖνος οὕτως ἐπὶ τὸ στῆθος τοῦ Ἰησοῦ λέγει

αὐτῷ «Κύριε, τίς ἐστιν;»

ἀγαπάω: to love
ἀνάκειμαι: to recline
ἀναπίπτω: to fall back on, lean back
ἀπορέω: to be at a loss
βλέπω: to see, have the power of sight
εἷς, μία, ἕν: one
κόλπος, ὁ: the bosom

λαμβάνω: to take, accept
νεύω: to nod or beckon
παραδίδωμι: to betray
πέμπω: to send
πνεῦμα, -ατος, τό: spirit
στῆθος, -εος, τό: the breast
ταράσσω: to stir, stir up, trouble

13:19 ἀπ᾽ ἄρτι: "henceforth"
πρὸ τοῦ γενέσθαι: aor. inf. articular, "before it has happened"
ἵνα πιστεύητε: pres. subj. in purpose clause, "so that you believe"
ὅταν γένηται: aor. subj. in general temporal clause, "when it happens
(whenever that is)"
ὅτι ἐγώ εἰμι: noun clause, object of πιστεύητε, "believe *that I am (the one)*"
13:20 ἄν τινα πέμψω: aor. subj. in general relative clause, "whomever I send"
13:21 ἐταράχθη: aor. pass. of ταράσσω, "he was troubled"
παραδώσει: fut. of παραδίδωμι, "say that one of you *will betray*"
13:22 περὶ τίνος λέγει: ind. quest. after ἀπορούμενοι, "being at a loss *about whom he
speaks*"
13:23 ἦν ἀνακείμενος: impf. periphrastic, "one was lying down"
13:24 περὶ οὗ λέγει: ind. quest., "say (i.e. ask) *about whom he speaks*"
13:25 ἀναπεσὼν: aor. part. circum. of ἀνα-πίπτω, "having fallen back on"

¹⁹ Amodo dico vobis priusquam fiat, ut credatis, cum factum fuerit, quia ego sum. ²⁰ Amen, amen dico vobis: Qui accipit, si quem misero, me accipit; qui autem me accipit, accipit eum, qui me misit."

²¹ Cum haec dixisset Iesus, turbatus est spiritu et protestatus est et dixit: "Amen, amen dico vobis: Unus ex vobis tradet me."

²² Aspiciebant ad invicem discipuli, haesitantes de quo diceret. ²³ Erat recumbens unus ex discipulis eius in sinu Iesu, quem diligebat Iesus. ²⁴ Innuit ergo huic Simon Petrus, ut interrogaret: "Quis est, de quo dicit?"

²⁵ Cum ergo recumberet ille ita supra pectus Iesu, dicit ei: "Domine, quis est?"

---

accipio, (3): to accept, receive
amodo: henceforth, from now
aspicio, (3): to look, gaze
dominus, -i *m*: lord
haesito, (1): to be undecided
innuo, (3), **innui, innutus**: to beckon
interrogo, (1): to ask, question
invicem: in turn, reciprocally, one another
ita: thus, therefore

mitto, (3) **misi, missus**: to send
pectus, pectoris *n*: breast, heart
priusquam: before; until; sooner than;
protestor, (1): to bear witness in public
recumbo, (3): to recline
sinus, -us *m*: lap
spiritus, -us *m*: soul, spirit
trado, (3): to betray, hand over
turbo, (1): to disturb, agitate, confuse

13:19 **fiat**: pres. subj. anticipatory after *priusquam*, "before it happens"
   ut credatis: pres. subj. in purpose clause, "in order that you believe"
   cum factum fuerit: fut. perf. in *cum* temporal clause, "once it has happened"
   quia ego sum: ind. st., "believe *that I am* (the one)"
13:20 **si quem misero**: fut. perf. in future more vivid protasis, "if I send someone"
   i.e. accepts *whomever I send*"
13:21 **cum... dixisset**: plupf. subj. in *cum* circumstantial clause, "*when he had said* these things"
13:22 **de quo diceret**: impf. subj. in relative clause of characteristic, "about that (which) he spoke"
13:24 **ut interrogaret**: impf. subj. in purpose clause, "beckoned him *to ask*"
13:25 **cum... recumberet**: impf. subj. in *cum* circumstantial clause, "when he was reclining"

²⁶ ἀποκρίνεται οὖν ὁ Ἰησοῦς «Ἐκεῖνός ἐστιν ᾧ ἐγὼ βάψω
τὸ ψωμίον καὶ δώσω αὐτῷ·» βάψας οὖν [τὸ] ψωμίον λαμβάνει καὶ δίδωσιν Ἰούδᾳ Σίμωνος Ἰσκαριώτου. ²⁷ καὶ μετὰ
τὸ ψωμίον τότε εἰσῆλθεν εἰς ἐκεῖνον ὁ Σατανᾶς.

λέγει οὖν αὐτῷ Ἰησοῦς «Ὃ ποιεῖς ποίησον τάχειον.»
²⁸ τοῦτο δὲ οὐδεὶς ἔγνω τῶν ἀνακειμένων πρὸς τί εἶπεν αὐτῷ·
²⁹ τινὲς γὰρ ἐδόκουν, ἐπεὶ τὸ γλωσσόκομον εἶχεν Ἰούδας, ὅτι
λέγει αὐτῷ Ἰησοῦς Ἀγόρασον ὧν χρείαν ἔχομεν εἰς τὴν ἑορτήν,
ἢ τοῖς πτωχοῖς ἵνα τι δῷ. ³⁰ λαβὼν οὖν τὸ ψωμίον ἐκεῖνος
ἐξῆλθεν εὐθύς· ἦν δὲ νύξ.

ἀγοράζω: to purchase
ἀνάκειμαι: to recline
βάπτω: to dip in water
γλωσσόκομος, ὁ: box
δοκέω: to suppose
εἰσῆλθον: to go into, enter (aor.)
ἐξῆλθον: to go out of (aor.)
ἑορτή, ἡ: festival

εὐθύς: (adv.) immediately
Ἰσκαριώτης, -ου, ὁ: the Iscariot
νύξ, νυκτός, ἡ: the night
πτωχός, ὁ: a beggar
Σατανᾶς, -ᾶ, ὁ: Satan
τάχειον (adv.): quickly
χρεία, ἡ: use, advantage, need
ψωμίον, τό: a piece of bread

13:26 βάψω: fut. of βάπτω, "that one for whom *I will dip*"
  δώσω: fut. of δίδωμι, "and *I will give* it to him"
  βάψας: aor. part., "having dipped"
  Σίμωνος Ἰσκαριώτου: gen., "to Judas (the son) *of Simon Iscariot*"
13:27 ποίησον: aor. imper., "what you are doing, *do it!*"
13:28 τῶν ἀνακειμένων: pres. part. gen. partitive, "no one *of those reclining* knew"
  πρὸς τί εἶπεν: ind. quest., "knew *about what he spoke*"
13:29 ἀγόρασον: aor. imper., "go buy!"
  ὧν: rel. pronoun whose antecedent is the object of ἀγόρασον, gen. after
    χρείαν, "buy (the things) *of which* we have need"
  ἵνα τι δῷ: aor. subj. in noun clause after λέγει, "some supposed that he told
    him *to give something* to the poor"

²⁶ Respondet Iesus: "Ille est, cui ego intinctam buccellam porrexero." Cum ergo intinxisset buccellam, dat Iudae Simonis Iscariotis. ²⁷ Et post buccellam tunc introivit in illum Satanas.

Dicit ergo ei Iesus: "Quod facis, fac citius." ²⁸ Hoc autem nemo scivit discumbentium ad quid dixerit ei; ²⁹ quidam enim putabant quia loculos habebat Iudas, quia dicit ei Iesus: "Eme ea, quae opus sunt nobis ad diem festum," aut egenis ut aliquid daret. ³⁰ Cum ergo accepisset ille buccellam, exivit continuo; erat autem nox.

---

accipio, (3) **accepi, acceptus**: to receive
buccella, -ae *f*: morsel, small piece of food
citius (*adv.*): quickly, swiftly
continuo (*adv.*): immediately
discumbo (3): to recline
egenus, -a, -um: in want of, poor
emo, (3): to buy, acquire
exeo, (4), exivi: to exit
intingo, (3), **intinxi, intinctus**: to dip

introeo, (2), **introivi, introitus**: to enter
loculus, -i *m*: money-box
nemo, neminis *n*: no one
nox, noctis *f*: night
opus, operis *n*: need
porrigo, (3), **porrexi, porrectus**: to stretch out, extend, offer
puto, (1): to think, believe
Satanas, -ae *m*: Satan
scio (4) **scivi**: to know

13:26 **cui ... porrexero**: fut. perf. in relative clause, "to whom I shall extend"
    cum... intinxisset: plupf. subj. in *cum* circumstantial clause, "when he had dipped"
13:28 **discumbentium**: pres. part. gen. partitive, "no one *of them reclining*"
    ad quid dixerit: perf. subj. in indirect question, "to what (purpose) he had spoken"
13:29 **eme**: pres. imper., "*buy* those things!"
    opus: nom. pred., "buy those things which are *necessary*"
    ut ... daret: impf. subj. in purpose clause, "or *to give* something to the poor"
13:30 **cum... accepisset**: plupf. subj. circumstantial clause, "when he had received"

Jesus Predicts Peter's Denial

³¹ ὅτε οὖν ἐξῆλθεν λέγει Ἰησοῦς «Νῦν ἐδοξάσθη ὁ υἱὸς τοῦ ἀνθρώπου, ³² καὶ ὁ θεὸς ἐδοξάσθη ἐν αὐτῷ· καὶ ὁ θεὸς δοξάσει αὐτὸν ἐν αὐτῷ, καὶ εὐθὺς δοξάσει αὐτόν.

³³ Τεκνία, ἔτι μικρὸν μεθ' ὑμῶν εἰμί· ζητήσετέ με, καὶ καθὼς εἶπον τοῖς Ἰουδαίοις ὅτι Ὅπου ἐγὼ ὑπάγω ὑμεῖς οὐ δύνασθε ἐλθεῖν, καὶ ὑμῖν λέγω ἄρτι.

³⁴ ἐντολὴν καινὴν δίδωμι ὑμῖν ἵνα ἀγαπᾶτε ἀλλήλους, καθὼς ἠγάπησα ὑμᾶς ἵνα καὶ ὑμεῖς ἀγαπᾶτε ἀλλήλους. ³⁵ ἐν τούτῳ γνώσονται πάντες ὅτι ἐμοὶ μαθηταί ἐστε, ἐὰν ἀγάπην ἔχητε ἐν ἀλλήλοις.»

³⁶ λέγει αὐτῷ Σίμων Πέτρος «Κύριε, ποῦ ὑπάγεις;»

ἀπεκρίθη Ἰησοῦς «Ὅπου ὑπάγω οὐ δύνασαί μοι νῦν ἀκολουθῆσαι, ἀκολουθήσεις δὲ ὕστερον.»

ἀγάπη, ἡ: love
ἀκολουθέω: to follow
ἀλλήλων: of one another
ἄρτι: just now
γινώσκω: to know
δοξάζω: to magnify
δύναμαι: to be able, capable, strong enough
ἐντολή, ἡ: an order, command

εὐθύς: (adv.) immediately
ζητέω: to seek
καινός, -ή, -όν: new, fresh
μικρός, -ά, -όν: small, little
τεκνίον, τό: a little child
υἱός, ὁ: a son
ὑπάγω: to go or withdraw
ὕστερος, -α, -ον: latter, last

13:31 ἐδοξάσθη: aor. pass. of δοξάζομαι, "he has been glorified"

13:32 αὐτὸν ἐν αὐτῷ: "will glorify *him* (the son) *in himself* (the father)"
   καθὼς εἶπον: "*as I said* to the Jews" i.e. in 8:22 above

13:33 ἐλθεῖν: aor. inf. after οὐ δύνασθε, "you cannot *come*"

13:34 ἵνα ἀγαπᾶτε: pres. subj. in noun clause explaining ἐντολὴν, "a new command *that you love each other*"

13:35 ἐν τούτῳ: "in this way"
   γνώσονται: fut. of γινώσκω, "all *will know*"
   ἐὰν ἀγάπην ἔχητε: pres. subj. in fut. more vivid protasis, "if you have love"

13:36 ἀκολουθῆσαι: aor. inf. after οὐ δύνασαί, "you cannot *follow*"

Jesus Predicts Peter's Denial

³¹ Cum ergo exisset, dicit Iesus: "Nunc clarificatus est Filius hominis, et Deus clarificatus est in eo; ³² si Deus clarificatus est in eo, et Deus clarificabit eum in semetipso et continuo clarificabit eum.

³³ Filioli, adhuc modicum vobiscum sum; quaeretis me, et sicut dixi Iudaeis: 'Quo ego vado, vos non potestis venire,' et vobis dico modo.

³⁴ Mandatum novum do vobis, ut diligatis invicem; sicut dilexi vos, ut et vos diligatis invicem. ³⁵ In hoc cognoscent omnes quia mei discipuli estis: si dilectionem habueritis ad invicem."

³⁶ Dicit ei Simon Petrus: "Domine, quo vadis?"

Respondit Iesus: "Quo vado, non potes me modo sequi, sequeris autem postea."

---

clarifico, (1): to make known
cognosco, (3): to know
continuo: (*adv.*) immediately
dilectio, -onis *f*: love, delight
diligo, (1): to love
exeo, (4) exii: to leave, depart
filiolus, -i *m*: little son
invicem: in turn, reciprocally, mutually
mandatum, -i *n*: a command

modicus, -a, -um: small, small amount
modo: just now, recently
novus, -a, -um: new
postea: afterwards
quaero, (3): to search for, seek
semetipse, -a, -um: one's self
sequor, (3) secutus sum: to follow
vado, (3): to go
venio (4): **to come**

13:31 **cum... exisset**: plupf. subj. circumstantial clause, "when he had left"

13:34 **ut diligatis**: pres. subj. noun clause explaining *mandatum*, "a new command, *namely that you love* each other"

13:35 **si... habueritis**: fut. perf. in fut. more vivid protasis, "*if you have* love for each other"

quia ... estis: ind. st. after *cognoscent*, "know *that you are*"

³⁷ λέγει αὐτῷ ὁ Πέτρος «Κύριε, διὰ τί οὐ δύναμαί σοι ἀκολουθεῖν ἄρτι; τὴν ψυχήν μου ὑπὲρ σοῦ θήσω.»

³⁸ ἀποκρίνεται Ἰησοῦς «Τὴν ψυχήν σου ὑπὲρ ἐμοῦ θήσεις; ἀμὴν ἀμὴν λέγω σοι, οὐ μὴ ἀλέκτωρ φωνήσῃ ἕως οὗ ἀρνήσῃ με τρίς.

Chapter 14

Jesus Comforts His Disciples

¹ Μὴ ταρασσέσθω ὑμῶν ἡ καρδία· πιστεύετε εἰς τὸν θεόν, καὶ εἰς ἐμὲ πιστεύετε. ² ἐν τῇ οἰκίᾳ τοῦ πατρός μου μοναὶ πολλαί εἰσιν· εἰ δὲ μή, εἶπον ἂν ὑμῖν, ὅτι πορεύομαι ἑτοιμάσαι τόπον ὑμῖν· ³ καὶ ἐὰν πορευθῶ καὶ ἑτοιμάσω τόπον ὑμῖν, πάλιν ἔρχομαι καὶ παραλήμψομαι ὑμᾶς πρὸς ἐμαυτόν, ἵνα ὅπου εἰμὶ

ἀλέκτωρ, -ορος, ἡ: a cock
ἀρνέομαι: to deny, disown
ἐμαυτοῦ: of me, of myself
ἑτοιμάζω: to make ready, prepare
ἕως: until (+ subj.)
ἠώς, ἡ: the morning red, daybreak, dawn
μονή, ἡ: a room

οἰκία, ἡ: a building, house, dwelling
πάλιν (adv.): again
παραλαμβάνω: to take along with
πορεύω: to make to go
τόπος, ὁ: a place
τρίς: thrice, three times
ψυχή, ἡ: soul, life

13:37 θήσω: fut. of τίθημι, "I will lay down my life"

13:38 οὐ μὴ ἀλέκτωρ φωνήσῃ: aor. subj. in strong denial, "the cock will not crow"
 ἕως οὗ ἀρνήσῃ: aor. subj. of ἀρνέομαι in general temporal clause, "until you deny me"

14:1 μὴ ταρασσέσθω: pres. pass. imper. 3 s., "let your heart not be troubled"

14:2 εἰ δὲ μή: "if it were not (true)" i.e. otherwise
 εἶπον ἂν: aor. in past contrafactual apodosis, "would I have told you?"
 ἑτοιμάσαι: aor. inf. of purpose, "that I go to prepare"

14:3 ἐὰν πορευθῶ καὶ ἑτοιμάσω: aor. subj. in fut. more vivid protasis, "If I go and make ready"
 ἔρχομαι καὶ παραλήμψομαι: note the mixture of present and future in the apodosis, "I am coming back and I will take you along"

³⁷ Dicit ei Petrus: "Domine, quare non possum te sequi modo? Animam meam pro te ponam."

³⁸ Respondet Iesus: "Animam tuam pro me pones? Amen, amen dico tibi: Non cantabit gallus, donec me ter neges.

Chapter 14

Jesus Comforts His Disciples

¹ Non turbetur cor vestrum. Creditis in Deum et in me credite. ² In domo Patris mei mansiones multae sunt; si quo minus, dixissem vobis, quia vado parare vobis locum? ³ Et si abiero et praeparavero vobis locum, iterum venio et accipiam vos ad meipsum, ut, ubi sum

---

abeo, (4) **abii:** to depart, go away
accipio, (3), to accept, receive
anima, -ae *f*: soul, spirit
canto, (1): to sing, recite
cor, cordis *n*: the heart
dico, (3) **dixi,** dictus: to say
domus, -us *f*: house
donec: while, until
gallus, galli *m*: cock, rooster
iterum (*adv.*): again
locus, -i *m*: place

mansio, -onis *f*: abode, quarters, dwelling
minor, minus: less
modo: presently, now
multus, -a -um: much, many
nego, (1): to deny
paro, (1): to prepare
pono, (3): to lay down, set
praeparo, (1): to prepare
quare: in what way? how?
ter: three times
turbo, (1): to trouble

13:38 **donec … neges:** pres. subj. anticipatory, "until you deny me" i.e. as I expect you will

14:1 **non turbetur:** pres. subj. jussive, "*let* your heart *not be troubled,*" where we would expect *ne* instead of *non*

    creditis … credite: Jerome translates πιστεύετε two different ways, but they are probably both imperatives, "*believe* in the father, *believe* in me"

14:2 **si quo minus (sc. esset):** pres. contrary to fact protasis, "if (it were) less by any" i.e. if it were not so

    dixissem: plupf. subj. in past contrary to fact apodosis, "would I have said?"

    parare: inf. of purpose, "I go *to prepare*"

14:3 **si abiero et praeparavero:** fut. perf. in fut. more vivid protasis, "if I depart and prepare"

    venio et accipiam: mixing pres. and fut. in the apodosis, "I am coming again and I will receive"

ἐγὼ καὶ ὑμεῖς ἦτε. ⁴ καὶ ὅπου ἐγὼ ὑπάγω οἴδατε τὴν ὁδόν.»

Jesus the Way to the Father

⁵ λέγει αὐτῷ Θωμᾶς «Κύριε, οὐκ οἴδαμεν ποῦ ὑπάγεις· πῶς οἴδαμεν τὴν ὁδόν;»

⁶ λέγει αὐτῷ Ἰησοῦς «Ἐγώ εἰμι ἡ ὁδὸς καὶ ἡ ἀλήθεια καὶ ἡ ζωή· οὐδεὶς ἔρχεται πρὸς τὸν πατέρα εἰ μὴ δι' ἐμοῦ. ⁷ εἰ ἐγνώκειτέ με, καὶ τὸν πατέρα μου ἂν ᾔδειτε· ἀπ' ἄρτι γινώσκετε αὐτὸν καὶ ἑωράκατε.»

⁸ λέγει αὐτῷ Φίλιππος «Κύριε, δεῖξον ἡμῖν τὸν πατέρα, καὶ ἀρκεῖ ἡμῖν.»

⁹ λέγει αὐτῷ ὁ Ἰησοῦς «Τοσοῦτον χρόνον μεθ' ὑμῶν εἰμὶ καὶ οὐκ ἔγνωκάς με, Φίλιππε; ὁ ἑωρακὼς ἐμὲ ἑώρακεν τὸν πατέρα· πῶς σὺ λέγεις Δεῖξον ἡμῖν τὸν πατέρα ; ¹⁰ οὐ πιστεύεις ὅτι ἐγὼ ἐν τῷ πατρὶ καὶ ὁ πατὴρ ἐν ἐμοί ἐστιν;

ἀλήθεια, ἡ: the truth
ἀρκέω: to be sufficient (+ *dat.*)
γινώσκω: to know
δείκνυμι: to show
ὁδός, ἡ: a way

πατήρ, πατρός, ὁ: a father
τοσοῦτος, -αύτη, -οῦτο: so much
ὑπάγω: to go, withdraw
χρόνος, ὁ: time

14:3 ἵνα ... καὶ ὑμεῖς ἦτε: pres. subj. in clause of purpose and result, "so that you too may be"

14:4-5 οἴδατε = ἴστε, "you know" οἴδαμεν = ἴσμεν, "we know"

14:6 εἰ μὴ δι' ἐμοῦ: "except through me"

14:7 εἰ ἐγνώκειτε: plupf. of γινώσκω in past contrafactual protasis, "if you had known me" where the aorist is normal
ἂν ᾔδειτε: plupf. of εἶδον with impf. force in present contrafactual apodosis, "you would now know"
ἀπ' ἄρτι: "from now on"

14:8 δεῖξον: aor. imper. of δείκνυμι, "show!"

14:9 τοσοῦτον χρόνον: acc. of duration, "I am with you *for such a long time*"
οὐκ ἔγνωκάς: perf. of γινώσκω, *"you have not come to know* me?"
ὁ ἑωρακὼς: perf. part. attrib. of ὁράω, "the one who has seen"

14:10 οὐ πιστεύεις; anticipating an affirmative answer, "don't you believe?"

ego, et vos sitis.   ⁴ Et quo ego vado, scitis viam."

Jesus the Way to the Father

⁵ Dicit ei Thomas: "Domine, nescimus quo vadis; quomodo possumus viam scire?"

⁶ Dicit ei Iesus: "Ego sum via et veritas et vita; nemo venit ad Patrem nisi per me.   ⁷ Si cognovistis me, et Patrem meum utique cognoscetis; et amodo cognoscitis eum et vidistis eum."

⁸ Dicit ei Philippus: "Domine, ostende nobis Patrem, et sufficit nobis."

⁹ Dicit ei Iesus: "Tanto tempore vobiscum sum, et non cognovisti me, Philippe? Qui vidit me, vidit Patrem. Quomodo tu dicis: 'Ostende nobis Patrem'?   ¹⁰ Non credis quia ego in Patre, et Pater in me est?

---

amodo: henceforth, from now
cognosco, (3) **cognovi**: to know
nemo, neminis *m/f*: no one, nobody
nescio, (4): to not know
ostendeo, (2): to show, reveal, make clear
Philippus, -i *m*: Philip
scio, (4): to know
sufficio, (3): to be sufficient to (+ *dat.*)

tantus, -a, -um: so great, so much
tempus, temporis *n*: time
Thomas (*indecl.*): Thomas
utique (*adv.*): certainly
veritas, -atis *f*: truth
via, -ae *f*: way
video, (2): to see
vita, -ae *f*: life

14:3   **ut... sitis**: pres. subj. mixing result and purpose clause, "*so that you may be where I go*"

14:9   **tanto tempore**: abl. where one would expect the acc. for duration of time, "*for such a great time* I have been with you"

non cognovisti: perf. with present meaning, "you have not come to know"

τὰ ῥήματα ἃ ἐγὼ λέγω ὑμῖν ἀπ’ ἐμαυτοῦ οὐ λαλῶ· ὁ δὲ πατὴρ ἐν ἐμοὶ μένων ποιεῖ τὰ ἔργα αὐτοῦ. ¹¹ πιστεύετέ μοι ὅτι ἐγὼ ἐν τῷ πατρὶ καὶ ὁ πατὴρ ἐν ἐμοί· εἰ δὲ μή, διὰ τὰ ἔργα αὐτὰ πιστεύετε. ¹² ἀμὴν ἀμὴν λέγω ὑμῖν, ὁ πιστεύων εἰς ἐμὲ τὰ ἔργα ἃ ἐγὼ ποιῶ κἀκεῖνος ποιήσει, καὶ μείζονα τούτων ποιήσει, ὅτι ἐγὼ πρὸς τὸν πατέρα πορεύομαι· ¹³ καὶ ὅτι ἂν αἰτήσητε ἐν τῷ ὀνόματί μου τοῦτο ποιήσω, ἵνα δοξασθῇ ὁ πατὴρ ἐν τῷ υἱῷ· ¹⁴ ἐάν τι αἰτήσητέ με ἐν τῷ ὀνόματί μου τοῦτο ποιήσω.

Jesus Promises the Holy Spirit

¹⁵ ἐὰν ἀγαπᾶτέ με, τὰς ἐντολὰς τὰς ἐμὰς τηρήσε-τε. ¹⁶ κἀγὼ ἐρωτήσω τὸν πατέρα καὶ ἄλλον παράκλητον δώσει ὑμῖν ἵνα ᾖ μεθ’ ὑμῶν εἰς τὸν αἰῶνα, ¹⁷ τὸ πνεῦμα τῆς ἀληθείας, ὃ ὁ κόσμος οὐ δύναται λαβεῖν, ὅτι οὐ θεωρεῖ αὐτὸ οὐδὲ γινώσκει· ὑμεῖς γινώσκετε αὐτό, ὅτι παρ’ ὑμῖν

αἰτέω: to ask, beg
αἰών, -ῶνος, ὁ: age
γινώσκω: to know
δίδωμι: to give
ἐντολή, ἡ: command, behest
ἔργον, τό: a work, deed
ἐρωτάω: to ask
θεωρέω: to look at, view, behold

κόσμος, ὁ: world
μένω: to remain
ὄνομα, -ατος, τό: a name
παράκλητος, ὁ: a helper
πνεῦμα, -ατος, τό: a spirit
ῥῆμα, -ατος, τό: word, saying
τηρέω: to watch over, protect, keep
υἱός, ὁ: a son

14:11 εἰ δὲ μή (sc. πιστεύετε): "if you do not (believe)" i.e. otherwise
δια τὰ ἔργα αὐτὰ: "because of the works themselves"
14:12 κἀκεῖνος (=καὶ ἐκεῖνος) ποιήσει: fut., "that one also will do"
μείζονα: n. pl. acc., "he will do (works) *greater* than these"
14:13 ὅτι ἂν αἰτήσητε: aor. subj. in general relative clause, "whatever you seek"
ἵνα δοξασθῇ: aor. pass. subj. in clause of purpose and result, "I will do *so that* the father *is glorified*"
14:14 ἐάν τι αἰτήσητέ με: aor. subj. in fut. more vivid protasis, "if you ask me for anything"
14:15 ἐὰν ἀγαπᾶτέ: pres. subj. in fut. more vivid protasis, "if you love"
14:16 ἵνα ᾖ: pres. subj. in result clause, "he will give a helper *to be* with you"
14:17 λαβεῖν: aor. of λαμβάνω complementing δύναται, "cannot *receive*"
14:18 ἀφήσω: fut. of ἀπο-ἵημι, "I will not abandon you"

Verba, quae ego loquor vobis, a meipso non loquor; Pater autem in me manens facit opera sua. ¹¹ Credite mihi quia ego in Patre, et Pater in me est; alioquin propter opera ipsa credite. ¹² Amen, amen dico vobis: Qui credit in me, opera, quae ego facio, et ipse faciet, et maiora horum faciet, quia ego ad Patrem vado. ¹³ Et quodcumque petieritis in nomine meo, hoc faciam, ut glorificetur Pater in Filio; ¹⁴ si quid petieritis me in nomine meo, ego faciam.

Jesus Promises the Holy Spirit

¹⁵ Si diligitis me, mandata mea servabitis; ¹⁶ et ego rogabo Patrem, et alium Paraclitum dabit vobis, ut maneat vobiscum in aeternum, ¹⁷ Spiritum veritatis, quem mundus non potest accipere, quia non videt eum nec cognoscit. Vos cognoscitis eum, quia apud vos

---

accipio, (3) **accepi**, **acceptus**: to receive, accept
alioquin: otherwise
alius, alia, aliud: other, another
credo, (3): to trust, believe in
diligo, (3): to love
glorifico, (1): to glorify
loquor, (3), **locutus sum**: speak
mandatum, -i *n*: command

maneo, (2): to remain
nomen, -inis *n*: name
opus, operis *n*: work, deed
paraclitus, -i *m*: helper, appellation for Holy Ghost
peto, (3), **petii**, **petitus**: to seek
servo, (1): to keep, preserve
spiritus -us *m*: spirit
veritas, -tatis *f*: the truth

14:12 **maiora horum**: "he will do things *greater than these*"
    et ipse faciet: fut., "he himself will also do (these things)"
14:13 **quodcumque petieritis**: fut. perf. in general relative clause, "whatever you seek"
    ut glorificetur: pres. subj. in purpose clause, "in order that he may be glorified"
14:14 **si quid petieritis**: fut. perf. in fut. more vivid protasis, "if you seek anything"
14:15 **si diligitis me**: pres. instead future in more vivid protasis, "if you love me"
14:16 **ut maneat**: pres. subj. purpose clause, "he will give a helper *to remain* with you"

223

μένει καὶ ἐν ὑμῖν ἐστίν. ¹⁸ οὐκ ἀφήσω ὑμᾶς ὀρφανούς, ἔρχομαι πρὸς ὑμᾶς. ¹⁹ ἔτι μικρὸν καὶ ὁ κόσμος με οὐκέτι θεωρεῖ, ὑμεῖς δὲ θεωρεῖτέ με, ὅτι ἐγὼ ζῶ καὶ ὑμεῖς ζήσετε. ²⁰ ἐν ἐκείνῃ τῇ ἡμέρᾳ ὑμεῖς γνώσεσθε ὅτι ἐγὼ ἐν τῷ πατρί μου καὶ ὑμεῖς ἐν ἐμοὶ κἀγὼ ἐν ὑμῖν. ²¹ ὁ ἔχων τὰς ἐντολάς μου καὶ τηρῶν αὐτὰς ἐκεῖνός ἐστιν ὁ ἀγαπῶν με· ὁ δὲ ἀγαπῶν με ἀγαπηθήσεται ὑπὸ τοῦ πατρός μου, κἀγὼ ἀγαπήσω αὐτὸν καὶ ἐμφανίσω αὐτῷ ἐμαυτόν.»

²² λέγει αὐτῷ Ἰούδας, οὐχ ὁ Ἰσκαριώτης, «Κύριε, τί γέγο-νεν ὅτι ἡμῖν μέλλεις ἐμφανίζειν σεαυτὸν καὶ οὐχὶ τῷ κόσμῳ;»

²³ ἀπεκρίθη Ἰησοῦς καὶ εἶπεν αὐτῷ «Ἐάν τις ἀγαπᾷ με τὸν λόγον μου τηρήσει, καὶ ὁ πατήρ μου ἀγαπήσει αὐτόν, καὶ πρὸς αὐτὸν ἐλευσόμεθα καὶ μονὴν παρ᾽ αὐτῷ ποιησόμεθα. ²⁴ ὁ μὴ ἀγαπῶν με τοὺς λόγους μου οὐ τηρεῖ· καὶ ὁ λόγος ὃν ἀκούετε οὐκ ἔστιν ἐμὸς ἀλλὰ τοῦ πέμψαντός με πατρός.

ἀκούω: to hear
ἀφίημι: to send forth, discharge
ἐμφανίζω: to make manifest, reveal
ἐντολή, ἡ: a command
ζάω: to live
ἥμερα, -ἡ: a day

μέλλω: to intend to do, to be about to + inf
μονή, ἡ: a home
ὀρφανός, ὁ: an orphan
οὐκέτι: no more, no longer
πέμπω: to send, despatch
τηρέω: to keep, preserve

14:19 ἔτι μικρὸν: acc. of duration, "for a little (time) yet"
14:21 ἀγαπηθήσεται: fut. pass. of ἀγαπάω, "*he will be loved* by the father"
   ἐμφανίσω: fut., "I will reveal myself"
14:22 τί γέγονεν: perf., "what happened?"
   ὅτι ... μέλλεις: noun clause with epexegetic force, "what happened *to the effect that you intend*" + inf.
14:23 ἐάν τις ἀγαπᾷ: pres. subj. in fut. more vivid protasis, "if anyone loves me"
   ἐλευσόμεθα ... ποιησόμεθα: fut., "*we will come ...we will make for ourselves* a home"
14:24 τοῦ πέμψαντός: aor. part. attrib. gen. s., "of the one who sent me"
14:25 λελάληκα: perf. of λαλέω, "I have said"

manet; et in vobis erit. ¹⁸ Non relinquam vos orphanos; venio ad vos. ¹⁹ Adhuc modicum, et mundus me iam non videt; vos autem videtis me, quia ego vivo et vos vivetis. ²⁰ In illo die vos cognoscetis quia ego sum in Patre meo, et vos in me, et ego in vobis. ²¹ Qui habet mandata mea et servat ea, ille est, qui diligit me; qui autem diligit me, diligetur a Patre meo, et ego diligam eum et manifestabo ei meipsum."

²² Dicit ei Iudas, non ille Iscariotes: "Domine, et quid factum est, quia nobis manifestaturus es teipsum et non mundo?"

²³ Respondit Iesus et dixit ei: "Si quis diligit me, sermonem meum servabit, et Pater meus diliget eum, et ad eum veniemus et mansionem apud eum faciemus; ²⁴ qui non diligit me, sermones meos non servat. Et sermo, quem auditis, non est meus, sed eius qui misit me, Patris.

---

apud: near, among (+ *acc.*)
dies, -diei *m/f*: day
diligo, (3): to love
mandatum, -i *n*: command
manifesto, (1): to make known, disclose
mansio, mansionis *f*: a home
mitto, (3) **misi, missus**: to send
modicus, -a, -um: a small amount

mundus, -i *m*: the world
orphanus, -i *m*: orphan
relinquo, (3): to leave behind, abandon
sermo, -onis *m*: words, sayings
servo, (1): to serve
venio, (4): to come
vivo, (3): to live, survive

14:18 **orphanos**: acc. pred. after *relinquat*, "leave you *as orphans*"
    venio: note the pres. with fut. meaning, "I will come"
14:22 **non ille Iscariotes:** "not the Iscariot," where *ille* is virtually the definite article
    quia manifestaturus es: fut. periphrastic in noun clause with epexegetic force, "what has happened *such that you are about to reveal yourself?*"
    nobis ... non mundo: dat. after *manifestaturus*, "reveal yourself *to us* ...*not to the world*"
    eius ... Patris: "the word *of him* who sent me, *the father*"

²⁵ ταῦτα λελάληκα ὑμῖν παρ᾽ ὑμῖν μένων· ²⁶ ὁ δὲ παράκλητος, τὸ πνεῦμα τὸ ἅγιον ὃ πέμψει ὁ πατὴρ ἐν τῷ ὀνόματί
μου, ἐκεῖνος ὑμᾶς διδάξει πάντα καὶ ὑπομνήσει ὑμᾶς πάντα
ἃ εἶπον ὑμῖν ἐγώ. ²⁷ εἰρήνην ἀφίημι ὑμῖν, εἰρήνην τὴν ἐμὴν
δίδωμι ὑμῖν· οὐ καθὼς ὁ κόσμος δίδωσιν ἐγὼ δίδωμι ὑμῖν.
²⁸ μὴ ταρασσέσθω ὑμῶν ἡ καρδία μηδὲ δειλιάτω. ἠκούσατε ὅτι ἐγὼ εἶπον ὑμῖν Ὑπάγω καὶ ἔρχομαι πρὸς ὑμᾶς. εἰ
ἠγαπᾶτέ με ἐχάρητε ἄν, ὅτι πορεύομαι πρὸς τὸν πατέρα, ὅτι
ὁ πατὴρ μείζων μού ἐστιν. ²⁹ καὶ νῦν εἴρηκα ὑμῖν πρὶν γενέσθαι, ἵνα ὅταν γένηται πιστεύσητε. ³⁰ οὐκέτι πολλὰ λαλήσω
μεθ᾽ ὑμῶν, ἔρχεται γὰρ ὁ τοῦ κόσμου ἄρχων· καὶ ἐν ἐμοὶ

ἅγιος, -α, -ον: sacred, holy	ὄνομα, -ατος, τό: name
δειλιάω: to be afraid	παράκλητος, ὁ: a helper
διδάσκω: to teach	πνεῦμα, -ατος, τό: spirit
εἰρήνη, ἡ: peace, time of peace	πρίν: before (+ *inf.*)
καθώς: just as	ταράσσω: to disturb
καρδια, ἡ: the heart	ὑπομιμνήσκω: to remind
μείζων, -ον: greater	χαίρω: to rejoice, be glad, be delighted

14:26 διδάξει ... ὑπομνήσει: fut., "he will teach ...he will remind you"
14:28 μὴ ταρασσέσθω: pres. imper. 3 s., "*let* your heart *not be troubled*"
    μηδὲ δειλιάτω: pres. imper. 3 s., "let it not be afraid"
    εἰ ἠγαπᾶτέ με ἐχάρητε ἄν: impf. in pres. contrafactual condition, "if you
    (now) loved me, you would be rejoicing"
14:29 εἴρηκα: perf. of λέγω, "I have said"
    πρὶν γενέσθαι: aor. inf., "before it happens"
    ἵνα ... πιστεύσητε: aor. subj. in clause of purpose and result, "so that you may
    believe"
    ὅταν γένηται: aor. subj. in general temporal clause, "when it happens
    (whenever that is)"
14:30 οὐκ ἔχει οὐδέν: "he has no power"

²⁵ Haec locutus sum vobis apud vos manens. ²⁶ Paraclitus autem, Spiritus Sanctus, quem mittet Pater in nomine meo, ille vos docebit omnia et suggeret vobis omnia, quae dixi vobis. ²⁷ Pacem relinquo vobis, pacem meam do vobis; non quomodo mundus dat, ego do vobis. Non turbetur cor vestrum neque formidet.

²⁸ Audistis quia ego dixi vobis: Vado et venio ad vos. Si diligeretis me, gauderetis quia vado ad Patrem, quia Pater maior me est. ²⁹ Et nunc dixi vobis, priusquam fiat, ut, cum factum fuerit, credatis. ³⁰ Iam non multa loquar vobiscum, venit enim princeps mundi et in me

---

audio, (4): to hear
cor, cordis *n*: heart
doceo, (2): to teach
formido, (1): to dread, fear, be afraid
gaudeo, (2): to rejoice
mitto, (3): to send
multus, -a, -um: much, many
mundus, -i *m*: world
paraclitus, -i *m*: helper, (appellation for Holy Ghost)

pater, patris *m*: father
pax, pacis *f*: peace
princeps, principis *m*: master, chief
priusquam: before (+ *subj.*)
quomodo: as
sanctus, -a, -um: divine, holy
suggero, (3): to suggest, remind
turbo, (1): to disturb

14:27 **non turbetur**: pres. subj. jussive, "*let* your heart *not be troubled*," where we would expect *ne* instead of *non*.

neque formidet: pres. subj. jussive, "nor let it be afraid"

14:28 **si diligeretis ... gauderetis**: impf. subj. in pres. contrary to fact condition, "if you (now) loved me ... you would rejoice"

me: abl. of comparison after *maior*, "the father is greater *than me*"

14:29 **fiat**: pres. subj. anticipatory after *priusquam*, "before it happens"

cum factum fuerit: fut. perf. *cum* temporal clause, "when it will have happened"

ut ... credatis: pres. subj. purpose clause, "so that you may believe"

14:30 **princeps mundi**: "master of the world," i.e. the devil

227

οὐκ ἔχει οὐδέν, ³¹ ἀλλ᾽ ἵνα γνῷ ὁ κόσμος ὅτι ἀγαπῶ τὸν πατέρα, καὶ καθὼς ἐντολὴν ἔδωκέν μοι ὁ πατὴρ οὕτως ποιῶ. Ἐγείρεσθε, ἄγωμεν ἐντεῦθεν.

Chapter 15

The Vine and the Branches

¹ ἐγώ εἰμι ἡ ἄμπελος ἡ ἀληθινή, καὶ ὁ πατήρ μου ὁ γεωργός ἐστιν· ² πᾶν κλῆμα ἐν ἐμοὶ μὴ φέρον καρπὸν αἴρει αὐτό, καὶ πᾶν τὸ καρπὸν φέρον καθαίρει αὐτὸ ἵνα καρπὸν πλείονα φέρῃ. ³ ἤδη ὑμεῖς καθαροί ἐστε διὰ τὸν λόγον ὃν λελάληκα ὑμῖν. ⁴ μείνατε ἐν ἐμοί, κἀγὼ ἐν ὑμῖν. καθὼς τὸ κλῆμα οὐ δύναται καρπὸν φέρειν ἀφ᾽ ἑαυτοῦ ἐὰν μὴ μένῃ ἐν τῇ ἀμπέλῳ, οὕτως οὐδὲ ὑμεῖς ἐὰν μὴ ἐν ἐμοὶ μένητε. ἐγώ εἰμι ἡ ἄμπελος, ὑμεῖς τὰ κλήματα.

ἄγω: to lead or go
ἀληθινός, -ή, -όν: true
ἄμπελος, ἡ: grapevine
γεωργός, ὁ: a farmer
ἤδη: now, already

καθαίρω: to clean, prune
καθαρός, -α, -ον: clean, spotless
καρπός, ὁ: a fruit
κλῆμα, -ατος, τό: a vine-twig, vine-branch
φέρω: to bear

14:31 ἵνα γνῷ: aor. subj. of γινώσκω in clause of purpose and result, "so that the world may know"

καθὼς ἔδωκέν: aor. of δίδωμι, "just as he gave"

οὕτως ποιῶ: "just so I do"

ἐγείρεσθε: pres. imper., "arise!"

ἄγωμεν: pres. subj. hortatory, "let us go"

15:2 μὴ φέρον: pres. part. conditional, *"if not bearing fruit"*

καὶ πᾶν (sc. κλῆμα): *and every branch* bearing fruit"

ἵνα ... φέρῃ: pres. subj. in purpose clause, "so that it may bear more"

15:3 λελάληκα: perf., "the word *I have spoken*"

15:4 μείνατε: aor. imper., "remain!"

καθὼς ... οὕτως: "just as ... so also"

ἐὰν μὴ μένῃ: pres. subj. in pres. general protasis, "if it does not remain"

ἐὰν μὴ μένητε: pres. subj., "if you do not remain"

15:5 οὐ ... οὐδέν: the double negative is cumulative, "you are able to do *nothing*"

non habet quidquam;   ³¹ sed, ut cognoscat mundus quia diligo Patrem, et sicut mandatum dedit mihi Pater, sic facio.

Surgite, eamus hinc.

Chapter 15

The Vine and the Branches

¹ Ego sum vitis vera, et Pater meus agricola est.   ² Omnem palmitem in me non ferentem fructum tollit eum; et omnem, qui fert fructum, purgat eum, ut fructum plus afferat.   ³ Iam vos mundi estis propter sermonem, quem locutus sum vobis.   ⁴ Manete in me, et ego in vobis. Sicut palmes non potest ferre fructum a semetipso, nisi manserit in vite, sic nec vos, nisi in me manseritis.

---

affero, afferre: to bring to, bear
agricola, -ae *m*: farmer
eo, (4): to go
fero, ferre, tuli, latus: to bring, bear
fructus, -us *m*: crops, fruit, reward
mandatum, -i *n*: order,; commandment
maneo, (2) mansi: to remain
mundus, -a, -um: clean

palmes, -itis *m*: young vine branch, shoot
plus, pluris (*gen.*): more
purgo, (1): to make clean, cleanse
semetipse, -a, -um: one's self
tollo, (3), sustuli, sublatus: to remove
verus, -a, -um: true, real
vitis, -is *f.*: vine

14:31 **ut cognoscat**: pres. subj. purpose clause, "in order that the world may understand"

eamus: pres. subj. hortatory, "let us go"

15:2 **non ferentem**: pres. part. modifying *palmitem*, conditional, "*if not bearing fruit*"

eum: antecedent is *palmitem*, "he removes *it*"

ut ... afferat: pres. subj. in purpose clause, "so that it may bear"

15:4 **sicut ... ut**: *just as* branches ...*just so* you"

nisi manserit ... nisi manseritis: fut. perf. in pres. general condition, "unless it remains ... unless you remain"

229

⁵ ὁ μένων ἐν ἐμοὶ κἀγὼ ἐν αὐτῷ οὗτος φέρει καρπὸν πολύν, ὅτι χωρὶς ἐμοῦ οὐ δύνασθε ποιεῖν οὐδέν. ⁶ ἐὰν μή τις μένῃ ἐν ἐμοί, ἐβλήθη ἔξω ὡς τὸ κλῆμα καὶ ἐξηράνθη, καὶ συνάγουσιν αὐτὰ καὶ εἰς τὸ πῦρ βάλλουσιν καὶ καίεται. ⁷ ἐὰν μείνητε ἐν ἐμοὶ καὶ τὰ ῥήματά μου ἐν ὑμῖν μείνῃ, ὃ ἐὰν θέλητε αἰτήσασθε καὶ γενήσεται ὑμῖν· ⁸ ἐν τούτῳ ἐδοξάσθη ὁ πατήρ μου ἵνα καρπὸν πολὺν φέρητε καὶ γένησθε ἐμοὶ μαθηταί.

⁹ καθὼς ἠγάπησέν με ὁ πατήρ, κἀγὼ ὑμᾶς ἠγάπησα, μείνατε ἐν τῇ ἀγάπῃ τῇ ἐμῇ. ¹⁰ ἐὰν τὰς ἐντολάς μου τηρήσητε, μενεῖτε ἐν τῇ ἀγάπῃ μου, καθὼς ἐγὼ τοῦ πατρὸς τὰς ἐντολὰς τετήρηκα καὶ μένω αὐτοῦ ἐν τῇ ἀγάπῃ.

ἀγαπάω: to love
ἀγάπη, ἡ: love
αἰτέω: to ask, beg
βάλλω: to throw
δύναμαι: to be able (+ *inf.*)
ἐντολή, ἡ: a command
καίω: to burn
κλῆμα, -ατος, τό: a vine-twig, vine-branch

μένω: to remain
ξηραίνω: to parch up, dry up
πολύς, πολλά, πολύ: many, much
πῦρ, πυρός, τό: fire
συνάγω: to gather together, collect
τηρέω: to keep, preserve
χωρίς: apart from (+ *gen.*)

15:6 ἐβλήθη ... ἐξηράνθη: aor. pass. gnomic with general force, "he is cast off ... he becomes withered"

15:7 ἐὰν μείνητε ... μείνῃ: aor. subj. in fut. more vivid protasis,"*if you remain* in me and if my words *remain*"

ὃ ἐὰν θέλητε: pres. subj., "(that) which if you wish it" i.e. whatever you wish

αἰτήσασθε: aor. imper., "ask for"

γενήσεται: fut. of γίνομαι, "*it will be* for you"

15:8 ἵνα φέρητε ... γένησθε: subj. in noun clause in apposition to τούτῳ, "in this, namely *that you bear fruit* ... and *that you become*"

15:9 μείνατε: aor. imper., "remain!"

15:10 ἐὰν ... τηρήσητε: aor. subj. in fut. more vivid protasis, "if you keep"

μενεῖτε; fut., "then *you will remain*"

τετήρηκα: perf., "just as *I have kept* the commands"

15:11 ἵνα ἡ χαρὰ ᾖ: pres. subj. in purpose clause, "*so that my joy be* in you"

⁵ Ego sum vitis, vos palmites. Qui manet in me, et ego in eo, hic fert fructum multum, quia sine me nihil potestis facere. ⁶ Si quis in me non manserit, missus est foras sicut palmes et aruit; et colligunt eos et in ignem mittunt, et ardent. ⁷ Si manseritis in me, et verba mea in vobis manserint, quodcumque volueritis, petite, et fiet vobis. ⁸ In hoc clarificatus est Pater meus, ut fructum multum afferatis et efficiamini mei discipuli.

⁹ Sicut dilexit me Pater, et ego dilexi vos; manete in dilectione mea. ¹⁰ Si praecepta mea servaveritis, manebitis in dilectione mea, sicut ego Patris mei praecepta servavi et maneo in eius dilectione.

---

affero, afferre: to bring to, carry forth
ardeo, (2): to burn
aresco, (3), **arui**: to become dry, dry up
clarifico, (1): to make famous, glorify
colligo, (3): to collect, gather
dilectio, dilectionis *f.*: love
diligo, (3), **dilexi, dilectus**: to love
efficio, (3): to prove
fero, ferre: to bear
foras (*adv.*): out of doors, out
fructus, -us *m*: fruit, reward

ignis, -is *m*: fire
maneo, (2), **mansi, mansus**: to remain, stay
mitto, (3), **misi, missus**: to send
multus, -a, -um: much
nihil: nothing
palmes, palmitis *m*: young vine branch
peto, (3): to desire
praeceptum, -i *n*: order, command
servo, (1): **to keep, preserve**
volo, velle, volui: to wish, want

15:6 **si quis manserit**: fut. perf. in pres. general protasis, "*if anyone does* not *remain*"
15:7 **si manseritis**: fut. perf. in future more vivid protasis, "if you remain"
   quodcumque volueritis: perf. subj. in general relative clause, "whatever you wish"
15:8 **ut ... afferatis ... efficiamini**: pres. subj. in noun clause in apposition to *hoc*, "he is glorified in this, namely, *that you bear fruit ... that you prove yourselves*"
15:10 **si ... servaveritis**: fut. perf. in fut. more vivid protasis, "if you keep"

¹¹ ταῦτα λελάληκα ὑμῖν ἵνα ἡ χαρὰ ἡ ἐμὴ ἐν ὑμῖν ᾖ καὶ ἡ χαρὰ ὑμῶν πληρωθῇ. ¹² αὕτη ἐστὶν ἡ ἐντολὴ ἡ ἐμὴ ἵνα ἀγαπᾶτε ἀλλήλους καθὼς ἠγάπησα ὑμᾶς· ¹³ μείζονα ταύτης ἀγάπην οὐδεὶς ἔχει, ἵνα τις τὴν ψυχὴν αὐτοῦ θῇ ὑπὲρ τῶν φίλων αὐτοῦ. ¹⁴ ὑμεῖς φίλοι μού ἐστε ἐὰν ποιῆτε ὃ ἐγὼ ἐντέλλομαι ὑμῖν. ¹⁵ οὐκέτι λέγω ὑμᾶς δούλους, ὅτι ὁ δοῦλος οὐκ οἶδεν τί ποιεῖ αὐτοῦ ὁ κύριος· ὑμᾶς δὲ εἴρηκα φίλους, ὅτι πάντα ἃ ἤκουσα παρὰ τοῦ πατρός μου ἐγνώρισα ὑμῖν. ¹⁶ οὐχ ὑμεῖς με ἐξελέξασθε, ἀλλ᾽ ἐγὼ ἐξελεξάμην ὑμᾶς, καὶ ἔθηκα ὑμᾶς ἵνα ὑμεῖς ὑπάγητε καὶ καρπὸν φέρητε καὶ ὁ καρπὸς ὑμῶν μένῃ, ἵνα ὅτι ἂν αἰτήσητε τὸν πατέρα ἐν τῷ ὀνόματί μου δῷ ὑμῖν. ¹⁷ ταῦτα ἐντέλλομαι ὑμῖν ἵνα ἀγαπᾶτε ἀλλήλους.

ἀγάπη, ἡ: love
αἰτέω: to ask, beg
γνωρίζω: to make known, point out, explain
δοῦλος, ὁ: a slave
ἐκλέγω: to choose

ἐντέλλομαι: to enjoin, command
πληρόω: to make full
φίλος, -η, -ον: loved, beloved, dear
χαρά, ἡ: joy, delight

πληρωθῇ: aor. subj. pass. in purpose clause, *"so that* your joy *be made full"*

15:12 ἵνα ἀγαπᾶτε: pres. subj. in noun clause in apposition to αὕτη, "this is my commnad, namely, *that you love"*

15:13 μείζονα: acc. s. f., "love *greater* than this"

ἵνα τις θῇ: aor. subj. of τίθημι in noun clause in apposition to ταύτης, "greater than this, *that he lay down* his life"

15:14 ἐὰν ποιῆτε: pres. subj. in pres. general protasis, "if you do"

15:15 εἴρηκα: perf., *"I have called* you friends"

ἐγνώρισα: aor. of γνωρίζω, *"I have made known* to you"

15:16 οὐχ ... ἐξελέξασθε: aor. of ἐκ-λέγω, "you have not chosen"

ἔθηκα: aor. of τίθημι, "I have placed you"

ἵνα ὑπάγητε: pres. subj. in purpose clause, "so that you would go"

ἵνα ... δῷ: aor. subj of δίδωμι in result clause, "so that he would give you"

ὅτι ἂν αἰτήσητε: aor. subj. in general relative clause, "whatever you ask"

τὸν πατέρα: acc. after αἰτήσητε, whatever you ask *the father"*

15:17 ἵνα ἀγαπᾶτε: pres. subj. in noun clause in apposition to ταῦτα, "I command these things, *that you love"*

¹¹ Haec locutus sum vobis, ut gaudium meum in vobis sit, et gaudium vestrum impleatur. ¹² Hoc est praeceptum meum, ut diligatis invicem, sicut dilexi vos; ¹³ maiorem hac dilectionem nemo habet, ut animam suam quis ponat pro amicis suis. ¹⁴ Vos amici mei estis, si feceritis, quae ego praecipio vobis. ¹⁵ Iam non dico vos servos, quia servus nescit quid facit dominus eius; vos autem dixi amicos, quia omnia, quae audivi a Patre meo, nota feci vobis. ¹⁶ Non vos me elegistis, sed ego elegi vos et posui vos, ut vos eatis et fructum afferatis, et fructus vester maneat, ut quodcumque petieritis Patrem in nomine meo, det vobis. ¹⁷ Haec mando vobis, ut diligatis invicem.

---

affero, afferre: to bear forth
amicus, -i *m*: friend, ally, disciple
anima, -ae *f*: soul, spirit
dilectio, dilectionis *f*: love
diligo, (1): to love
eligo, (3), **elegi**: to pick out, choose
fructus, -us *m*: fruit, profit, reward
gaudium, -i *n*: joy
impleo, (2): to fill , become complete

invicem: in turn, reciprocally, mutually
mando, (1): to order, command
notus, -a, -um: well known, familiar
peto, (3) **petii**: to desire, seek
pono, (3) **posui**: to place, lay down
praeceptum, -i *n*: order, command
praecipio, (3): to order, teach, instruct
servus, -i *m*: servant, slave

15:11 **ut ... sit ... impleatur**: pres. subj. in purpose clause, "I have spoken *so that* my joy *is* in you... *so that* your joy *may be complete*"

15:12 **ut diligatis**: pres. subj. in noun clause in apposition to *hoc*, "this is my command, *namely, that you love*"

15:13 **hac**: abl. of comparison after *maiorem*, "greater love *than this*"

  ut ... ponat: pres. subj. in noun clause in apposition to *hac* "namely, that someone lay down"

  quis: (= **quisque**) "anyone"

15:14 **si feceritis**: fut. perf. in pres. general condition, "if you do"

15:15 **servos**: acc. predicate, "I call you *servants*"

  nota: predicate acc., "I have made all *known*"

15:16 **ut ... eatis ... afferatis ... maneat**: pres. subj. in purpose clause, "so that you would go ... so that you would bear ... so that it would remain"

  quodcumque petieritis: perf. subj. in general relative clause, "whatever you seek"

  ut ... det: pres. subj. purpose clause, "so that he would give"

15:17 **ut diligatis**: pres. subj. in noun clause in apposition to *haec*, "I command these things, *namely, that you love* one another"

The World Hates the Disciples

¹⁸ εἰ ὁ κόσμος ὑμᾶς μισεῖ, γινώσκετε ὅτι ἐμὲ πρῶτον ὑμῶν

μεμίσηκεν. εἰ ἐκ τοῦ κόσμου ἦτε, ὁ κόσμος ἂν τὸ ἴδιον ἐφίλει·

¹⁹ ὅτι δὲ ἐκ τοῦ κόσμου οὐκ ἐστέ, ἀλλ᾽ ἐγὼ ἐξελεξάμην ὑμᾶς

ἐκ τοῦ κόσμου, διὰ τοῦτο μισεῖ ὑμᾶς ὁ κόσμος. ²⁰ μνημονεύετε

τοῦ λόγου οὗ ἐγὼ εἶπον ὑμῖν Οὐκ ἔστιν δοῦλος μείζων τοῦ

κυρίου αὐτοῦ· εἰ ἐμὲ ἐδίωξαν, καὶ ὑμᾶς διώξουσιν· εἰ τὸν

λόγον μου ἐτήρησαν, καὶ τὸν ὑμέτερον τηρήσουσιν. ²¹ ἀλλὰ

ταῦτα πάντα ποιήσουσιν εἰς ὑμᾶς διὰ τὸ ὄνομά μου, ὅτι οὐκ

οἴδασιν τὸν πέμψαντά με. ²² εἰ μὴ ἦλθον καὶ ἐλάλησα αὐτοῖς,

ἁμαρτίαν οὐκ εἴχοσαν· νῦν δὲ πρόφασιν οὐκ ἔχουσιν περὶ τῆς

ἁμαρτίας αὐτῶν. ²³ ὁ ἐμὲ μισῶν καὶ τὸν πατέρα μου μισεῖ.

²⁴ εἰ τὰ ἔργα μὴ ἐποίησα ἐν αὐτοῖς ἃ οὐδεὶς ἄλλος ἐποίησεν,

ἁμαρτία, ἡ: a failure, fault, sin	οἶδα: to know (*perf.*)
διώκω: to pursue	ὄνομα, -ατος, τό: a name
ἐκλέγω: to pick or single out	πρόφασις, -εως, ἡ: excuse
ἵστημι: to make to stand	τηρέω: to keep, preserve
μισέω: to hate	ὑμέτερος, -α, -ον: your, yours
μνημονεύω: to call to mind, remember	φιλέω: to love, regard with affection

15:18 μεμίσηκεν: perf. of μισέω, "that it *has hated* me"
  εἰ ... ἦτε, ἂν ἐφίλει: impf. in pres. contrafactual condition, "*if you were* of the world ... the world *would love* you"
15:19 ἐξελεξάμην: aor. mid. of ἐκ-λέγω, "I have chosen"
15:20 τοῦ λόγου οὗ: gen., "*the word which* I spoke," the relative pronoun is attracted into the case of its antecedent
  διώξουσιν: fut., "they will chase you too"
15:21 ποιήσουσιν: fut., "they will do"
  οὐκ οἴδασιν: perf. (=ἴσασι), "they do not know"
15:22 εἰ μὴ ἦλθον καὶ ἐλάλησα: aor. in past contrafactual protasis,"if I had not come and spoken"
  οὐκ εἴχοσαν impf. 3 pl. (=εἶχον) in present contrafactual apodosis (expecting ἄν), "they would not (now) have"

The World Hates the Disciples

¹⁸ Si mundus vos odit, scitote quia me priorem vobis odio habuit. ¹⁹ Si de mundo essetis, mundus, quod suum est, diligeret; quia vero de mundo non estis, sed ego elegi vos de mundo, propterea odit vos mundus. ²⁰ Mementote sermonis, quem ego dixi vobis: Non est servus maior domino suo. Si me persecuti sunt, et vos persequentur; si sermonem meum servaverunt, et vestrum servabunt. ²¹ Sed haec omnia facient vobis propter nomen meum, quia nesciunt eum, qui misit me. ²² Si non venissem et locutus fuissem eis, peccatum non haberent; nunc autem excusationem non habent de peccato suo. ²³ Qui me odit et Patrem meum odit. ²⁴ Si opera non fecissem in eis, quae nemo alius fecit,

---

eligo, (3), **elegi, electus**: to pick out, choose
excusatio, -onis *f*: excuse
habeo, (2) **habui**: to have, hold
memini, -isse (*perf.*): to remember (+ *gen.*)
mundus, -i *m*: the world
nescio, (4): to not know
nomen, -inis *n*: name
odi, odisse: to hate (*perf.*)
odium, -i *n*: hatred, contempt

opus, operis *n*: need, work
peccatum, -i *n*: sin; moral offense
persequor, (3), **persecutus sum**: to persecute, attack
prior, prius: earlier, prior
scio, (4): know, understand
vero: certainly, truly

15:18 **scitote**: fut. imper., "*know that!*"
    odio: abl. of manner with *habuit*, "the world held me *in contempt*"
15:19 **si ... essetis ... diligeret**: impf. subj. in pres. contrary to fact condition, "*if you were* of the world ...the world *would love you*"
    quod suum est: (*quod = quoad*), "would love you *as its own*"
15:20 **mementote**: pres. imper. of defective *memini*, "remember!" + gen.
    maior: pred. nom., "is not *greater than*" + abl. of comparison
15:22 **si non venissem et locutus fuissem**: plupf. subj. in past contrary to fact protasis, "If I had not come and spoken"
    non haberent: impf. subj. in present contrary to fact apodosis, "they would not (now) have"
15:24 **si ... non fecissem**: plupf. subj. in contrary to fact protasis, "if I had not done"

ἁμαρτίαν οὐκ εἴχοσαν· νῦν δὲ καὶ ἑωράκασιν καὶ μεμισήκασιν καὶ ἐμὲ καὶ τὸν πατέρα μου. ²⁵ ἀλλ᾽ ἵνα πληρωθῇ ὁ λόγος ὁ ἐν τῷ νόμῳ αὐτῶν γεγραμμένος ὅτι Ἐμίσησάν με δωρεάν.

The Work of the Holy Spirit

²⁶ ὅταν ἔλθῃ ὁ παράκλητος ὃν ἐγὼ πέμψω ὑμῖν παρὰ τοῦ πατρός, τὸ πνεῦμα τῆς ἀληθείας ὃ παρὰ τοῦ πατρὸς ἐκπορεύεται, ἐκεῖνος μαρτυρήσει περὶ ἐμοῦ· ²⁷ καὶ ὑμεῖς δὲ μαρτυρεῖτε, ὅτι ἀπ᾽ ἀρχῆς μετ᾽ ἐμοῦ ἐστέ.

ἀλήθεια, ἡ; the truth
ἀρχή, ἡ: a beginning
γράφω: to write
δωρεά, ἡ: gift
μαρτυρέω: to bear witness

νόμος, ὁ: custom, law
παράκλητος, ὁ: a helper
πέμπω: to send
πληρόω: to fill
πνεῦμα, -ατος, τό: a spirit

15:24 οὐκ εἴχοσαν impf. 3 pl. (=εἶχον) in present contrafactual apodosis (expecting ἄν), "they would not (now) have sin"

ἑωράκασιν: perf. of ὁράω, "they have seen"

μεμισήκασιν: perf. of μισέω, "they have hated"

καὶ ...καὶ: "*both* the father *and* me"

15:25 ἵνα πληρωθῇ: aor. subj. in purpose clause, "(these things are done) so the word is fufilled"

ὁ γεγραμμένος: perf. part. agreeing with λόγος, "the word *written* in the law" Ps. 69:4

δωρεάν: adverbial acc., "as a gift" i.e. freely

15:26 ὅταν ἔλθῃ: aor. subj. in general temporal clause, "whenever he comes"

peccatum non haberent; nunc autem et viderunt et oderunt et me et Patrem meum. ²⁵ Sed ut impleatur sermo, qui in lege eorum scriptus est: 'Odio me habuerunt gratis.'

The Work of the Holy Spirit

²⁶ Cum autem venerit Paraclitus, quem ego mittam vobis a Patre, Spiritum veritatis, qui a Patre procedit, ille testimonium perhibebit de me; ²⁷ sed et vos testimonium perhibetis, quia ab initio mecum estis.

---

et ...et: both ...and
gratia, -ae f: grace, a gift
initium, -i n: beginning
lex, legis f: law
mitto, (3): to send
odi, odisse: to hate (perf.)
odium, -i n: hatred, contempt
paraclitus, -i m: helper

perhibeo, (2): to present, give, bestow
procedo, (3): to proceed, appear
scribo, (3), scripsi, scriptus: to write
sermo, sermonis m: speech, the word
spiritus, -us m: soul, spirit
testimonium, -i n: testimony
venio, (4) veni: to come

15:24 **non haberent**: impf. subj. in present contrary to fact apodosis, "*they would not have* sin"

15:25 **ut impleatur**: pres. subj. in purpose clause, "so that it is fulfilled"

   odio ... gratis: abl. of manner, "they held me *in contempt ...freely*""

15:26 **cum ... venerit**: fut. perf. in *cum* temporal clause, "when he comes"

Chapter 16

¹ ταῦτα λελάληκα ὑμῖν ἵνα μὴ σκανδαλισθῆτε. ² ἀποσυναγώγους ποιήσουσιν ὑμᾶς· ἀλλ᾽ ἔρχεται ὥρα ἵνα πᾶς ὁ ἀπο-
κτείνας ὑμᾶς δόξῃ λατρείαν προσφέρειν τῷ θεῷ. ³ καὶ ταῦτα
ποιήσουσιν ὅτι οὐκ ἔγνωσαν τὸν πατέρα οὐδὲ ἐμέ. ⁴ ἀλλὰ
ταῦτα λελάληκα ὑμῖν ἵνα ὅταν ἔλθῃ ἡ ὥρα αὐτῶν μνημονεύητε
αὐτῶν ὅτι ἐγὼ εἶπον ὑμῖν· ταῦτα δὲ ὑμῖν ἐξ ἀρχῆς οὐκ εἶπον,
ὅτι μεθ᾽ ὑμῶν ἤμην. ⁵ νῦν δὲ ὑπάγω πρὸς τὸν πέμψαντά με
καὶ οὐδεὶς ἐξ ὑμῶν ἐρωτᾷ με Ποῦ ὑπάγεις; ⁶ ἀλλ᾽ ὅτι ταῦτα
λελάληκα ὑμῖν ἡ λύπη πεπλήρωκεν ὑμῶν τὴν καρδίαν. ⁷ ἀλλ᾽
ἐγὼ τὴν ἀλήθειαν λέγω ὑμῖν, συμφέρει ὑμῖν ἵνα ἐγὼ ἀπέλθω.
ἐὰν γὰρ μὴ ἀπέλθω, ὁ παράκλητος οὐ μὴ ἔλθῃ πρὸς ὑμᾶς·

ἀποκτείνω: to kill, slay
ἀποσυνάγωγος, -ον: put out of the
  synagogue
ἀρχή, ἡ: a beginning, origin
λαλέω: to talk
λατρεία, ἡ: service, servitude
λύπη, ἡ: grief

μνημονεύω: to call to mind, remember
πᾶς, πᾶσα, πᾶν: all, every
πληρόω: to fill, complete
προσφέρω: to provide, apply to
σκανδαλίζω: to give offence to
συμφέρω: to be advantageous to (+ *dat.*)
ὥρα, ἡ: hour

16:1 ἵνα μὴ σκανδαλισθῆτε: aor. pass. subj. in purpose clause, "lest you be
     scandalized"

16:2 ἀποσυναγώγους: acc. pred., "will make you *put out of the synagogue*"
     ἵνα δόξῃ: aor. subj. of δοκέω in result clause, "so that he will think"
     ὁ ἀποκτείνας: aor. part. attributive, "anyone one who kills"
     προσφέρειν: pres. inf. in ind. st. after δόξῃ, "will think *that he provides* service"

16:3 οὐκ ἔγνωσαν: aor. of γινώσκω, "they did not know"

16:4 ἵνα ... μνημονεύητε: pres. subj. in purpose clause, "I spoke *in order that you
     remember*"
     ὅταν ἔλθῃ: aor. subj. in general temporal clause, "whenever the time comes"
     ἤμην: impf. of εἰμι (= ἦ), "because *I was* with you"

16:6 πεπλήρωκεν: perf. act., "grief *has filled*"

16:7 ἵνα ἐγὼ ἀπέλθω: aor. subj. in noun clause as subject of συμφέρει, "*that I go
     away* is to your advantage"
     ἐὰν γὰρ μὴ ἀπέλθω: aor. subj. in fut. more vivid protasis, "unless I depart"
     οὐ μὴ ἔλθῃ: aor. subj. in strong denial, "he will certainly not come"

Chapter 16

¹ Haec locutus sum vobis, ut non scandalizemini. ² Absque synagogis facient vos; sed venit hora, ut omnis, qui interficit vos, arbitretur obsequium se praestare Deo. ³ Et haec facient, quia non noverunt Patrem neque me. ⁴ Sed haec locutus sum vobis, ut, cum venerit hora eorum, reminiscamini eorum, quia ego dixi vobis. Haec autem vobis ab initio non dixi, quia vobiscum eram. ⁵ At nunc vado ad eum, qui me misit, et nemo ex vobis interrogat me: 'Quo vadis?› ⁶ Sed quia haec locutus sum vobis, tristitia implevit cor vestrum. ⁷ Sed ego veritatem dico vobis: Expedit vobis, ut ego vadam. Si enim non abiero, Paraclitus non veniet ad vos;

---

abeo, (4), **abii**: to depart, go away
arbitror, (1): to judge, believe, think
expedio, (4): to be expedient
impleo, (2), **implevi**: to complete
initium, **-i** *n*: beginning
interficio, (3): to kill, destroy
nosco, (3), **novi**, **notus**: to know

obsequium, **-i** *n*: services, obedience
praesto, (1): to offer, present X (*acc.*) to Y (*dat.*)
reminiscor, (3): to call to mind, recollect
scandalizo, (1): to tempt to evil, scandalize
synagoga, **-ae** *f*: synagogue
tristitia, **-ae** *f*: sadness
veritas, **-tatis** *f*: truth

16:1 **ut non scandalizemini**: pres. subj. in negative purpose clause, "lest you be tempted"

16:2 **absque synagogis**: prepositional phrase as a predicate, "will make you *from the synagogue*," i.e. expelled from the synagogue

ut ... arbitretur: pres. subj. in purpose/result clause, "the hour *so that he will think*" i.e. when he will think

se praestare: pres. inf. in indirect statement after *arbitretur*, "*each* thinks *that he presents* obedience"

16:4 **ut ... reminiscamini**: pres. subj. in purpose clause, "I have spoken *so that you remember*" + gen.

cum ... venerit: fut. perf. in *cum* temporal clause, "when the hour comes"

16:7 **ut ... vadam**: pres. subj. in noun clause as subject of *expedit*, "*that I leave* is expedient to you"

si ... non abiero: fut. perf. in fut. more vivid protasis, "if I do not leave"

239

ἐὰν δὲ πορευθῶ, πέμψω αὐτὸν πρὸς ὑμᾶς. ⁸ καὶ ἐλθὼν ἐκεῖνος
ἐλέγξει τὸν κόσμον περὶ ἁμαρτίας καὶ περὶ δικαιοσύνης καὶ
περὶ κρίσεως· ⁹ περὶ ἁμαρτίας μέν, ὅτι οὐ πιστεύουσιν εἰς
ἐμέ· ¹⁰ περὶ δικαιοσύνης δέ, ὅτι πρὸς τὸν πατέρα ὑπάγω
καὶ οὐκέτι θεωρεῖτέ με· ¹¹ περὶ δὲ κρίσεως, ὅτι ὁ ἄρχων τοῦ
κόσμου τούτου κέκριται.

¹² ἔτι πολλὰ ἔχω ὑμῖν λέγειν, ἀλλ᾽ οὐ δύνασθε βαστά-
ζειν ἄρτι· ¹³ ὅταν δὲ ἔλθῃ ἐκεῖνος, τὸ πνεῦμα τῆς ἀληθείας,
ὁδηγήσει ὑμᾶς εἰς τὴν ἀλήθειαν πᾶσαν, οὐ γὰρ λαλήσει ἀφ᾽
ἑαυτοῦ, ἀλλ᾽ ὅσα ἀκούει λαλήσει, καὶ τὰ ἐρχόμενα ἀναγγελεῖ
ὑμῖν. ¹⁴ ἐκεῖνος ἐμὲ δοξάσει, ὅτι ἐκ τοῦ ἐμοῦ λήμψεται καὶ
ἀναγγελεῖ ὑμῖν. ¹⁵ πάντα ὅσα ἔχει ὁ πατὴρ ἐμά ἐστιν· διὰ
τοῦτο εἶπον ὅτι ἐκ τοῦ ἐμοῦ λαμβάνει καὶ ἀναγγελεῖ ὑμῖν.

ἀναγγέλλω: to carry back tidings of, report
ἄρχων, -οντος, ὁ: a ruler, commander
βαστάζω: to lift, bear
δικαιοσύνη, ἡ: righteousness, justice
δύναμαι: to be able, capable
ἐλέγχω: to refute

κρίνω: to judge
κρίσις: a judgement
λαμβάνω: to take
ὁδηγέω: to lead, guide
ὅσος, -η, -ον: how much
πνεῦμα, -ατος, τό: a spirit

16:7 ἐὰν δὲ πορευθῶ: aor. subj. in fut. more vivid protasis, "if I go"
16:8 ἐλθὼν: aor. part. instrumental, "by coming" or temporal, "once he comes"
    ἐλέγξει: fut. of ἐλέγχω, "he will refute"
16:9 μέν ... δέ ... δέ: a rare use of this particle combination in John
16:10 ὅτι ... ὑπάγω: causal, "because I go"
16:11 κέκριται: perf. of κρίνω, "he has judged"
16:12 λέγειν: inf. after ἔχω, "I am able *to say*"
16:13 ὅταν δὲ ἔλθῃ: aor. subj. in general temporal clause, "whenever he comes"
    τὰ ἐρχόμενα: pres. part. attrib., "he will report *the things coming*" i.e. the future
16:14 λήμψεται: fut. of λαμβάνω, "he will take"
16:15 ὅτι ... λαμβάνει καὶ ἀναγγελεῖ: ind. st. after εἶπον, "I said *that he takes and
    will report*" note the mix of future and present

si autem abiero, mittam eum ad vos. ⁸ Et cum venerit ille, arguet mundum de peccato et de iustitia et de iudicio: ⁹ de peccato quidem, quia non credunt in me; ¹⁰ de iustitia vero, quia ad Patrem vado, et iam non videtis me; ¹¹ de iudicio autem, quia princeps mundi huius iudicatus est.

¹² Adhuc multa habeo vobis dicere, sed non potestis portare modo. ¹³ Cum autem venerit ille, Spiritus veritatis, deducet vos in omnem veritatem; non enim loquetur a semetipso, sed quaecumque audiet, loquetur et, quae ventura sunt, annuntiabit vobis. ¹⁴ Ille me clarificabit, quia de meo accipiet et annuntiabit vobis. ¹⁵ Omnia, quaecumque habet Pater, mea sunt; propterea dixi quia de meo accipit et annuntiabit vobis.

---

accipio, (3): to receive, accept
adhuc: thus far, till now
annuntio, (1): to announce, say
arguo, (3): to accuse, charge, convict
audio, (4): to hear
deduco, (3): to lead
iudicium, -i *n*: judgment
iudico, (1): to judge
iustitia, -ae *f*: righteousness, justice

modo: just now
porto, (1): to carry, bring
possum, posse, potui: be able, can
propterea: therefore, for this reason
quidem: indeed, certainly
semetipse, -a, -um: one's self
spiritus -us *m*: soul, spirit
vero: certainly, truly

16:8 **cum venerit**: fut. perf. in *cum* temporal clause, "when he comes"

16:11 **princeps mundi**: "prince of this world," i.e. the devil

16:12 **dicere**: inf. complementing *habeo*, "I am able *to tell* many things"

16:13 **cum ... venerit**: fut. perf. in *cum* temporal clause, "when he comes" cf. vs. 8 above

    deducet: "he will lead;" this has been corrected from Jerome's erroneous *docebit*, "he will teach" as a translation of the verb ὁδηγήσει

    quae ventura sunt: fut. periphrastic, "he will announce *what is about to come*"

The Disciples' Grief Will Turn to Joy

¹⁶ μικρὸν καὶ οὐκέτι θεωρεῖτέ με, καὶ πάλιν μικρὸν καὶ ὄψεσθέ με.

¹⁷ εἶπαν οὖν ἐκ τῶν μαθητῶν αὐτοῦ πρὸς ἀλλήλους «Τί ἐστιν τοῦτο ὃ λέγει ἡμῖν Μικρὸν καὶ οὐ θεωρεῖτέ με, καὶ πάλιν μικρὸν καὶ ὄψεσθέ με; καί Ὅτι ὑπάγω πρὸς τὸν πατέρα;» ¹⁸ ἔλεγον οὖν «Τί ἐστιν τοῦτο ὃ λέγει μικρόν ; οὐκ οἴδαμεν τί λαλεῖ.»

¹⁹ ἔγνω Ἰησοῦς ὅτι ἤθελον αὐτὸν ἐρωτᾶν, καὶ εἶπεν αὐτοῖς «Περὶ τούτου ζητεῖτε μετ᾽ ἀλλήλων ὅτι εἶπον Μικρὸν καὶ οὐ θεωρεῖτέ με, καὶ πάλιν μικρὸν καὶ ὄψεσθέ με; ²⁰ ἀμὴν ἀμὴν λέγω ὑμῖν ὅτι κλαύσετε καὶ θρηνήσετε ὑμεῖς, ὁ δὲ κόσμος χαρήσεται· ὑμεῖς λυπηθήσεσθε, ἀλλ᾽ ἡ λύπη ὑμῶν εἰς χαρὰν γενήσεται. ²¹ ἡ γυνὴ ὅταν τίκτῃ λύπην ἔχει, ὅτι ἦλθεν ἡ ὥρα αὐτῆς· ὅταν δὲ γεννήσῃ τὸ παιδίον,

---

ἀλλήλων: of one another	λυπέω: to pain, grieve
γεννάω: to beget, engender	μικρός, -α, -ον: small
γυνή, γυναικός, ἡ: a woman	ὄψομαι: to see (*fut.*)
ζητέω: to seek, seek for	παιδίον, τό: little or young child
θρηνέω: to sing a dirge, to wail	τίκτω: to bring into the world
κλαίω: to weep, lament, wail	

16:16 **μικρὸν**: acc. of duration, "for a short time"
   ὄψεσθε: fut., "you will see"
16:17 **ἐκ τῶν μαθητῶν**: partitive, "(some) of his disciples"
   Μικρὸν ...ὄψεσθε.: note the direct speech quoted within direct speech
16:19 **ἔγνω**: aor. of γινώσκω, "Jesus knew"
   ἐρωτᾶν: pres. inf. after ἤθελον, "that they wished *to ask*"
   Μικρὸν... με;: Jesus now quotes himself
16:20 **κλαύσετε**: fut. of κλαίω, "you will weep"
   χαρήσεται: fut. mid. of χαίρω, "but the world *will rejoice*"
   λυπηθήσεσθε: fut. pass. of λυπέω, "you will be grieved"
16:21 **ὅταν τίκτῃ**: pres. subj. in general temporal clause, "when she is giving birth"
   ὅταν δὲ γεννήσῃ: aor. subj. of γεννάω in general temporal clause, "when she has borne"

242

The Disciples' Grief Will Turn to Joy

¹⁶ Modicum, et iam non videtis me; et iterum modicum, et videbitis me."

¹⁷ Dixerunt ergo ex discipulis eius ad invicem: "Quid est hoc, quod dicit nobis: 'Modicum, et non videtis me; et iterum modicum, et videbitis me' et 'Vado ad Patrem'?" ¹⁸ Dicebant ergo: "Quid est hoc, quod dicit: 'Modicum'? Nescimus quid loquitur."

¹⁹ Cognovit Iesus quia volebant eum interrogare et dixit eis: "De hoc quaeritis inter vos, quia dixi: 'Modicum, et non videtis me; et iterum modicum, et videbitis me'? ²⁰ Amen, amen dico vobis quia plorabitis et flebitis vos, mundus autem gaudebit; vos contristabimini, sed tristitia vestra vertetur in gaudium. ²¹ Mulier, cum parit, tristitiam habet, quia venit hora eius; cum autem pepererit puerum,

---

cognosco, (3) cognovi: to know
contristo, (1): to sadden, depress, discourage
fleo, (2): to cry, weep
gaudeo, (2), gavisus sum: to be glad, rejoice
gaudium, -i *n*: joy, gladness
interrogo, (1): to question, ask
invicem: in turn, reciprocally, among themselves
modicus, -a, -um: short time, small amount
mulier, mulieris *f*: woman

pario, (3), peperi, partum: to bear, give birth to
ploro, (1): to cry over, lament
puer, -i *m*: boy
quaero, (3): to search for, seek
tristitia, -ae *f*: sadness
verto, (3): to turn, change
video, (2) vidi: to see
volo, velle: to wish, want

16:16 **modicum**: acc. duration of time, "for a little while"
16:18 **quid loquitur**: indic. in vivid indirect question, "do not know *what he is saying*"
16:21 **cum parit**: pres., "when she is in the process of giving birth"
    cum ... pepererit: fut. perf. in *cum* temporal clause, "when she has given birth"

οὐκέτι μνημονεύει τῆς θλίψεως διὰ τὴν χαρὰν ὅτι ἐγεννήθη ἄνθρωπος εἰς τὸν κόσμον. ²² καὶ ὑμεῖς οὖν νῦν μὲν λύπην ἔχετε· πάλιν δὲ ὄψομαι ὑμᾶς, καὶ χαρήσεται ὑμῶν ἡ καρδία, καὶ τὴν χαρὰν ὑμῶν οὐδεὶς ἀρεῖ ἀφ᾽ ὑμῶν. ²³ καὶ ἐν ἐκείνῃ τῇ ἡμέρᾳ ἐμὲ οὐκ ἐρωτήσετε οὐδέν· ἀμὴν ἀμὴν λέγω ὑμῖν, ἄν τι αἰτήσητε τὸν πατέρα δώσει ὑμῖν ἐν τῷ ὀνόματί μου. ²⁴ ἕως ἄρτι οὐκ ἠτήσατε οὐδὲν ἐν τῷ ὀνόματί μου· αἰτεῖτε καὶ λήψεσθε, ἵνα ἡ χαρὰ ὑμῶν ᾖ πεπληρωμένη.

²⁵ ταῦτα ἐν παροιμίαις λελάληκα ὑμῖν· ἔρχεται ὥρα ὅτε οὐκέτι ἐν παροιμίαις λαλήσω ὑμῖν ἀλλὰ παρρησίᾳ περὶ τοῦ πατρὸς ἀπαγγελῶ ὑμῖν. ²⁶ ἐν ἐκείνῃ τῇ ἡμέρᾳ ἐν τῷ ὀνόματί μου αἰτήσεσθε, καὶ οὐ λέγω ὑμῖν ὅτι ἐγὼ ἐρωτήσω τὸν πατέρα

αἴρω: to take up, remove
αἰτέω: to ask, beg
ἀπαγγέλλω: to report, announce
ἄρτι: just now
γεννάω: to bear (a child)
ἐρωτάω: to ask
ἕως: until, till
θλῖψις, -εως, ἡ: pain, affliction

καρδία, ἡ: the heart
λύπη, ἡ: pain of body
μνημονεύω: to call to mind, remember
παροιμία, ἡ: a proverb, maxim
παρρησία, ἡ: freespokenness, openness
χαίρω: to gladden
χαρά, ἡ: joy
ὥρα, ἡ: period of time, hour

16:22 τῆς θλίψεως: gen. after μνημονεύει, "she remembers *the pain*"

ὅτι ἐγεννήθη: aor. pass. in epexegetic clause, "the joy *that a man has been born*"

16:22 νῦν μὲν ... πάλιν δὲ: "while now ... but later"

ὄψομαι ...χαρήσεται ... ἀρεῖ: fut., "I will see ... your heart *will be gladdened* ..."no one *will remove* from you"

16:23 ἐμὲ ... οὐδέν: double acc. after ἐρωτήσετε, "you will ask me (for) nothing"

ἄν τι αἰτήσητε: aor. subj. in general relative clause, "*whatever you ask* the father"

16:24 αἰτεῖτε: imper., "*ask!*"

λήψεσθε: fut. of λαμβάνω, "ask and *you shall receive*"

ἵνα ᾖ πεπληρωμένη: perf. subj. periphrastic of πληρόω in result clause, "so that your joy *may be filled*"

16:25 ἀπαγγελῶ: fut., "I will speak and *I will announce* to you"

iam non meminit pressurae propter gaudium, quia natus est homo

in mundum. ²² Et vos igitur nunc quidem tristitiam habetis; iterum

autem videbo vos, et gaudebit cor vestrum, et gaudium vestrum

nemo tollit a vobis. ²³ Et in illo die me non rogabitis quidquam.

Amen, amen dico vobis: Si quid petieritis Patrem in nomine meo,

dabit vobis. ²⁴ Usque modo non petistis quidquam in nomine meo.

Petite et accipietis, ut gaudium vestrum sit plenum.

²⁵ Haec in proverbiis locutus sum vobis; venit hora, cum iam non

in proverbiis loquar vobis, sed palam de Patre annuntiabo vobis. ²⁶ Illo

die in nomine meo petetis, et non dico vobis quia ego rogabo Patrem

---

accipio, (3) **accepi**, **acceptus**: to receive, accept
annuntio, (1): to announce, say
dies, diei *m/f*: day
gaudeo, (2): to rejoice
gaudium, -i *n*: joy, gladness
memini, meminisse: to remember, recall (+ *gen.*) (*perf.*)
nascor, (3), **natus sum**: to be born, begotten

palam (*adv.*): openly, plainly
peto, (3), **petii**, **petitus**: to desire, seek
plenus, -a, -um: full
pressura, -ae *f.*: pressure, burden, distress
proverbium, -i *n*: proverb, saying
rogo, (1): to ask
tollo, (3), **sustuli**, **sublatus**: to remove
tristitia, -ae *f.*: sadness
usque: continuously

16:21 **pressurae**: gen. after meminit, "she remembers *the pain*"
16:22 **nunc quidam ... iterum autem**: "while now ...but later," translating νῦν μὲν ... πάλιν δὲ
16:23 **me ... quidam**: double acc., "you will not ask *me anything*"
 si quid petieritis: fut. perf. in fut. more vivid protasis, "if you seek anything"
16:24 **usque modo non petistis**: perf, "up till now you have not asked"
 ut ... sit: pres. subj. in result clause, "*so that* your joy *is* full"
16:25 **cum ... loquar**: fut. in *cum* temporal clause, "when I will speak"

περὶ ὑμῶν· ²⁷ αὐτὸς γὰρ ὁ πατὴρ φιλεῖ ὑμᾶς, ὅτι ὑμεῖς ἐμὲ πεφιλήκατε καὶ πεπιστεύκατε ὅτι ἐγὼ παρὰ τοῦ πατρὸς ἐξῆλθον. ²⁸ ἐξῆλθον ἐκ τοῦ πατρὸς καὶ ἐλήλυθα εἰς τὸν κόσμον· πάλιν ἀφίημι τὸν κόσμον καὶ πορεύομαι πρὸς τὸν πατέρα.»

²⁹ λέγουσιν οἱ μαθηταὶ αὐτοῦ «Ἴδε νῦν ἐν παρρησίᾳ λαλεῖς, καὶ παροιμίαν οὐδεμίαν λέγεις. ³⁰ νῦν οἴδαμεν ὅτι οἶδας πάντα καὶ οὐ χρείαν ἔχεις ἵνα τίς σε ἐρωτᾷ· ἐν τούτῳ πιστεύομεν ὅτι ἀπὸ θεοῦ ἐξῆλθες.»

³¹ ἀπεκρίθη αὐτοῖς Ἰησοῦς «Ἄρτι πιστεύετε; ³² ἰδοὺ ἔρχεται ὥρα καὶ ἐλήλυθεν ἵνα σκορπισθῆτε ἕκαστος εἰς τὰ ἴδια κἀμὲ μόνον ἀφῆτε· καὶ οὐκ εἰμὶ μόνος, ὅτι ὁ πατὴρ μετ᾽ ἐμοῦ ἐστίν.

³³ ταῦτα λελάληκα ὑμῖν ἵνα ἐν ἐμοὶ εἰρήνην ἔχητε· ἐν τῷ κόσμῳ θλῖψιν ἔχετε, ἀλλὰ θαρσεῖτε, ἐγὼ νενίκηκα τὸν κόσμον.»

ἀφίημι: to release, leave behind
ἕκαστος, -η, -ον: each, each one
ἐξῆλθον: to depart (aor.)
θαρσέω: to be of good courage, take courage
θλῖψις, -εως, ἡ: affliction
μόνος, -η, -ον: alone, left alone
νικάω: to conquer, prevail, vanquish

οἶδα: to know (perf.)
παρρησία, ἡ: frankness, openness
πορεύω: to make to go
σκορπίζω: to scatter, disperse
φιλέω: to love
χρεία, ἡ: use, advantage, service

16:27 πεφιλήκατε καὶ πεπιστεύκατε: perf., "you have loved and have believed"
16:28 ἐλήλυθα: perf., "I have come"
16:29 ἴδε: aor. imper. of εἶδον, "behold!"
16:30 ἵνα τίς σε ἐρωτᾷ: pres. subj. in noun clause, explaining χρείαν, "no need *for anyone to ask*"
16:31 ἄρτι πιστεύετε: "now you believe?"
16:32 ἔρχεται καὶ ἐλήλυθεν: pres. and perf., "the hour *is coming and it has come*"
     ἵνα σκορπισθῆτε: aor. pass. subj. explaining ὥρα, "the hour that (i.e. when) you will be scattered," with the idea of purpose and result
     ἀφῆτε: aor. subj. of ἀπο-ίημι, "and (when) *you will leave* me alone"
16:33 ἵνα ... ἔχητε: pres. subj. in purpose clause, "*so that you will have* peace"

de vobis; ²⁷ ipse enim Pater amat vos, quia vos me amastis et

credidistis quia ego a Deo exivi. ²⁸ Exivi a Patre et veni in mundum;

iterum relinquo mundum et vado ad Patrem."

²⁹ Dicunt discipuli eius: "Ecce nunc palam loqueris, et proverbium

nullum dicis. ³⁰ Nunc scimus quia scis omnia, et non opus est tibi,

ut quis te interroget; in hoc credimus quia a Deo existi."

³¹ Respondit eis Iesus: "Modo creditis? ³² Ecce venit hora et

iam venit, ut dispergamini unusquisque in propria et me solum

relinquatis; et non sum solus, quia Pater mecum est.

³³ Haec locutus sum vobis, ut in me pacem habeatis; in mundo

pressuram habetis, sed confidite, ego vici mundum."

---

amo, (1): to love
confido, (3): to trust in, believe
dispergo, (3): to scatter, disperse
ecce: behold! see!
exeo, (4), **exivi, exitus:** to exit, depart
loquor, (3) **locutus sum:** to speak
modo: only, just now
nullus, -a, -um: no, none
opus, operis *n*: need, necessity
palam (*adv.*): openly, plainly

pax, pacis *f*: peace
pressura, -ae *f*: burden, distress
proprius, -a, -um: own, very own
proverbium, -i *n*: proverb, saying
relinquo, (3): to leave behind, abandon
scio, (4): to know
solus, -a, -um: only, alone
unusquisque: each one
venio, (4) **veni:** to come
vinco, (3), **vici, victus:** to conquer

16:27 **amastis:** syncopated perf. (= *amavistis*), "you have loved"

16:30 **ut ... interroget:** pres. subj. noun clause after *opus*, "no need *to interrogate*"

16:32 **venit hora et iam venit:** pres. and perf. respectively, "the hour is coming and already has come"

    ut dispergamini ... relinquatis: pres. subj. explaining *hora*, "the hour *when you will be scattered ...when you will abandon*" with the idea of purpose and result

    unusquisque: nom. subject singular in form but plural in sense and the subject of *dispergamini* and *relinquatis*, "*each one* (of you) will be scattered"

    solum: acc. pred., "abandon me *alone*"

16:33 **ut ... habeatis:** pres. subj. in purpose clause, "I spoke *in order that you may have*"

Chapter 17

Jesus Prays to Be Glorified

¹ ταῦτα ἐλάλησεν Ἰησοῦς, καὶ ἐπάρας τοὺς ὀφθαλμοὺς αὐτοῦ εἰς τὸν οὐρανὸν εἶπεν

«Πάτερ, ἐλήλυθεν ἡ ὥρα· ² δόξασόν σου τὸν υἱόν, ἵνα ὁ υἱὸς δοξάσῃ σέ, καθὼς ἔδωκας αὐτῷ ἐξουσίαν πάσης σαρκός, ἵνα πᾶν ὃ δέδωκας αὐτῷ δώσῃ αὐτοῖς ζωὴν αἰώνιον. ³ αὕτη δέ ἐστιν ἡ αἰώνιος ζωὴ ἵνα γινώσκωσι σὲ τὸν μόνον ἀληθινὸν θεὸν καὶ ὃν ἀπέστειλας Ἰησοῦν Χριστόν. ⁴ ἐγώ σε ἐδόξασα ἐπὶ τῆς γῆς, τὸ ἔργον τελειώσας ὃ δέδωκάς μοι ἵνα ποιήσω· ⁵ καὶ νῦν δόξασόν με σύ, πάτερ, παρὰ σεαυτῷ τῇ δόξῃ ᾗ εἶχον πρὸ τοῦ τὸν κόσμον εἶναι παρὰ σοί.

αἰώνιος, -α, -ον: eternal	ζωή, ἡ: life
ἀποστέλλω: to send off	κόσμος, ὁ: world
γῆ, ἡ: earth	οὐρανός, ὁ: heaven
γινώσκω: to know	ὀφθαλμός, ὁ: the eye
δοξά, ἡ: glory	σάρξ, -κος, ἡ: flesh
δοξάζω: to magnify, glorify	τελειόω: to make perfect, complete
ἐξουσία, ἡ: power or authority	χριστός, -ή, -όν: annointed
ἐπαίρω: to lift up and set on	

17:1   **ἐπάρας**: aor. part. of ἐπι-αίρω, "*having lifted* his eyes"

17:2   **δόξασόν**: aor. imper., "*glorify* your son!"

     ἵνα ὁ υἱὸς δοξάσῃ: aor. subj. in purpose clause, "so that the son may glorify"

     πᾶν ὃ δέδωκας ... αὐτοῖς: the n. s. **πᾶν** is the antecedent of **αὐτοῖς** by sense, "*everyone whom you* (the father) *have given* to him (the son), he will give *to them* eternal life"

     ἵνα ... δώσῃ: aor. subj. in purpose clause, "*so that he may give* to them"

17:3   **ἵνα γινώσκωσι**: pres. subj. in appositive clause, "this is eternal life, *namely, that they might know*"

     ὃν ἀπέστειλας: aor., "whom you sent"

17:4   **τελειώσας**: aor. part. instrumental, "I glorified you *by having accomplished*"

     ἵνα ποιήσω: aor. subj. purpose clause, "gave *in order to do*"

17:5   **δόξῃ ᾗ**: rel. pron. attracted into the case (dat.) of its antecedent, "glorify me *with the glory which* I had"

     πρὸ τοῦ τὸν κόσμον εἶναι: articular inf., "before the world to be" i.e. before the world was

Chapter 17

Jesus Prays to Be Glorified

¹ Haec locutus est Iesus; et, sublevatis oculis suis in caelum, dixit:

"Pater, venit hora: clarifica Filium tuum, ut Filius clarificet te,

² sicut dedisti ei potestatem omnis carnis, ut omne, quod dedisti ei,

det eis vitam aeternam. ³ Haec est autem vita aeterna, ut cognoscant

te solum verum Deum et, quem misisti, Iesum Christum. ⁴ Ego te

clarificavi super terram; opus consummavi, quod dedisti mihi, ut

faciam; ⁵ et nunc clarifica me tu, Pater, apud temetipsum claritate,

quam habebam, priusquam mundus esset, apud te.

---

apud: at, by, near (+ *acc.*)
caro, carnis *f*: flesh, body
claritas, -atis *f*: glory, fame
consummo, (1): to finish, end, complete
do, (1) **dedi, datus**: to give
filius, fili *m*: son
oculus, -i *m*: eye

potestas, -tatis *f*: power, strength
priusquam: before (+ *subj.*)
solus, -a, -um: alone
sublevo, (1): to lift up, raise
terra, -ae *f*: earth, land
verus, -a, -um: true, real
vita, -ae *f*: life

17:1   **sublevatis oculis**: abl. abs., "his eyes having been lifted"
      ut ... clarificet: pres. subj. in result clause, "glorify! *so that he may glorify*"
17:2   **omnis carnis**: objective gen., "power *over all flesh*"
      ut ... det: pres. subj. in purpose clause, "so that he may give"
      omne, quod dedisti ... eis: the antededent of both *quod* and *eis* is *omne*,
        "*everyone whom you gave* to him, he will give *to them* eternal life"
17:3   **ut cognoscant**: pres. subj. in noun clause of apposition, "this is life, *that they*
        know you, the one true God"
17:4   **ut faciam**: pres. subj. in ind. com. after *dedisti*, "you gave me (the order) *to do*"
17:5   **te-met-ipsum**: acc. emphatic, "you yourself"
      priusquam ... esset: impf. subj. indicating design or anticipation, "*before the
        world existed*"

Jesus Prays for His Disciples

⁶ ἐφανέρωσά σου τὸ ὄνομα τοῖς ἀνθρώποις, οὓς ἔδωκάς μοι ἐκ τοῦ κόσμου. σοὶ ἦσαν κἀμοὶ αὐτοὺς ἔδωκας, καὶ τὸν λόγον σου τετήρηκαν. ⁷ νῦν ἔγνωκαν ὅτι πάντα ὅσα ἔδωκάς μοι παρὰ σοῦ εἰσίν· ⁸ ὅτι τὰ ῥήματα ἃ ἔδωκάς μοι δέδωκα αὐτοῖς, καὶ αὐτοὶ ἔλαβον καὶ ἔγνωσαν ἀληθῶς ὅτι παρὰ σοῦ ἐξῆλθον, καὶ ἐπίστευσαν ὅτι σύ με ἀπέστειλας. ⁹ ἐγὼ περὶ αὐτῶν ἐρωτῶ· οὐ περὶ τοῦ κόσμου ἐρωτῶ ἀλλὰ περὶ ὧν δέδωκάς μοι, ὅτι σοί εἰσιν, καὶ τὰ ἐμὰ πάντα σά ἐστιν ¹⁰ καὶ τὰ σὰ ἐμά, καὶ δεδόξασμαι ἐν αὐτοῖς. ¹¹ καὶ οὐκέτι εἰμὶ ἐν τῷ κόσμῳ, καὶ αὐτοὶ ἐν τῷ κόσμῳ εἰσίν, κἀγὼ πρὸς σὲ ἔρχομαι.

δοξάζομαι: to be magnified, glorified
ἐμός, -α, -ον: my
ἐρωτάω: to ask
ὄνομα, -ατος, τό: a name
πιστεύω: to trust in, believe in

ῥῆμα, -ατος, τό: a word, saying
σός, -α, -ον: your
τηρέω: to guard, keep
φανερόω: to make manifest

17:6   κἀμοὶ: (= καὶ ἐμοὶ) *"and to me* you gave them"
      τετήρηκαν: perf., "they have kept"
17:7   ἔγνωκαν: perf., "they have come to know"
      πάντα ... παρὰ σοῦ εἰσίν: "all things are from you;" usually a neuter plural
        subject takes a singular verb, not plural (see πάντα ἐστιν in verse 9 below)
17:8   ἔλαβον ... ἔγνωσαν: aor., "they received ... they knew"
17:9   περὶ αὐτῶν: "I ask *on their behalf*"
      περὶ ὧν: "on behalf of those whom" the rel. is attracted to the case (gen.) of its
        antecedent
      σοί: nom. pred., "because they are *yours*"
17:10 καὶ τὰ σὰ ἐμά: "and yours are mine"
      δεδόξασμαι: perf., "I have been glorified"

Jesus Prays for His Disciples

⁶ Manifestavi nomen tuum hominibus, quos dedisti mihi de mundo. Tui erant, et mihi eos dedisti, et sermonem tuum servaverunt. ⁷ Nunc cognoverunt quia omnia, quae dedisti mihi, abs te sunt, ⁸ quia verba, quae dedisti mihi, dedi eis; et ipsi acceperunt et cognoverunt vere quia a te exivi et crediderunt quia tu me misisti. ⁹ Ego pro eis rogo; non pro mundo rogo, sed pro his, quos dedisti mihi, quia tui sunt; ¹⁰ et mea omnia tua sunt, et tua mea; et clarificatus sum in eis. ¹¹ Et iam non sum in mundo, et hi in mundo sunt, et ego ad te venio.

---

accipio, (3), **accepi**: accept, receive
cognosco, (3), **cognovi**: to know
do, (1) **dedi**: to give
exeo, (4), **exivi**: to go out
homo, hominis *m*: a person
manifesto, (1): to make known, clarify
meus, -a, -um: my
mitto, (3), **misi**: to sent

mundus, -i *m*: world
nomen, -inis *n*: a name
rogo, (1): to ask
sermo, -onis *m*: speech
servo (1): to preserve, keep
tuus, -a, -um: your
verbum, -i *n*: word, proverb
vere: really, truly

17:6: **tui**: nom. pred,, "they were *yours*"
17:7-8 **quia ... quia ... quia**: introducing ind. st., "they know *that* ... believe *that*"
17:10 **mea omnia tua sunt, et tua mea**: "all mine are yours, and yours mine"

πάτερ ἅγιε, τήρησον αὐτοὺς ἐν τῷ ὀνόματί σου ᾧ δέδωκάς μοι,
ἵνα ὦσιν ἓν καθὼς ἡμεῖς. ¹² ὅτε ἤμην μετ᾽ αὐτῶν ἐγὼ ἐτήρουν
αὐτοὺς ἐν τῷ ὀνόματί σου ᾧ δέδωκάς μοι, καὶ ἐφύλαξα, καὶ
οὐδεὶς ἐξ αὐτῶν ἀπώλετο εἰ μὴ ὁ υἱὸς τῆς ἀπωλείας, ἵνα ἡ
γραφὴ πληρωθῇ.

¹³ νῦν δὲ πρὸς σὲ ἔρχομαι, καὶ ταῦτα λαλῶ ἐν τῷ κόσμῳ
ἵνα ἔχωσιν τὴν χαρὰν τὴν ἐμὴν πεπληρωμένην ἐν ἑαυτοῖς.
¹⁴ ἐγὼ δέδωκα αὐτοῖς τὸν λόγον σου, καὶ ὁ κόσμος ἐμίσησεν
αὐτούς, ὅτι οὐκ εἰσὶν ἐκ τοῦ κόσμου καθὼς ἐγὼ οὐκ εἰμὶ ἐκ
τοῦ κόσμου. ¹⁵ οὐκ ἐρωτῶ ἵνα ἄρῃς αὐτοὺς ἐκ τοῦ κόσμου
ἀλλ᾽ ἵνα τηρήσῃς αὐτοὺς ἐκ τοῦ πονηροῦ. ¹⁶ ἐκ τοῦ κόσμου
οὐκ εἰσὶν καθὼς ἐγὼ οὐκ εἰμὶ ἐκ τοῦ κόσμου. ¹⁷ ἁγίασον
αὐτοὺς ἐν τῇ ἀληθείᾳ· ὁ λόγος ὁ σὸς ἀλήθειά ἐστιν. ¹⁸ καθὼς

ἁγιάζω: to make holy
ἀληθεῖα, ἡ: the truth
ἀπολεῖα, ἡ: perdition
ἀπόλλυμι: to destroy utterly, kill, slay
γραφή, ἡ: a writing, scripture

καθὼς: just as
κόσμος, ὁ: the world
πονηρός, ὁ: the evil one
φυλάσσω: to keep guard

17:11 τήρησον: aor. imper., "*care for* them!"

   ἐν τῷ ὀνόματι ᾧ δέδωκάς: "in your name which you gave me" the relative
     pronoun is attracted into the case (dat.) of its antecedent ὀνόματι.

   ἵνα ὦσιν: pres. subj. in purpose clause, "care for them *so that they be* one"

17:12 ἤμην: impf. of εἰμί (= ἦ), "when *I was* with them"

   ἐφύλαξα: aor., "I guarded"

   ἀπώλετο: aor. mid. of ἀπόλλυμι, "none *was lost*"

   εἰ μὴ ὁ υἱός: "none was lost *except the son* of perdition" i.e. Judas Iscariot

   ἵνα πληρωθῇ: aor. subj. pass. in purpose clause, "so that scripture *be fulfilled*"

17:13 ἵνα ἔχωσιν: pres. subj. in purpose clause, "I speak *so that they have*"

   πεπληρωμένην: perf. part. serving as predicate, "so that they have my joy
     fufilled"

17:15 ἵνα ἄρῃς ... τηρήσῃς: aor. subj. in ind. command after ἐρωτῶ, "I do not ask
     that you remove ... but *that you keep* them"

17:17 ἁγίασον: aor. imper., "make holy!"

Pater sancte, serva eos in nomine tuo, quod dedisti mihi, ut sint unum sicut nos. ¹² Cum essem cum eis, ego servabam eos in nomine tuo, quod dedisti mihi, et custodivi, et nemo ex his periit, nisi filius perditionis, ut Scriptura impleatur.

¹³ Nunc autem ad te venio et haec loquor in mundo, ut habeant gaudium meum impletum in semetipsis. ¹⁴ Ego dedi eis sermonem tuum, et mundus odio eos habuit, quia non sunt de mundo, sicut ego non sum de mundo. ¹⁵ Non rogo, ut tollas eos de mundo, sed ut serves eos ex Malo. ¹⁶ De mundo non sunt, sicut ego non sum de mundo. ¹⁷ Sanctifica eos in veritate; sermo tuus veritas est. ¹⁸ Sicut

custodio, (4), **custodivi**: to guard, protect	**pereo**, (4), **perii, peritus**: to die, pass away
gaudium, **-i** *n*: joy	**sanctifico**, (1): to sanctify, make holy
impleo, (2), **implevi, impletus**: to fill	**sanctus**, **-a, -um**: divine, holy
malus, **-a, -um**: bad, evil	**scriptura**, **-ae** *f*: writing, scripture
nomen, **-inis** *n*: name	**semetipse**, **-a, -um**: one's self
odium, **-i** *n*: hate	**servo**, (1): to keep, preserve
perditio, **-onis** *f*: destruction, ruin	**veritas**, **-tatis** *f*: the truth

17:11 **ut sint**: pres. subj. in purpose clause, "keep them *so that they be*"
    unum: predicate nom., "so that they may be *one*"
17:12 **cum essem**: impf. subj. in *cum* circumstantial clause, "*when I was* with them"
    nemo ex his: partitive, "none of these"
    ut ... impleatur: pres. subj. in purpose clause, "I speak so that it may be fulfilled"
17:13 **ut habeant**: pres. subj. in purpose clause, "I speak *so they may have*"
17:14 **odio**: abl. of manner, "the world has them *in contempt*"
17:15 **ut tollas ... serves**: pres. subj. in ind. quest. after *rogo*, "I ask *that you raise them ...that you preserve* them""

ἐμὲ ἀπέστειλας εἰς τὸν κόσμον, κἀγὼ ἀπέστειλα αὐτοὺς εἰς τὸν κόσμον· ¹⁹ καὶ ὑπὲρ αὐτῶν ἐγὼ ἁγιάζω ἐμαυτόν, ἵνα ὦσιν καὶ αὐτοὶ ἡγιασμένοι ἐν ἀληθείᾳ.

²⁰ οὐ περὶ τούτων δὲ ἐρωτῶ μόνον, ἀλλὰ καὶ περὶ τῶν πιστευόντων διὰ τοῦ λόγου αὐτῶν εἰς ἐμέ, ²¹ ἵνα πάντες ἓν ὦσιν, καθὼς σύ, πατήρ, ἐν ἐμοὶ κἀγὼ ἐν σοί, ἵνα καὶ αὐτοὶ ἐν ἡμῖν ὦσιν, ἵνα ὁ κόσμος πιστεύῃ ὅτι σύ με ἀπέστειλας. ²² κἀγὼ τὴν δόξαν ἣν δέδωκάς μοι δέδωκα αὐτοῖς, ²³ ἵνα ὦσιν ἓν καθὼς ἡμεῖς ἕν, ἐγὼ ἐν αὐτοῖς καὶ σὺ ἐν ἐμοί, ἵνα ὦσιν τετελειωμένοι εἰς ἕν, ἵνα γινώσκῃ ὁ κόσμος ὅτι σύ με ἀπέστειλας καὶ ἠγάπησας αὐτοὺς καθὼς ἐμὲ ἠγάπησας.

²⁴ πατήρ, οὓς δέδωκάς μοι, θέλω ἵνα ὅπου εἰμὶ ἐγὼ κἀκεῖνοι ὦσιν μετ᾽ ἐμοῦ, ἵνα θεωρῶσιν τὴν δόξαν τὴν ἐμὴν ἣν δέδωκάς μοι, ὅτι ἠγάπησάς με πρὸ καταβολῆς κόσμου.

ἀγαπάω: to love	θέλω: to wish
ἁγιάζω: to make holy	θεωρέω: to look at, view, behold
ἀλήθεια, ἡ: the truth	καθώς: just as, just like
γινώσκω: to know	καταβολή, ἡ: a throwing down, founding
δόξα, ἡ: glory, opinion	πιστεύω: to believe in
εἷς, μία, ἕν: one	τελειόω: to complete, perfect

17:18 ἀπέστειλας: aor., "just as *you* sent me"

κἀγὼ = (καὶ ἐγώ) "*so also I* sent them"

17:19 ἵνα ὦσιν ἡγιασμένοι: perf.. subj. periphrastic in purpose clause, "so that they may be made holy"

17:20 οὐ μόνον ...ἀλλὰ καὶ: "not only ...but also"

17:21 ἵνα πάντες ἓν ὦσιν ...ὦσιν...πιστεύῃ: pres. subj. in purpose clause, "*so that all may be one* ...*so that they be* with us ...*so that* the would *may believe*""

17:23 ἵνα ὦσιν τετελειωμένοι: perf. subj. periphrastic in purpose clause, "*so that they become perfected* into one"

ἵνα γινώσκῃ: pres. subj. in result clause, "*so that* the world *knows*"

17:24 ἵνα ... ὦσιν: pres. subj. in noun clause obj. of θέλω, "I wish *that they be* where I am"

ἵνα θεωρῶσιν: pres. subj. in purpose clause, "be where I am *in order to see*"

me misisti in mundum, et ego misi eos in mundum; ¹⁹ et pro eis ego sanctifico meipsum, ut sint et ipsi sanctificati in veritate.

²⁰ Non pro his autem rogo tantum, sed et pro eis, qui credituri sunt per verbum eorum in me, ²¹ ut omnes unum sint, sicut tu, Pater, in me et ego in te, ut et ipsi in nobis unum sint; ut mundus credat quia tu me misisti. ²² Et ego claritatem, quam dedisti mihi, dedi illis, ut sint unum, sicut nos unum sumus; ²³ ego in eis, et tu in me, ut sint consummati in unum; ut cognoscat mundus, quia tu me misisti et dilexisti eos, sicut me dilexisti.

²⁴ Pater, quod dedisti mihi, volo, ut ubi ego sum, et illi sint mecum, ut videant claritatem meam, quam dedisti mihi, quia dilexisti me ante constitutionem mundi.

---

claritas, claritatis *f.*: glory
constitutio, constitutionis *f.*: creation
consummo, (1): to finish, bring about
diligo, (3), **dilexi, dilectus**: to love
omnis, -e: all

pater, patris *m*: father
rogo, (1): to ask
veritas, -tatis *f*: the truth
volo, velle: to wish, want

17:19 **ut sint sanctificati**: perf. subj. periphrastic in purpose clause, "in order that they be made holy"

17:20 **non tantum ... sed et**: "not only ...but also"

credituri sunt: fut. periphrastic, "those who believe"

17:21 **ut ... sint ... sint ... credat**: pres. subj. in mixture of purpose and result, "*so that all may be* one ... *so that they* themselve *may be one ...so that* the world *may believe*"

17:23 **ut sit consummati**: perf. subj. periphrastic in purpose clause, "*in order that they be made* into one"

ut cognoscat: pres. subj. in purpose clause, "*so that* world *may know*"

17:24 **ut et illi sint** : pres. subj. in noun jussive clause after *volo*, "wish *that they too would be* with me"

ut videant: pres. subj. in purpose clause, "be with me so *that they would see*""

255

²⁵ πατὴρ δίκαιε, καὶ ὁ κόσμος σε οὐκ ἔγνω, ἐγὼ δέ σε ἔγνων, καὶ οὗτοι ἔγνωσαν ὅτι σύ με ἀπέστειλας, ²⁶ καὶ ἐγνώρισα αὐτοῖς τὸ ὄνομά σου καὶ γνωρίσω, ἵνα ἡ ἀγάπη ἣν ἠγάπησάς με ἐν αὐτοῖς ᾖ κἀγὼ ἐν αὐτοῖς.»

Chapter 18

Jesus Arrested

¹ ταῦτα εἰπὼν Ἰησοῦς ἐξῆλθεν σὺν τοῖς μαθηταῖς αὐτοῦ πέραν τοῦ χειμάρρου τῶν Κέδρων ὅπου ἦν κῆπος, εἰς ὃν εἰσῆλθεν αὐτὸς καὶ οἱ μαθηταὶ αὐτοῦ.

² ᾔδει δὲ καὶ Ἰούδας ὁ παραδιδοὺς αὐτὸν τὸν τόπον, ὅτι πολλάκις συνήχθη Ἰησοῦς ἐκεῖ μετὰ τῶν μαθητῶν αὐτοῦ. ³ ὁ οὖν Ἰούδας λαβὼν τὴν σπεῖραν καὶ ἐκ τῶν ἀρχιερέων καὶ ἐκ τῶν Φαρισαίων ὑπηρέτας ἔρχεται ἐκεῖ μετὰ φανῶν καὶ λαμπάδων καὶ ὅπλων.

ἀγάπη, ἡ: love
ἀρχιερεύς, -έως, ὁ: a chief-priest
δίκαιος, -η, -ον: just
εἰσῆλθον: to go in or into, enter (*aor.*)
κέδρος, ἡ: the cedar-tree
κῆπος, ὁ: a garden, orchard
λαμπάς, -άδος, ἡ: a torch
ὅπλον, τό: a tool, arms

παραδίδωμι: to betray
πέραν: on the other side, across, beyond
σπεῖρα, ἡ: a tactical unit, a band
συνάγω: to gather together, convene
τόπος, ὁ: a place
ὑπηρέτης, -ου, ὁ: a public official
φανός, ὁ: a torch
χειμάρρους, ὁ: a brook

17:25 οὐκ ἔγνω ... ἔγνων ... ἔγνωσαν: aor. of γινώσκω, "the world *did not know* ...but I knew ...these knew"

17:26 ἐγνώρισα ... γνωρίσω: aor. and fut. of γνωρίζω, "I made known ...I will make known"

ἵνα ... ᾖ: pres. subj. in purpose clause, "*so the love may be*"

ἀγαπή ἣν: internal acc. with ἠγάπησας, "*the love which* you loved"

18:1 τοῦ χειμάρρου τῶν Κέδρων: "across *the brook of the Kidron*," lit. "of the cedars," a brook outside Jerusalem

ὅπου ἦν κῆπος: "where there was a garden," i.e., the garden of Gethsemane

18:2 ὁ παραδιδοὺς: pres. part. attributive, "Judas, *the one who was betraying him*"

συνήχθη: aor. pass. of συν-άγω, "Jesus *gathered* there"

18:3 λαβὼν: aor. part. of λαμβάνω, "*having secured* a band"

ἔρχεται: "goes there" note the vivid present tense

²⁵ Pater iuste, et mundus te non cognovit; ego autem te cognovi, et hi cognoverunt quia tu me misisti;   ²⁶ et notum feci eis nomen tuum et notum faciam, ut dilectio, qua dilexisti me, in ipsis sit, et ego in ipsis."

Chapter 18

Jesus Arrested

¹ Haec cum dixisset Iesus, egressus est cum discipulis suis trans torrentem Cedron, ubi erat hortus, in quem introivit ipse et discipuli eius.

² Sciebat autem et Iudas, qui tradebat eum, locum, quia frequenter Iesus convenerat illuc cum discipulis suis.   ³ Iudas ergo, cum accepisset cohortem et a pontificibus et pharisaeis ministros, venit illuc cum lanternis et facibus et armis.

---

accipio, (3) **accepi, acceptus**: to receive, accept
arma, -orum *n*: arms, weapons
cognosco, (3), **cognovi**: to know
cohors, -tis *f*: cohort, band of men
convenio, (4), **conveni**: to meet, assemble
dilectio, -onis *f*: love, goodwill
egredior, (3), **egressus sum**: to go
fax, facis *f*: torch
frequenter (*adv.*): often, frequently
hortus, horti *m*: garden

introeo, (4), **introivi, introitus**: enter, go into
iustus, -a, -um: just, fair
lanterna, -ae *f*: lantern
locus, loci *m*: location, place
minister, -tri *m*: attendant, minister
notus, -a, -um: well known
pharisaeus, -i *m*: Pharisee
pontifex, -ficis *m*: high priest
scio, (4): to know
torrens, -entis *m*: wash, brook
trado, (3): to hand over, betray

17:26 **notum**: predicate acc., "made your name *known*"
    ut ... sit: pres. subj. in result clause, "*so that* the love *may be* in them"
18:1 **cum dixisset**: plupf. subj. in *cum* circumstantial clause, "when Jesus had spoken"
    Cedron: gen. pl., "brook *of the Cedars*"
    introivit: singular verb takes both *ipse* and *discipuli* as its subject
18:3 **cum accepisset**: plupf. subj. in cum circumstantial clause, "when he had received"

⁴ Ἰησοῦς οὖν εἰδὼς πάντα τὰ ἐρχόμενα ἐπ' αὐτὸν ἐξῆλθεν, καὶ λέγει αὐτοῖς «Τίνα ζητεῖτε;»

⁵ ἀπεκρίθησαν αὐτῷ «Ἰησοῦν τὸν Ναζωραῖον.»

λέγει αὐτοῖς «Ἐγώ εἰμι.» εἱστήκει δὲ καὶ Ἰούδας ὁ παραδιδοὺς αὐτὸν μετ' αὐτῶν. ⁶ ὡς οὖν εἶπεν αὐτοῖς «Ἐγώ εἰμι,» ἀπῆλθαν εἰς τὰ ὀπίσω καὶ ἔπεσαν χαμαί.

⁷ πάλιν οὖν ἐπηρώτησεν αὐτούς «Τίνα ζητεῖτε;»

οἱ δὲ εἶπαν «Ἰησοῦν τὸν Ναζωραῖον.»

⁸ ἀπεκρίθη Ἰησοῦς «Εἶπον ὑμῖν ὅτι ἐγώ εἰμι· εἰ οὖν ἐμὲ ζητεῖτε, ἄφετε τούτους ὑπάγειν·» ⁹ ἵνα πληρωθῇ ὁ λόγος ὃν εἶπεν ὅτι «Οὓς δέδωκάς μοι οὐκ ἀπώλεσα ἐξ αὐτῶν οὐδένα.»

¹⁰ Σίμων οὖν Πέτρος ἔχων μάχαιραν εἵλκυσεν αὐτὴν καὶ ἔπαισεν τὸν τοῦ ἀρχιερέως δοῦλον καὶ ἀπέκοψεν αὐτοῦ τὸ ὠτάριον τὸ δεξιόν. ἦν δὲ ὄνομα τῷ δούλῳ Μάλχος.

ἀπῆλθον: to go away (aor.)
ἀποκόπτω: to cut off, hew off
ἀφίημι: to send forth, allow (+ inf.)
δεξιός, -ά, -όν: on the right side
ἕλκω: to draw, drag
ἐξῆλθον: to go out (aor.)
ἐπερωτάω: to inquire of, about
Μάλχος, ὁ: Malchos

μάχαιρα, ἡ: a large knife
Ναζωραῖος, -ον: of Nazareth
ὀπίσω (adv.): backwards
παίω: to strike, smite
πίπτω: to fall
χαμαί: on the earth, on the ground (dv.)
ὠτάριον, τό: a small part of the ear

18:4 εἰδὼς: perf. part. caual, "since he knew""
 τὰ ἐρχόμενα: pres. part. n. pl., "knew *all the things coming*" i.e. the future
18:5 εἱστήκει: plupf., "Judas *was standing*"
18:6 ἀπῆλθαν ... ἔπεσαν: aor.with weak ending, "*they drew back ... they fell* to the ground"
18:8 ἄφετε: aor. imper., "*allow* these to go"
18:9 ἵνα πληρωθῇ: aor. pass. subj. in purpose clause, "so that the word be fulfilled"
 οὓς δέδωκάς: perf., "whom you have given" see above John 17:6-8
18:10 εἵλκυσεν ... ἔπαισεν ... ἀπέκοψεν: aor., "*he drew* his knife ...*he struck* the servant ... *he cut off* his ear"

⁴ Iesus itaque sciens omnia, quae ventura erant super eum, processit et dicit eis: "Quem quaeritis?"

⁵ Responderunt ei: "Iesum Nazarenum."

Dicit eis: "Ego sum!" Stabat autem et Iudas, qui tradebat eum, cum ipsis. ⁶ Ut ergo dixit eis: "Ego sum!" abierunt retrorsum et ceciderunt in terram.

⁷ Iterum ergo eos interrogavit: "Quem quaeritis?"

Illi autem dixerunt: "Iesum Nazarenum."

⁸ Respondit Iesus: "Dixi vobis: Ego sum! Si ergo me quaeritis, sinite hos abire," ⁹ ut impleretur sermo, quem dixit: "Quos dedisti mihi, non perdidi ex ipsis quemquam."

¹⁰ Simon ergo Petrus, habens gladium, eduxit eum et percussit pontificis servum et abscidit eius auriculam dextram. Erat autem nomen servo Malchus.

---

abeo, (4), **abii**, **abitum**: to depart
abscido, (3), **abscidi**, **abscisus**: to cut off
auricula, -ae *f*: ear
cado, (3), **cecidi**, **casus**: to fall, sink, drop
dexter, -**a**, -**um**: right
educo, (3), **eduxi**, **eductus**: to draw out
gladius, -**i** *m*: sword
interrogo, (1): to question, ask
Nazarenus, -**i** *m*: the Nazarene
percutio, (3), **percussi**: to beat, strike
perdo, (3), **perdidi**, **perditus**: to ruin, destroy

Petrus, -**i** *m*: Peter
pontifex, -**ficis** *m*: high p.riest
procedo, (3), **processi**: to proceed, advance
quaero, (3): to seek
retrorsum (*adv.*): back, backwards
scio, (4): to know
servus, -**i** *m*: slave, servant
Simon, **Simonis** *m*: Simon
sino, (3): to allow, permit (+ *inf.*)
sto, (1): to stand

18:4 **ventura**: fut. part. in periphrastic with *erant*, "which were *about to come*" i.e. the future

18:9 **ut impleretur**: impf. subj. in purpose clause, "so that it may be fulfilled"
    quos dedisti: *whom you gave me*" see above John 17:6-8

18:10 **servo**: dat. of possession, "the *servant's* name was Malchus

¹¹ εἶπεν οὖν ὁ Ἰησοῦς τῷ Πέτρῳ «Βάλε τὴν μάχαιραν εἰς τὴν θήκην· τὸ ποτήριον ὃ δέδωκέν μοι ὁ πατὴρ οὐ μὴ πίω αὐτό;»

¹² ἡ οὖν σπεῖρα καὶ ὁ χιλίαρχος καὶ οἱ ὑπηρέται τῶν Ἰουδαίων συνέλαβον τὸν Ἰησοῦν καὶ ἔδησαν αὐτὸν ¹³ καὶ ἤγαγον πρὸς Ἄνναν πρῶτον· ἦν γὰρ πενθερὸς τοῦ Καιάφα, ὃς ἦν ἀρχιερεὺς τοῦ ἐνιαυτοῦ ἐκείνου. ¹⁴ ἦν δὲ Καιάφας ὁ συμβουλεύσας τοῖς Ἰουδαίοις ὅτι «συμφέρει ἕνα ἄνθρωπον ἀποθανεῖν ὑπὲρ τοῦ λαοῦ.»

Peter's First Denial

¹⁵ ἠκολούθει δὲ τῷ Ἰησοῦ Σίμων Πέτρος καὶ ἄλλος μαθητής. ὁ δὲ μαθητὴς ἐκεῖνος ἦν γνωστὸς τῷ ἀρχιερεῖ, καὶ συνεισῆλθεν τῷ Ἰησοῦ εἰς τὴν αὐλὴν τοῦ ἀρχιερέως, ¹⁶ ὁ δὲ Πέτρος εἱστήκει πρὸς τῇ θύρᾳ ἔξω. ἐξῆλθεν οὖν

ἄγω: to lead or carry
ἀκολουθέω: to follow
Ἄνναν, ὁ: Annan
ἀποθνῄσκω: to die off, die
αὐλή, ἡ: a forecourt
γνωστός, -ή, -όν: known to (+ *dat.*)
δέω: to bind
ἐνιαυτός, ὁ: year
ἔξω: outside
θήκη, ἡ: a case, scabbard
θύρα, ἡ: a door
Καιάφα, -ας, ὁ: Caiaphas

λαός, λαοῦ, ὁ: the people
μάχαιρα, ἡ: a large knife
πενθερός, ὁ: a father-in-law
πίνω: to drink
ποτήριον, τό: a drinking-cup, wine-cup
σπεῖρα, ἡ: band
συλλαμβάνω: to collect, gather together
συμβουλεύω: to advise, counsel
συμφέρω: to be expedient
συνεισῆλθον: to enter along with (+ *dat.*) (*aor.*)
χιλίαρχος, ὁ: a commander of a thousand men

18:11 βάλε: aor. imper., "*put* your sword"

οὐ μὴ πίω: aor. subj. of πίνω in a rhetorical question, "shall I not drink it?"

18:12-13 συνέλαβον ... ἔδησαν ... ἤγαγον: aor., "*they apprehended* him ... *they bound* him ... *they led* him"

18:13 τοῦ ἐνιαυτοῦ ἐκείνου: gen. of time within which, "high priest *during that year*"

18:14 ὁ συμβουλεύσας: aor. part. pred., "Caiaphas was *the one who counseled*" see John 11:49-59

ἕνα ἀποθανεῖν: aor. inf. after impers. συμφέρει, "it is expedient *that one die*"

18:15 συνεισῆλθεν: aor., "he entered along with" + dat.

18:16 εἱστήκει: plupf., "he was standing"

^{11} Dixit ergo Iesus Petro: "Mitte gladium in vaginam; calicem, quem dedit mihi Pater, non bibam illum?"

^{12} Cohors ergo et tribunus et ministri Iudaeorum comprehenderunt Iesum et ligaverunt eum ^{13} et adduxerunt ad Annam primum; erat enim socer Caiphae, qui erat pontifex anni illius. ^{14} Erat autem Caiphas, qui consilium dederat Iudaeis: "Expedit unum hominem mori pro populo."

Peter's First Denial

^{15} Sequebatur autem Iesum Simon Petrus et alius discipulus. Discipulus autem ille erat notus pontifici et introivit cum Iesu in atrium pontificis; ^{16} Petrus autem stabat ad ostium foris. Exivit ergo

---

adduco, (3), **adduxi, adductus**: to lead up, bring
alius, alia, aliud: other, another
Annan (*indecl.*): Annas
annus, -i *m*: year
atrium, -i *n*: atrium, reception hall
bibo, (3): to drink
Caiphas, -ae *m*: Caiphas
calix, calicis *m*: cup, a vessel for drinking
cohors, cohortis *f*: band, cohort
comprehendo, (3): to catch, seize
consilium, -i *n*: advice, recommendation

foris, foris, *f*. a door
homo, hominis *m*: man
ligo, (1): to bind, tie
minister, -tri *m*: minister, guard
notus, -a, -um: well known, familiar
ostium, -i *n*: doorway, front door
populus, -i *m*: people, nation, state
primum (*adv.*): first
sequor, (3), **secutus sum**: follow
socer, soceri *m*: father in law
tribunus, -i *m*: tribune
vagina, -ae *f*. sheath, scabbard

18:11 **bibam**: pres. subj. deliberative, "*should I not drink?*"

18:14 **unum hominem mori**: acc. + inf. after *expedit*, it is expedient *that one man die* for his poeple" cf. John 11:49-59

18:15 **sequebatur**: singular verb with compound subject, "Peter *was following* and other apostle"

    pontifici: dat. after *notus*, "the disciple known *to the high priest*"

261

ὁ μαθητὴς ὁ ἄλλος ὁ γνωστὸς τοῦ ἀρχιερέως καὶ εἶπεν τῇ θυρωρῷ καὶ εἰσήγαγεν τὸν Πέτρον.

¹⁷ λέγει οὖν τῷ Πέτρῳ ἡ παιδίσκη ἡ θυρωρός «Μὴ καὶ σὺ ἐκ τῶν μαθητῶν εἶ τοῦ ἀνθρώπου τούτου;»

λέγει ἐκεῖνος «Οὐκ εἰμί.»

¹⁸ εἱστήκεισαν δὲ οἱ δοῦλοι καὶ οἱ ὑπηρέται ἀνθρακιὰν πεποιηκότες, ὅτι ψῦχος ἦν, καὶ ἐθερμαίνοντο· ἦν δὲ καὶ ὁ Πέτρος μετ᾽ αὐτῶν ἑστὼς καὶ θερμαινόμενος.

The High Priest Questions Jesus

¹⁹ ὁ οὖν ἀρχιερεὺς ἠρώτησεν τὸν Ἰησοῦν περὶ τῶν μαθητῶν αὐτοῦ καὶ περὶ τῆς διδαχῆς αὐτοῦ.

²⁰ ἀπεκρίθη αὐτῷ Ἰησοῦς «Ἐγὼ παρρησίᾳ λελάληκα τῷ κόσμῳ· ἐγὼ πάντοτε ἐδίδαξα ἐν συναγωγῇ καὶ ἐν τῷ ἱερῷ, ὅπου πάντες οἱ Ἰουδαῖοι συνέρχονται, καὶ ἐν κρυπτῷ ἐλάλησα οὐδέν. ²¹ τί με ἐρωτᾷς; ἐρώτησον τοὺς ἀκηκοότας τί ἐλάλησα αὐτοῖς· ἴδε οὗτοι οἴδασιν ἃ εἶπον ἐγώ.»

ἀκούω: to hear
ἀνθρακιά, ἡ: a heap of hot charcoal
γνωστός, -ή, -όν: known, to be known
διδάσκω: to teach
διδαχή, ἡ: teaching
δοῦλος, ὁ: a slave
εἰσάγω: to lead in or into
θερμαίνω: to warm, heat
θυρωρός, ἡ: a door-keeper, porter

ἱερόν, τό: temple
ἵστημι: to make to stand
κρυπτός, -ή, -όν: hidden, secret
παιδίσκη, ἡ: a young girl, maiden
πάντοτε: at all times, always
παρρησια, ἡ: openness
συναγωγή, ἡ: a bringing together, uniting
συνέρχομαι: to come together
ψῦχος, -εος, τό: cold

18:16 εἰσήγαγεν: aor., "he *led inside* Peter"
18:17 ἡ παιδίσκη ἡ θυρωρός: hendiadys, "the maid doorkeeper"
  μὴ ... εἶ: expecting an affirmative answer, "*are you not* also one of his?"
18:18 εἱστήκεισαν: plupf., "they were standing"
  πεποιηκότες: perf. part., "they *having made* a charcoal fire"
  ἑστὼς: perf. part., circum., "Peter was with them, *standing* and warming"
18:21 ἐρώτησον: aor. imper., "ask!"
  τοὺς ἀκηκοότας: perf. part. of ἀκούω, "ask *those who have heard!*"
  οἴδασιν: perf. of εἶδον (= ἴσασι), "they know"

discipulus alius, qui erat notus pontifici, et dixit ostiariae et introduxit Petrum.

¹⁷ Dicit ergo Petro ancilla ostiaria: "Numquid et tu ex discipulis es hominis istius?"

Dicit ille: "Non sum!"

¹⁸ Stabant autem servi et ministri, qui prunas fecerant, quia frigus erat, et calefaciebant se; erat autem cum eis et Petrus stans et calefaciens se.

The High Priest Questions Jesus

¹⁹ Pontifex ergo interrogavit Iesum de discipulis suis et de doctrina eius.

²⁰ Respondit ei Iesus: "Ego palam locutus sum mundo; ego semper docui in synagoga et in templo, quo omnes Iudaei conveniunt, et in occulto locutus sum nihil.   ²¹ Quid me interrogas? Interroga eos, qui audierunt quid locutus sum ipsis; ecce hi sciunt, quae dixerim ego."

---

ancilla, -ae *f.*: slave girl, maid servant
audio, (4), **audii**: to hear
calefacio, (3): to make warm, heat
convenio, (4): to meet, assemble
doceo, (2), **docui, doctus**: to teach, show, point out
doctrina, -ae *f.*: teaching, instruction
frigus, -oris *n.*: cold
introduco, (3), **introduxi**: to lead in
loquor, (3), **locutus sum**: to speak

nihil: nothing
numquid: is it possible? can it be that?
occultum, -i *n.*: secrecy, hiding
ostiarius, -a, -um: belonging to the door
palam (*adv.*): openly, plainly
pruna, -ae *f.*: a live coal, fire
scio, (4): to know
semper (*adv.*): always
synagoga, -ae *f.*: synagogue
templum, -i *n.*: temple

18:16 **ostiariae**: dat. used substantively as ind. obj., "he said *to the doorkeeper*"

18:18 **stans et calefaciens**: pres. part. circum., "he was with them, *standing and warming* himself"

18:21 **quae dixerim**: perf. subj. in relative clause of characeristic, "they know (the things) which I said"

²² ταῦτα δὲ αὐτοῦ εἰπόντος εἷς παρεστηκὼς τῶν ὑπηρετῶν ἔδωκεν ῥάπισμα τῷ Ἰησοῦ εἰπών «Οὕτως ἀποκρίνῃ τῷ ἀρχιερεῖ;»

²³ ἀπεκρίθη αὐτῷ Ἰησοῦς «Εἰ κακῶς ἐλάλησα, μαρτύρησον περὶ τοῦ κακοῦ· εἰ δὲ καλῶς, τί με δέρεις;» ²⁴ ἀπέστειλεν οὖν αὐτὸν ὁ Ἅννας δεδεμένον πρὸς Καιάφαν τὸν ἀρχιερέα.

Peter's Second and Third Denials

²⁵ ἦν δὲ Σίμων Πέτρος ἑστὼς καὶ θερμαινόμενος. εἶπον οὖν αὐτῷ «Μὴ καὶ σὺ ἐκ τῶν μαθητῶν αὐτοῦ εἶ;»

ἠρνήσατο ἐκεῖνος καὶ εἶπεν «Οὐκ εἰμί.»

²⁶ λέγει εἷς ἐκ τῶν δούλων τοῦ ἀρχιερέως, συγγενὴς ὢν οὗ ἀπέκοψεν Πέτρος τὸ ὠτίον «Οὐκ ἐγώ σε εἶδον ἐν τῷ κήπῳ μετ᾽ αὐτοῦ;» ²⁷ πάλιν οὖν ἠρνήσατο Πέτρος· καὶ εὐθέως ἀλέκτωρ ἐφώνησεν.

ἀλέκτωρ, -ορος, ἡ: a cock
ἀποκόπτω: to cut off, hew off
ἀποκρίνομαι: to answer
ἀρνέομαι: to deny, disown
δέρω: to flay, strike
δίδωμι: to give
δοῦλος, ὁ: a slave servant
εἶδον: to see (*aor.*)
εὐθέως (*adv.*): immediately

θερμαίνω: to warm, heat
κακός, -ή, -όν: bad
κῆπος, ὁ: a garden, orchard
παρίστημι: to make to stand beside
ῥάπισμα, -ατος, τό: a slap on the face
συγγενής, ὁ: a kinsman
φωνέω: to speak, make a sound
ὠτίον, τό: the ear

18:22 **αὐτοῦ εἰπόντος**: aor. part. in gen. abs., "him having said"
  παρεστηκὼς: perf. part. intransitive of παρα-ἵστημι, "one of the officers *standing by*"
18:23 **μαρτύρησον**; aor. imper., "bear witness!"
  εἰ δὲ καλῶς: "but if (I spoke) well"
  δεδεμένον: perf. of δέω circum., "he sent him *having been bound*"
18:25 **ἠρνήσατο**: aor. mid. of ἀρνέομαι, "he denied"
18:26 **οὗ**: rel. pron. gen., "being a realtive (of the one) *whose* ear"
  ἀπέκοψεν: aor. of ἀπο-κόπτω, "Peter *cut off*"
  οὐκ ἐγώ σε εἶδον: "did I not see you?" expecting "yes"

²² Haec autem cum dixisset, unus assistens ministrorum dedit alapam Iesu dicens: "Sic respondes pontifici?"

²³ Respondit ei Iesus: "Si male locutus sum, testimonium perhibe de malo; si autem bene, quid me caedis?" ²⁴ Misit ergo eum Annas ligatum ad Caipham pontificem.

Peter's Second and Third Denials

²⁵ Erat autem Simon Petrus stans et calefaciens se. Dixerunt ergo ei: "Numquid et tu ex discipulis eius es?"

Negavit ille et dixit: "Non sum!"

²⁶ Dicit unus ex servis pontificis, cognatus eius, cuius abscidit Petrus auriculam: "Nonne ego te vidi in horto cum illo?" ²⁷ Iterum ergo negavit Petrus; et statim gallus cantavit.

---

abscido, (3), **abscidi**: to cut off, separate
alapa, -ae *f*: a blow, slap
assisto, (3): to assist, attend to
auricula, -ae *f*: the ear
bene: well, good
caedo (3): to strike, beat
calefacio, (3): to make warm, heat
canto, (1): to sing, crow
cognatus, -i *m*: relation, kinsman
gallus, -i *m*: cock, rooster

hortus, horti *m*: garden
iterum (*adv.*): again, for the second time
ligo, (1): to bind, tie
malus, -a, -um: bad, evil
nego, (1): to deny, say ... not
numquid: is it possible? can it be that?
pontifex, -**ficis** *m*: a high priest
servus, -i *m*: servant, slave
statim (*adv.*): at once, immediately
testimonium, -i *n*: testimony

18:22 **cum dixisset**: plupf. subj. in *cum* circumstantial clause, "when he had said"
18:25 **erat autem Simon**: returning to and repeating the situation above verse 18 (*q.v.*)
18:26 **nonne vidi**: expecting "yes" answer, "did I not see you?"

Jesus Before Pilate

²⁸ ἄγουσιν οὖν τὸν Ἰησοῦν ἀπὸ τοῦ Καιάφα εἰς τὸ πραι-
τώριον· ἦν δὲ πρωί· καὶ αὐτοὶ οὐκ εἰσῆλθον εἰς τὸ πραιτώριον,
ἵνα μὴ μιανθῶσιν ἀλλὰ φάγωσιν τὸ πάσχα. ²⁹ ἐξῆλθεν οὖν
ὁ Πειλᾶτος ἔξω πρὸς αὐτοὺς καί φησιν «Τίνα κατηγορίαν
φέρετε τοῦ ἀνθρώπου τούτου;»

³⁰ ἀπεκρίθησαν καὶ εἶπαν αὐτῷ «Εἰ μὴ ἦν οὗτος κακὸν
ποιῶν, οὐκ ἄν σοι παρεδώκαμεν αὐτόν.»

³¹ εἶπεν οὖν αὐτοῖς Πειλᾶτος «Λάβετε αὐτὸν ὑμεῖς, καὶ
κατὰ τὸν νόμον ὑμῶν κρίνατε αὐτόν.»

εἶπον αὐτῷ οἱ Ἰουδαῖοι «Ἡμῖν οὐκ ἔξεστιν ἀποκτεῖναι
οὐδένα·» ³² ἵνα ὁ λόγος τοῦ Ἰησοῦ πληρωθῇ ὃν εἶπεν σημαίνων
ποίῳ θανάτῳ ἤμελλεν ἀποθνήσκειν.

ἄγω: to lead
εἰσῆλθον: to enter (aor.)
ἔξεστι: it is in one's power (+ inf.)
ἐξῆλθον: to depart (aor.)
ἔφαγον: to eat (aor.)
θάνατος, ὁ: death
κακός, -ή, -όν: bad
κατηγορία, ἡ: an accusation, charge
κρίνω: to judge
μέλλω: to intend to do, to be about to do

μιαίνω: to stain, pollute
νόμος, ὁ: custom, law
πάσχα, τό (indecl.): Passover (dinner)
Πειλᾶτος: Pilate, the Roman governor
πληρόω: to make full
ποῖος, -α, -ον: of what nature? of what sort?
πραιτώριον, τό: palace of the governor
πρωί (adv.): early
σημαίνω: to, indicate
φημί: to declare, make known

18:28 ἵνα μὴ μιανθῶσιν: aor. pass. subj. in purpose clause, "lest they be defiled"
(ἵνα) φάγωσιν: aor. subj. in purpose clause, "but in order to eat"

18:29 τοῦ ἀνθρώπου: gen. of the person charged, "what charge do you bring against *this man*"

18:30 εἰ μὴ ἦν ... ποιῶν: pres. part. in periphrastic impf. (=ἐποίει) in present contrafactual protasis, "if he were not doing"
οὐκ ἄν σοι παρεδώκαμεν: aor. in past contrafactual apodosis, "we would not have handed him over to you"

18:31 λάβετε ... κρίνατε: aor. imper., "take him! ... judge him!" where a participle would be normal, i.e. λαβὼν κρίνατε, "having taken, judge!"
ἀποκτεῖναι: aor. inf. complementing ἔξεστιν, "it is not possible *to kill*"

18:32 ἵνα ... πληρωθῇ: aor. pass. subj. in purpose clause, "(this was) in order for the word to be fulfilled"
ποίῳ θανάτῳ ἤμελλεν: ind. quest. after σημαίνων, "indicating *by what sort of death he was about to*" + inf.

Jesus Before Pilate

²⁸ Adducunt ergo Iesum a Caipha in praetorium. Erat autem mane. Et ipsi non introierunt in praetorium, ut non contaminarentur, sed manducarent Pascha. ²⁹ Exivit ergo Pilatus ad eos foras et dicit: "Quam accusationem affertis adversus hominem hunc?"

³⁰ Responderunt et dixerunt ei: "Si non esset hic malefactor, non tibi tradidissemus eum."

³¹ Dixit ergo eis Pilatus: "Accipite eum vos et secundum legem vestram iudicate eum!"

Dixerunt ei Iudaei: "Nobis non licet interficere quemquam," ³² ut sermo Iesu impleretur, quem dixit, significans qua esset morte moriturus.

---

accipio, (3): **to receive, accept**
accusatio, -onis *f.*: accusation
adduco, (3): to lead
adversus: against (+ *acc.*)
affero, afferre: to allege
contamino, (1): to defile dishonor
exeo, (4), **exivi**: to depart
foras (*adv.*): out of doors, outside
impleo, (2): to fulfill
interficio, (3): to kill, execute
introeo, (4), **introii**: to enter
iudico (1): to judge
lex, legis *f.*: law

licet, (2): it is permitted (+ *inf.*)
malefactor, -oris *m*: wrongdoer, criminal
manduco, (1): to eat
mane *n* (*indecl.*): early morning
morior, (3), **mortuus sum**: to die
mors, mortis *f.*: death
Pascha, -atis *n*: Passover
Pilatus, -i *m*: Pontius Pilate a prefect for Judea in 26- 36 AD
praetorium, -i *n*: Roman govenor's palace
secundum: according to (+ *acc.*)
significo, (1): to indicate, show

18:28 **ut non ... contaminarentur**: impf. subj. in purpose clause, "lest they be defiled," expecting *ne*

ut ... manducarent: impf. subj. in purpose clause, "but so that they could eat"

18:30 **si non esset**: impf. subj in pres. contrary to fact protasis, "*unless he were* (now) a criminal"

non tradidissemus: plupf. subj. in past contrary to fact apodosis, "we would not have handed over him"

18:32 **ut ... impleretur**: impf. subj. in purpose clause ,"so that it may be fulfilled"

Iesu: gen., "the word *of Jesus*"

qua ... morte: abl. of means in ind. quest., "*by what sort of death* he was"

moriturus: fut. perf. part. periphrastic with *esset*, in ind. quest., "by what death he was *about to die*"

267

³³ εἰσῆλθεν οὖν πάλιν εἰς τὸ πραιτώριον ὁ Πειλᾶτος καὶ ἐφώνησεν τὸν Ἰησοῦν καὶ εἶπεν αὐτῷ «Σὺ εἶ ὁ βασιλεὺς τῶν Ἰουδαίων;»

³⁴ ἀπεκρίθη Ἰησοῦς «Ἀπὸ σεαυτοῦ σὺ τοῦτο λέγεις ἢ ἄλλοι εἰπόν σοι περὶ ἐμοῦ;»

³⁵ ἀπεκρίθη ὁ Πειλᾶτος «Μήτι ἐγὼ Ἰουδαῖός εἰμι; τὸ ἔθνος τὸ σὸν καὶ οἱ ἀρχιερεῖς παρέδωκάν σε ἐμοί· τί ἐποίησας;»

³⁶ ἀπεκρίθη Ἰησοῦς «Ἡ βασιλεία ἡ ἐμὴ οὐκ ἔστιν ἐκ τοῦ κόσμου τούτου· εἰ ἐκ τοῦ κόσμου τούτου ἦν ἡ βασιλεία ἡ ἐμή, οἱ ὑπηρέται οἱ ἐμοὶ ἠγωνίζοντο ἄν, ἵνα μὴ παραδοθῶ τοῖς Ἰουδαίοις· νῦν δὲ ἡ βασιλεία ἡ ἐμὴ οὐκ ἔστιν ἐντεῦθεν.»

³⁷ εἶπεν οὖν αὐτῷ ὁ Πειλᾶτος «Οὐκοῦν βασιλεὺς εἶ σύ;»

ἀγωνίζομαι: to contend
ἄλλος, -η, -ον: an other
βασιλεία, ἡ: a kingdom, dominion
βασιλεύς, -έως, ὁ: a king, chief
ἔθνος, -εος, τό: a nation
εἰσῆλθον: to enter (aor.)

ἐντεῦθεν: hence, from here
κόσμος, ὁ: the world
παραδίδωμι: to betray, hand over
ποιέω: to do, make
ὑπηρέτης, ὁ: a public servant
φωνέω: to address

18:34 **ἢ ἄλλοι**: "*or did others* say to you?"

18:35 **μήτι εἰμι**; a rhetorical question, "Am I a Jew?" i.e. I am not!

18:36 **εἰ ἦν ... ἠγωνίζοντο ἄν**: impf. tenses in a present contrafactual condition, "if my kingdom were ... my servants would be fighting for me"

ἵνα μὴ παραδοθῶ: aor. pass. subj. of **παρα-δίδωμι** in purpose clause, "lest I be handed over"

³³ Introivit ergo iterum in praetorium Pilatus et vocavit Iesum et dixit ei: "Tu es rex Iudaeorum?"

³⁴ Respondit Iesus: "A temetipso tu hoc dicis, an alii tibi dixerunt de me?"

³⁵ Respondit Pilatus: "Numquid ego Iudaeus sum? Gens tua et pontifices tradiderunt te mihi; quid fecisti?"

³⁶ Respondit Iesus: "Regnum meum non est de mundo hoc; si ex hoc mundo esset regnum meum, ministri mei decertarent, ut non traderer Iudaeis; nunc autem meum regnum non est hinc."

³⁷ Dixit itaque ei Pilatus: "Ergo rex es tu?"

---

an: or (interog.)
decerto, (1): to fight
facio, (3), **feci**: to do, manke
gens, gentis *f*: people
hinc (*adv.*): from here
itaque: and so, therefore
mundus, -i *m*: the world

nascor, (3), **natus sum**: to be born, begotten
numquid: is it possible? can it be that?
pontifex, -ficis *m*: a chief priest
regnum, -i *n*: power, kingdom
rex, regis *m*: king
trado, (3), **tradidi**: to hand over, betray
voco, (1): to call, summon

18:34 **a te-met-ipso**: "from your very self" emphatic
18:36 **si ... esset**: impf. subj. in pres. contrary to fact protasis, "*if* my kingdom *were* of this world"

 decertarent: impf. subj. in present contrary to fact apodosis, "then my servants *would be contending*"

 ut non traderer: impf. subj. in mixed purpose and result clause, "contending *so that I would not be delivered*"

ἀπεκρίθη ὁ Ἰησοῦς «Σὺ λέγεις ὅτι βασιλεύς εἰμι. ἐγὼ εἰς τοῦτο γεγέννημαι καὶ εἰς τοῦτο ἐλήλυθα εἰς τὸν κόσμον ἵνα μαρτυρήσω τῇ ἀληθείᾳ· πᾶς ὁ ὢν ἐκ τῆς ἀληθείας ἀκούει μου τῆς φωνῆς.»

³⁸ λέγει αὐτῷ ὁ Πειλᾶτος «Τί ἐστιν ἀλήθεια;» καὶ τοῦτο εἰπὼν πάλιν ἐξῆλθεν πρὸς τοὺς Ἰουδαίους, καὶ λέγει αὐτοῖς «Ἐγὼ οὐδεμίαν εὑρίσκω ἐν αὐτῷ αἰτίαν· ³⁹ ἔστιν δὲ συνήθεια ὑμῖν ἵνα ἕνα ἀπολύσω ὑμῖν ἐν τῷ πάσχα· βούλεσθε οὖν ἀπολύσω ὑμῖν τὸν βασιλέα τῶν Ἰουδαίων;»

⁴⁰ ἐκραύγασαν οὖν πάλιν λέγοντες «Μὴ τοῦτον ἀλλὰ τὸν Βαραββᾶν.» ἦν δὲ ὁ Βαραββᾶς λῃστής.

αἴτια, ἡ: guilt, cause
ἀλήθεια, ἡ: the truth
ἀπολύω: to loose from
Βαραββᾶς, ὁ: Barabbas
βούλομαι: to will, wish, be willing
γεννάω: to give birth
ἐξῆλθον: to go out of (aor.)
εὑρίσκω: to find

κραυγάζω: to shout
λῃστής, -οῦ, ὁ: a robber, thief
μαρτυρέω: to bear witness to (+ dat.)
πάλιν (adv.): again
πάσχα, τό (indecl.): Passover
Πειλᾶτος: Pilate
συνήθεια, ἡ: custom
φωνή, ἡ: a sound, tone

18:37 γεγέννημαι: perf., "I was born for this"
ἐλήλυθα: perf., "I have come"
ἵνα μαρτυρήσω: aor. subj. in purpose clause, "I have come in order to witness to the truth"
πᾶς ὁ ὤν: pres. part. attricutive, "everyone who is"
18:39 ἵνα ἕνα ἀπολύσω: aor. subj. of ἀπο-λύω in noun clause explaining συνήθεια, "it is your custom to release one"
ἀπολύσω: aor. subj. after βούλεσθε where an infinitive would be normal, "do you wish that I release?"

Respondit Iesus: "Tu dicis quia rex sum. Ego in hoc natus sum et ad hoc veni in mundum, ut testimonium perhibeam veritati; omnis, qui est ex veritate, audit meam vocem."

[38] Dicit ei Pilatus: "Quid est veritas?" Et cum hoc dixisset, iterum exivit ad Iudaeos et dicit eis: "Ego nullam invenio in eo causam. [39] Est autem consuetudo vobis, ut unum dimittam vobis in Pascha; vultis ergo dimittam vobis regem Iudaeorum?"

[40] Clamaverunt ergo rursum dicentes: "Non hunc sed Barabbam!" Erat autem Barabbas latro.

---

audio (4): to hear
Barabbas *m*: Barabbas
causa, -ae *f*: accusation, charge
clamo, (1): to proclaim, declare shout
consuetudo, -inis *f*: customary practice
dimitto, (3): to send down
exeo, (4) **exivi**: to exit

invenio, (4): to discover, find
iterum (*adv.*): again
latro, latronis *m*: robber
nullus, -a, -um: none, not any, nothing
rursum (*adv.*): turned back, backward
veritas, -tatis *f*: the truth
vox, vocis *f*: voice

18:37 **ut ... perhibeam**: pres. subj. in purpose clause, "I came *in order to present*"
18:38 **cum ... dixisset**: plupf. subj. in cum circumstantial clause, "when he had said"
18:39 **ut ... dimittam**: pres. subj. in noun result clause, "your custom *that I release*"
    dimittam: pres. subj. in noun clause after *vultis* where we would expect an infinitive, "do you wish me *to release*?"

Chapter 19

Jesus Sentenced to Be Crucified

¹ τότε οὖν ἔλαβεν ὁ Πειλᾶτος τὸν Ἰησοῦν καὶ ἐμαστίγωσεν. ² καὶ οἱ στρατιῶται πλέξαντες στέφανον ἐξ ἀκανθῶν ἐπέθηκαν αὐτοῦ τῇ κεφαλῇ, καὶ ἱμάτιον πορφυροῦν περιέβαλον αὐτόν, ³ καὶ ἤρχοντο πρὸς αὐτὸν καὶ ἔλεγον «Χαῖρε ὁ βασιλεὺς τῶν Ἰουδαίων·» καὶ ἐδίδοσαν αὐτῷ ῥαπίσματα.

⁴ καὶ ἐξῆλθεν πάλιν ἔξω ὁ Πειλᾶτος καὶ λέγει αὐτοῖς «Ἴδε ἄγω ὑμῖν αὐτὸν ἔξω, ἵνα γνῶτε ὅτι οὐδεμίαν αἰτίαν εὑρίσκω ἐν αὐτῷ.» ⁵ ἐξῆλθεν οὖν ὁ Ἰησοῦς ἔξω, φορῶν τὸν ἀκάνθινον στέφανον καὶ τὸ πορφυροῦν ἱμάτιον. καὶ λέγει αὐτοῖς «Ἰδοὺ ὁ ἄνθρωπος.»

ἄγαμαι: to wonder, be astonished	μαστιγόω: to whip, flog
ἄγω: to lead or carry	ὅτε: when
αἴτια, ἡ: blame, guilt	οὐδείς, -οὐδεμία, οὐδέν: no one
ἄκανθα, -ης, ἡ: a thorn, prickle	περιβάλλω: to throw round
ἀκάνθινος, -η, -ον: of thorns	πλέκω: to twist, weave
βασιλεύς, ὁ: a king	πορφύρεος, -ον: purple
ἐξῆλθον: to exit, go out (aor.)	ῥάπισμα, -ατος, τό: a slap on the face
ἐπιτίθημι: to lay, put or place upon	στέφανος, ὁ: a crown, garland
εὑρίσκω: to find	στρατιώτης, -ου, ὁ: a soldier
ἱμάτιον, τό: a cloak or mantle	φορέω: to bear, wear
κεφαλή, ἡ: the head	χαίρω: to rejoice, be glad, be delighted

19:1 ἔλαβεν: aor., "he *took* Jesus and whipped him.

19:2 πλέξαντες: aor. of πλέκω, "having woven"

ἐπέθηκαν: aor. of ἐπι-τίθημι, "they placed upon"

περιέβαλον: aor. of περι-βάλλω, "they cast X (acc.) around Y (acc.)"

19:3 ἤρχοντο: impf. of ἔρχομαι, "*they kept approaching* him and kept saying"

ἐδίδοσαν: impf. of δίδωμι, "*they kept giving* him slaps"

19:4 ἵνα γνῶτε: aor. subj. in purpose clause, "I lead him out *so that you know*"

19:5 λέγει αὐτοῖς: "(Pilate) says to them" note the lack of indication of change of subject

ἰδού: aor. mid. imper., "*behold* the man!"

Chapter 19

Jesus Sentenced to Be Crucified

¹ Tunc ergo apprehendit Pilatus Iesum et flagellavit.   ² Et milites, plectentes coronam de spinis, imposuerunt capiti eius et veste purpurea circumdederunt eum;   ³ et veniebant ad eum et dicebant: "Ave, rex Iudaeorum!" et dabant ei alapas.

⁴ Et exiit iterum Pilatus foras et dicit eis: "Ecce adduco vobis eum foras, ut cognoscatis quia in eo invenio causam nullam."   ⁵ Exiit ergo Iesus foras, portans spineam coronam et purpureum vestimentum. Et dicit eis: "Ecce homo!"

---

adduco, (3): to lead, bring up
alapa, **-ae** *f*: blow, slap, smack
apprehendo, (3): to seize, apprehend
ave: hail! (*imper.*)
caput, **capitis** *n*: head
causa, **-ae** *f*: accusation, charge
circumdo, (1), **circumdedi**: to surround, encircle
corona, **-ae** *f*: crown, garland
flagello, (1): to flog, whip, lash
foras (*adv.*): outside
impono, (3), **imposui**, **impositus**: to impose, set

invenio, (4) to find
miles, **militis** *m*: soldier, foot soldier
nullus, **-a**, **-um**: no, none
Pilatus, **-i** *m*: Pontius Pilate a prefect of Judea in 26- 36 AD
plecto, (3): to weave, twist
porto, (1): to carry, bring
purpureus, **-a**, **-um**: purple
spina, **-ae** *f*: thorn
spineus, **-a**, **-um**: thorny
vestimentum, **-i** *n*: garment, robe
vestis, **vestis** *f*: garment, robe

19:2   **capiti**: dat. with compound verb, "he placed *on his head*"
       veste purpurea: abl. of means, "dressed him *with a purple garment*"
19:4   **ut cognoscatis**: pres. subj. in purpose clause, "I lead out *in order that you understand*"

⁶ ὅτε οὖν εἶδον αὐτὸν οἱ ἀρχιερεῖς καὶ οἱ ὑπηρέται ἐκραύγασαν λέγοντες «Σταύρωσον σταύρωσον.»

λέγει αὐτοῖς ὁ Πειλᾶτος «Λάβετε αὐτὸν ὑμεῖς καὶ σταυρώσατε, ἐγὼ γὰρ οὐχ εὑρίσκω ἐν αὐτῷ αἰτίαν.»

⁷ ἀπεκρίθησαν αὐτῷ οἱ Ἰουδαῖοι «Ἡμεῖς νόμον ἔχομεν,
καὶ κατὰ τὸν νόμον ὀφείλει ἀποθανεῖν, ὅτι υἱὸν θεοῦ ἑαυτὸν
ἐποίησεν.»

⁸ ὅτε οὖν ἤκουσεν ὁ Πειλᾶτος τοῦτον τὸν λόγον, μᾶλλον
ἐφοβήθη, ⁹ καὶ εἰσῆλθεν εἰς τὸ πραιτώριον πάλιν καὶ λέγει τῷ
Ἰησοῦ «Πόθεν εἶ σύ;» ὁ δὲ Ἰησοῦς ἀπόκρισιν οὐκ ἔδωκεν αὐτῷ.

¹⁰ λέγει οὖν αὐτῷ ὁ Πειλᾶτος «Ἐμοὶ οὐ λαλεῖς; οὐκ οἶδας ὅτι
ἐξουσίαν ἔχω ἀπολῦσαί σε καὶ ἐξουσίαν ἔχω σταυρῶσαί σε;»

αἴτια, ἡ: blame	νόμος, ὁ: a law
ἀπόκρισις, ἡ: an answer	ὀφείλω: to owe, ought to (+ *inf.*)
ἀρχιερεύς, -έως, ὁ: chief-priest	πόθεν: whence?
εἰσῆλθον: to enter (*aor.*)	σταυρόω: to crucify
εὑρίσκω: to find	ὑπερέτης, ὁ: a public servant
λαλέω: to talk	φοβέομαι: to fear
μᾶλλον (*adv.*): more	

19:6 **σταύρωσον**: aor. imper. s., "crucify!"

   λάβετε ... σταυρώσατε: aor. imper. pl., "take! ...crucify!" where a participle
   would normally be used for the first action

19:7 **ἀποθανεῖν**: aor. inf. complementing **ὀφείλει**, "it is fitting (for him) *to die*"

   υἱόν: acc. pred., "he made himself *the son* of God"

19:8 **ἐφοβήθη**: aor. pass., "Pilate *became afraid*"

19:9 **οὐκ ἔδωκεν**: aor., "Jesus *did not give* an answer"

19:10 **ἀπολῦσαι ... σταυρῶσαι**: aor. inf. epexegetic after **ἐξουσίαν**, "the power *to
   release ...to crucify*"

⁶ Cum ergo vidissent eum pontifices et ministri, clamaverunt dicentes: "Crucifige, crucifige!"

Dicit eis Pilatus: "Accipite eum vos et crucifigite; ego enim non invenio in eo causam."

⁷ Responderunt ei Iudaei: "Nos legem habemus, et secundum legem debet mori, quia Filium Dei se fecit."

⁸ Cum ergo audisset Pilatus hunc sermonem, magis timuit ⁹ et ingressus est praetorium iterum et dicit ad Iesum: "Unde es tu?" Iesus autem responsum non dedit ei. ¹⁰ Dicit ergo ei Pilatus: "Mihi non loqueris? Nescis quia potestatem habeo dimittere te et potestatem habeo crucifigere te?"

---

accipio, (3) **accepi, acceptus**: to receive, accept
audio, (4), **audivi, auditus**: to hear
causa, -ae *f*: charge
crucifigo, (3): to crucify
debeo, (2): ought to (+ *inf.*)
dimitto, (3): to send away, release
habeo, (2): to have
ingredior, (3), **ingressus sum**: to advance, enter

loquor, (3), **locutus sum**: to speak
magis: to greater extent, more greatly
morior, (3): to die
nescio, (4): to not know
potestas, potestatis *f*: power
responsum, -i *n*: answer, response
secundum: according to (+ *acc.*)
sermo, sermonis *m*: speech, the word
timeo, (2), **timui**: to fear, dread, be afraid
unde: from where, whence

19:6 **cum ... vidissent**: plupf. subj. in *cum* circumstantial clause, "when they had seen"
19:7 **filium**: predicate noun, "he made himself *the son* of god"
19:8 **cum ... audisset**: plupf. subj. in *cum* circumstantial clause, "when he had heard"
19:10 **dimittere ... crucifigere**: pres. inf. epexegetic with *potestatem*, "the power *to release ...to crucify*"

275

¹¹ ἀπεκρίθη αὐτῷ Ἰησοῦς «Οὐκ εἶχες ἐξουσίαν κατ' ἐμοῦ οὐδεμίαν εἰ μὴ ἦν δεδομένον σοι ἄνωθεν· διὰ τοῦτο ὁ παραδούς μέ σοι μείζονα ἁμαρτίαν ἔχει.»

¹² ἐκ τούτου ὁ Πειλᾶτος ἐζήτει ἀπολῦσαι αὐτόν· οἱ δὲ Ἰουδαῖοι ἐκραύγασαν λέγοντες «Ἐὰν τοῦτον ἀπολύσῃς, οὐκ εἶ φίλος τοῦ Καίσαρος· πᾶς ὁ βασιλέα ἑαυτὸν ποιῶν ἀντιλέγει τῷ Καίσαρι.»

¹³ ὁ οὖν Πειλᾶτος ἀκούσας τῶν λόγων τούτων ἤγαγεν ἔξω τὸν Ἰησοῦν, καὶ ἐκάθισεν ἐπὶ βήματος εἰς τόπον λεγόμενον Λιθόστρωτον, Ἑβραϊστὶ δὲ Γαββαθά. ¹⁴ ἦν δὲ παρασκευὴ τοῦ πάσχα, ὥρα ἦν ὡς ἕκτη.

καὶ λέγει τοῖς Ἰουδαίοις «Ἴδε ὁ βασιλεὺς ὑμῶν.»

ἄγω: to lead or carry
ἁμαρτία, ἡ: a fault, sin
ἀντιλέγω: to speak against
ἄνωθεν (adv.): from above, from on high
βῆμα, -ατος, τό: a seat, stand
δίδωμι: to give
ἕκτος, -η, -ον: sixth
ζητέω: to seek, seek for
καθίζω: to make to sit down, seat

Καῖσαρ, -αρος, ὁ: Caesar, the emperor
κραύγω: to cry out
λιθόστρωτος, -ον: paved with stones
μείζων, -ον: greater
παραδίδωμι: to hand over, betray
παρασκευή, ἡ: preparation
τόπος, ὁ: a place
φίλος, ὁ: a friend
ὥρα, ἡ: hour

19:11 οὐκ εἶχες: impf. in contrafactual apodosis (expecting ἄν), "you would have no power"

εἰ μὴ ἦν δεδομένον: plupf. periphrastic in past contrafactual protasis: "unless it had been given"

ὁ παραδούς: aor. part. of παρα-δίδωμι, "the one who betrayed" i.e. Judas

σοι: pred. dat. after μείζονα, "greater *than your* (sin)"

19:12 ἐὰν τοῦτον ἀπολύσῃς: aor. subj. in pres. general protasis, "*if you release him,* you are no friend"

πᾶς ὁ ... ποιῶν: pres. part. attrib., "*anyone who makes* himself king"

19:13 ἤγαγεν: aor. of ἄγω, "*he led* him outside"

ἐκάθισεν: aor., "he caused him (Jesus) to sit" or "he (himself) sat"

εἰς τόπον: "placed him *into the seat*," whereas "he sat *in the seat*" would take ἐν with the dative, but these differences are often not observed

Λιθόστρωτον: "the Pavement" in Hebrew *Gabbatha*

19:14 παρασκευὴ τοῦ πάσχα: "it was *the preparation for the Passover*"

276

¹¹ Respondit Iesus: "Non haberes potestatem adversum me ullam, nisi tibi esset datum desuper; propterea, qui tradidit me tibi, maius peccatum habet."

¹² Exinde quaerebat Pilatus dimittere eum; Iudaei autem clamabant dicentes: "Si hunc dimittis, non es amicus Caesaris! Omnis, qui se regem facit, contradicit Caesari."

¹³ Pilatus ergo, cum audisset hos sermones, adduxit foras Iesum et sedit pro tribunali in locum, qui dicitur Lithostrotos, Hebraice autem Gabbatha. ¹⁴ Erat autem Parasceve Paschae, hora erat quasi sexta.

Et dicit Iudaeis: "Ecce rex vester!"

---

adduco, (3), **adduxi**: to lead, bring
adversum: opposite, against (+ *acc.*)
amicus, -i *m*: friend, ally
audio, (4), **audivi**: to hear
Caesar, Caesaris *m*: Caesar
contradico, (3): to oppose
desuper (*adv.*): from above
do, (1) **dedi, datus**: to give
exinde: thence, after that
hora, -ae *f*: hour, time

locus, loci *m*: seat, place
maior, –us: greater, larger
parasceves, -ae *f*: day of preparation
peccatum, -i *n*: sin
quasi: about
sedeo, (2): to sit
sex: six
trado, (3), **tradidi**: to hand over, surrender
tribunal, -alis *n*: tribunal, judgement seat
ullus, -a, -um: any

19:11 **non haberes**: impf. subj. in pres. contrary to fact apodosis, "you would not have"

nisi ... esset datum: plupf. subj. in past contrary to fact protasis, "unless it had been given"

19:12 **si ... dimittis**: an instance in which a pres. general condition is translated with a pres. indic. instead of a fut. perf., "if you release"

Caesari: dat. with compound verb, "opposes *Caesar*"

19:13 **cum audisset**: plupf. subj. in *cum* circumstantial clause, "when he had heard"

in locum: the acc. where we would expect an abl. of place., "he sits *in the place* before the tribunal"

Hebraice autem Gabbatha: "which is called *Gabbatha in Hebrew*"

19:14 **Parascevem**: "the preparation," the day before the Passover, a transliteration of the Greek word for preparation.

277

¹⁵ ἐκραύγασαν οὖν ἐκεῖνοι «Ἆρον ἆρον, σταύρωσον αὐτόν.»

λέγει αὐτοῖς ὁ Πειλᾶτος «Τὸν βασιλέα ὑμῶν σταυρώσω;»

ἀπεκρίθησαν οἱ ἀρχιερεῖς «Οὐκ ἔχομεν βασιλέα εἰ μὴ Καίσαρα.»

¹⁶ τότε οὖν παρέδωκεν αὐτὸν αὐτοῖς ἵνα σταυρωθῇ.

The Crucifixion of Jesus

παρέλαβον οὖν τὸν Ἰησοῦν· ¹⁷ καὶ βαστάζων αὐτῷ τὸν σταυρὸν ἐξῆλθεν εἰς τὸν λεγόμενον Κρανίου Τόπον, ὃ λέγεται Ἑβραϊστὶ Γολγοθά, ¹⁸ ὅπου αὐτὸν ἐσταύρωσαν, καὶ μετ᾽ αὐτοῦ ἄλλους δύο ἐντεῦθεν καὶ ἐντεῦθεν, μέσον δὲ τὸν Ἰησοῦν.

αἴρω: to take up, raise, lift up
βαστάζω: to lift, lift up, raise
Γολγοθά (*indecl.*): Golgatha
ἐντεῦθεν: hence or thence
ἐξῆλθον: to exit (*aor.*)

Καῖσαρ, -αρος, ὁ: Caesar, the emperor
κρανίον, τό: the skull
μέσος, -η, -ον: middle, in the middle
παραδίδωμι: to hand over
σταυρός, ὁ: a cross

19:15 ἆρον ... σταύρωσον: aor. imper. of αἴρω, "away with him! ... crucify him!"
σταυρώσω: aor. subj. in deliberative quest., *"should I crucify* your king?"
19:16 παρέδωκεν: aor., *"he handed over* him to them"
ἵνα σταυρωθῇ: aor. subj. pass. in purpose clause, "handed him over *in order to be crucified"*
παρέλαβον: aor. of παρα-λαμβάνω, "and so *they received* Jesus"
19:17 αὐτῷ (=ἑαυτῷ): lifting the cross *for himself*
Κρανίου Τόπον: "the place of the skull" in Hebrew *Golgotha*
19:18 ἐσταύρωσαν: aor., "where *they crucified* him"
ἐντεῦθεν καὶ ἐντεῦθεν: "one on each side"

¹⁵ Clamaverunt ergo illi: "Tolle, tolle, crucifige eum!"

Dicit eis Pilatus: "Regem vestrum crucifigam?"

Responderunt pontifices: "Non habemus regem, nisi Caesarem."

¹⁶ Tunc ergo tradidit eis illum, ut crucifigeretur.

The Crucifixion of Jesus

Susceperunt ergo Iesum. ¹⁷ Et baiulans sibi crucem exivit in eum, qui dicitur Calvariae locum, quod Hebraice dicitur Golgotha, ¹⁸ ubi eum crucifixerunt et cum eo alios duos hinc et hinc, medium autem Iesum.

---

alius, alia, aliud: other, another
baiulo, (1): to carry, bear
calvaria, -ae *f*: skull
crux, crucis *f*: cross
duo, duae, duo: two
exeo, (4), **exivi**: to exit, depart

locus, -i *m*: location, place
medius, -a, -um: middle, middle of
nisi: except for, if not
suscipio, (3), **suscepi**: to receive
tollo, (3), to remove, take away
trado, (3), **tradidi**: to hand over, betray

19:15 **crucifigam**: pres. subj. deliberative, "*should I crucify* your king?"
19:16 **ut crucifigeretur**: impf. subj. in purpose clause, "he handed him over to be crucified"
19:18 **hinc et hinc**: "on one side and the other"

279

¹⁹ ἔγραψεν δὲ καὶ τίτλον ὁ Πειλᾶτος καὶ ἔθηκεν ἐπὶ τοῦ σταυροῦ· ἦν δὲ γεγραμμένον ΙΗΣΟΥΣ Ο ΝΑΖΩΡΑΙΟΣ Ο ΒΑΣΙΛΕΥΣ ΤΩΝ ΙΟΥΔΑΙΩΝ. ²⁰ τοῦτον οὖν τὸν τίτλον πολλοὶ ἀνέγνωσαν τῶν Ἰουδαίων, ὅτι ἐγγὺς ἦν ὁ τόπος τῆς πόλεως ὅπου ἐσταυρώθη ὁ Ἰησοῦς· καὶ ἦν γεγραμμένον Ἑβραϊστί, Ῥωμαϊστί, Ἑλληνιστί. ²¹ ἔλεγον οὖν τῷ Πειλάτῳ οἱ ἀρχιερεῖς τῶν Ἰουδαίων «Μὴ γράφε Ὁ βασιλεὺς τῶν Ἰουδαίων, ἀλλ᾽ ὅτι ἐκεῖνος εἶπεν Βασιλεὺς τῶν Ἰουδαίων εἰμί.»

²² ἀπεκρίθη ὁ Πειλᾶτος «Ὃ γέγραφα γέγραφα.»

²³ οἱ οὖν στρατιῶται ὅτε ἐσταύρωσαν τὸν Ἰησοῦν ἔλαβον τὰ ἱμάτια αὐτοῦ καὶ ἐποίησαν τέσσερα μέρη, ἑκάστῳ στρατιώτῃ μέρος, καὶ τὸν χιτῶνα. ἦν δὲ ὁ χιτὼν ἄραφος, ἐκ τῶν ἄνωθεν ὑφαντὸς δι᾽ ὅλου·

ἀναγινώσκω: to read
ἄραφος, -ον: seamless
ἀρχιερεύς, ὁ: the high priest
γράφω: to write
ἐγγύς: near, nigh (+ gen.)
ἕκαστος, -η, -ον: each, each one
ἱμάτιον, τό: clothing
μέρος, -εος, τό: a part, share
ὅλος, -η, -ον: whole, entire

πόλις, πόλεως, ἡ : a city
σταυρός, ὁ: a cross
στρατιώτης, -ου, ὁ: a soldier
τέσσαρες, -ων, οἱ: four
τίθημι: to set, put, place
τίτλος, ὁ: title, inscription
ὑφαντός, -ή, -όν: woven
χιτών, -ῶνος, ὁ: a frock

19:19 ἔγραψεν ... ἔθηκεν: aor., "Pilate *wrote ... he placed*"
ἦν γεγραμμένον: perf. part. in plupf. periphrastic, "it had been written"
19:20 ἀνέγνωσαν: aor. ἀνα-γινώσκω, "many of the Jews *read*"
ἐγγὺς ... τῆς πόλεως: "was *near the city*"
Ἑβραϊστί, Ῥωμαϊστί, Ἑλληνιστί: "in Hebrew, Latin and Greek"
19:21 μὴ γράφε: pres. imper. in prohibition where aor. subj. is more normal, "don't write!"
ὅτι ἐκεῖνος εἶπεν Βασιλεὺς τῶν Ἰουδαίων εἰμί: note the triple direct speech, "write that 'he said "I am the king"'"
19:22 ὃ γέγραφα: perf., "*what I have written* I have written"
19:23 δι᾽ ὅλου: "completely" i.e. all in one piece

[19] Scripsit autem et titulum Pilatus et posuit super crucem; erat autem scriptum: "IESUS NAZARENUS REX IUDAEORUM."

[20] Hunc ergo titulum multi legerunt Iudaeorum, quia prope civitatem erat locus, ubi crucifixus est Iesus; et erat scriptum Hebraice, Latine, Graece. [21] Dicebant ergo Pilato pontifices Iudaeorum: "Noli scribere: 'Rex Iudaeorum', sed: 'Ipse dixit: Rex sum Iudaeorum'."

[22] Respondit Pilatus: "Quod scripsi, scripsi!"

[23] Milites ergo cum crucifixissent Iesum, acceperunt vestimenta eius et fecerunt quattuor partes, unicuique militi partem, et tunicam. Erat autem tunica inconsutilis, desuper contexta per totum.

---

accipio, (3), **accepi**: to receive, accept
civitas, civitatis *f*: community, city, town
consutilis, -e: sewed together
contexo, (3), **contexui, contextus**: to weave
desuper (*adv.*): from above, from overhead
lego, (3), **legi**: to read
locus, -i *m*: location, place
miles, militis *m*: a soldier
multus, -a, -um: much, many
Nazarenus, -i *m*: the Nazarene
nolo, nolle: be unwilling, do not wish

pars, partis *f*: part, share
pono, (3), **posui, positus**: to put, place
prope: near (+ *acc.*)
quattuor: four
rex, regis *m*: a king
scribo, (3), **scripsi, scriptus**: to write
titulus, -i *m*: label, sign
totus, -a, -um: whole, entire
tunica, tunicae *f*: undergarment, shirt, tunic
unusquisque, unumquidque: each one
vestimentum, -i *n*: clothing

19:20 **Hebraice, Latine, Graece**: "it was written *in Hebrew, Latin, and Greek*"
19:21 **sed Ipse dixit: Rex ...** : "But write: 'he said, "I am king"'"; note the triple direct speech
19:23 **cum crucifixissent**: cum circumstantial clause, "when they had crucified"
    unicuique: dat. of adv. of *unusquisque*, "a part *for each* soldier"
    per totum: "completely" i.e. all in one piece with no seams

²⁴ εἶπαν οὖν πρὸς ἀλλήλους «Μὴ σχίσωμεν αὐτόν, ἀλλὰ λάχωμεν περὶ αὐτοῦ τίνος ἔσται·»

ἵνα ἡ γραφὴ πληρωθῇ

«Διεμερίσαντο τὰ ἱμάτιά μου ἑαυτοῖς

καὶ ἐπὶ τὸν ἱματισμόν μου ἔβαλον κλῆρον.»

οἱ μὲν οὖν στρατιῶται ταῦτα ἐποίησαν·

²⁵ εἱστήκεισαν δὲ παρὰ τῷ σταυρῷ τοῦ Ἰησοῦ ἡ μήτηρ αὐτοῦ καὶ ἡ ἀδελφὴ τῆς μητρὸς αὐτοῦ, Μαρία ἡ τοῦ Κλωπᾶ καὶ Μαρία ἡ Μαγδαληνή. ²⁶ Ἰησοῦς οὖν ἰδὼν τὴν μητέρα καὶ τὸν μαθητὴν παρεστῶτα ὃν ἠγάπα λέγει τῇ μητρί «Γύναι, ἴδε ὁ υἱός σου·» ²⁷ εἶτα λέγει τῷ μαθητῇ «Ἴδε ἡ μήτηρ σου.» καὶ ἀπ᾽ ἐκείνης τῆς ὥρας ἔλαβεν ὁ μαθητὴς αὐτὴν εἰς τὰ ἴδια.

ἀγαπάω: to love, be fond of
ἀδελφή, ἡ: a sister
βάλλω: to throw, cast
γραφή, ἡ: a writing, scripture
γυνή, γυναικός, ἡ: a woman
διαμερίζω: to distribute
ἴδιος, -α, -ον: one's own
ἱματισμός, ὁ: clothing
κλῆρος, -ου, ὁ: a lot
Κλωπᾶς, Κλωπᾶ, ὁ: Clopas

λαγχάνω: to obtain by lot
λαμβάνω: to take, receive
Μαγδαληνή, ἡ: the Magdalene
μαθητής, -οῦ, ὁ: a disciple
Μαρία, -ας, ἡ: Mary
μήτηρ, μητρός, ἡ: a mother
παρίστημι: to make to stand beside
σταυρός, ὁ: a cross
σχίζω: to split, cleave
υἱός, ὁ: a son

19:24 **μὴ σχίσωμεν ... λάχωμεν**: aor. subj. in hortatory clause, "let's not split it ...let's cast lots"

    τίνος ἔσται: ind. quest., "(in order to see) *whose it will be*"

    ἵνα ἡ γραφὴ πληρωθῇ: aor. pass. subj. in result clause, "(this was) so that the scripture be fulfilled" Ps. 22:18

    διεμερίσαντο: aor. of **δια-μερίζω**, "they divided up"

    ἔβαλον: aor., "they cast a lot"

19:25 **εἱστήκεισαν**: plupf. of **ἵστημι**, "they were standing"

    ἡ τοῦ Κλωπᾶ: "Mary, *the (wife) of Clopas*"

19:26 **παρεστῶτα**: perf. part. circum. of **παρα-ἵστημι** with present meaning, "seeing the disciple *standing*"

19:27 **εἰς τὰ ἴδια**: "he received him *into his own* (household)"

²⁴ Dixerunt ergo ad invicem: "Non scindamus eam, sed sortiamur de illa, cuius sit,"

ut Scriptura impleatur dicens:

"Partiti sunt vestimenta mea sibi

et in vestem meam miserunt sortem."

Et milites quidem haec fecerunt.

²⁵ Stabant autem iuxta crucem Iesu mater eius et soror matris eius, Maria Cleopae, et Maria Magdalene.   ²⁶ Cum vidisset ergo Iesus matrem et discipulum stantem, quem diligebat, dicit matri: "Mulier, ecce filius tuus."   ²⁷ Deinde dicit discipulo: "Ecce mater tua." Et ex illa hora accepit eam discipulus in sua.

---

accipio, (3) **accepi, acceptus**: to receive, accept
Cleopas, Cleopae *m*: Cloepas
hora, -ae *f*: an hour, period of time
invicem: in turn, reciprocally, mutually
iuxta: near (+ *acc.*)
Magdalene (*indecl.*): Magdalene
Maria, -ae *f*: Mary
mater, matris *f*: mother

mulier, mulieris *f*: woman
partior, (4), **partitus sum**: to divide up
quidem: indeed
scindo, (3): to tear, cut to pieces
scriptura, -ae *f*: scripture
soror, sororis *f*: sister
sors, sortis *f*: lot, fate
sortior, (4), **sortitus sum**: to cast lots
vestis, vestis *f*: clothing

19:24 **non scindamus**: pres. subj. hortatory where one would expect *ne*, "let us not divide"

    sortiamur: pres. subj. hortatory: "let us cast lots"

    cuius sit: pres. subj. indirect question, "(to see) whose it will be"

    ut ... impleatur: pres. subj. purpose clause, "so that it may be fulfilled" Ps 22:18

    in vestem meam: "for the sake of my garment"

19:25 **Cleopae**: "Mary, (the wife) *of Clopa*"

19:26 **cum vidisset**: plupf. subj. *cum* circumstantial clause, "when he had seen"

    stantem: pres. part. circum. after *vidisset*, "saw him *standing*"

19:27 **in sua**: neuter pl. acc., "into his own (household)"

The Death of Jesus

²⁸ μετὰ τοῦτο εἰδὼς ὁ Ἰησοῦς ὅτι ἤδη πάντα τετέλεσται ἵνα τελειωθῇ ἡ γραφὴ λέγει «Διψῶ.» ²⁹ σκεῦος ἔκειτο ὄξους μεστόν· σπόγγον οὖν μεστὸν τοῦ ὄξους ὑσσώπῳ περιθέντες προσήνεγκαν αὐτοῦ τῷ στόματι. ³⁰ ὅτε οὖν ἔλαβεν τὸ ὄξος ὁ Ἰησοῦς εἶπεν «Τετέλεσται,» καὶ κλίνας τὴν κεφαλὴν παρέδωκεν τὸ πνεῦμα.

διψάω: to thirst
ἤδη: now, already
κεῖμαι: to be laid
κλίνω: to make to bend, slope
μεστός, -ή, -όν: full of (+ gen.)
ὄξος, -εος, τό: vinegar
ὅτε: when
παραδίδωμι: to give over
περιτίθημι: to place round

πνεῦμα, -ατος, τό: spirit
προσήνεγκα: to place near to (aor.)
σκεῦος, -εος, τό: a vessel
σπόγγος, ὁ: a sponge
στόμα, τό: the mouth
τελειόω: to make perfect, complete
τελέω: to fulfil, accomplish
ὕσσωπος, ἡ: hyssop

19:28 εἰδὼς: perf. part. with present sense, "Jesus *knowing*"
τετέλεσται: perf., "knowing that all things *were accomplished*"
ἵνα τελειωθῇ: aor. pass. subj. of τελειόω in purpose/result clause, "so that the scripture might be fulfilled" Ps. 69:21
διψῶ: fut., "I thirst"
19:29 ὄξους: gen. after μεστόν, "full *of vinegar*"
περιθέντες: aor. part. of περι-τίθημι, "having placed X (acc.) on Y (dat.)"
προσήνεγκαν: aor., "they placed it near" + dat.
19:30 κλίνας: aor. part. of κλίνω, "*having bowed* his head"
παρέδωκεν: aor., "*he gave up* his spirit"

The Death of Jesus

²⁸ Post hoc sciens Iesus quia iam omnia consummata sunt, ut consummaretur Scriptura, dicit: "Sitio." ²⁹ Vas positum erat aceto plenum; spongiam ergo plenam aceto hyssopo circumponentes, obtulerunt ori eius. ³⁰ Cum ergo accepisset acetum, Iesus dixit: "Consummatum est!" Et inclinato capite tradidit spiritum.

---

acetum, -i *n*: vinegar
caput, capitis *n*: head
circumpono, (3): to placed X (*acc.*) around Y (*dat.*)
consummo, (1): to finish off, end
hyssopus: the Hyssop plant
inclino, (1): to bend, lower
offero, offerre, obtuli: to offer, present

os, oris *n*: mouth
plenus, -a, -um: full
scio, (4): to know
sitio, (4), **sitivi**: to be thirsty
spiritus, -us *m*: spirit
spongia, -ae *f*: sponge
trado, (3), **tradidi**: to hand over, give up
vas, vasis *n*: vessel, jar

19:28 **ut consummaretur**: impf. subj. purpose clause, "in order for scripture to be fulfilled" Ps. 22:15
19:29 **aceto**: abl. after *plenum*, "there was a jar full *of vinegar*"
   hyssopo: dat. after *circumponentes*, "placing the sponge on *a hyssop stem*"
   ori: dat. after compound verb, "they offered it *to his mouth*"
19:30 **cum... accepisset**: plupf. subj. in *cum* circumstantial clause, "when he had received"
   inclinato capite: abl. abs., "his head having been inclined"

³¹ οἱ οὖν Ἰουδαῖοι, ἐπεὶ παρασκευὴ ἦν, ἵνα μὴ μείνῃ ἐπὶ
τοῦ σταυροῦ τὰ σώματα ἐν τῷ σαββάτῳ, ἦν γὰρ μεγάλη ἡ
ἡμέρα ἐκείνου τοῦ σαββάτου, ἠρώτησαν τὸν Πειλᾶτον ἵνα
κατεαγῶσιν αὐτῶν τὰ σκέλη καὶ ἀρθῶσιν. ³² ἦλθον οὖν οἱ
στρατιῶται, καὶ τοῦ μὲν πρώτου κατέαξαν τὰ σκέλη καὶ
τοῦ ἄλλου τοῦ συνσταυρωθέντος αὐτῷ· ³³ ἐπὶ δὲ τὸν Ἰησοῦν
ἐλθόντες, ὡς εἶδον ἤδη αὐτὸν τεθνηκότα, οὐ κατέαξαν αὐτοῦ τὰ
σκέλη, ³⁴ ἀλλ᾽ εἷς τῶν στρατιωτῶν λόγχῃ αὐτοῦ τὴν πλευρὰν
ἔνυξεν, καὶ ἐξῆλθεν εὐθὺς αἷμα καὶ ὕδωρ. ³⁵ καὶ ὁ ἑωρακὼς
μεμαρτύρηκεν, καὶ ἀληθινὴ αὐτοῦ ἐστιν ἡ μαρτυρία, καὶ ἐκεῖνος

αἷμα, -ατος, τό: blood	μένω: to remain
ἀληθινός, -ή, -όν: true	νύσσω: to prick, pierce
εἷς, μία, ἕν: one	παρασκευή, ἡ: preparation
ἐρατάω: to ask	πλευρά, -ᾶς, ἡ: a rib
εὐθύς: (adv.) immediately	πρωτός, -ή, -όν: first
ἦλθον: to go (aor.)	Σάββατον, τό: sabbath
ἡμέρα, ἡ: day	σκέλος, -εος, τό: the leg
κατάγνυμι: to break in pieces	σταυρός, ὁ: a cross
λόγχη, ἡ: a spear-head	συνσταυρόω: to crucify along with
μαρτυρέω: to bear witness	σῶμα, -ατος, τό: body
μαρτυρία, ἡ: witness, testimony, evidence	ὕδωρ, ὕδατος, τό: water

19:31 παρασκευὴ: "it was *the preparation* (of the passover)"
ἵνα μὴ μείνῃ: aor. subj. of μένω in purpose clause, "lest the bodies remain"
ἵνα κατεαγῶσιν ... ἀρθῶσιν: aor. subj. pass. in ind. quest. after ἠρώτησαν,
"they asked *that they be broken* and *that they be removed*"
19:32 κατέαξαν: aor. of κατα-άγνυμι, "so they came and *they broke*"
τοῦ μὲν πρώτου: gen., "bones *of the first* (thief)"
συνσταυρωθέντος: aor. pass. part. gen. s. of συν-σταυρόω, "and the bones *of
the one crucified with*"
19:33 τεθνηκότα: perf. part. in ind. st. after εἶδον, "they saw *that he was dead*"
19:34 λόγχῃ: dat. of means, "pierced *with his spear*"
19:35 ὁ ἑωρακὼς: perf. part. of ὁράω, "the one who has seen"
μεμαρτύρηκεν: perf. of μαρτυρέω, "he has witnessed"

³¹ Iudaei ergo, quoniam Parasceve erat, ut non remanerent in cruce corpora sabbato, erat enim magnus dies illius sabbati, rogaverunt Pilatum, ut frangerentur eorum crura, et tollerentur. ³² Venerunt ergo milites et primi quidem fregerunt crura et alterius, qui crucifixus est cum eo; ³³ ad Iesum autem cum venissent, ut viderunt eum iam mortuum, non fregerunt eius crura, ³⁴ sed unus militum lancea latus eius aperuit, et continuo exivit sanguis et aqua. ³⁵ Et qui vidit, testimonium perhibuit, et verum est eius testimonium, et ille

---

alter, altera, alterum: one of two, the second
aperio, (4), **aperui, apertus**: to open
aqua, **-ae** *f.*: water
continuo (*adv.*): immediately
corpus, -oris *n*: body
crus, cruris *n*: leg
fero, ferre, tuli, latus: to bring
frango, (3) **fregi**: to break, shatter
lancea, -ae *f.*: lance
latus, lateris *n*: side
magnus, -a, -um: great

parasceves, -ae *f.*: day before the Sabbath
perhibeo, (2), **perhibui**: to present, give
primus, -a, -um: first
quidem: indeed, certainly
quoniam: because, since
remaneo, (2): to stay behind, remain
rogo, (1): to ask
sabbatum, -i *n*: Sabbath
sanguis, -inis *m*: blood
verus, -a, -um: true, real

19:31 **ut non remanerent**: impf. subj. purpose clause, *lest* the bodies *remain*" expecting *ne*

  ut frangerent... tollerentur: impf. subj. in ind. quest., "asked *whether they could break... and take away*"

19:32 **primi ...alterius**: gen., "the legs *of the first ...of the second*"

19:33 **cum venissent**: plupf. subj. in *cum* circumstantial clause, "when they had come"

  ut viderunt: perf. in temporal clause, "when they saw"

  eum mortuum (sc. **esse**): ind. st., "saw *that he was dead*"

19:34 **lancea**: abl. of means, "pierced *with a lance*"

19:35 **qui vidit**: perf., "*he who has seen*, that one give testimony"

οἶδεν ὅτι ἀληθῆ λέγει, ἵνα καὶ ὑμεῖς πιστεύητε. ³⁶ ἐγένετο γὰρ ταῦτα ἵνα ἡ γραφὴ πληρωθῇ «ὀστοῦν οὐ συντριβήσεται αὐτοῦ.» ³⁷ καὶ πάλιν ἑτέρα γραφὴ λέγει «Ὄψονται εἰς ὃν ἐξεκέντησαν.»

The Burial of Jesus

³⁸ μετὰ δὲ ταῦτα ἠρώτησεν τὸν Πειλᾶτον Ἰωσὴφ ἀπὸ Ἁριμαθαίας, ὢν μαθητὴς [τοῦ] Ἰησοῦ, κεκρυμμένος δὲ διὰ τὸν φόβον τῶν Ἰουδαίων, ἵνα ἄρῃ τὸ σῶμα τοῦ Ἰησοῦ· καὶ ἐπέτρεψεν ὁ Πειλᾶτος. ἦλθεν οὖν καὶ ἦρεν τὸ σῶμα αὐτοῦ. ³⁹ ἦλθεν δὲ καὶ Νικόδημος, ὁ ἐλθὼν πρὸς αὐτὸν νυκτὸς τὸ πρῶτον, φέρων ἕλιγμα σμύρνης καὶ ἀλόης ὡς λίτρας ἑκατόν.

ἀληθής, -ές: unconcealed, true
ἀλόη, ἡ: aloe
Ἁριμαθαία, -ας, η: Aramathia
ἐγκεντέω: to stab
ἑκατόν (*indecl.*): a hundred
ἕλιγμα, -ατος, τό: a packet
ἐπιτρέπω: to turn towards, yield
Ἰωσὴφ: Joseph
κρύπτω: to hide, cover, cloak
λίτρα, ἡ: a silver coin, a pound

Νικόδημος: Nicodemus
νύξ, νυκτός, ἡ: the night
ὀστέον, τό: bone
ὄψομαι: to see (*fut.*)
σμύρνα, ἡ: myrrh
συντρίβω: to rub together, shatter
σῶμα, τὸ: a body
φέρω: to bear
φόβος, ὁ: fear

19:35 ἵνα καὶ ὑμεῖς πιστεύητε: pres. subj. in purpose clause, "so that you might believe"

19:36 ἵνα ἡ γραφὴ πληρωθῇ: aor. subj. pass. in purpose clause, "these things happened *in order that the scripture be fulfilled*" Ex. 12:46

οὐ συντριβήσεται: fut. of συν-τρίβω, "his bones *will not be shattered*"

19:37 ἑτέρα γραφὴ: Zech. 12:10

ἐξεκέντησαν: aor. of ἐκ-κεντέω, "they will look upon whom *they stabbed*"

19:38 κεκρυμμένος: perf. part. concessive, "although having kept it secret"

ἵνα ἄρῃ: aor. subj. of αἴρω in noun clause after ἠρώτησεν, "he asked *to take the body*"

ἐπέτρεψεν: aor. of ἐπιτρέπω, "Pilate *yielded*"

ἦρεν: aor. of αἴρω, "he (Joseph) removed"

19:39 νυκτὸς: gen. of time within which, "during the night"

ἕλιγμα: "a packet of" + gen.

ὡς λίτρας ἑκατόν: "about 100 pounds (in value)" where genitive is normal

288

scit quia vera dicit, ut et vos credatis.   ³⁶ Facta sunt enim haec, ut

Scriptura impleatur: "Os non comminuetur eius,"   ³⁷ et iterum alia

Scriptura dicit: "Videbunt in quem transfixerunt."

The Burial of Jesus

³⁸ Post haec autem rogavit Pilatum Ioseph ab Arimathaea, qui

erat discipulus Iesu, occultus autem propter metum Iudaeorum, ut

tolleret corpus Iesu; et permisit Pilatus. Venit ergo et tulit corpus

eius.   ³⁹ Venit autem et Nicodemus, qui venerat ad eum nocte

primum, ferens mixturam myrrhae et aloes quasi libras centum.

---

aloe, aloes *f.*: aloe plant
Arimathaea (*indecl.*): Arimathea
centum: one hundred
comminuo, (3): to break
ferro, ferre, tuli, latus: to carry
Ioseph (*indecl.*): Joseph
libra, -ae *f.*: Roman coin
metus, metus *m.*: fear
mixtura, -ae *f.*: mixture
myrrha, -ae *f.*: myrrh
Nicodemus, -i *m.*: Nicodemus

nox, noctis *f.*: night
occultus, -a, -um: hidden, in secret
os, ossis *n.*: bone
permitto, (3), **permisi**: to permit, allow
primum: at first, earlier
quasi: about, approximately
scio, (4): to know, understand
tollo, (3), **sustuli**: to remove
transfigo, (3): to transfix, pierce through
verus, -a, -um: true

19:35 **ut... credatis**: pres. subj. in purpose clause, "speaks *in order that you believe*"

19:36 **ut... impleatur**: pres. subj. in purpose clause, "these things were done *in order that scripture be fulfilled*" Ps. 34:20

19:37 **alia scriptura**: Zech. 12:10

19:38 **ut tolleret**: impf. subj. in ind. quest. after *rogavit*, "asked *whether he could take away*"

19:39 **quasi libras centum**: "about 100 pounds (in value)" where the genitive is normal

289

⁴⁰ ἔλαβον οὖν τὸ σῶμα τοῦ Ἰησοῦ καὶ ἔδησαν αὐτὸ ὀθονίοις μετὰ τῶν ἀρωμάτων, καθὼς ἔθος ἐστὶν τοῖς Ἰουδαίοις ἐντα-φιάζειν. ⁴¹ ἦν δὲ ἐν τῷ τόπῳ ὅπου ἐσταυρώθη κῆπος, καὶ ἐν τῷ κήπῳ μνημεῖον καινόν, ἐν ᾧ οὐδέπω οὐδεὶς ἦν τεθειμένος· ⁴² ἐκεῖ οὖν διὰ τὴν παρασκευὴν τῶν Ἰουδαίων, ὅτι ἐγγὺς ἦν τὸ μνημεῖον, ἔθηκαν τὸν Ἰησοῦν.

Chapter 20

The Empty Tomb

¹ τῇ δὲ μιᾷ τῶν σαββάτων Μαρία ἡ Μαγδαληνὴ ἔρχεται πρωὶ σκοτίας ἔτι οὔσης εἰς τὸ μνημεῖον, καὶ βλέπει τὸν λίθον ἠρμένον ἐκ τοῦ μνημείου. ² τρέχει οὖν καὶ ἔρχεται πρὸς Σίμωνα

ἄρωμα, -ατος, τό: spice
βλέπω: to see, have the power of sight
δέω: to bind, wrap
ἔθος, -εος, τό: custom, habit
ἐνταφιάζω: to prepare for burial
καθώς: just as
καινός, -ή, -όν: new, fresh
κῆπος, ὁ: a garden

λίθος, ὁ: a stone
μνημεῖον, τό: a monument
ὀθόνιον, τό: a piece of fine linen
παρασκευή, ἡ: preparation day
πρωί (adv.): early in the day
σκοτία, ἡ: darkness, gloom
τρέχω: to run

19:40 ἔδησαν: aor. of δέω, "*they wrapped* it (the body)"
  ὀθονίοις: dat.of means, "they wrapped it *with cloth*"
  μετὰ τῶν ἀρωμάτων: "together with spices"
  ἐνταφιάζειν: pres. inf. after ἔθος ἐστὶν, "as is the custom *to prepare to bury*"
19:41 ὅπου ἐσταυρώθη: aor. pass. in local relative clause, "the place *where he was crucified*"
  ἦν τεθειμένος: perf. part. of τίθημι in plupf. periphrastic, "in which no one *had been placed*"
19:42 διὰ τὴν παρασκευὴν: "because of the preparation (of the Passover)"
  ἔθηκαν: aor. of τίθημι, "they placed"
20:1 τῇ δὲ μιᾷ (sc. ὥρᾳ): dat. of time when, "at the first hour"
  σκοτίας ἔτι οὔσης: gen. abs., "there still being darkness"
20:1 ἠρμένον: perf. part. circum. of αἴρω, "she sees the stone *having been removed*"

⁴⁰ Acceperunt ergo corpus Iesu et ligaverunt illud linteis cum aromatibus, sicut mos Iudaeis est sepelire.   ⁴¹ Erat autem in loco, ubi crucifixus est, hortus, et in horto monumentum novum, in quo nondum quisquam positus erat.   ⁴² Ibi ergo propter Parascevem Iudaeorum, quia iuxta erat monumentum, posuerunt Iesum.

Chapter 20

The Empty Tomb

¹ Prima autem sabbatorum Maria Magdalene venit mane, cum adhuc tenebrae essent, ad monumentum et videt lapidem sublatum a monumento.   ² Currit ergo et venit ad Simonem

---

accipio, (3) **accepi**, **acceptus**: to receive,
    accept
adhuc: thus far, till now
aroma, aromatis *n*: spice
corpus, -oris *n*: a body
curro, (3): to run
hortus, -i *m*: garden
ibi: there, in that place
iuxta: nearly, close by (+ *acc.*)
lapis, lapidis *m*: stone
ligo, (1): to bind, tie
linteum, -i *n*: linen cloth, linen

locus, -i *m*: place
Magdalene (*indecl.*): Magdalene
mane (indecl) *n*: in the morning
Maria, -ae *f*: Mary
monumentum, -i *n*: tomb
mos, moris *m*: custom, habit
nondum: not yet
novus, -a, -um: new, fresh
pono, (3), **posui, positus**: to place, put
sepelio, (4): to bury
subferro, -ferre, sustuli, sublatus: to remove
tenebrae, -arum *f*: darkness (*pl.*)

19:40 **linteis**: abl. means, "they wrapped *with cloths*"
    sepelire: epexegetic inf., "it is the custom *to bury*"
19:41 **monumentum**: properly a tomb-marker, but here an empty tomb
19:42 **quia**: causal, "*because* the tomb was nearby"
20:1 **prima (sc. hora)**: abl. of thime when, "at the first hour"
    cum... essent: impf. subj. in *cum* circumstanital clause, "*when there was* still darkness"
20:1 **lapidem sublatum**: ind. st., "see *that the stone has been removed*"

Πέτρον καὶ πρὸς τὸν ἄλλον μαθητὴν ὃν ἐφίλει ὁ Ἰησοῦς, καὶ λέγει αὐτοῖς «Ἦραν τὸν κύριον ἐκ τοῦ μνημείου, καὶ οὐκ οἴδαμεν ποῦ ἔθηκαν αὐτόν.»

³ ἐξῆλθεν οὖν ὁ Πέτρος καὶ ὁ ἄλλος μαθητής, καὶ ἤρχοντο εἰς τὸ μνημεῖον. ⁴ ἔτρεχον δὲ οἱ δύο ὁμοῦ· καὶ ὁ ἄλλος μαθητὴς προέδραμεν τάχειον τοῦ Πέτρου καὶ ἦλθεν πρῶτος εἰς τὸ μνημεῖον, ⁵ καὶ παρακύψας βλέπει κείμενα τὰ ὀθόνια, οὐ μέντοι εἰσῆλθεν. ⁶ ἔρχεται οὖν καὶ Σίμων Πέτρος ἀκολουθῶν αὐτῷ, καὶ εἰσῆλθεν εἰς τὸ μνημεῖον· ⁷ καὶ θεωρεῖ τὰ ὀθόνια κείμενα, καὶ τὸ σουδάριον, ὃ ἦν ἐπὶ τῆς κεφαλῆς αὐτοῦ, οὐ μετὰ τῶν ὀθονίων κείμενον ἀλλὰ χωρὶς ἐντετυλιγμένον εἰς ἕνα τόπον. ⁸ τότε οὖν εἰσῆλθεν καὶ ὁ ἄλλος μαθητὴς ὁ ἐλθὼν

αἴρω: to take
ἀκολουθέω: to follow
βλέπω: to see
εἰσῆλθον: to go into (*aor.*)
ἐντυλίσσω: to wrap up
ἐξῆλθον: to go out (*aor.*)
ἦλθον: to go or come (*aor.*)
θεωρέω: to look at, view, behold
κεῖμαι: to be laid
κεφαλή, ἡ: the head
κύριος, ὁ: a lord, master
ὀθόνιον, τό: a piece of fine linen

οἶδα: to know (*perf.*)
ὁμοῦ: together,
παρακύπτω: to stoop sideways (to peek)
προέδραμον: to run forward (*aor.*)
πρῶτος, -η, -ον: first
σουδάριον, τό: towel, cloth
ταχύς, -εῖα, ύ: swift, fast
τόπος, ὁ: the place
τότε: at that time, then
φιλέω: to love, regard with affection
χωρίς (*adv.*): separately, apart from

20:2 ἦραν: aor. of αἴρω, "they took"

πoῦ ἔθηκαν: aor. of τίθημι in ind. quest., "we don't know *where they placed him*"

20:4 ἔτρεχον: impf., "they were running"

τοῦ Πέτρου; gen. of comparison after τάχειον, "faster *than Peter*"

20:5 παρακύψας: aor. part. of παρακύπτω, "having stooped sideways"

20:7 κείμενα: pres. part. circum. agreeing with ὀθόνια, "he saw the linen cloth *lying* not with the others"

κείμενον ...ἐντετυλιγμένον: perf. part. circum. agreeing with σουδάριον, "he saw the cloth not *lying ... having been rolled up*"

ἀλλὰ χωρὶς: adverbial, "*but* rolled up *apart*"

20:8 ὁ ἐλθὼν: aor. part. attributive, "*the one who went* first"

Petrum et ad alium discipulum, quem amabat Iesus, et dicit eis:

"Tulerunt Dominum de monumento, et nescimus, ubi posuerunt eum!"

³ Exiit ergo Petrus et ille alius discipulus, et veniebant ad

monumentum. ⁴ Currebant autem duo simul, et ille alius discipulus

praecucurrit citius Petro et venit primus ad monumentum; ⁵ et cum

se inclinasset, videt posita linteamina, non tamen introivit. ⁶ Venit

ergo et Simon Petrus sequens eum et introivit in monumentum;

et videt linteamina posita ⁷ et sudarium, quod fuerat super caput

eius, non cum linteaminibus positum, sed separatim involutum in

unum locum. ⁸ Tunc ergo introivit et alter discipulus, qui venerat

---

alter, -a, -um: other
amo, (1): to love
autem: but
caput, capitis *n*: head
citus, -a, -um: quick, swift
duo, duae, duo: two
exeo, (4), exii: to depart
ferro, ferre, tuli: to carry away
inclino, (1): to bend, lower
involvo, (3), involvi, involutus: to wrap

linteamen, -inis *n*: linen cloth
locus, loci *m*: place
nescio, (4): not to know
pono, (3) posui: to put, place
praecurro, (3), -cucurri: to run before
separatim (*adv.*): apart, separately
sequor, (3), secutus sum: follow
simul (*adv.*): at same time
sudarium, -i *n*: cloth

20:3 **ille alius:** "that other," corresponding to ὁ ἄλλος, with *ille* indicating that it refers to the very "other" disciple previously mentioned
20:4 **Petro:** abl. of comparison after *citius*, "he ran faster *than Peter*"
venit primus: nom. adj. with adverbial force, "he came first" i.e. arrived first
20:5 **cum... inclinasset:** plupf. subj. in *cum* circumstantial clause, "when he had bent over"
20:5-6 **posita** (*bis*): perf. part. circum., "sees the linens *set aside*"

293

πρῶτος εἰς τὸ μνημεῖον, καὶ εἶδεν καὶ ἐπίστευσεν· ⁹ οὐδέπω γὰρ ᾔδεισαν τὴν γραφὴν ὅτι δεῖ αὐτὸν ἐκ νεκρῶν ἀναστῆναι. ¹⁰ ἀπῆλθον οὖν πάλιν πρὸς αὐτοὺς οἱ μαθηταί.

Jesus Appears to Mary Magdalene

¹¹ Μαρία δὲ εἱστήκει πρὸς τῷ μνημείῳ ἔξω κλαίουσα. ὡς οὖν ἔκλαιεν παρέκυψεν εἰς τὸ μνημεῖον, ¹² καὶ θεωρεῖ δύο ἀγγέλους ἐν λευκοῖς καθεζομένους, ἕνα πρὸς τῇ κεφαλῇ καὶ ἕνα πρὸς τοῖς ποσίν, ὅπου ἔκειτο τὸ σῶμα τοῦ Ἰησοῦ.

¹³ καὶ λέγουσιν αὐτῇ ἐκεῖνοι «Γύναι, τί κλαίεις;»

λέγει αὐτοῖς ὅτι «Ἦραν τὸν κύριόν μου, καὶ οὐκ οἶδα ποῦ ἔθηκαν αὐτόν.» ¹⁴ ταῦτα εἰποῦσα ἐστράφη εἰς τὰ ὀπίσω, καὶ θεωρεῖ τὸν Ἰησοῦν ἑστῶτα, καὶ οὐκ ᾔδει ὅτι Ἰησοῦς ἐστίν.

ἄγγελος, ὁ: a messenger, envoy
ἀνίστημι: to make to stand up, raise up
ἀπῆλθον: to go away (aor.)
δεῖ: it is necessary
εἶδον: to see (aor.)
ἵστημι: to make to stand
κεφαλή, ἡ: the head
κλαίω: to weep, lament, wail

λευκός, -ή, -όν: light, bright
νεκρός, ὁ: a corpse
ὀπίσω: backwards
παρακύπτω: to stoop sideways
πούς, ποδός, ὁ: a foot
πρῶτος, -η, -ον: first
στρέφω: to turn about or aside, turn
τίθημι: to put or place

20:9 ᾔδεισαν: plupf. of οἶδα, "*they knew* not yet"
    ἀναστῆναι: aor. inf. intransitive of ἀνα-ίστημι with δεῖ, "that it is necessary for him *to rise*"
20:11 πρὸς αὐτοὺς: (= ἑαυτοὺς) "they went back *to themselves*" i.e. to their homes
20:11 εἱστήκει: plupf. of ἵστημι with imperfect meaning, "she was standing"
    παρέκυψεν: aor. of παρακύπτω, "she stooped sideways (to peek in)"
20:12 θεωρεῖ: note the switch to vivid present tense, "she sees"
    καθεζομένους: pres. part. circum., "sees angels *sitting*"
    ἔκειτο: impf. with pluperfect meaning, "where *he had been laid*"
20:13 ὅτι ἦραν: aor. of αἴρω, "they removed," where ὅτι introduces direct speech
20:14 ἐστράφη: aor. pass. of στρέφω, "she turned herself around"
    ἑστῶτα: perf. part. circum. of ἵστημι, "sees Jesus *standing*"
    οὐκ ᾔδει: plupf. of οἶδα, "she did not know"

primus ad monumentum, et vidit et credidit. ⁹ Nondum enim sciebant Scripturam, quia oportet eum a mortuis resurgere. ¹⁰ Abierunt ergo iterum ad semetipsos discipuli.

Jesus Appears to Mary Magdalene

¹¹ Maria autem stabat ad monumentum foris plorans. Dum ergo fleret, inclinavit se in monumentum ¹² et videt duos angelos in albis sedentes, unum ad caput et unum ad pedes, ubi positum fuerat corpus Iesu.

¹³ Et dicunt ei illi: "Mulier, quid ploras?"

Dicit eis: "Tulerunt Dominum meum, et nescio, ubi posuerunt eum." ¹⁴ Haec cum dixisset, conversa est retrorsum et videt Iesum stantem; et non sciebat quia Iesus est.

---

abeo, (4), abii: to depart, go away
albus, -a, -um: white
angelus, -i *m*: angel, messenger
caput, capitis *n*: head
convertor, (3), conversus sum: to turn oneself around
corpus, -oris *n*: a body, corpse
duo, duae, duo: two
fero, ferre, tuli: to bear away
fleo, (2): to cry, weep
foris, foris *f*: a door
inclino, (1): to bend down, stoop
iterum (*adv.*): again

Maria, -ae *f*: Mary
mortuus, -i *m*: the dead, corpse
mulier, -eris *f*: a woman
nescio, (4): to not know
oportet, (2): it is necessary, ought
pes, pedis *m*: foot
ploro, (1): to cry, weep
pono, (3), posui: to put, place
primus, -a, -um: first
resurgo, (3): to rise
retrorsum (*adv.*): back, backwards
sedeo, (2): to sit, remain
sto, (1): to stand

20:9 **eum ... resurgere**: acc. + inf. after *oportet*, "know that it was necessary *for him to rise again*"

20:10 **ad semetipsos**: "back *to themselves*" i.e. to where they were staying

20:11 **dum... fleret**: impf. subj. in temporal clause, "while she was crying," where indicative would be expected

20:12 **positum fuerat**: plupf. (= *positum erat*), "where *he had been laid*"

20:14 **cum dixisset**: plupf. subj. in cum circumstantial clause, "when she had said"

¹⁵ λέγει αὐτῇ Ἰησοῦς «Γύναι, τί κλαίεις; τίνα ζητεῖς;»

ἐκείνη δοκοῦσα ὅτι ὁ κηπουρός ἐστιν, λέγει αὐτῷ «Κύριε, εἰ σὺ ἐβάστασας αὐτόν, εἰπέ μοι ποῦ ἔθηκας αὐτόν, κἀγὼ αὐτὸν ἀρῶ.»

¹⁶ λέγει αὐτῇ Ἰησοῦς «Μαριάμ.»

στραφεῖσα ἐκείνη λέγει αὐτῷ Ἑβραϊστί «Ῥαββουνεί» (ὃ λέγεται «Διδάσκαλε.»)

¹⁷ λέγει αὐτῇ Ἰησοῦς «Μή μου ἅπτου, οὔπω γὰρ ἀναβέ-βηκα πρὸς τὸν πατέρα· πορεύου δὲ πρὸς τοὺς ἀδελφούς μου καὶ εἰπὲ αὐτοῖς Ἀναβαίνω πρὸς τὸν πατέρα μου καὶ πατέρα ὑμῶν καὶ θεόν μου καὶ θεὸν ὑμῶν .»

¹⁸ ἔρχεται Μαριὰμ ἡ Μαγδαληνὴ ἀγγέλλουσα τοῖς μαθη-ταῖς ὅτι «Ἑώρακα τὸν κύριον» καὶ ταῦτα εἶπεν αὐτῇ.

ἀγγέλλω: to bear a message	εἶπον: to say (aor)
ἀδελφός, ὁ: brother	κηπουρός, ὁ: a gardener.
ἀναβαίνω: to go up, mount, to go up to	ὁράω: to see
ἅπτω: to fasten, touch	οὔπω: not yet
βαστάζω: to carry off	πατήρ, πατρός, ὁ: a father
διδάσκαλος, ὁ: a teacher, master	πορεύω: to make to go
δοκέω: to have an opinion, suppose	Ῥαββουνεί: teacher (Hebrew)

20:15 δοκοῦσα: pres. part., "she, *supposing* that"

ἀρῶ: fut. of αἴρω, "and *I will take* him *away*"

20:16 στραφεῖσα: aor. part. pass. of στρέφω, "and she *having turned herself*"

20:17 μή μου ἅπτου: pres. imper. mid., "don't touch me!"

ἀναβέβηκα: perf. of ἀνα-βαίνω, "I have not yet ascended"

πορεύου: pres. mid. imper., "make your way"

20:18 ἀγγέλλουσα: pres. part. expressing purpose, "goes in order to announce"

ὅτι ἑώρακα: perf. with ὅτι introducing direct speech, "to announce '*I have seen* the lord'"

¹⁵ Dicit ei Iesus: "Mulier, quid ploras? Quem quaeris?"

Illa, existimans quia hortulanus esset, dicit ei: "Domine, si tu sustulisti eum, dicito mihi, ubi posuisti eum, et ego eum tollam."

¹⁶ Dicit ei Iesus: "Maria!"

Conversa illa dicit ei Hebraice: "Rabbuni!" quod dicitur "Magister."

¹⁷ Dicit ei Iesus: "Iam noli me tenere, nondum enim ascendi ad Patrem; vade autem ad fratres meos et dic eis: 'Ascendo ad Patrem meum et Patrem vestrum, et Deum meum et Deum vestrum'."

¹⁸ Venit Maria Magdalene annuntians discipulis: "Vidi Dominum!" et quia haec dixit ei.

---

annuntio, (1): to announce, say
ascendo, (3), **ascendi**, **ascensus**: to rise, ascend
enim: indeed, in fact
existimo, (1): to think, suppose
frater, fratris *m*: brother
Hebraice: in Hebrew

hortulanus, -i *m*: gardener
magister, magistri *m*: teacher
ploro, (1): to cry, weep
quaero, (3): to search for, seek
teneo, (2): to hold
vado, (3), **vasi**: go

20:15 **quia esset**: impf. subj. in ind. st. indicating an alleged perception, "thinking *that he was*"

  dicito: fut. imper., "*tell me*"

20:16 **conversa**: circumstantial part., "she *having turned around*"

20:17 **tenere**: inf. after *noli*, "don't touch"

20:18 **quia... dixit**: indirect statement, "announced to the disciples *that he said these things to her*"

Jesus Appears to His Disciples

¹⁹ οὔσης οὖν ὀψίας τῇ ἡμέρᾳ ἐκείνῃ τῇ μιᾷ σαββάτων, καὶ τῶν θυρῶν κεκλεισμένων ὅπου ἦσαν οἱ μαθηταὶ διὰ τὸν φόβον τῶν Ἰουδαίων, ἦλθεν ὁ Ἰησοῦς καὶ ἔστη εἰς τὸ μέσον, καὶ λέγει αὐτοῖς «Εἰρήνη ὑμῖν.» ²⁰ καὶ τοῦτο εἰπὼν ἔδειξεν καὶ τὰς χεῖρας καὶ τὴν πλευρὰν αὐτοῖς. ἐχάρησαν οὖν οἱ μαθηταὶ ἰδόντες τὸν κύριον.

²¹ εἶπεν οὖν αὐτοῖς [ὁ Ἰησοῦς] πάλιν «Εἰρήνη ὑμῖν· καθὼς ἀπέσταλκέν με ὁ πατήρ, κἀγὼ πέμπω ὑμᾶς.» ²² καὶ τοῦτο εἰπὼν ἐνεφύσησεν καὶ λέγει αὐτοῖς «Λάβετε πνεῦμα ἅγιον· ²³ ἄν τινων ἀφῆτε τὰς ἁμαρτίας ἀφέωνται αὐτοῖς· ἄν τινων κρατῆτε κεκράτηνται.»

ἅγιος, -α, -ον: sacred, holy
ἁμαρτία, ἡ: a sin
ἀποστέλλω: to send off or away from
ἀφίημι: to send forth, discharge
δείκνυμι: to bring to light, display, exhibit
εἰρήνη, ἡ: peace, time of peace
ἐμφυσάω: to blow in, inspire
ἤμερα, ἡ: a day
θύρα, ἡ: a door
κλήζω: to shut

κρατέω: to keep, retain
λαμβάνω: to take, receive
μέσος, -η, -ον: middle, in the middle
ὀψία, ἡ: the latter part of day, evening
πέμπω: to send, despatch
πλευρά, ἡ: a rib
πνεῦμα, -ατος, τό: a spirit
φόβος, ὁ: fear
χαίρω: to rejoice, be glad, be delighted
χείρ, χειρός, ἡ: a hand

20:19 οὔσης οὖν ὀψίας: gen. abs., "it being evening"

τῇ μιᾷ σαββάτων: dat. of time when, "on the first (day) of the week"

κεκλεισμένων: perf. part. of κλήζω in gen. abs., "the doors *having been closed*"

ἔστη: aor. intransitive of ἵστημι, "Jesus came and *stood*"

20:20 ἔδειξεν: aor. of δείκνυμι, "*he showed* to them"

ἐχάρησαν: aor. of χαίρω, "they rejoiced"

20:21 ἀπέσταλκέν: perf. of ἀπο-στέλλω, "as the father *has sent* me"

20:22 ἐνεφύσησεν: aor. of ἐν-φυσάω, "he breathed into them"

20:23 ἄν τινων ἀφῆτε: aor. subj. of ἀπο-ἵημι in present general relative clause with conditional force, "whoever's sins you forgive" (i.e. if you forgive)

ἀφέωνται: perf. of ἀπο-ἵημι with force of an apodosis, "(then) they are forgiven"

ἄν τινων κρατῆτε: pres. subj. of κρατέω in pres. general relative clause with conditional force, "whose sins you keep" (i.e. if you keep)

κεκράτηνται: perf. with force of an apodosis, "(then) they are retained"

Jesus Appears to His Disciples

¹⁹ Cum esset ergo sero die illa prima sabbatorum, et fores essent clausae, ubi erant discipuli, propter metum Iudaeorum, venit Iesus et stetit in medio et dicit eis: "Pax vobis!" ²⁰ Et hoc cum dixisset, ostendit eis manus et latus. Gavisi sunt ergo discipuli, viso Domino.

²¹ Dixit ergo eis iterum: "Pax vobis! Sicut misit me Pater, et ego mitto vos." ²² Et cum hoc dixisset, insufflavit et dicit eis: "Accipite Spiritum Sanctum. ²³ Quorum remiseritis peccata, remissa sunt eis; quorum retinueritis, retenta sunt."

---

clausus, -a, -um: closed
foris, foris *f.*: door
gaudeo, (2), **gavisus sum**: to be glad, rejoice
insufflo, (1): to blow, inspire
latus, lateris *n*: side
manus, -us *f*: hand
medium, -i *n*: midst
metus, metus *m*: fear
mitto, (3), **misi, missus**: to send
ostendeo, (2), **ostendi**: to show, reveal

pax, pacis *f.*: peace
peccatum, -i *n*: sin
remitto, (3), **remisi, remissus**: to send back, remit
retineo, (2), **retinui, retentus**: to hold back, restrain, retain
sabbata, -orum *n*: a week
sanctus, -a, -um: sacred, holy
sero (*adv.*): late, at a late hour
sto, (1), **steti**: to stand
video, (2), **visi, visus**: to see

20:19 **cum esset ... essent**: impf. subj. in *cum* circumstantial clause, "*when it was* late ... *when* the doors *were* closed"
    die illa prima: abl. of time when, "*on that first day* of the week"
20:20 **cum dixisset**: plupf. subj. in circumstantial clause, "when he had said"
    gavisi sunt: perf. of *gaudeo*, "they were gladdened"
    viso Domino: abl. absolute, "the Lord having been seen"
20:22 **cum... dixisset**: plupf. subj. in cum circumstantial clause, "when he had said"
20:23 **remiseritis ...retinueritis**: perf. subj. in general relative clause, "whoever's sins *you forgive ...you retain*"

Jesus Appears to Thomas

²⁴ Θωμᾶς δὲ εἷς ἐκ τῶν δώδεκα, ὁ λεγόμενος Δίδυμος, οὐκ ἦν μετ' αὐτῶν ὅτε ἦλθεν Ἰησοῦς. ²⁵ ἔλεγον οὖν αὐτῷ οἱ ἄλλοι μαθηταί «Ἑωράκαμεν τὸν κύριον.»

ὁ δὲ εἶπεν αὐτοῖς «Ἐὰν μὴ ἴδω ἐν ταῖς χερσὶν αὐτοῦ τὸν τύπον τῶν ἥλων καὶ βάλω τὸν δάκτυλόν μου εἰς τὸν τύπον τῶν ἥλων καὶ βάλω μου τὴν χεῖρα εἰς τὴν πλευρὰν αὐτοῦ, οὐ μὴ πιστεύσω.»

²⁶ καὶ μεθ' ἡμέρας ὀκτὼ πάλιν ἦσαν ἔσω οἱ μαθηταὶ αὐτοῦ καὶ Θωμᾶς μετ' αὐτῶν. ἔρχεται ὁ Ἰησοῦς τῶν θυρῶν κεκλεισμένων, καὶ ἔστη εἰς τὸ μέσον καὶ εἶπεν «Εἰρήνη ὑμῖν.» ²⁷ εἶτα λέγει τῷ Θωμᾷ «Φέρε τὸν δάκτυλόν σου ὧδε καὶ ἴδε τὰς χεῖράς μου, καὶ φέρε τὴν χεῖρά σου καὶ βάλε εἰς τὴν πλευράν μου, καὶ μὴ γίνου ἄπιστος ἀλλὰ πιστός.»

ἄπιστος, -ον: unbelieving
δάκτυλος, ὁ: a finger
δίδυμος, -ος, -ον: double, twin
δώδεκα: twelve
εἰρήνη, ἡ: peace, time of peace
ἔσω: to the interior
ἧλος, ὁ: a nail
ἡμέρα, ἡ: day

Θωμᾶς: Thomas
κλῄζω: to shut
μέσος, -η, -ον: middle, in the middle
ὀκτώ (indecl.): eight
πιστός, -η, -ον: believing
πλευρά, -ᾶς, ἡ: a rib
τύπος, ὁ: a blow
ὧδε: hither, to this place

20:25 ἑωράκαμεν: perf., "we have seen"

ἐὰν μὴ ἴδω ... βάλω: aor. subj. in future more vivid protases, "unless I see" ...unless I put my finger"

εἰς τὸν τύπον τῶν ἥλων: "put my finger into the mark of the nails"

οὐ μὴ πιστεύσω: aor. subj. of πιστεύω in strong denial, "I surely will not believe"

20:26 κεκλεισμένων: perf. part. of κλῄζω in gen. abs., "the doors having been closed"

ἔστη: aor. intransitive of ἵστημι, "he stood"

20:27 φέρε ...ἴδε ...φέρε ...βάλε: imper. Usually φέρε before another imperative is almost adverbial ("come on now!") but here it takes an object and retains its verbal force, "take your finger and look! ...take your hand and put it!"

μὴ γίνου: pres. imper. of γίνομαι, "don't be unbelieving!"

Jesus Appears to Thomas

²⁴ Thomas autem, unus ex Duodecim, qui dicitur Didymus, non erat cum eis, quando venit Iesus. ²⁵ Dicebant ergo ei alii discipuli: "Vidimus Dominum!"

Ille autem dixit eis: "Nisi videro in manibus eius signum clavorum et mittam digitum meum in signum clavorum et mittam manum meam in latus eius, non credam."

²⁶ Et post dies octo iterum erant discipuli eius intus, et Thomas cum eis. Venit Iesus ianuis clausis et stetit in medio et dixit: "Pax vobis!" ²⁷ Deinde dicit Thomae: "Infer digitum tuum huc et vide manus meas et affer manum tuam et mitte in latus meum; et noli fieri incredulus sed fidelis!"

---

affero, aferre: to bring to
alius, alia, aliud: other
clausus, -a, -um: closed
clavus, -i *m*: nail, spike
credo, (3): to believe
deinde: then, after
didymus, -i *m*: twin
digitus, -i *m*: finger
duodecim: twelve
fidelis, -e: faithful
fio, fieri: to become, be

ianua, -ae *f*: door, entrance
incredulus, -a, -um: unbelieving, incredulous
inferro, inferre: to bring into
intus (*adv.*): within, inside
latus, lateris *n*: side
medium, -i *n*: middle, center
nolo, nolle: be unwilling, do not
octo: eight
pax, pacis *f*: peace
signum, -i *n*: sign
Thomas (*indecl.*): Thomas

20:25 **nisi... videro... mittam**: fut. perf. and fut. in fut. more vivid protasis, "Unless I see and place"
   non credam: fut. in fut. more vivid apodosis, "I will not believe"
20:26 **ianuis clausis**: abl. abs., "the doors having been closed"
   infer ... vide ...affer ...mitte: pres. imper. with the two forms of *fero* retaining verbal force of Greek φέρε (instead of the adverbial *age*), "*take* your finger and *look*! ...*take* your hand and *put* it!"!
20:27 **fieri**: pres. inf. after *noli* in prohibition, "do not wish *to become!*"

²⁸ ἀπεκρίθη Θωμᾶς καὶ εἶπεν αὐτῷ «Ὁ κύριός μου καὶ ὁ θεός μου.»

²⁹ λέγει αὐτῷ ὁ Ἰησοῦς «Ὅτι ἑώρακάς με πεπίστευκας; μακάριοι οἱ μὴ ἰδόντες καὶ πιστεύσαντες.»

The Purpose of John's Gospel

³⁰ πολλὰ μὲν οὖν καὶ ἄλλα σημεῖα ἐποίησεν ὁ Ἰησοῦς ἐνώπιον τῶν μαθητῶν, ἃ οὐκ ἔστιν γεγραμμένα ἐν τῷ βιβλίῳ τούτῳ· ³¹ ταῦτα δὲ γέγραπται ἵνα πιστεύητε ὅτι Ἰησοῦς ἐστὶν ὁ χριστὸς ὁ υἱὸς τοῦ θεοῦ, καὶ ἵνα πιστεύοντες ζωὴν ἔχητε ἐν τῷ ὀνόματι αὐτοῦ.

βιβλίον, τό: a paper, scroll, letter
ἐνώπιον: face to face (+ gen.)
ζωή, ἡ: life
μακάριος, -α, -ον: blessed, happy

ὄνομα, -ατος, τό: name
πολύς, πολλά, πολύ: many
σημεῖον, τό: a sign, a mark, token
χριστός, -ή, -όν: annointed

20:29 ἑώρακας ...ἐπίστευκας: perf., "because *you have seen ...you have believed*"
    οἱ μὴ ἰδόντες: aor. part. attributive with conditional force, "blessed are *the ones who (if) not having seen*"
    πιστεύσαντες: aor. part., "yet *having believed*"
20:30 ἃ οὐκ ἔστιν γεγραμμένα: perf. periphrastic of γράφω, "which have not been written"
20:31 γέγραπται: perf. of γράφω, "these *have been written*"
    ἵνα πιστεύητε ...ἔχητε: pres. subj. in purpose clause, "in order that you believe ...in order that you have"
    ὁ χριστὸς ὁ υἱὸς: nom. pred., "that Jesus is *the Annointed one, the Son*"
    πιστεύοντες: pres. part. instrumental, "so that you have life *by believing*"

²⁸ Respondit Thomas et dixit ei: "Dominus meus et Deus meus!"

²⁹ Dicit ei Iesus: "Quia vidisti me, credidisti. Beati, qui non viderunt et crediderunt!"

The Purpose of John's Gospel

³⁰ Multa quidem et alia signa fecit Iesus in conspectu discipulorum suorum, quae non sunt scripta in libro hoc;   ³¹ haec autem scripta sunt, ut credatis quia Iesus est Christus Filius Dei et ut credentes vitam habeatis in nomine eius.

---

beatus, -a, -um: blessed
conspectus, conspectus *m*: view
credo, (3), **credidi**: to trust, believe
liber, libri *m*: book, volume
multus, -a, -um: many

nomen, nominis *n*: name
scribo, (3) **scripsi, scriptus**: to write
signum, -i *m*: a sign
video, (2), **vidi, visus**: to see
vita, -ae *f*: life

20:31   **ut credatis ... habeatis**: pres. subj. in purpose clause, "these things were written *in order that you believe ...in order that you have*"
    credentes: pres. part. instrumental, "have life *by believing*"

303

Chapter 21

Jesus and the Miraculous Catch of Fish

¹ μετὰ ταῦτα ἐφανέρωσεν ἑαυτὸν πάλιν Ἰησοῦς τοῖς μαθηταῖς ἐπὶ τῆς θαλάσσης τῆς Τιβεριάδος· ἐφανέρωσεν δὲ οὕτως. ² ἦσαν ὁμοῦ Σίμων Πέτρος καὶ Θωμᾶς ὁ λεγόμενος Δίδυμος καὶ Ναθαναὴλ ὁ ἀπὸ Κανὰ τῆς Γαλιλαίας καὶ οἱ τοῦ Ζεβεδαίου καὶ ἄλλοι ἐκ τῶν μαθητῶν αὐτοῦ δύο. ³ λέγει αὐτοῖς Σίμων Πέτρος Ὑπάγω ἁλιεύειν· λέγουσιν αὐτῷ Ἐρχόμεθα καὶ ἡμεῖς σὺν σοί. ἐξῆλθαν καὶ ἐνέβησαν εἰς τὸ πλοῖον, καὶ ἐν ἐκείνῃ τῇ νυκτὶ ἐπίασαν οὐδέν.

⁴ πρωίας δὲ ἤδη γινομένης ἔστη Ἰησοῦς εἰς τὸν αἰγιαλόν· οὐ μέντοι ᾔδεισαν οἱ μαθηταὶ ὅτι Ἰησοῦς ἐστίν.

⁵ λέγει οὖν αὐτοῖς Ἰησοῦς «Παιδία, μή τι προσφάγιον ἔχετε;»

αἰγιαλός, ὁ: the sea-shore, beach	παιδίον, τό: little or young child
ἁλιεύω: to fish	πιάζω: to catch
Γαλιλαία, -ας, ἡ: Galilee	πλοῖον, τό: a ship, vessel
ἐμβαίνω: to step in	προσφάγιον, τό: relish, side dish
ἔρχομαι: to come or go	πρωία, -ας, ἡ: early morning
θάλασσα, ἡ: the sea	Τιβεριάς, -άδος, ἡ: Tiberias
Κανά, ὁ: Cana	ὑπάγω: to go, withdraw
νύξ, νυκτός, ἡ: the night	φανερόω: to make manifest
ὁμοῦ: at the same place, together	

21:1 ἐφανέρωσεν: aor. of φανερόω, "he showed himself"

21:3 ἁλιεύειν: pres. inf. expressing purpose, "I go to fish"
    ἐνέβησαν: aor. of ἐν-βαίνω, "they boarded"
    ἐπίασαν: aor. of πιάζω, "they caught nothing"

21:4 πρωίας δὲ ἤδη γινομένης: gen. abs., "early morning already happening" i.e. at daybreak
    ἔστη: aor. intransitive, "Jesus stood"
    ᾔδεισαν: plupf. of οἶδα, "they did not know"

21:5 μή τι ... ἔχετε: "don't you have any?" expecting a negative answer

Chapter 21

Jesus and the Miraculous Catch of Fish

¹ Postea manifestavit se iterum Iesus discipulis ad mare Tiberiadis; manifestavit autem sic. ² Erant simul Simon Petrus et Thomas, qui dicitur Didymus, et Nathanael, qui erat a Cana Galilaeae, et filii Zebedaei et alii ex discipulis eius duo. ³ Dicit eis Simon Petrus: "Vado piscari." Dicunt ei: "Venimus et nos tecum." Exierunt et ascenderunt in navem; et illa nocte nihil prendiderunt.

⁴ Mane autem iam facto, stetit Iesus in litore; non tamen sciebant discipuli quia Iesus est.

⁵ Dicit ergo eis Iesus: "Pueri, numquid pulmentarium habetis?"

---

ascendo, (3), **ascendi**: to rise, ascend
Cana (*indecl.*): Cana
exeo, (4), **exii**: to exit, depart
filius, fili *m*: son
Galilaea, -ae *f*: Galilee
litus, litoris *n*: shore
mane (*indecl.*): early in the morning
manifesto, (1): to reveal, manifest
mare, maris *n*: sea
navis, navis *f*: ship
nihil: nothing, no

nox, noctis *f*: night
numquid: can it be that?
piscor, (1): to fish
postea: afterwards
prendo, (3), **prendidi**: to catch
puer, -i *m*: boy
pulmentarium, -i *n*: relish, food
sic: thus, so
simul: at same time, likewise
sto, (1), **steti**: to stand
venio, (4), **veni, ventus**: to come

21:1 **ad mare**: acc. place to which without a verb of motion used in place of an abl. of place where, "at the sea"

21:3 **piscari**: inf. of purpose, "I am going *in order to fish*"
illa nocte: abl. of time within which, "*in the course of that night*"

21:4 **mane... facto**: abl. abs., "morning having broken"

305

ἀπεκρίθησαν αὐτῷ «Οὔ.»

⁶ ὁ δὲ εἶπεν αὐτοῖς «Βάλετε εἰς τὰ δεξιὰ μέρη τοῦ πλοίου τὸ δίκτυον, καὶ εὑρήσετε.» ἔβαλον οὖν, καὶ οὐκέτι αὐτὸ ἑλκύσαι ἴσχυον ἀπὸ τοῦ πλήθους τῶν ἰχθύων.

⁷ λέγει οὖν ὁ μαθητὴς ἐκεῖνος ὃν ἠγάπα ὁ Ἰησοῦς τῷ Πέτρῳ «Ὁ κύριός ἐστιν.» Σίμων οὖν Πέτρος, ἀκούσας ὅτι ὁ κύριός ἐστιν, τὸν ἐπενδύτην διεζώσατο, ἦν γὰρ γυμνός, καὶ ἔβαλεν ἑαυτὸν εἰς τὴν θάλασσαν· ⁸ οἱ δὲ ἄλλοι μαθηταὶ τῷ πλοιαρίῳ ἦλθον, οὐ γὰρ ἦσαν μακρὰν ἀπὸ τῆς γῆς ἀλλὰ ὡς ἀπὸ πηχῶν διακοσίων, σύροντες τὸ δίκτυον τῶν ἰχθύων. ⁹ ὡς οὖν ἀπέβησαν εἰς τὴν γῆν βλέπουσιν ἀνθρακιὰν κειμένην καὶ ὀψάριον ἐπικείμενον καὶ ἄρτον.

ἀνθρακιά, ἡ: a heap of charcoal, hot embers
ἀποβαίνω: to step off from
ἄρτος, ὁ: a loaf of wheat-bread
βάλλω: to cast
βλέπω: to see
γῆ, ἡ: earth
γυμνός, -ή, -όν: naked, unclad
δεξιός, -ά, -όν: on the right side
διαζώννυμι: to gird round the middle
διακόσιοι, -αι, -α: two hundred
δίκτυον, τό: a casting-net, a net
ἕλκω: to draw, drag
ἐπενδύτης, -ου, ὁ: outer garment

ἐπίκειμαι: to be laid upon
εὑρίσκω: to find
ἰσχύω: to be strong, able (+ *inf.*)
ἰχθύς, -ύος, ὁ: a fish
μακρός, ά, -όν: large
μέρος, -εος, τό: a part, share
οὐκέτι: no more, no longer, no further
ὀψάριον, τό: food (eaten with bread)
πῆχυς, -εος, ὁ: a cubit
πλῆθος, -εος, τό: a great number
πλοιάριον, τό: a skiff, boat
πλοῖον, τό: a small boat
σύρω: to draw, drag

21:6 βάλετε: aor. imper. of βάλλω, "cast!"
   εὑρήσετε: fut. of εὑρίσκω, "you will find"
   ἑλκύσαι: aor. inf. with ἴσχυον, "they were not able *to drag*"
21:7 διεζώσατο: aor. of δια-ζώννυμι, "he placed X (acc) around himself"
21:8 τῷ πλοιαρίῳ: dat. of means, "came *by boat*"
   οὐ μακρὰν: acc. of extent, "not a great (distance)"
   ὡς ἀπὸ πηχῶν διακοσίων, "about 200 cubits away"
21:9 ἀπέβησαν: aor. of ἀπο-βαίνω, "as *they stepped off* (the boat) onto the land"
   κειμένην ... ἐπικείμενον: pres. part. circum., "they see the embers *placed* ...the food *placed upon*"

Responderunt ei: "Non."

⁶ Ille autem dixit eis: "Mittite in dexteram navigii rete et invenietis." Miserunt ergo et iam non valebant illud trahere a multitudine piscium.

⁷ Dicit ergo discipulus ille, quem diligebat Iesus, Petro: "Dominus est!" Simon ergo Petrus, cum audisset quia Dominus est, tunicam succinxit se, erat enim nudus, et misit se in mare; ⁸ alii autem discipuli navigio venerunt, non enim longe erant a terra, sed quasi cubitis ducentis, trahentes rete piscium. ⁹ Ut ergo descenderunt in terram, vident prunas positas et piscem superpositum et panem.

---

audio, (4), **audii:** to hear
cubitus, -i *m*: a cubit (a length of about 18 inches)
descendo, (3), **descendi:** to descend
dextera, -ae *f*: right side
diligo, (1): to love
ducenti, -ae, –a: 200
invenio, (4): to come upon
longe (*adv.*): far off
mare, maris *n*: the sea
mitto, (3): to send
multitudo, -inis *f*: multitude, great number
navigium, -i *n*: vessel, ship
nudus, -a, -um: nude, bare

panis, panis *m*: bread
piscis, piscis *m*: fish
pono, (3), **posui, positus:** to put, place
pruna, -ae *f*: glowing charcoal, fire
quasi: about
rete, retis *n*: net
succingo, (3), **succinxi:** to gather up with a belt or girdle
superpono, (3), **superposui, superpositus:** to place over
terra, -ae *f*: land
traho, (3): to draw, drag
tunica, -ae *f*: undergarment, shirt, tunic
valeo, (2): to be strong, able

21:6 **rete:** n. acc. obj. of *mittite*, "cast *your net*"
  a multitudine piscium: *a* + abl. with a causal force, "from the number," i.e. because of the number
21:7 **cum audisset:** plupf. subj. in *cum* circumstantial clause, "when he had heard"
21:8 **navigio:** abl. of means, "they came *by boat*"
21:9 **ut ... descenderunt:** *ut* temporal, "as they descended"
  positas ...superpositum: perf. part. circum., "they saw the coals *placed* and the fish *placed upon*"

¹⁰ λέγει αὐτοῖς ὁ Ἰησοῦς «Ἐνέγκατε ἀπὸ τῶν ὀψαρίων ὧν ἐπιάσατε νῦν.» ¹¹ ἀνέβη οὖν Σίμων Πέτρος καὶ εἵλκυσεν τὸ δίκτυον εἰς τὴν γῆν μεστὸν ἰχθύων μεγάλων ἑκατὸν πεντήκοντα τριῶν· καὶ τοσούτων ὄντων οὐκ ἐσχίσθη τὸ δίκτυον. ¹² λέγει αὐτοῖς ὁ Ἰησοῦς «Δεῦτε ἀριστήσατε.» οὐδεὶς ἐτόλμα τῶν μαθητῶν ἐξετάσαι αὐτόν «Σὺ τίς εἶ;» εἰδότες ὅτι ὁ κύριός ἐστιν. ¹³ ἔρχεται Ἰησοῦς καὶ λαμβάνει τὸν ἄρτον καὶ δίδωσιν αὐτοῖς, καὶ τὸ ὀψάριον ὁμοίως. ¹⁴ τοῦτο ἤδη τρίτον ἐφανερώθη Ἰησοῦς τοῖς μαθηταῖς ἐγερθεὶς ἐκ νεκρῶν.

ἀριστάω: to take breakfast
δεῦτε: hither! come on! come here!
δίδωμι: to give
ἐγείρω: to awaken, wake up, rouse
ἑκατόν (indecl.): a hundred
ἐξετάζω: to examine closely, inquire
ἤνεγχα: to fetch (aor.)
μεστός, -ή, -όν: full of (+ gen.)
νεκρός, ὁ: a corpse, the dead

οἶδα: to know (perf.)
ὁμοίως: similarly
πεντήκοντα (indecl.): fifty
πιάζω: to catch
σχίζω: to split, cleave
τολμάω: to undertake, dare
τοσοῦτος, -αύτη, -οῦτο: so large
τρεῖς, τρία: three
τρίτος, -η, -ον: the third (time)

21:10 ἐνέγκατε: weak aor. imper., "fetch"
   ὧν ἐπιάσατε: pron. attracted into the case (gen.) of the antecedent ὀψαρίων, "the food *which* you caught"
21:11 ἀνέβη: aor. of ἀνα-βαίνω, "he went aboard"
   εἵλκυσεν: aor. of ἕλκω, "he dragged"
   ἑκατὸν πεντήκοντα τριῶν: "153"
   τοσούτων ὄντων: gen. abs. concessive, "despite being so many"
   οὐκ ἐσχίσθη: aor. pass. of σχίζω, "the net *was not torn*"
21:12 ἀριστήσατε: aor. imper. of ἀριστάω, "take your meal"
   ἐξετάσαι: aor. inf. complementing ἐτόλμα, "no one dared *to ask* him"
   εἰδότες: perf. part. causal, "since they knew"
21:14 ἐφανερώθη: aor. pass. of φανερόω, "the third time *he appeared*"
   ἐγερθεὶς: aor. pass. part. temporal, "after having been raised"

¹⁰ Dicit eis Iesus: "Afferte de piscibus, quos prendidistis nunc."

¹¹ Ascendit ergo Simon Petrus et traxit rete in terram, plenum magnis piscibus centum quinquaginta tribus; et cum tanti essent, non est scissum rete. ¹² Dicit eis Iesus: "Venite, prandete." Nemo autem audebat discipulorum interrogare eum: "Tu quis es?" scientes quia Dominus est. ¹³ Venit Iesus et accipit panem et dat eis et piscem similiter. ¹⁴ Hoc iam tertio manifestatus est Iesus discipulis, cum resurrexisset a mortuis.

---

accipio, (3): to receive, accept
affero, afferre: to bring to
audeo, (2), ausus sum: to dare (+ *inf.*)
centum: one hundred
interrogo, (1): to ask, question
magnus, -a, -um: large, great
mortuus, -i *m*: the dead, a corpse
nemo, neminis *m/f.*: no one, nobody
plenus, -a, -um: full
prandeo, (2): to a meal

prendo, (3), prendidi, prenditus:to catch
quinquaginta: fifty
resurgo, (3), resurrexi, resurrectus: to rise
scindo, (3), scidi, scissus: to tear, split
scio, (4): to know
similiter: similarly
tantus, -a, -um: so great, so many
tertius, -a, -um: third
traho, (3), traxi: to draw, drag
tres, -ia: three

21:10 **de piscibus**: with a partitive sense, "some *of the fish*"
21:11 **piscibus**: abl. after *plenum*, "full *of fish*"
  cum tanti essent: impf. subj. in *cum* concessive clause, "although they were so great"
21:14 **hoc iam tertio**: abl. of time when, "on this third occasion"
  cum resurrexisset: plupf. subj. in *cum* temporal clause, "since he had risen"

Jesus Reinstates Peter

¹⁵ ὅτε οὖν ἠρίστησαν λέγει τῷ Σίμωνι Πέτρῳ ὁ Ἰησοῦς «Σίμων Ἰωάνου, ἀγαπᾷς με πλέον τούτων;»

λέγει αὐτῷ «Ναί, κύριε, σὺ οἶδας ὅτι φιλῶ σε.»

λέγει αὐτῷ «Βόσκε τὰ ἀρνία μου.»

¹⁶ λέγει αὐτῷ πάλιν δεύτερον «Σίμων Ἰωάνου, ἀγαπᾷς με;»

λέγει αὐτῷ «Ναί, κύριε, σὺ οἶδας ὅτι φιλῶ σε.»

λέγει αὐτῷ «Ποίμαινε τὰ προβάτιά μου.»

¹⁷ λέγει αὐτῷ τὸ τρίτον «Σίμων Ἰωάνου, φιλεῖς με;»

ἐλυπήθη ὁ Πέτρος ὅτι εἶπεν αὐτῷ τὸ τρίτον «Φιλεῖς με;» καὶ εἶπεν αὐτῷ «Κύριε, πάντα σὺ οἶδας, σὺ γινώσκεις ὅτι φιλῶ σε.»

ἀριστάω: to take a meal	ναί: yes
ἀρνίον, τό: a lamb	οἶδα: to know (*perf.*)
βόσκω: to feed, tend	πλέων, πλέον: more
γινώσκω: to know	ποιμαίνω: to shepherd, herd
δεύτερος, -α, -ον: second	προβάτιον, τό: a little sheep
κύριος, ὁ: a lord	τρίτος, -η, -ον: third
λυπέω: to pain, distress, grieve	φιλέω: to love

21:15 ἠρίστησαν: aor. of ἀριστάω, "when they had eaten"

Ἰωάνου: gen., "Simon (son) *of John*"

τούτων: gen. after πλέον: "do you love me more *than these*"

βόσκε: pres. imper., "*feed* my lambs"

21:16 ποίμαινε: pres. imper., "*herd* my sheep"

21:17 ἐλυπήθη: aor. pass. of λυπέω, "he was grieved"

ὅτι εἶπεν: causal, "because he said" either because he asked a third time or because he changed from the verb ἀγαπάω to φιλέω

Jesus Reinstates Peter

¹⁵ Cum ergo prandissent, dicit Simoni Petro Iesus: "Simon Ioannis, diligis me plus his?"

Dicit ei: "Etiam, Domine, tu scis quia amo te."

Dicit ei: "Pasce agnos meos."

¹⁶ Dicit ei iterum secundo: "Simon Ioannis, diligis me?"

Ait illi: "Etiam, Domine, tu scis quia amo te."

Dicit ei: "Pasce oves meas."

¹⁷ Dicit ei tertio: "Simon Ioannis, amas me?"

Contristatus est Petrus quia dixit ei tertio: "Amas me?" et dicit ei: "Domine, tu omnia scis, tu cognoscis quia amo te."

---

agnus, -i *m*: lamb
amo (1): to love
cognosco (3): to know
contristo, (1): to sadden
diligo (3), **dilexi, dilectus**: to love
etiam: and also, besides
iterum (*adv.*): again; a second time

ovis, ovis *f*: sheep
pasco (3): to feed, graze
plus, pluris (*gen.*): more, more than
prandeo, (2), **prandi**: to eat a meal
scio, (4): to know
secundus, -a, -um: second
tertius, -a, -um: third

21:15 **cum... prandissent**: plupf. subj. in *cum* circumstantial clause, "when they had eaten"
    Simon Ioannis: "Simon, (the son) of John"
    his: abl. comparison after *plus*, "do you love me more *than these*"
21:17 **tertio**: abl., "for the third time"
    amas: the third time the verb *amo* is used instead of *diligo*, corresponding to the variation in the Greek

λέγει αὐτῷ Ἰησοῦς «Βόσκε τὰ προβάτιά μου. ¹⁸ ἀμὴν

ἀμὴν λέγω σοι, ὅτε ἦς νεώτερος, ἐζώννυες σεαυτὸν καὶ περι-

επάτεις ὅπου ἤθελες· ὅταν δὲ γηράσῃς, ἐκτενεῖς τὰς χεῖράς

σου, καὶ ἄλλος ζώσει σε καὶ οἴσει ὅπου οὐ θέλεις.» ¹⁹ τοῦτο

δὲ εἶπεν σημαίνων ποίῳ θανάτῳ δοξάσει τὸν θεόν. καὶ τοῦτο

εἰπὼν λέγει αὐτῷ «Ἀκολούθει μοι.»

²⁰ ἐπιστραφεὶς ὁ Πέτρος βλέπει τὸν μαθητὴν ὃν ἠγάπα

ὁ Ἰησοῦς ἀκολουθοῦντα, ὃς καὶ ἀνέπεσεν ἐν τῷ δείπνῳ ἐπὶ

τὸ στῆθος αὐτοῦ καὶ εἶπεν «Κύριε, τίς ἐστιν ὁ παραδιδούς

σε;» ²¹ τοῦτον οὖν ἰδὼν ὁ Πέτρος λέγει τῷ Ἰησοῦ «Κύριε,

οὗτος δὲ τί;»

ἀκολουθέω: to follow
ἀναπίπτω: to fall back, recline
βλέπω: to look at, see
γηράσκω: to grow old, become old
δεῖπνον, τό: the principal meal
δοξάζω: to magnify, glorify
ἐθέλω: to will, wish, purpose
ἐκτείνω: to stretch out (the hands)
ἐπιστρέφω: to turn about, turn round
ζώννυμι: to gird

θάνατος, ὁ: death
μαθητής, -οῦ, ὁ: a disciple
νεώτερος, -α, -ον: younger
οἴσω: to bear (fut.)
παραδίδωμι: to betray
περιπατέω: to walk about
ποῖος, -α, -ον: of what nature? of what sort?
σημαίνω: to indicate, make known
στῆθος, -εος, τό: the breast

21:18 ὅταν δὲ γηράσῃς: aor. subj. in general temporal clause, "when you become old" i.e. whenever that is

ἐκτενεῖς ... ζώσει ... οἴσει: fut., "you will extend your hands ... another *will gird* you ... *he will bring* you"

21:19 ποίῳ θανάτῳ: dat. of manner introducing ind. quest., "indicating *by what sort of death* he will glorify"

21:20 ἐπιστραφεὶς: aor. pass. part. of ἐπιστρέπω, "Peter *having turned*"

ἀκολουθοῦντα: pres. part. circum., "sees the disciple *following*"

ἀνέπεσεν: aor. of ἀνα-πίπτω, "who had reclined" cf. John 13:25

ὁ παραδιδούς: pres. part. of παρα-δίδωμι, "the one who is betraying"

21:21 οὗτος δὲ τί: a colloquial expression, "but this one, what (about him)?"

Dicit ei: "Pasce oves meas. ¹⁸ Amen, amen dico tibi: Cum esses iunior, cingebas teipsum et ambulabas, ubi volebas; cum autem senueris, extendes manus tuas, et alius te cinget et ducet, quo non vis." ¹⁹ Hoc autem dixit significans qua morte clarificaturus esset Deum. Et hoc cum dixisset, dicit ei: "Sequere me."

²⁰ Conversus Petrus videt illum discipulum, quem diligebat Iesus, sequentem, qui et recubuit in cena super pectus eius et dixit: "Domine, quis est qui tradit te?" ²¹ Hunc ergo cum vidisset Petrus, dicit Iesu: "Domine, hic autem quid?"

---

ambulo, (1): to walk
cena, -ae f: dinner
cingo, (3): to dress
clarifico, (1): to make known, glorify
convertor (3), coversus: to turn around
duco, (3): to lead
extendo, (3): to stretch
iunior, iunius: younger
manus, -us m: a hand

mors, mortis f: death
pectus, pectoris n: breast, chest
recumbo, (1), recubui: to lie back, recline
senesco, (3), senui: to grow old
sequor, (3), secutus sum: to follow
significo, (1): to signify
trado, (3): to hand over, surrender
volo, velle: to wish, want

21:18 cum esses: impf. subj. in *cum* circumstantial clause, "*when you were* younger"
cum ... senueris: fut. perf. in *cum* circumstantial clause, "when you become old"
quo non vis: in local relative clause, "will lead you *whither you do not wish*"
21:19 qua morte clarificaturus esset: impf. subj. + fut. part. periphrastic in indirect question, "indicating *by what death he was about to be glorified*"
cum dixisset: plupf. subj in *cum* circumstantial clause, "when he had said"
21:20 qui et recubuit ...tradit te?: cf. John 13:25
21:21 cum vidisset: plupf. subj. in *cum* circumstantial clause, "when he had seen"
hic autem quid?: a colloquial *non sequitur*, "but this one, what (about him)?"

²² λέγει αὐτῷ ὁ Ἰησοῦς «Ἐὰν αὐτὸν θέλω μένειν ἕως

ἔρχομαι, τί πρὸς σέ; σύ μοι ἀκολούθει.» ²³ ἐξῆλθεν οὖν οὗτος ὁ

λόγος εἰς τοὺς ἀδελφοὺς ὅτι ὁ μαθητὴς ἐκεῖνος οὐκ ἀποθνῄσκει.

οὐκ εἶπεν δὲ αὐτῷ ὁ Ἰησοῦς ὅτι οὐκ ἀποθνῄσκει, ἀλλ᾽ «Ἐὰν

αὐτὸν θέλω μένειν ἕως ἔρχομαι, τί πρὸς σέ;»

²⁴ οὗτός ἐστιν ὁ μαθητὴς ὁ μαρτυρῶν περὶ τούτων καὶ ὁ

γράψας ταῦτα, καὶ οἴδαμεν ὅτι ἀληθὴς αὐτοῦ ἡ μαρτυρία ἐστίν.

²⁵ ἔστιν δὲ καὶ ἄλλα πολλὰ ἃ ἐποίησεν ὁ Ἰησοῦς, ἅτινα

ἐὰν γράφηται καθ᾽ ἕν, οὐδ᾽ αὐτὸν οἶμαι τὸν κόσμον χωρήσειν

τὰ γραφόμενα βιβλία.

ἀληθής, -ες: true
ἀποθνῄσκω: to die off, die
βιβλίον, τό: a paper, scroll
γράφω: to write
εἷς, μία, ἕν: one
ἐξῆλθον: to go out of (*aor.*)

ἔρχομαι: to come
ἕως: until, till
κόσμος, ὁ: world
μαρτυρία, ἡ: witness, testimony
οἶμαι: to suppose
χωρέω: to make room for, contain

21:22 ἐὰν θέλω: pres. subj. in pres. general protasis, "if I wish"
  αὐτὸν μένειν: pres. inf. complementing θέλω, "if I wish *him to remain*"
  ἕως ἔρχομαι: the indicative signals a definite moment, "until I come"
21:23 ἐξῆλθεν: aor., "the account *went forth*" i.e. circulated
  οὐκ ἀποθνῄσκει: pres. with fut. force, "did not say *that he will not die*"
21:24 ὁ γράψας: aor. part. of γράφω, "the one who wrote," the author identifies the
  beloved disciple as the source for the gospel
21:25 ἐὰν γράφηται: pres. subj. pass. of γράφω in fut. more vivid protasis, "(which)
  if they are written"
  κατὰ ἕν: "one by one"
  τὸν κόσμον χωρήσειν: fut. inf. in ind. st. after οἶμαι, representing a fut. more
  vivid apodosis, "I do not suppose *that the world would contain*"

²² Dicit ei Iesus: "Si eum volo manere donec veniam, quid ad te? Tu me sequere." ²³ Exivit ergo sermo iste in fratres, quia discipulus ille non moritur. Non autem dixit ei Iesus: "Non moritur," sed "Si eum volo manere donec veniam, quid ad te?"

²⁴ Hic est discipulus, qui testimonium perhibet de his et scripsit haec; et scimus quia verum est testimonium eius.

²⁵ Sunt autem et alia multa, quae fecit Iesus; quae, si scribantur per singula, nec ipsum arbitror mundum capere eos, qui scribendi sunt, libros.

---

arbitro, (1): to think, judge
capio, (3), **cepi**, **captus**: to take hold, grasp
donec: while, until
exeo, (4), **exivi**: to go out
liber, **libri** *m*: book
maneo, (2): to remain, stay
morior, (3), **mortuus sum**: to die
multus, **-a**, **-um**: many
mundus, **-i** *m*: world

perhibeo, (2), **perhibui**, **perhibitus**: to present, give
scribo, (3), **scripsi**, **scriptus**: to write
sequor, (3): to follow
sermo, **sermonis** *m*: speech, the word
singulus, **-a**, **-um**: single, one
testimonium, **-i** *n*: testimony
verus, **-a**, **-um**: true, real
volo, **velle**: to wish

21:22 **si ... volo**: an instance in which a pres. general condition is translated with a pres. indic. instead of a fut. perf., "if I wish." This sentence became famous in the renaissance discussion of the primacy of the Greek text over the Latin text. In the Old Latin versions, there is a variation between the word *si* and the word *sic*, but Jerome conflated them and wrote *si sic* even though there is no Greek word corresponding to the word *sic*.

    donec veniam: pres. subj. anticipatory, "remain *until such time as I come*"

    quid ad te?: "what (is that) to you?"

21:25 **exivit**: "this word *went out*" i.e. circulated

21:25 **si scribantur**: pres. subj. in fut. less vivid protasis, "if they were to be written"

    per singula: neuter pl., "one by one"

    capere: inf. in ind. st. after *arbitor*, "think that the world *would hold*"

    scribendi sunt: pass. periphrastic, "the book which *would have to be written*"

Proper Names

Greek	Latin		Origin
Ἀβραάμ, ὁ	Abraham *m*	Abraham, the Old Testament patriarch	Hebrew
Αἰνών, ἡ	Enon	Aenon, a place in the Jordan Valley	Aramaic
Ἀνδρέας, -ου, ὁ	Andreas, -ae *m*	Andrew, one of the apostles	Greek
Ἄννας, -α, ὁ	Annan	Annas, High Priest of Judea (6–15 A.D.), appointed by the Roman legate Quirinus, governor of Syria	
Ἀριμαθαία, -ας, ἡ	Arimathaea, -ae *f*	Arimathea, a city in Judea mentioned only as the home of Joseph of Arimathea	Hebrew
Βαραββᾶς, -ᾶ, ὁ	Barabbas, -ae *m*	Barabbas, "son of Abba," the prisoner released instead of Christ	Aramaic
Βηθανία, -ας, ἡ	Bethania, -a *f*	"house of affliction" or "house of dates;" Bethany, a village near Jerusalem; home of Mary, Martha, and Lazarus	Aramaic
Βηθλεέμ, ἡ	Bethlehem *f*	"house of bread," Bethlehem, a city near Jerusalem	Hebrew
Βηθσαϊδά, ἡ	Bethsaida *f*	"house of fishing," Bethsaida, the name of two cities on the shore of the Sea of Galilee	Aramaic
Γαββαθά, ἡ	Gabbatha	"Gabbatha", a paved square, on which the Roman procurator had his judgment seat	Aramaic
Γαλιλαία, -ας, ἡ	Galilaea, -ae *f*	Galilee, a district towards the southern end of the Roman province Syria; the northern division of Palestine; also, the sea bearing the same name	Hebrew

319

Γολγοθᾶ, ἡ	Golgotha	Golgotha, a hill outside the walls of Jerusalem where Jesus was crucified	Aramaic
Δαυείδ, ὁ	David *m*	David, a king of Israel	Hebrew
Ἐλαιών, τὸ Ὄρος τῶν	Oliveti, Mons	The Mount of Olives; a mountain ridge east of Jerusalem, named for the olive groves which covered its slopes	Greek
Ἕλλην, -ηνος, ὁ	Graecus, -i *m*	A Greek	
Ἐφραίμ, ὁ	Ephraim *m*	Ephraim, a city near Jerusalem(John 11:54)	Hebrew
Ζεβεδαῖος, -ου, ὁ	Zebedaeus, -i *m*	Zebedee, father of the apostles James and John	Hebrew
Ἠλείας, -ου, ὁ	Elias, -ae *m*	Elijah, an Old Testament prophet	Hebrew
Ἠσαίας, -α, ὁ	Isaia, -ae *m*	Isaiah, an Old Testament prophet	Hebrew
Θωμᾶς, -ᾶ, ὁ	Thomas *m*	"the twin," one of the twelve apostles	Hebrew
Ἰακώβ, ὁ	Iacob *m*	Jacob, the Hebrew patriarch; the second son of Isaac	Hebrew
Ἱεροσόλυμα, -ύμων, τά	Hierosolyma, -orum *n*; Hierosolyma, -ae *f*	The city of Jerusalem, capital of Israel and Judah, site of the crucifixion and resurrection	Hebrew
Ἱεροσολυμείτης, -ου, ὁ	Hierosolymis, -itis *m*	An inhabitant of the city of Jerusalem	Hebrew
Ἰησοῦς, οῦ, ὁ	Iesus, Iesu *m*	Jesus, the Greek form of Joshua; the Messiah	Hebrew
Ἰορδάνης, -ου, ὁ	Iordanes, -is *m*	the River Jordan, flowing from the Sea of Galilee to the Dead Sea, in which Jesus was baptized by John the Baptist	Hebrew
Ἰουδαία, -ας, ἡ	Iudaea, -ae *f*	Judea	Hebrew
Ἰουδαῖος, Ἰουδαίου ὁ	Iudaeus, -i *m*	a Jew	Hebrew
Ἰούδας, -α, ὁ	Iudas, -ae *m*	Judas, the apostle who betrayed and handed him over to the Roman authorities	Hebrew

Greek	Latin	Meaning	Language
Ἰσκαριώτης, -ου, ὁ	Iscariotes, -tis, *m*	Iscariot, an epithet of the apostle Judas and his father Simon; of uncertain meaning	
Ἰσραήλ, ὁ	Israel	the kingdom of Israel	Hebrew
Ἰωάννης, ου, ὁ	Ioannes, Ioannis *m*	John	Hebrew
Ἰωσήφ, ὁ	Ioseph *m*	Joseph	Hebrew
Καϊάφας, -ᾶ, ὁ	Caiphas, -ae, *m*	Caiaphas, a Jewish high priest	Aramaic
Καῖσαρ, -αρος, ὁ	Caesar, Caesaris *m*	Caesar, referring to the Roman emperor; in John, Tiberius (r. 14–37 AD)	Latin
Κανά, ἡ	Cana	Cana, a town in Galilee	Hebrew
Καπερναούμ, ἡ	Capharnaum *f*	Capernaum, a city in Galilee	Hebrew
Κεδρών, ὁ	Cedron *m*	Kidron, a brook and valley near Jerusalem	Hebrew
Κηφᾶς, -ᾶ, ὁ	Caiphas, -ae, *m*	"a rock," Cephas, a name given to the apostle Peter	Aramaic
Κλωπᾶς, ᾶ, ὁ	Cleopas, Cleopae, *m*	Clopas, the husband of Mary, the sister of the mother of Jesus, who stood at the foot of the cross	Aramaic
Λάζαρος, ου, ὁ	Lazarus, -i *m*	a friend of Jesus, whom he raised from the dead at Bethany (John 11:1-44)	Hebrew
Λευΐτης, ου, ὁ	Levita, -ae *m*	a Levite; properly a member of the Israelite tribe of Levi; those who assist in the priestly duties during worship in the Temple	Hebrew
λιθόστρωτον, -ου, τό	Lithostrotos	"the paved (place)"; see Γαββαθά/Gabbatha	Greek
Μαγδαληνή,-ῆς,ἡ	Magdalene *f*	Magdalene; a woman of Magdala, a place on the coast of the Sea of Galilee near Tiberias; referring to Mary, a disciple of Jesus (John 19:25; John 20:1, 18)	
Μάλχος, -ου, ὁ	Malchus, -i *m*	Malchus, a slave of the high priest	Hebrew

Μάρθα, -ας, ἡ	Martha, -ae *f*	Martha, the sister of Lazarus (John 11:1, 5, 19-39)	Aramaic
Μαρία(μ), -ας, ἡ	Maria, -ae *f*	Mary; one of several women mentioned in the Gospels; in John, 1.) Mary Magdalene (John 19:25; John 20:1, 11, 16, 18); 2.) Mary, the sister of Lazarus (John 11:1–45; John 12:3); 3.) Mary, the mother of James the less and sister of Jesus' mother (John 19:25)	Hebrew
Μεσσίας, -ου, ὁ	Messias, -ae *m*	Messiah, "the annointed one," the Old Testament title corresponding to Greek Χριστός ("Christ")	Hebrew
Μωσῆς, -έως, ὁ	Moyses, -is, *m*	Moses, the Hebrew patriarch who led the Jews out of Egypt in the book of Exodus	Hebrew
Ναζαρὲτ, ἡ	Nazareth *f*	Nazareth, a city in Galilee and hometown of Jesus	Uncertain
Ναθαναήλ, ὁ	Nathanael *m*	Nathanael, an early disciple of Jesus (John 1:45–49, 21:2), commonly identified with Bartholomew	Hebrew
Νικόδημος, -ου, ὁ	Nicodemus, -i *m*	A Pharisee and member of the Sanhedrin (John 3:1–21, 7:50–51, 19:39–42)	Greek
Πέτρος, -ου, ὁ	Petrus, -i *m*	"a rock," Peter, one of the twelve apostles	Greek
Πιλᾶτος, -ου, ὁ	Pilatus, -i *m*	Pontius Pilate a prefect for Judea in 26–36 AD	Latin
Ῥαββεί (*emph.*, Ῥαββουνεί)	Rabbi (*emph.* Rabbuni)	"teacher," a title of respect often applied to Jesus	Aramaic
Ῥωμαῖος, -α, -ον	Romanus, -a, -um	Roman	Latin
σάββατον, ου, τό	Sabbatum, -i *n*	the Sabbath; the seventh day of the week; a sacred day on which the Jews were required to abstain from all work; also the word for week	Hebrew
Σαλείμ, τό	Salim	Salim (John 3:23)	

Σαμάρεια, -ας, ἡ	Samaria, -ae *f*	Samaria; a small district of Palestine, located between Galilee (to the north) and by Judaea (to the south)	Hebrew
Σατανᾶς, -ᾶ, ὁ	Satanas, -ae *m*	Satan, the devil (John 13:27)	Hebrew
Σιλωάμ, ὁ	Siloa, -ae *f*	Siloam, a pool in the south of Jerusalem	Hebrew
Σίμων, -ωνος, ὁ	Simon, Simonis *m*	Simon; in John, 1.) a name of Peter, the apostle or 2.) the father of Judas Iscariot (John 6:71; 12:4; 13:2, 26)	Hebrew
Σιών, ἡ	Sion	Zion, the hill upon which Jerusalem was built; the city itself (John 12:15)	Hebrew
Σολομῶν, -ῶνος, ὁ	Salomon, -is *m*	Solomon; son of David and king of ancient Israel, famed for his wisdom and building the Temple in Jerusalem (John 10:23)	Hebrew
Συχάρ, ἡ	Sichar	Sychar, a city in Samaria	Hebrew
Τιβεριάς, -άδος, ἡ	Tiberias, -adis *f*	Tiberias, a city in Galilee; a name for the Sea of Galilee, on the western shore of which the city is located	Latin
Φαρισαῖος, -ου, ὁ	Pharisaeus, -i *m*	a Pharisee, a member of an ancient Jewish sect	Hebrew
Φίλιππος, -ου, ὁ	Philippus, -i *m*	Phillip of Bethsaida, one of the apotles	Greek
Χριστός, -οῦ, ὁ	Christus, -i *m*	Christ, "the annointed one;" epithet for Jesus translating the Hebrew "Messiah"	Greek

Glossary: Greek

A α

ἀγαπάω: to love

ἀγγέλλω, ἀγγελῶ, ἤγγειλα, ἤγγελκα: to send

ἄγω, ἄξω, ἤγαγον: to lead

αἴρω, ἀρῶ, ἦρα, ἦρκα: to take up, raise, lift

αἰτέω: to ask, beg

αἰών, -ῶνος, ὁ: time, age

αἰώνιος, -ία, -ιον: eternal

ἀκολουθέω: to follow

ἀκούω, ἀκούσομαι, ἤκουσα, ἀκήκοα: to hear

ἀλήθεία, -ας, ἡ: the truth

ἀλλά: but

ἀλλήλων (gen.): of one another

ἄλλος, -η, -ο: other

ἁμαρτία, ἡ: a failure, fault, sin

ἀμήν: amen

ἄν: would, might (conditional particle)

ἀναβαίνω: to go up, ascend

ἀνήρ, ἀνδρός, ὁ: a man, husband

ἄνθρωπος, -ου, ὁ: man

ἀπό: from (+ gen.)

ἀποθνήσκω, -θανοῦμαι, -έθανον, -τέθνηκα: to die off, die

ἀποκρίνομαι: to answer

ἀπόλλυμι, -ολῶ, -ώλεσα, -ολώλεκα: to destroy utterly, kill, slay

ἀποστέλλω, -στελῶ, - ἔστειλα: to send away or forth

ἄρτι (adv.): just now

ἄρτος, ὁ: a loaf of wheat-bread

ἀρχιερεύς, -έως, ὁ: high priest

αὐτός, -ή, -ό: he, she, it (self, same)

ἀφίημι, -ήσω, -ῆκα, -εῖκα: to release, let go

B β

βαίνω, βήσομαι, ἔβην, βέβηκα: to step, walk, go

βάλλω, βαλῶ, ἔβαλον, βέβληκα,: to cast

βλέπω: to see

Γ γ

Γαλιλαία, -ας, ἡ: Galilee, the northern region of Palestine

γάρ: for, so, then (postpositive)

γεννάω: to bear (a child)

γῆ, γῆς, ἡ: earth, land

γίνομαι, γενήσομαι, ἐγενόμην, γέγονα: to become, happen

γινώσκω, γνώσομαι, ἔγνων, ἔγνωκα: to know

γράφω, γράψω, ἔγραψα, γέγραφα, γέγραμμαι, ἐγράφην: to write

γυνή, γυναικός, ἡ: a woman

Δ δ

δέ: but, and

δεῖ: it is necessary

διά: through (+ gen.); because of (+ acc.)

δίδωμι, δώσω, ἔδωκα, δέδωκα, δέδομαι, ἐδόθην: to give

δοκέω: to have an opinion, suppose

δόξα, -ης, ἡ: glory

δοξάζω: to magnify, glorify

δύναμαι: to be able, be possible

δύο: two

E ε

ἐάν: if (ever), when(ever)

ἐγώ, μοῦ, μοί, μέ: I, me

εἰ: if

εἶδον: to see (aor.)

εἰμί: to be

εἶμι: to go (fut.)

εἶπον: to speak, say (*aor.*)

εἶς, μία, ἕν: one

εἰς: into

ἐκ, ἐξ: from, out of, of, by

ἐκεῖ: there

ἐκεῖνος, -η, -ο: that

ἐμαυτοῦ: of me, of myself (ἐμοῦ + αὐτός)

ἐν: in, on, by

ἐξέρχομαι: to go out

ἔξω: outside

ἐπί: on, over (+ *gen.*) ; on, at (+ *dat.*); on, to, for(+ *acc.*)

ἔργον, -ου, τό: work, deed

ἐρέω: to say or speak (*fut.*)

ἔρχομαι: to go, come

ἐρωτάω: to ask

εὑρίσκω, εὑρήσω, ηὗρον, ηὕρηκα: to find

ἔφαγον: to eat (*aor.*)

ἔχω, ἕξω, ἔσχον, ἔσχηκα: to have, to be in a certain condition, to be able to (+ *inf.*)

ἕως (*adv.*): until

Z ζ

ζητέω: to seek, seek for

ζωή, -ῆς, ἡ: life

H η

ἤ (*conj.*): than, or

ἤδη: now

ἦλθον, (*aor.*), ἐλήλυθα (*perf.*): to come

ἡμεῖς, ἡμῶν, ἡμῖν, ἡμᾶς: we, us

ἡμέρα, -ας, ἡ: day

ἤνεγκα or ἤνεγκον (*aor.*), ἐνήνοχα (*perf.*): to bear, carry

Θ θ

θέλημα, -ατος, τό: will

θέλω: to will, wish (+ *inf.*)

θεός, -οῦ, ὁ: God, a god

θεωρέω: to look at, view, behold

θύρα, -ας, ἡ: a door

I ι

ἴδιος, -α, -ον: one's own

ἰδού: look! behold! (*imper. of* εἶδον)

Ἰησοῦς, -οῦ, ὁ: Jesus

ἵνα: in order that, that

Ἰουδαῖος, -α, -ον: Jewish

ἵστημι, στήσω, ἔστησα (1 *aor.*), ἔστην (2 *aor.*) ἔστηκα: to set up, cause to stand

K κ

καθώς: just as

καί: and, even, also

καταβαίνω: to go down, come down

κόσμος, -ου, ὁ: the world

κρίνω, κρινῶ, ἔκρινα, κέκρικα, ἐκρίθην: to judge

κύριος, ὁ: Lord

Λ λ

λαλέω: to speak

λαμβάνω, λήψομαι, ἔλαβον, εἴληφα, ἐλήφθην: to take, receive

λέγω: to say, speak

λόγος, -ου, ὁ: a word, matter

M μ

μαθητής, -οῦ, ὁ: disciple, student

μαρτυρέω: to bear witness

μένω, μενῶ, ἔμεινα: to remain, abide

μετά: with (+ *gen.*); after (+ *acc.*)

μή: not

μικρός, -ά, -όν: small, little

μνημεῖον, -ου, τό: a memorial, tomb

μόνος, -η, -ον: alone, only

N ν

νόμος, ὁ: custom, law
νῦν: now
νύξ, νυκτός, ἡ: the night

O o

ὁ, ἡ, τό: the definite article
οἶδα: to know (perf.)
ὄνομα, -ατος, τό: a name
ὅπου: where
ὁράω, ἑώρακα (perf.): to see
ὅς, ἥ, ὅ: who, which
ὅταν: whenever
ὅτε: when
ὅτι: because; that
οὐ, οὐκ, οὐχ: not
οὐδέ: and not; neither
οὐδείς, οὐδεμία, οὐδέν: no one, nothing
οὐκέτι: no longer, no more
οὖν: therefore
οὐρανός, -οῦ, ὁ: heaven, sky
οὗτος, αὕτη, τοῦτο: this
οὕτως: in this way, thus
ὀφθαλμός, -οῦ, ὁ: an eye
ὄψομαι: to see (fut.)

Π π

πάλιν (adv.): again
παρά: from (+ gen.); with, beside (+ dat.); other than (+ acc.)
παραδίδωμι: to hand over, betray
πᾶς, πᾶσα, πᾶν: all, every, each
πάσχα, τό (indecl.): the Passover, Passover meal
πατήρ, πατρός, ὁ: father
πέμπω, πέμψω, ἔπεμψα: to send
περί: about (+ gen.); near (+ acc.)
Πέτρος, -ου, ὁ: Peter
πίνω, πιομαι, ἔπιον: to drink
πιστεύω: to trust, believe in

πνεῦμα, -ατος, τό: spirit
πόθεν: whence, from where?
ποιέω: to do, make
πολύς, πολλή, πολύ: many; much
πορεύω: to go
ποῦ: where?
πρόβατον, -ου, τό: a sheep
πρός: for (+ gen.); at (+ dat.); to, against (+ acc.)
πῶς: how?

Σ σ

σημεῖον, -ου, τό: a sign
σύ, σοῦ, σέ, σοί: you (singular)
σύν: with (+ dat.)
συνάγω: to bring together, collect

T τ

τηρέω: to keep, preserve
τίθημι, θήσω, ἔθηκα, τέθηκα: to put or place
τις, τι: someone, anyone; something
τίς, τί: who? which?
τόπος, ὁ: a place
τοσοῦτος, τοσαύτη, τοσοῦτο: so large
τότε: then

Υ υ

ὕδωρ, ὕδατος, τό: water
υἱός, -οῦ, ὁ: son
ὑμεῖς, ὑμῶν, ὑμᾶς, ὑμῖν: you (pl.)
ὑπάγω: to withdraw, depart
ὑπέρ: on behalf of (+ gen.); above (+ acc.)

Φ φ

Φαρισαῖος, -ου, ὁ: a Pharisee, a member of an ancient Jewish sect
φέρω: to bear, bring
φημί: to say

329

φωνέω: to address

φωνή, ῆς, ἡ: voice

φῶς, φωτός, τό: light

Χ χ

χείρ, χειρός, ἡ: a hand

χριστός, -ή, -όν: anointed; ὁ Χριστός:
Christ, "the annointed one"

Ω ω

ὥρα, ἡ: hour, period of time

ὡς: (*adv.*) as, so, approximately (with a
number); (*conj.*) that, in order that,
since, when; (*prep.*) to (+ *acc.*); as if,
as (+ *part.*); as _____ as possible (+
superlative)

Glossary: Latin

A a

a, ab: from, by, with (+ *abl.*)

abeo, (4), **abi(v)i, abitum**: to depart, go forth

accipio, (3), **accepi, acceptus**: to receive, accept

ad: to, up to, towards (+ *acc.*)

aeternus, -a, -um: eternal, everlasting

aio, (3): to say

alius, alia, aliud: other, another

amen: amen (*exclamation*)

ante: before, in front of (+ *acc.*)

apud: near, in the presence of (+ *acc.*)

aqua, -ae *f.*: water

ascendo, (3): to climb, ascend

audio, (4): to hear, listen, accept

autem: moreover, however

C c

caelus, -i *m*: heaven, sky

Christus, -i *m*: Christ

cognosco, (3) **cognovi, cognitum**: to know

credo, (3), **credidi, creditum**: to believe

cum: with (+ *abl.*);

D d

de: down from, about, concerning (+ *abl.*)

descendo, (3), **descendi, descensum**: to descend, go down

deus, -i *m*: God

dico, (3), **dixi, dictum**: to say, speak

dies, diei *m/f.* day

diligo, (3), **dilexi, dilectum**: to love

discipulus, -i *m*: student, disciple

do, (1), **dedi, datum**: to give

doceo, (2), **docui, doctum**: to teach

dominus, -i *m*: lord

E e

ecce: behold! (*exclamation*)

ego, mei, mihi, me: I, me

enim: for, indeed

ergo: therefore

et: and, also

ex, e: out of, from (+ *abl.*)

exeo, (4), **exi(v)i, exitum**: to come, go

F f

facio, (3), **feci, factus**: to do, make

fero, ferre, tuli, latus: to bring

filius, filii *m*: son

fio, (3): to become

foras (*adv.*): outside

G g

gloria, -ae *f.* glory

H h

habeo, (2), **habui, habitum**: to have, hold

hic, haec, hoc: this

homo, hominis m: a man

hora, -ae *f.* hour

I i

iam: already, now

ibi: here

Iesus, Iesu, m: Jesus

ille, illa, illud: that

impleo, (2), **implevi, impletum**: to fill

in: in, on

inter: between

interficio, (3) **interfeci, interfectum**: to kill, destroy

interrogo, (1): to ask, question

invicem (*adv.*): in turns, alternately

is, ea, id: he, she, it

itaque: and so, therefore

iterum (*adv.*): again

Iudaeus, -i *m*: Jew

iudico, (1): to judge, give judgment

L l

locus, -i *m*: place, location

loquor, (3), **locutus sum**: to speak, talk

lux, lucis *f*: light

M m

manduco, (1): to eat

maneo, (2), **mansi, mansum**: to remain, stay

meus, -a, -um: my, mine

mitto, (3), **misi, missum**: to send

modicus, -a, -um: moderate, short, small

monumentum, -i *n*: monument, tomb

morior, (3), **mortuus sum**: to die

mulier, -eris *f*: a woman

multus, -a, -um: much, many

mundus, -i *m*: world

mundus, -a, -um: clean

N n

nascor, (3) **natus sum**: to be born

nemo, neminis, *m/f*: no one

neque: and not, nor

nescio, (4), **nescivi**: to not know

nisi, ni: if not, unless

nolo, nolle, nolui: wish not to (+ *inf.*)

nomen, -inis *n*: a name

non: not

nondum: not yet

nonne: not? (*interrogative particle expecting an affirmative answer*)

numquid: surely not? (*interrogative particle expecting a negative answer*)

nunc: now

O o

oculus, -i *m*: an eye

omnis, -e: all, every, the whole

oportet, (2), **oportuit**: it is necessary, ought

opus, operis *n*: work

ovis, ovis *f*: a sheep

P p

palam (*adv.*): openly, plainly

pater, patris *m*: father

per: through (+ *acc.*)

perhibeo, (2), **perhibui**: to present, give

pes, pedis *m*: a foot

peto, (3) **petii**: to beg, entreat, ask

pono, (3), **posui, positum**: to lay down, set

pontifex, -icis *m*: high priest

possum, posse, potui: to be able, be possible

post: after (+ *acc.*)

primum (*adv.*): at first, before

pro: for, on behalf of (+ *abl.*)

propter: on account of, because of (+ *acc.*)

propterea: therefore, for that reason

Q q

quaero, (3), **quaesivi, quaesitum**: to seek, ask

quasi: as if

qui, quae, quod: who, which, what

quia: because

quidam, quaedam, quoddam: a certain one, someone

quis, quid: who? which? what?

quomodo: in what way? how?

R r

respondeo, (3), **respondi**, **responsum**: to answer

rex, **regis** m: a king

rogo, (1): to ask

S s

sanctus, -a, -um: divine, holy

scio, (4), **scivi**, **scitum**: to know, understand

scribo, (3) **scripsi**, **scriptum**: to write

sed: but

semetipse, -a, -um: one's self

sequor, (3), **secutus sum**: follow

sermo, **sermonis** *m*: speech, talk, word

servo (1): to preserve, keep

si: if

sic: in this way, thus

sicut: just as, like

signum, -i *n*: sign

sine: without (+ *abl.*)

sto, (1), **steti**, **statum**: to stand

sum, **esse**, **fui**, **futurum**: to be

super: over (+ *acc.*)

T t

tantus, -a, -um: so great, so much

testimonium, -i *n*: testimony, witness

trado, (3): to betray, hand over

tu, **tui**, **tibi**, **te**: you (*s.*)

tunc: then

turba, -ae *f*: a crowd, multitude

U u

ubi: where

unde: whence, from where

unus, -a, -um: one

ut: in order to, so that (+ subj.)

V v

vado, (3), **vasi**: to go, walk

venio, (4), **veni**, **ventum**: to come

verbum, -i *n*: a word

veritas, -**tatis** *f*: the truth

verus, -a, -um: true

vester, **vestra**, **vestrum**: your

video, (2), **vidi**, **visum**: to see

vita, -ae *f*: life

voco, (1): to call, summon

volo, **velle**, **volui**: to wish, want

vos, **vobis**: you (*pl.*)

vox, **vocis** *f*: voice, utterance

Made in the USA
Columbia, SC
22 October 2024

44903208R00207